Human Demography and Disease offers an interdisciplinary and integrated perspective on the relationship between historical populations and the dynamics of epidemiological processes. It brings the techniques of time-series analysis and computer matrix modelling to historical demography and geography to extract detailed information concerning the oscillations in births, deaths, migrations and epidemics from parish registers and other data series and to build mathematical models of the population cycles. This book presents a new way of studying pre-industrial communities and explores the subtle, and hitherto undetected, effects of fluctuating nutritional levels on mortality patterns and the dynamics of infectious diseases. This fascinating piece of detective work will be of interest to researchers, teachers and students in the fields of demography, anthropology, historical geography, social history, population biology, public health and epidemiology.

HUMAN DEMOGRAPHY AND DISEASE

HUMAN DEMOGRAPHY
AND DISEASE

SUSAN SCOTT
AND CHRISTOPHER J. DUNCAN

School of Biological Sciences,
University of Liverpool

CAMBRIDGE
UNIVERSITY PRESS

PUBLISHED BY THE PRESS SYNDICATE OF THE UNIVERSITY OF CAMBRIDGE
The Pitt Building, Trumpington Street, Cambridge CB2 1RP, United Kingdom

CAMBRIDGE UNIVERSITY PRESS
The Edinburgh Building, Cambridge CB2 2RU, United Kingdom
40 West 20th Street, New York, NY 10011-4211, USA
10 Stamford Road, Oakleigh, Melbourne 3166, Australia

© Susan Scott and C. J. Duncan 1998

First published 1998

Printed in the United Kingdom at the University Press, Cambridge

Typeset in Times 10/13 pt   [SE]

A catalogue record for this book is available from the British Library

Library of Congress cataloguing in publication data
Scott, Susan, 1953–
Human demography and disease / Susan Scott and C. J. Duncan.
p. cm.
Includes bibliographical references and index.
ISBN 0 521 62052 X (hb)
1. Epidemiology – England, North West – History.   2. Epidemiology –
England, North West – Mathematical models.   3. England, North West –
Population – History.   4. England, North West – Population –
Mathematical models.   5. Epidemics – England, North West – History.
6. Malnutrition – England, North West – History.   7. Famine – England,
North West – History.   I. Duncan, C. J. (Christopher John)   II. Title.
[DNLM: 1. Disease Outbreaks – history – England.   2. Epidemiology –
history – England.   3. Models, Biological.   WA 11 FE5 S4h 1998]
RA650.6.G6S33   1998
614.4'242 – dc21
DNLM/DLC
for Library of Congress   97-41912 CIP

ISBN 0 521 62052 X hardback

Contents

Preface   *page* xv
Conversion table for imperial to metric units   xvi

1 Introduction   1
   1.1   Mortality and demographic theory   3
   1.2   Malnutrition and famine   5
   1.3   Lethal infectious diseases   8
   1.4   Readership   10

2 Tools for demography and epidemiology   16
   2.1   Parish registers – a valuable data base for theoretical
        population study   16
   2.2   Time-series analysis – a valuable tool for historical
        demography   18
   2.3   Matrix modelling of human populations   31

3 Identification of population oscillations: a case study   34
   3.1   Marginal farming conditions in northwest England   34
   3.2   Annual burials in the parish register series of Penrith,
        1557–1812   38
   3.3   Annual baptisms in the parish register series of
        Penrith, 1557–1812   39
   3.4   Cross-correlations between the burial and baptism
        series   43
   3.5   Endogenous versus exogenous oscillations   44
   3.6   Anatomy of a mortality crisis: the plague at Penrith   47
   3.7   The births loop at Penrith during the period
        1557–1750   49

3.8   Are endogenous oscillations detectable in other
      communities?   51
3.9   Conclusions   53

4   Density-dependent control and feedback   **55**
4.1   Use of a Leslie matrix to model the endogenous
      oscillations   55
4.2   The 30-year cycle in baptisms   58
4.3   Feedback: model no. 2   60
4.4   Homeostasis and density-dependent constraints in a
      single human population   64
4.5   Use of the family reconstitution study to validate the
      model   64
4.6   The role of migration   69
4.7   A migratory feedback vector for the matrix model   71
4.8   Conclusions   74

**5   Modelling the endogenous oscillations and predictions from time-
series analysis**   **75**
5.1   30-year cycles   77
5.2   Estimations of the fertility function   77
5.3   Mean age at marriage   80
5.4   Estimations of the mortality function of a population
      by time-series analysis   81
5.5   Why is the wavelength of endogenous oscillations
      approximately 43 years?   83

6   Cycles in the grain price series   **87**
6.1   Sources for the data series   89
6.2   Cycles in the wheat price index   90
6.3   Oats and barley price indices   92
6.4   Correspondence between the grain price indices   94
6.5   The effect of seasonal temperature on wheat prices   97
6.6   The effect of rainfall on wheat prices   101
6.7   Wheat prices and short wavelength temperature cycles   102
6.8   Use of a predicted wheat prices series: distinction
      between the medium and short wavelength oscillations
      in the wheat price series   103
6.9   What drove the different cycles in wheat prices?   104
6.10 Rust and other parasitic infestations of grain crops   106

| 6.11 | Conclusions | 109 |
| 6.12 | Appendix: Statistical considerations | 110 |

7 Interactions of exogenous cycles: a case study — 113
7.1	Introduction	113
7.2	Driving the short wavelength population oscillations at Penrith	114
7.3	Short wavelength mortality oscillations in the population dynamics	115
7.4	Infant mortality at Penrith	120
7.5	How does malnutrition affect child and infant mortality?	125
7.6	Analysis of neonatal and post-neonatal mortality in the crisis of 1623 at Penrith	127
7.7	Conclusions: the effects of malnutrition on infant mortality	129
7.8	The short wavelength oscillation in baptisms at Penrith	131
7.9	Short wavelength oscillation in immigration at Penrith	131
7.10	Medium wavelength oscillations in adult burials at Penrith	132
7.11	Medium wavelength oscillations in migration at Penrith	132
7.12	Interactions between the different oscillations: an overview	132
7.13	Variation in the interaction of exogenous cycles in different cohorts	137
7.14	Summary of exogenous cycles at Penrith	140
7.15	Appendix: Stationarity of the Penrith data series	142

8 Mortality crises and the effects of the price of wool — 145
8.1	Mortality crises in northwestern England	145
8.2	Other economic factors affecting the population dynamics	146
8.3	The effect of wool prices on the mortality cycles at Penrith, 1587–1643	147
8.4	Computation of a 'hardship index'	151
8.5	Did wheat prices drive wool prices during the period before 1650?	153
8.6	Effects of wool prices on the economy and demography of Penrith after 1650	155
8.7	The mortality crisis of 1623 in northwestern England	157

8.8   Wheat versus wool: factors determining mortality in
       six northwestern parishes, 1587–1643   161
8.9   Interaction of the economic factors that affect the
       population dynamics at Lancaster, 1600–1785   163
8.10   Paradoxical effect of wool prices on infant mortality
       at York   165

9   **Modelling epidemics for the demographer: the dynamics of
    smallpox in London**   169
9.1   Smallpox mortality in London, 1650–1900   171
9.2   Modelling the smallpox epidemics   173
9.3   Theory of the dynamics of infectious diseases   175
9.4   Conclusions from the linearised model of infectious
       diseases   177
9.5   Changes in the interepidemic interval   180
9.6   Driving the epidemics, 1647–1800   181
9.7   The effects of vaccination (cohorts IV and V)   183
9.8   Change to SEIR dynamics in cohorts V and VI   184
9.9   Age of catching smallpox   184
9.10   Is there an underlying 5-year oscillation in smallpox
       epidemics?   185
9.11   Long wavelength oscillations in smallpox mortality   186
9.12   Conclusions   188

10   **Non-linear modelling of the 2-yearly epidemics of smallpox:
     the genesis of chaos?**   189
10.1   Deaths in smallpox epidemics in Scotland   189
10.2   Smallpox epidemics at Chester   190
10.3   Drivers for the smallpox epidemics at Chester   195
10.4   Smallpox at York   197
10.5   Linear versus non-linear models of the 2-yearly
       smallpox epidemics   201
10.6   Conclusions from the non-linear model   205
10.7   Can white noise pump up the smallpox epidemics?   207
10.8   Examples of modelling the London smallpox epidemics:
       can the system be driven by an oscillation in $\delta\beta$ that
       is not at the resonant frequency?   208
10.9   The response of the non-linear model to a progressive
       increase in $\delta\beta$ 211
10.10 Chaos and epidemics of infectious diseases   214

10.11	Chaos and the modelling of smallpox epidemics	216
10.12	Do the theoretical models of chaos in epidemic systems have any basis in reality?	217
10.13	Theoretical considerations of the effects of population size and density	218
10.14	Comparison of the linearised and non-linear models of infectious diseases	219

11   Measles and whooping cough in London | **222**
11.1	Measles epidemics in London, 1630–1837	222
11.2	Annual measles deaths in London	224
11.3	The interepidemic interval	225
11.4	Effects of population size and density on the biology of the measles epidemics	225
11.5	Were the measles epidemics driven?	228
11.6	Effects of malnutrition during pregnancy on measles epidemics	229
11.7	Whooping cough epidemics in London	231
11.8	Annual whooping cough death series in London, 1701–1812	231
11.9	Periodicity of whooping cough epidemics	233
11.10	Driving the epidemics	234
11.11	Dynamics of whooping cough epidemics after 1785	236
11.12	Conclusions: whooping cough in underdeveloped countries today	238
11.13	Demographic analysis of the interacting effects of three lethal infectious diseases	238

12   Integration of the dynamics of infectious diseases with the demography of London | **244**
12.1	Incorporation of the death rate from the disease into the mathematical model	245
12.2	Criteria to be satisfied by the model	248
12.3	Modelling the London smallpox mortality in 1750–1780	248
12.4	Modelling smallpox mortality in London during cohort II (1710–1740)	252
12.5	The effect of changing the variables on the response of the model	254
12.6	Modelling the measles epidemics in London	263

12.7   Theoretical considerations of the effect of vaccination   264
12.8   Conclusions: interacting effects of nutrition on the
          detailed epidemiology of infectious diseases   267

13   Smallpox in rural towns in England in the 17th and 18th centuries   270
13.1   Smallpox epidemics in a rural town   271
13.2   What drives the smallpox epidemics at Penrith?   272
13.3   Dominant effect of the size of the pool of susceptibles   275
13.4   Did infants have a natural immunity to smallpox?   276
13.5   Non-linear modelling of the smallpox epidemics in
          rural towns   276
13.6   Could a noisy input drive the epidemics in rural towns?   280
13.7   Case fatality rate from smallpox   281
13.8   Smallpox at Thornton-in-Lonsdale   283
13.9   Driving the epidemics at Thornton-in-Lonsdale   286
13.10 Smallpox in other rural communities   290
13.11 Classification of smallpox epidemics and integration
          with population dynamics   299

14   Infectious diseases in England and Wales in the 19th century   303
14.1   Measles in England and Wales, 1847–1893   304
14.2   Modelling the measles epidemics in England and Wales   306
14.3   Smallpox deaths in England and Wales, 1847–1893   309
14.4   Scarlet fever in England and Wales   310
14.5   Annual scarlet fever deaths in England and Wales,
          1847–1893   310
14.6   Seasonal drivers for the scarlet fever epidemics   311
14.7   Effects of malnutrition on the biology of scarlet fever   311
14.8   Age of children dying of scarlet fever   314
14.9   Modelling the dynamics of scarlet fever in England
          and Wales, 1847–1877   314
14.10 Reasons for the decline in scarlet fever mortality   315
14.11 Diphtheria in England and Wales, 1855–1893   316
14.12 Overview of the interactions of lethal infectious
          diseases in England and Wales in the 19th century:
          effects of malnutrition   319

15   Prospectives – towards a metapopulation study   321
15.1   Mortality cycles in 404 aggregated parishes   324
15.2   Metapopulation dynamics   325

15.3 The spread of the plague in northwest England, a study
in metapopulation dynamics 328
15.4 Migration and dispersion in the metapopulation 330

References 335
Index 348

Preface

This book had its origins when we combined our interests in historical demography (S.S.) and in the modelling of biological systems (C.J.D.). We discovered that the parish registers of England from 1550 to 1812 contain very valuable data series which were readily studied by the statistical technique of time-series analysis, providing a fully quantitative and statistical approach to studies in human demography in the past. The results were ideal for the mathematical modelling of population cycles. We hope that this novel approach to the integration of historical demography and the epidemiology of infectious diseases will be of value to readers from a variety of disciplines.

We are grateful to the following for their encouragement and advice: Professor D. J. P. Barker, Dr D. Baxby, Dr Mary Dobson, Dr C. Galley, Professor Sir Robert May, FRS, Mr J. Oeppen, Dr M. J. Power, Dr G. Twigg and Professor R. I. Woods.

Our most profound thanks go to Dr S. R. Duncan of the University of Manchester Institute of Science and Technology, our co-author on many papers, for his unstinted assistance and advice. He introduced us to the intricacies of time-series analysis and dealt with all our mistakes in the early days with endless patience; he developed the mathematical modelling which forms a major part of this monograph. Without his continuing help, this book would not have been written.

S.S.
C.J.D

Conversion table for imperial to metric units

Imperial unit	Metric equivalent
1 inch	25.4 millimetres
1 foot	0.3048 metre
1 yard	0.9144 metre
1 mile	1.609 kilometres
1 acre	0.405 hectare
1 square mile	259 hectares

1

Introduction

Anderson (1994) suggested that 'Most of the infections that have attracted the greatest attention in the historical literature on human demography and disease are epidemic in character where the infection sweeps through a population . . . inducing high mortality. To examine their potential impact on human populations a model that combines both epidemiological and demographic processes is ideally required'; we hope to rise to the challenge in this study of the demography of historic populations. A new approach to historical epidemiology is attempted in which we apply the statistical technique of time-series analysis to a range of different data series to elicit quantitative information concerning not only population cycles but also the occurrence and biology of the epidemics of lethal infectious diseases, comparing the findings with mathematical models. In this way, we try to bridge the gap between historical studies of diseases and the current interest in the mathematical modelling of epidemics that occurred in the 20th century.

The publication of *The Population History of England 1541–1871* (Wrigley & Schofield, 1981) represented a landmark for the study of historical demography. These authors showed that the parish registers of baptisms, marriages and burials in earlier centuries contain a wealth of valuable information and that, by using relatively simple (although time-consuming) techniques, it is possible to extract detailed demographic data and to reconstruct the population history. Much can be achieved by aggregative analysis but to determine many of the demographic characteristics it is necessary to employ family reconstitution.

Wrigley & Schofield worked with the aggregative monthly and annual totals of baptisms, marriages and burials of 404 sample parishes in England; when these data are pooled the resulting plots suggest a slowly rising trend in population numbers in England from 1640 to 1740 which accelerated sharply thereafter. However, this pooling of aggregative data obscures the clear differences between individual communities; it is better to consider England in earlier centuries as a metapopulation, i.e. a population of populations, an ecological approach that is discussed in Chapter 15. When an individual community (usually a parish) is studied in detail, the rather static view is replaced by a dynamic picture of the population: cycles in births, deaths and migratory movements can be detected, the community (depending on its underlying dynamics) may have been stricken by regular epidemics of lethal infectious diseases; major mortality crises may have had an impact on the parish. All these factors would affect the overall population dynamics of a single community and, in turn, may be explicable in terms of its demography, geographical location and local economy. It is the oscillating biological systems that are the most interesting.

A study of the dynamics of a community, based on its burial and baptism records, therefore, begins with the elucidation of the underlying cycles in births and deaths. At first sight, most parish register series are very 'noisy' (i.e. contain much random variation) and appear as something of a jumble. We hope to show in this book how time-series analysis can be used to identify and characterise the different cycles (or oscillations) in a parish register series. It is a computer-based, statistical technique that permits a careful analysis of a data series, the separation of cycles of different wavelengths and the evaluation of confidence limits, so replacing anecdotal evidence and supposition with a firm quantitative approach. Time-series is used here to analyse a variety of data series: Bills of Mortality, temperature, rainfall and annual commodity prices as well as the baptisms, marriages and burials listed in parish registers.

It will be suggested that two completely different types of cycle can be detected by this means in single historical populations: exogenous and endogenous. The exogenous cycle is the more common and is the term that is given to fluctuations in the population that are driven by external factors. The second role for time-series analysis is the determination, with confidence limits, of the possible correlation between an exogenous cycle in baptisms or burials with cycles in environmental factors, such as seasonal weather conditions.

Endogenous cycles are less commonly detected in parish register series and are dependent on the inherent properties of the dynamics of the population. Once endogenous cycles in baptisms and burials in a community have been identified and characterised, it is possible, as we describe in Chapter 4, to construct matrix models of the population dynamics and to compare the results of running the model with the historic events determined by time-series analysis.

1.1 Mortality and demographic theory

Malthus (1798) suggested that population growth is regulated by the relative strengths of positive and preventive checks, and believed that the very slow rise in the population of European countries was the result mainly of a positive check that linked poverty and high mortality. He therefore placed greater emphasis on mortality, especially among the lower orders of society, but conceded that the process of delaying marriage (a preventive check) did operate to some extent. Landers (1993) pointed out that the progress that has been achieved in historical demography has been accomplished largely at the price of excluding mortality from the domain of structural analysis, concentrating instead almost exclusively on fertility and, in particular, nuptiality. Thus, Wrigley & Schofield (1981) have changed the emphasis from the Malthusian view, suggesting that the demographic pattern was determined more by fertility than mortality; from 1551–1751, England appears to have been controlled by an effective preventive check homeostatic equilibrium, with an intrinsic growth rate of approximately 0.5% per year. The changes in fertility were determined almost entirely by changes in nuptiality. Age at marriage was relatively stable and fertility responded closely to changes in the proportion marrying; there was an accelerated growth rate particularly during the late 18th century (Wrigley & Schofield, 1981). Landers (1993), working on the data from London for the period 1670 to 1830, presented the opposite viewpoint and analysed the available data within the framework of a structural model of mortality change which describes the specific demographic and epidemiological characteristics of early modern metropolitan centres. Both viewpoints may be correct, although we have found (see Chapters 7 and 8), following a family reconstitution study of a rural town in Cumberland, northwest England, that mortality was of overriding importance in determining the population dynamics there, illustrating the importance of studying individual populations and not pooling the data from communities where the underlying demography may be very different.

Historical mortality patterns are still little understood and the demographic parameters of mortality decline are unclear. A reduction in the intensity of mortality fluctuations in England spanned the latter part of the 17th century to the beginning of the 19th and was, apparently, characterised by a marked reduction in the crisis mortality that was caused by infectious epidemic diseases with, firstly, the disappearance of plague and then, a century later, the substantial decline in smallpox and typhus. However, the level of non-crisis mortality, in fact, increased during this period (Wrigley & Schofield, 1981). Wrigley & Schofield (1981) suggested that the lulls between mortality crises allowed the population to recover; they found that mortality in England worsened between 1580–1680 such that life expectancy declined from nearly 40 years to just above 30 years. From 1740–1820, there was a sharp improvement and expectation of life at birth rose from 31.7 to 39.2 years. Between these two periods, however, there was little discernible long-term trend, although this was a time of worsening mortality levels for both infants and for children aged 1–4 years (Wrigley & Schofield, 1981).

Two themes that run through this book are the role of homeostasis in populations in steady-state and the importance of the interaction of the different mortality cycles in population dynamics. Human populations often appear to fluctuate in cycles. Oscillations with a periodicity of 15 years have been imposed, it is suggested, on demographic rates by the climate or by fluctuations in the quality of the harvest, and a 20-year Kuznets cycle has been found which may reflect economic–demographic interactions (Easterlin, 1968). Longer wavelength oscillations have been detected in different historical periods; a 30-year cycle is found in the plotted data of baptisms from preindustrial parishes (Lee, 1974); other cycles have a periodicity of one generation, but longer cycles of 40 to 60 years that are closer to two generations have also been described and the 50-year Kondratieff cycle runs through the demographic variables of 19th century Europe (Lee, 1974; Herlihy, 1977). These latter oscillations have attracted most attention and two types of cycle have been identified. Firstly, transient, or generation-long, oscillations which reflect the intrinsic dynamics of population renewal and can occur in populations growing without effective constraint, such as might occur temporarily in newly settled areas; these oscillations taper over time (Lee, 1974, 1987). Secondly, control (or limit) cycles which differ from generation-long cycles in that they have no tendency to damp or decay (Wachter & Lee, 1989) and demographers such as Malthus and Easterlin have suggested theories for the existence of a steady-state population size or growth rate in which oscillations are driven by feedback (Easterlin, 1980). Although the factors causing these cycles are unclear, changes in fertility and birth rate within a controlled system have been advanced as the most probable underlying control mechanism (Lee, 1974). These cycles can continue unabated as long as the feedback factor is dominant (Wachter, 1991). The baby boom and bust pattern in the fertility of the USA in the 20th century is an example; the series displays a trough in the mid-thirties, a rise to a peak in the late fifties and a further decline thereafter (Lee, 1974). The cyclic pattern of these detrended US births 'is as clear a sinusoidal curve as any social scientist could dream of' (Wachter, 1991); the cycles have a periodicity of about 44 years, although the years covered, 1900–1984, allow for only two oscillations.

Demographic feedback models have been used to reproduce the regularity of these cycles (Lee, 1974; Wachter & Lee, 1989), but the models were all deficient in one way or another and the strength of feedback response either failed to generate control cycles or produced a periodicity of 90 years (Frauenthal & Swick, 1983). It has been concluded: 'A few models, in their pure form, do generate cycles of appropriate period and amplitude when fertility response takes on the strength observed. These are rather special models. Moderate changes in specification spoil the success' (Wachter, 1991). Questions still arise as to how far the intrinsic tendencies of the population may be affected by temporary conditions, by declining mortality or by waves of immigrants, and whether in human populations there are feedback mechanisms of sufficient sensitivity to generate self-sustaining cycles (Wachter & Lee, 1989). The identification and characterisation of population cycles, their interactions with one another, the reasons for their genesis and the validation of the conclusions advanced by the construction of mathematical models are the subject of this book.

1.2 Malnutrition and famine

Malthus (1798) suggested that the children of the poor suffered from malnutrition, which undermined their health and stunted their growth and the result was a high mortality. From this time, many demographers have considered the insufficient supply of food resources to be the main constraint of population growth and the main cause of the high mortality prevailing in pre-industrial times. McKeown (1976) believed that the effect was indirect and that population growth was mainly the consequence of the decline in mortality caused by the reduction in infectious diseases following an improvement in nutrition. Progress in transport and agriculture in the 18th century, particularly the creation of national grain markets, produced a more even distribution of grain and the enhanced nutritional status led to an increased resistance to infectious organisms. In support of this theory, research from developing countries affirms a clear relationship between malnutrition and susceptibility to infectious diseases and mortality (see section 11.12). The synergism between malnutrition and infection

is particularly apparent in young children; not only are they more predis-
posed to infectious diseases, but the illnesses are likely to be more severe
and with a higher risk of death. Babies with low birthweights in developing countries are eight times more likely to die as neonates and four times
more likely to die during the post-neonatal period (Ashworth & Feacham,
1985). The relationship extends beyond infancy, and low body weight
increases a child's susceptibility to illnesses such as diarrhoea (Scrimshaw,
Taylor & Gordon, 1968). Nutritional levels have also been indirectly linked
to mortality in adult populations and there are positive associations
between short-term fluctuations in grain prices and adult mortality both at
the time and in subsequent years (Lee, 1981; Galloway, 1988). More
recently, this theme has been taken up by the work of Barker and his colleagues who have found ecological correlations in the 20th century between
mortality rates by geographical regions in a given modern cohort and
mortality rates in the same region at the time that the cohort was born.
Death rates from diseases such as bronchitis, heart disease and strokes were
linked to the body weight at birth and it is suggested that nutritional
deprivation at different stages during pregnancy could affect developing
organs and the consequences were then expressed in adult life (Barker &
Osmond, 1986a,b; Barker, 1992a).

Livi-Bacci (1991) presented a different viewpoint. He analysed the available evidence over the period from the Black Death to the industrial revolution, interpreting the scanty quantitative information concerning calorific
budgets and food supply, prices and wages, changes in body weight and epidemiological history and the contrasting demographic behaviours of the
rich and poor. Livi-Bacci cast doubt upon the existence of any long-term
interrelationships between nutritional levels and mortality, showing that
the level of the latter was determined more by epidemiological cycles than
by the nutritional level of the population. He suggested that the permanent
potential conflict between food supply and population growth was also
mediated by the biological adaptability of the human species to nutritional
stress.

Because malnutrition and famine could potentially have had important
effects on the population dynamics of a community, the area chosen for
special study and reported in this book was northwestern England in the
17th and 18th centuries. Following the pioneering work of Appleby (1978),
the northwest of England has been suspected to be subject to famine and
sensitive to malnutrition (Howson, 1961; Rogers, 1975; Millward, 1983).
The Eden Valley (Cumbria, England) was backward, the farming conditions were marginal (Searle, 1983, 1986) and mortality crises occurred at

the end of the 16th and the start of the 17th centuries. Penrith is a market town that lies at the centre of the region and the derivation by a family reconstitution study of the demographic parameters of the community reveals a deprived society with low marital fertility where the dynamics were governed first by infant and then by child mortality. However, as we show in Chapter 8, the mortality crises in the northwest were not triggered solely by high grain prices, but occurred only in years where these coincided with low wool prices. Malnutrition is shown in Chapter 7 to have had a profound, but subtle, effect on mortality cycles that is not readily detectable by conventional demographic analysis; it is suggested that nutritive levels were particularly important during pregnancy and the first year of life (Scott, Duncan & Duncan, 1995; section 7.7), in agreement with current studies of historical epidemiology of the 20th century (Barker, 1992a). It is clear from Chapter 7 that an understanding of infant and child mortality is the key to population dynamics in the 16th and 17th centuries and it must be remembered that deaths in infancy can normally be determined only after a family reconstitution study.

Fogel (1994) has surveyed the extensive literature concerning the secular decline in mortality in western Europe during the late 19th and early 20th centuries and concluded that the elimination of crisis mortality accounted for less than 10% of the reduction in mortality rates. He suggested that by demonstrating that famine mortality was a secondary issue in the escape from the high mortality rates of the early modern era, these studies have shifted attention to the neglected issue of the principal contribution of *chronic* malnutrition to the high mortality rates of the past. Malnutrition and famine are contributors to a complex syndrome of multiple interconnecting effects involving three major demographic variables mortality, fertility and migration (Chen & Chowdhury, 1977) and there has been a call for a conceptual framework to examine the complicated interrelationships between demographic processes and famine (Hugo, 1984). As Fogel (1994) has pointed out, we have not yet completed the escape from hunger and premature death that began nearly three centuries ago and chronic diseases and early death are still occurring, even in the rich countries. He suggested that economists need to take account of long-run dynamic processes through a study of history, although uncovering what actually happened in the past requires an enormous investment in time and effort. As Walter & Schofield (1989) have emphasized

the incidence of crises only provides information on the more extreme consequences of famine in the form of exceptionally high mortality. There may also have been a less obvious, yet systematic, relationship between the availability of food and death operating across the whole range of fluctuations in prices and mortality. Such a relationship would be difficult to detect by scanning long series of data with the naked eye, especially if the effects of fluctuations in food prices on mortality were spread over several years. Its investigation, therefore, requires a careful statistical analysis of the covariation of food prices and series of vital events.

An attempt will be made to meet these challenges and to provide a description and a matrix model of the population dynamics of a community living in Cumbria, northwestern England, under conditions of hardship and deprivation over a long period of time (Appleby, 1978; Walter & Schofield, 1989) and determining the statistical correlation between mortality and grain prices. We believe that this is the first time that the dynamics of a homeostatic population have been explored in this way.

1.3 Lethal infectious diseases

Livi-Bacci (1991) has drawn attention to a possible synergy in the short term between famine and epidemic infections in determining mortality crises, and Chapters 9 to 13 are based on the mathematical modelling of the epidemics of lethal infectious diseases and the exogenous factors by which they were maintained. Historical demographers have suggested correlations between food intake and disease and the mechanisms that push or pull populations (Rotberg, 1983) and recent research indicates that in many European nations before the middle of the 19th century, the national production of food was at such low levels that the poorer classes must have been malnourished and this led to the high incidence of disease (Fogel, 1994; Duncan, Scott & Duncan, 1994a). Malnutrition *in utero* may predispose young children to certain epidemic diseases such as whooping cough (Duncan, Duncan & Scott, 1996a), measles (Duncan, Duncan & Scott, 1997) and scarlet fever (Duncan, Duncan & Scott, 1996b).

Diseases that are mostly associated with crisis mortality, with the exception of typhus, have been suggested to be relatively insensitive to nutritional levels (Rotberg & Rabb, 1985) and other factors have been advanced. For instance, it has been suggested that a colder climate may have helped to mute the effect of disease (Perrenoud, 1991), although this is contrary to the idea that colder winters are associated with increased mortality (Lee, 1981; Wilmshurst, 1994; Duncan *et al.*, 1996a). Government intervention with improvements in public health may have reduced the effects of epidemics and lessened the consequences by the introduction of quarantine measures, improved sanitation and more efficient methods of burial. However, although it has been shown that government intervention was decisive in reducing the consequences of the crisis in the early 1740s (Post, 1985), this argument is still speculative.

We show in Chapters 9 to 14, by using time-series analysis, that seasonal weather conditions were significantly correlated with the maintenance of the epidemics of certain lethal infectious diseases, but nutritional levels could also have had important effects on the dynamics of these diseases in different ways. Again, these effects are subtle and are not readily detectable by conventional historical analysis. Malnutrition has its effects on infection particularly in young children and these have been ignored previously because analyses of burial series have not separated children and adults (Chapter 13) and because the mathematics of the dynamics of epidemics (Chapter 9) have not been properly understood. We show that malnutrition can potentially (a) increase general susceptibility to the disease, (b) increase the chance of an infective dying, (c) act as a driver for the epidemics, (d) increase susceptibility in children indirectly via an effect in pregnancy, and (e) promote migration in search of jobs and food, so increasing the spread of infectives and susceptibles (Landers, 1987).

An understanding of the dynamics of lethal infections in earlier centuries is relevant to Third World countries today where conditions approximate to those of England in the 17th century. Malnutrition and overcrowding, both important determinants of the dynamics of epidemics in earlier centuries, are rife today. Smallpox has now been conquered but the World Health Organization reports that we face a global crisis with more than 17 million people dying from infectious diseases each year. New diseases, such as hepatitis C, ebola, haemorrhagic fever and the new strain of Creutzfeldt–Jakob disease are emerging; acquired human immunodeficiency syndrome (AIDS) has transformed into a global pandemic in just a few years. Some diseases have developed serious drug resistance. A vaccination programme for the world-wide elimination of measles is under consideration and there is also the real possibility of eliminating poliomyelitis and leprosy within a few years. Any such control measures depend crucially on an integrated understanding of the dynamics of the disease and of the population dynamics, an analysis that we have attempted in this book for populations living under broadly comparable conditions of hardship and deprivation in England in the 17th and 18th centuries. Modelling of the demographic impact of AIDS today, including its rate of spread in different subcontinents, the role of female prostitutes, age distribution of the population and the rates of change of sexual partner, is now being presented (Anderson, 1994; Garnett & Anderson, 1993a,b; Anderson *et al.*, 1991).

Even more exciting is the combination of molecular biology, ecology and epidemiology in studies in which mosquitoes are genetically engineered to secrete chosen proteins in their saliva. These proteins could be vaccines which would then be transmitted in the saliva of the mosquito which had thus been designed to act as a 'flying hypodermic syringe'. The scheme could be used to immunise humans or other mammals against a wide range of diseases, and any biting insect, not only mosquitoes, could be used to carry the vaccine. The appropriate gene has already been introduced into a mosquito and it produces antigen in sufficient amounts (Crampton, 1994; Crampton *et al.*, 1994). Again, the success of such schemes is dependent on an understanding of the underlying demography and epidemiology in Third World countries.

1.4 Readership

This book attempts to provide a new and integrated approach to human demography and infectious diseases in England in earlier centuries. It begins with detailed studies of single populations in the northwest and is set against the marginal economy of the region where mortality was of central importance in demographic control. Extensive use has been made of conventional time-series analysis to elucidate the nature of the interactions of the different oscillations that can be detected in the baptisms and burials series. The study investigates the nature of famine, food shortage and malnutrition, the prevalence and characteristics of infectious diseases and their impact on the population and on the mechanisms of homeostatic regulation. It is believed that this is the first description of a human population in steady-state, and computer simulation models are presented (Chapter 4) to describe the underlying population dynamics and the nature of the feedback mechanisms involved.

Smallpox was a major cause of childhood death in earlier centuries and the dynamics of this and other lethal, infectious diseases and their integration with the demography of populations ranging in size from small communities through rural towns and cities to London is discussed in the second part of the book. We hope that this quantitative, interdisciplinary approach will be of interest to a spectrum of readers:

Theoretical population biology

Ecologists have long been interested in population cycles, and the interrelationships of predator–prey cycles is used as an introductory example of the use of time-series analysis in section 2.2.1. However, one difficulty in such studies lies in obtaining satisfactory data series over several generations, and ecologists have to adopt sampling techniques to provide estimates of population numbers. A parish register series provides excellent data over some 10 generations of *identified* individuals, forming suitable material for theoretical population biologists to build mathematical models and to study the underlying dynamics.

One question that has motivated a thriving body of theoretical research in ecology for two decades is whether animal populations display chaotic dynamics (Ferrier & Gatto, 1993). A variety of ecological models have been suggested to exhibit chaotic dynamics because of non-linearities in population growth and interspecific interactions (Gilpin, 1979; Hastings & Powell, 1991; Pascual, 1993) although unambiguous evidence for chaos in the wild remains scarce (Ferriere & Gatto, 1993). The concept of chaos being displayed in the epidemics of infectious diseases is discussed in sections 10.10 and 10.11.

The term metapopulation arrived in the ecological literature in 1970 to describe a population of populations, an abstraction of the concept of the population to a higher level (Hanski & Gilpin, 1991). The term was coined by Levins (1969, 1970), who initially formulated a simple model to investigate the basic dynamic properties of metapopulations. Metapopulation theory has not previously been applied to human populations and in this book we are concerned primarily with the dynamics of individual populations but, in Chapter 15, the groundwork is laid for considering the different regions of England in the past as being metapopulations, and analysing migratory movements and the spread of infectious diseases between the constituent communities.

Historical demography; studies in economic and social history

As explained above, we present a new, statistical and strictly quantitative approach to the analysis of the valuable data contained in parish registers, bills of mortality, grain price series and meteorological readings and we produce mathematical models of the dynamics of epidemics and population cycles and integrate these in an overview in a case study of a rural market town in Chapters 7 and 8. We believe that this approach adds considerably to a study of regional economic and social history.

History of agriculture

One of the themes of this book is the importance of short wavelength *cycles* of malnutrition, which had subliminal, but important, effects in driving exogenous oscillations. It is suggested that malnutrition was associated with high grain prices and that oscillations in this series were intrinsically correlated with mortality cycles. Agriculturalists have been interested in the causes of the fluctuations of grain prices since the work of Hoskins (1964, 1968) and this problem is addressed in Chapter 6.

Historical geography

Each region of England in earlier centuries had its characteristic weather and economy as, for example, the marginal conditions of the Northern Province of England (an area that encompassed Cumberland, Westmorland, Furness, Durham and Northumberland), which were reflected in the demography of the constituent populations. Any study of the historical demography of a community must be firmly based on the geography of the region. Furthermore, it is possible to show by time-series analysis that cycles of seasonal meteorological variables had subtle effects on demographic features as diverse as grain prices and driving infectious epidemics. Finally, geographers (Cliff *et al.*, 1981) are interested in the complex pattern of the waves of spatial diffusion, whether they be of migratory movements between communities (see Chapter 4) or the spread of an infection within (Scott *et al.*, 1996) or between populations (Chapters 13 and 14).

Epidemiology

Two different approaches to epidemiological study have emerged in recent years. Firstly, in an innovative series of papers, Barker has analysed the splendid data sets available for the births in Hertfordshire early in the 20th century, following through the medical history of each individual to the present day. This work is discussed in Chapter 7. Secondly, following the earlier work of Bartlett (1957), the modelling of the epidemics of infectious diseases, based on simple, coupled equations that describe the movement of the infection through a population, has expand d our understanding of the underlying dynamics. The most commonly used data series comprises the recorded cases of measles in England and Wales in the 20th century. The epidemiological historian of earlier centuries has no comparable detailed data series with which to work but we show that, by using time-series analysis and other novel approaches, it is possible to identify the periodicity of lethal epidemics and to relate this to environmental factors and to the demography of the population. Finally, the changing dynamics of the disease and of the population can be integrated within a mathematical model (Chapter 12).

Medical historians

The dynamics of lethal, infectious diseases in England in earlier centuries, from 1600 to 1900, forms an important part of this book (see above) and we have employed different statistical and modelling techniques to provide a new perspective on these problems. Exogenous and endogenous mortality cycles and the subtle effects of malnutrition in earlier centuries are also of interest to medical historians and these are discussed and analysed in detail in Chapters 3 to 8.

Eco-sociological behaviour

There is currently considerable interest among biologists concerning parental investment strategies and the optimization of the possible allocation of their limited investment possibilities (Clutton-Brock, 1991). Animals theoretically face a variety of 'decisions' concerning their optimal life history strategies, i.e. how many offspring should they produce? should they make distinctions between their offspring? what is the optimal interreproductive interval? In reality, these strategies shown by animal species are determined by natural selection and are built into specific behaviour patterns by evolution. However, human populations have a genuine choice in their parental investment strategies and provide good examples for these studies in behavioural ecology from which interesting results have recently emerged (Dunbar, 1982; Hughes, 1986; Hill & Kaplan, 1988; Voland, 1988; Gaulin & Robbins, 1991). The data base that can be developed for a parish by family reconstitution is ideal for exploring the changes in parental investment strategies and resource competition within the family and the population, for example:

(1) Family limitation practices versus natural fertility (Scott & Duncan, 1996).
(2) The effect of malnutrition on pregnancy, neonatal mortality and post neonatal mortality (see Barker, 1992a; Barker & Martyn, 1992; Scott *et al.*, 1995; and Chapter 7).
(3) Migration patterns in response to cycles of resource availability. We have derived a vector that can be applied to a matrix population model which predicts the immigration/emigration of women in a community in each age group when acting as the feedback component. See section 4.7 and also the work of Espenshade, Bouvier & Arthur (1982) for an analysis of the effects of immigration and the stable population model.
(4) Was the low age-specific marital fertility in communities living under marginal conditions the consequences of the effects of malnutrition (Chapter 7)?

(5) Family fortunes through successive generations.
(6) Success of step-children in second marriages (which were found to be common after mortality crises).
(7) Time of weaning.
(8) Child's probability of surviving; were boys or girls favoured?
(9) Variations in the age of mating.
(10) Patterns of illegitimacy and the correlation with major migratory movements and the establishment of a frontier society (see Scott & Duncan, 1997a). Any metapopulation study (Chapter 15) will need to incorporate such eco-sociological behaviour.
(11) Was Penrith, 1550–1750 (Chapters 7 and 8), with a very low age-specific marital fertility (Scott & Duncan, 1996), high cyclical migration and a steady-state population, a situation in which Darwinian competition was expressed as displacement competition (Voland, 1988; Hill & Kaplan, 1988)?

We have started to address some of these questions (Scott *et al.*, 1995; Scott & Duncan, 1996, 1997a,b; Scott, Duncan & Duncan, 1997) in what promises to be an exciting and interdisciplinary field.

It is hoped that the investigations described in this book would also be appropriate for final-year undergraduate projects in any of the disciplines enumerated above. They would be inexpensive and require few facilities. A community would be chosen and a preliminary aggregative analysis from the printed parish registers of the burials and baptisms (family reconstitution would not be necessary) could be readily performed. The project should be firmly based on the geography and economy of the region. The following suggestions are examples of possible studies using conventional time-series analysis:

(1) Steady-state conditions versus rising or falling trends.
(2) Is there evidence of endogenous oscillations triggered by a mortality crisis?
(3) Characteristics of short wavelength oscillations. Were they driven by external factors?
(4) Correlation between cycles of births and deaths.
(5) Was mortality in the community sensitive to the prices of wool or other commodities?
(6) Is there evidence of smallpox mortality epidemics among the children?
(7) Do the dynamics change with population size or with time?

(8) Did the community suffer from mortality crises as, for example between August 1727 to February 1730 or June 1741 to October 1742 (see Wrigley & Schofield, 1981).

(9) Did the underlying demographic and epidemiological regimes uncovered lead to specific parental investment strategies in accordance with current sociobiological theory?

2

Tools for demography and epidemiology

2.1 Parish registers – a valuable data base for theoretical population study

The parish register series of England, many of which began in the 16th century, represent a data series of immense value to workers in historical demography and have been fully exploited by Wrigley & Schofield (1981) in their seminal work *The Population History of England 1541–1871*. They showed that by using such relatively simple techniques as aggregative analysis and family reconstitution it is possible to extract and synthesise a wealth of data. A study of the demography must begin with aggregative analysis and, as we describe in the following chapters, this can form the basis for a detailed investigation by time-series analysis. Wrigley (1966) provided a comprehensive description of the techniques of aggregative analysis, covering such topics as choice of parish and the extraction and tabulation of data. The information derived has previously been limited to annual or monthly totals of baptisms, burials and marriages, and it is used primarily to examine short-term fluctuations and their interrelationships, to give an impression of overall long-run trends and to highlight major demographic events such as mortality crises. It is a useful method to examine large-scale changes in demographic behaviour, but it is not possible to study the economic and demographic forces at the level of the individual family nor, for example, the series of infant deaths, and its effectiveness is hindered by underregistration of events and by breaks in record-keeping. Wrigley & Schofield (1981) and Razzell (1994, 1995) have taken great care in assessing the accuracy of their data. It has been suggested that Anglican parish registers may not be a reliable source of information for the study of historical demography (Razzell, 1995). However, Wrigley *et al.* (1997) concluded that although parish registers should be used with discretion and with an appreciation of their shortcomings, 'the comparative precision with which population characteristics can be defined from the information contained in Anglican parish registers is striking'. Furthermore, in this book, the data obtained from the aggregative analyses, family reconstitution and time-series analysis based on the entries in the parish register series were reproduced and validated (with confidence limits) by the independent techniques of computer simulation and mathematical modelling.

The technique of family reconstitution has considerably expanded the scope of aggregative analysis and is now central to current research in historical demography in the past, and some of the pitfalls and difficulties that have been encountered were described by Banks (1968) and Hollingsworth (1968), who observed that error, bias, uncertainty, mistakes and outright lies can all contaminate historical demographic data, with the most difficult problem resulting from a failure to record relevant events. The methods for family reconstitution are described in detail in Wrigley (1966) but, briefly, each event listed in the parish registers is transferred onto separate slips, which are then collated onto family reconstitution forms (FRFs). These forms contain the following information on each family grouping: dates and place of baptisms and burials for each marriage partner; date and place of marriage; occupation of couple and place of residence; names and professions of parents of the married couple; name, dates of birth (and/or baptism), marriage and burial of all children of the marriage. The resultant set of linked information permits a far greater depth of analysis than is possible through earlier conventional approaches to the use of parish registers, such as aggregative analysis, and a greatly expanded number of demographic measures can now be calculated, e.g. birth intervals, age-specific marital fertility and age at first marriage.

Additional information was added to the FRFs in the family reconstitution study of the parish of Penrith in Cumbria which forms the basis for part of this book by searching of adjacent parishes on the International Genealogical Index; although analysis was based largely on local records, dates of events occurring outside the parish were included to provide details of, for instance, migratory patterns. A small proportion of baptism dates were found in other parishes for marriage partners but was used only when the parish of origin was stated at time of marriage and usually when an unusual christian or surname made identification possible without ambiguity.

The valuable population data series derived in this way from parish registers form the basis for the technique of time-series analysis which is described in the following section. These data series are potentially of equal value to theoretical population biologists who are usually handicapped by the lack of comparable runs of data. An exception would be the detailed studies of Red Deer on the Island of Rhum, where individual animals can be identified, but more often ecologists have had to rely on regular sampling at the study site to obtain an estimate of population numbers. Parish registers can provide almost complete data for baptisms and burials over some ten generations and, if a family reconstitution is carried out, the history of identified individuals and families can be followed, the equivalent of colour-marking individual animals in ecological studies.

2.2 Time-series analysis – a valuable tool for historical demography

Cycles in population data series have frequently been identified, indeed a population would be remarkable if it did not exhibit fluctuations of some sort. Cycles can also be detected in the long-term records of natural (e.g. sunspot cycles), meteorological, human and economic (e.g. prices) events. Furthermore, the picture may be complicated because any data series may be compounded of two or more independent cycles.

Time-series analysis is a computer-based statistical technique that can be applied to phenomena that fluctuate or oscillate regularly with time. The standard oscillation (or cycle) considered by physicists and mathematicians is a sine wave (generated by plotting the sine of an angle against the angle itself). It is illustrated in Fig. 2.1 and is described as a sinusoidal waveform; a household example is the sine wave oscillation of the AC mains. Figure 2.1 shows the size of the sinusoidal oscillation (termed the amplitude), which fluctuates with precise regularity; it is plotted against time on the abscissa. The wavelength (λ) is the time taken for one complete oscillation and is measured from cycle peak to cycle peak; λ is 7 years in the example shown in Fig. 2.1. An oscillation is defined by its frequency, i.e. the number of complete cycles in unit time (e.g. cycles per second; middle C is a vibration at 256 cycles per second). From this it follows that the frequency $= 1/\lambda$. Many biological systems oscillate at a specific frequency (called the resonant or natural frequency, ω_r) which is predetermined by its inherent characteristics. An everyday example is a tuning fork or cut-glass vase, which oscillate at their resonant frequency when struck. Biological systems that have a resonant frequency of oscillation are as diverse as populations and the epidemics of infectious diseases. Time-series analysis is based on the fast Fourier transform, which regards any complex waveform or oscillation as the sum of sine waves. It is based on the concept of least squares, which, briefly, involves an estimation of the departure from a linear relationship in terms of sums of the squares of the deviations from values predicted by the regression line.

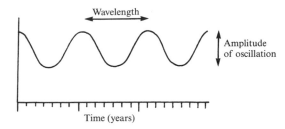

Figure 2.1. Diagram of a simple sinusoidal (= sine wave) oscillation in a data series (plotted on the ordinate) to explain the basic characteristics of a cycle. The wavelength (λ, measured in years) = the time between two successive peaks. Frequency = $1/\lambda$ (measured in cycles per year). Amplitude of the oscillation (measured off the ordinate) = the difference between a peak and a trough. In this example, the sine wave is shown superimposed on a basal level, i.e. the oscillation does not go to zero in the troughs.

It will be shown that a number of characteristic oscillations can be detected in the time-series of baptisms and burials and, since several oscillations are present together but are driven independently, the resulting fluctuations are difficult to distinguish. Furthermore, since these series represent human behaviour, the initial picture is inevitably confusing. Such cycles are described as 'noisy' or as a 'white noise series'. It is the function of time-series analysis to eliminate the noise and to distinguish the individual oscillations contained therein and to describe them as approximating to sine waves whose frequency (number of oscillations/unit time) and wavelength (duration of a single cycle, λ) can be determined and characterised. The time-series may also show gradual shifts or movements to relatively higher or lower values over a longer period of time. This gradual shifting is usually due to long-term factors such as, for example, changes in population size, changes in the demographic characteristics of the population, or changes in technology and is referred to as the trend in the time-series. A stable time-series exhibits no significant trend. In this study of cycles in human populations in historic times we identify the following different oscillations: (a) short wavelength, where the period is less than 8 years and often 5 to 6 years (although 3- and 2-yearly epidemics are found), (b) medium wavelength, where the period is between 10 and 32 years, and (c) long wavelength, where the period is greater than 40 years (commonly 43 or 44 years).

A very clear introduction to time-series analysis is given by Gottman (1981), who said 'In describing variation, the basic objective is to construct a model for the process that may have generated our observed data set.' This is accomplished by using either time-domain models (by autocorrelation and cross-correlation functions, see below) or frequency-domain models (by spectral density functions, see below). In this book, we follow Gottman by integrating the use of both time- and frequency-domain model-building. A number of computer packages for time-series analysis are available and in this book we have used the method of Shumway (1988) and the MATLAB package. The techniques available are summarised below and their use is illustrated by worked examples.

(1) *Spectral analysis.* The data series is fed into the computer program which analyses the relative importance (or strength) of the different cycles contained within the series and identifies their wavelength or period (i.e. the number of years for a complete cycle or oscillation). The significance of these cycles can be tested on the MATLAB program.

(2) *Coherence (or input–output functions).* This programme tests whether the oscillations of one data series are driving a second series and provides an estimate of the significance of the correlation of separate cycles within complex (and frequently noisy) waveforms. One series acts as the input (or independent process) and the other is regarded as the output (or dependent process). For example, one might wish to test the statistical significance of whether mean winter temperature drove adult burials in an historical population. The squared coherence function gives a measure of how well the input and output series are linearly related in much the same way as the ordinary correlation test used in classical statistics. The input–output regression relation is estimated by computing the impulse response function relating input to output. Finally, the squared coherence relating input and output is printed, so that the significance in the different frequency bands may be determined. Of course, a highly significant coherence does not necessarily indicate causality.

(3) *Filtering.* It is difficult to observe specific cycles in data by visual inspection because of random variability and, under such circumstances, smoothing the white noise series by a moving average, or by the more sophisticated process of filtering, removes unwanted oscillations and also, if desired, the trend. In this way, the use of linear filters can enhance the interesting part of the data. Filters may be designed to be low-pass, band-pass or high-pass, i.e. a low-pass filter eliminates short wavelength (or high frequency) oscillations while retaining the longer wavelength (or low frequency) cycles, and may cover a wide (or narrow) range of wavelengths.

(4) *Autocorrelation function (acf)*. The filtered data can be fed into a program which determines the wavelength of the resulting oscillation, the acf. Difficulties for the demographer arise when (as would be expected in human populations) the cycles detected have a period which varies slightly (e.g. a 6-year cycle may fluctuate between 5 and 8 years) and in these circumstances only a poor value for the acf at a specific wavelength is obtained. This non-stationary oscillation will show as a flat-topped acf, whereas a more regular cycle with a strong amplitude will show as a sharper peak.

(5) *Cross-correlation function (ccf)*. This program compares two filtered data series over a standard time period and provides an estimate of the significance of the correlation between them (the larger the cross-correlation value, the stronger the relationship) and of the delay (or lag) between the two cycles. Again, a significant correlation does not necessarily indicate causality.

The use of these techniques is illustrated in the following worked examples.

2.2.1 The lynx versus the hare

The first example of the use of time-series analysis is a simple one, beloved of animal population ecologists, in which the annual records of the Hudson Bay Co. for trapping fur pelts (an ingenious method of sampling population numbers, the validity of which has been exhaustively examined by Royama (1992)) were used in a classic study to estimate the fluctuating populations of the lynx and its prey, the hare (MacLulich, 1937). The raw data, printed out from the computer program are shown in Fig. 2.2 and it is obvious by eye (a) that there is a single, major oscillation in both which has peaks occurring about every 10 years, (b) that there is no clear trend in either series, and (c) that the peaks in the two series occurred in the same years.

The results of spectral analysis are shown in Fig. 2.3; the ordinates give the relative power of the identified wavebands and the abscissa shows the frequency of the oscillations from which the wavelength (1/frequency) can be readily determined. Each series obviously has a single, dominant peak, showing that the wavelengths of the oscillations are 10 years (hare) and 9 years (lynx). Both these oscillations were significant at the 99.5% confidence level ($P < 0.005$). The series are now filtered to display the dominant oscillation and to remove unwanted short wavelength oscillations, noise,

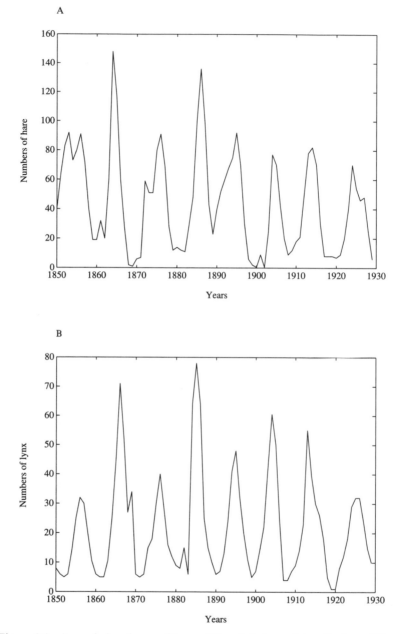

Figure 2.2. Annual abundance of hares (A) and their predator, the lynx (B), estimated from the Hudson's Bay Co. fur returns, 1850–1930. Recalculated from the
data given by MacLulich (1937).

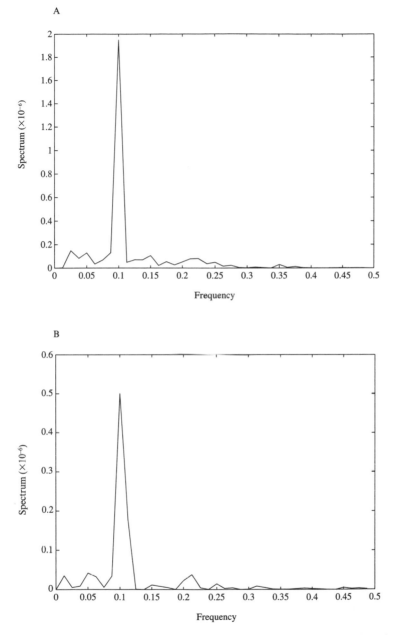

Figure 2.3. Spectral analysis of the unfiltered data series shown in Figure 2.2; abundance of hares (A) and lynx (B). The power of the spectrum is shown in the ordinate; the frequency (cycles/year) is shown on the abscissa; the wavelength (λ) = 1/frequency. There is a clear peak at a wavelength of about 10 years.

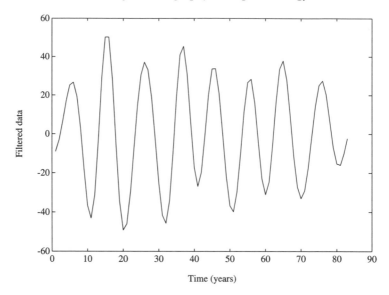

Figure 2.4. The series of the annual numbers of hares (shown in Fig. 2.2A) filtered to show cycles of wavelength between 8 and 16 years ('the filter window').

longer wavelength oscillations and trend. The print out for the hare is shown in Fig. 2.4 and since the wavelength had been identified as 10 years the chosen 'filter window' was for wavelengths lying between 8 and 16 years.

The series for lynx and hare can now be compared by the cross-correlation function (ccf) program which determines the degree of correlation between them and also the time (in years) by which one series precedes the other, termed the lag. The ccf can be computed with either filtered or unfiltered data series. Since there is only a single oscillation, the unfiltered data are preferred here and the ccf is shown in Fig. 2.5, which is interpreted as follows. The ordinate shows the strength of dominant peak (0.6), and hence of the cross-correlation, which is located at zero years on the abscissa, showing that the two series are synchronous (or at zero lag). If the major peak is displaced from the central axis (to the left or right) the delay or lag between the two series (in years) may be read off the abscissa. It is interesting that this time-series analysis reveals that the cycles of population numbers of the lynx and hare are synchronous because earlier ecological work, with the same data series, has suggested that the peak abundance of the hare generally preceded that of the lynx by a year or more (Young, 1950; Odum, 1959). Figure 2.5 also shows that the oscillation decays ('rolls off') on the positive and negative sides with the peaks located 10 years apart, confirming that this is a 10-year oscillation.

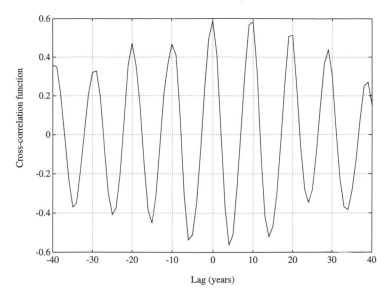

Figure 2.5. Cross-correlation function (ccf) of the unfiltered lynx (see Fig. 2.2B) versus the hare (Figure 2.2A) series. The maximum value of the ccf (+0.6) is at zero lag (0 years on the abscissa) showing that the two cycles are in synchrony. The roll-off (see the text) is at 10 years, confirming that the wavelengths of the cycles are 10 years (see Fig. 2.3).

2.2.2 Burial records at Thornton-in-Lonsdale

Thornton-in-Lonsdale is a small parish on the Lancashire and Yorkshire borders and one that has several interesting characteristics that will be described in Chapter 8 and section 13.8. The application of time-series analysis to the burial records for 1576–1812 is given here as our second worked example, where the data series is considerably more complex than in section 2.1.1. Initially, aggregative analysis is used to separate the series into annual child and adult burials and these are shown in Figs. 2.6 and 2.7, respectively. As might be expected, these data series are obviously noisy and contain intermittent peaks of burials. A comparison of the two figures suggests that years of mortality crises are not the same for children and adults; for example, compare years 1598 and 1664 (see arrows on figures) both of which were periods of high mortality for adults but, apparently, not especially hazardous for children. At this stage in the analysis, it is difficult to discern any regularity or the possibility of different kinds of oscillation that may correspond to different cyclical fluctuations. However, visual inspection suggests that after 1750 the behaviour of the child burial series is different from the earlier years and this change does not appear to be duplicated in the series of adult burials.

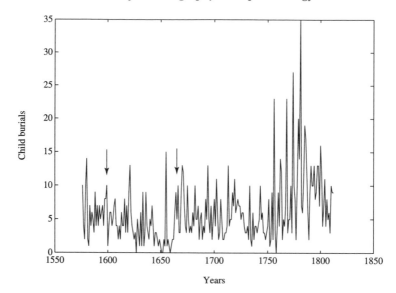

Figure 2.6. Child burials at Thornton-in-Lonsdale, 1576–1812. The years 1598 and 1664 are indicated by arrows and may be compared with the adult burials in these years shown in Fig. 2.7. Note the mortality peaks after 1750. Data source: Parish Register Series, Chippindall (1931).

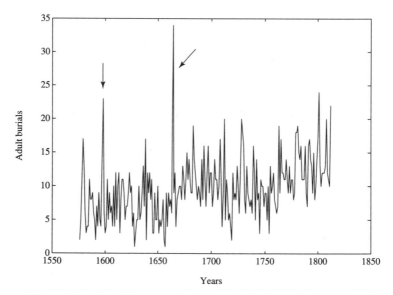

Figure 2.7. Adult burials, Thornton-in-Lonsdale, 1576–1812. The years 1598 and 1664 are indicated by arrows. Data source: Chippindall (1931).

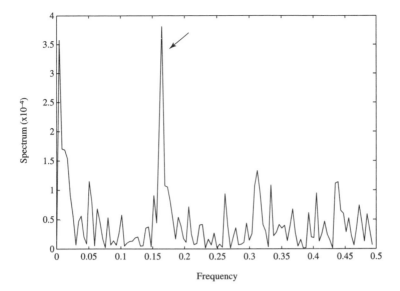

Figure 2.8. Spectral analysis of the child burial series at Thornton-in-Lonsdale shown in Fig. 2.6. Major peak at a wavelength of 6 years ($P < 0.05$) indicated by arrow. The trend also shows as a dominant peak at very low frequency (long wavelength). Compare with Fig. 2.9.

The following questions can be asked: are there any regular oscillations contained within these noisy data series? Is child mortality correlated with adult mortality?

Spectral analysis of child burials (Fig. 2.8) shows a major peak at 6 years, suggesting that this is the dominant oscillation contained within the data series shown in Fig. 2.6; it is significant at the 95% confidence level. Further spectral analysis carried out for separate periods reveals that the 6-year oscillation appears during the middle of the 17th century and is strongly developed after 1750. The periodicity and characteristics of this important cycle are not readily apparent from visual inspection of the raw data. The spectrum of adult burials, on the other hand, shows a multiplicity of different oscillations and none is significant (Fig. 2.9); the biggest peak, which is at approximately 128 years, reflects the rising trend of the data series after 1754 (see Fig. 2.7); the next largest peak is at 21 years, followed by 5 and 7 years.

Since the wavelength of the major oscillation detected in child burials was 6 years, the filter was chosen to cover wavelengths between 4 and 10 years (the filter window). Both data series are filtered and clear oscillations are revealed and the result for child burials is shown in Fig. 2.10. The annual

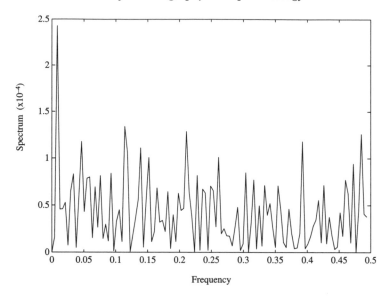

Figure 2.9. Spectral analysis of the adult burial series at Thornton-in-Lonsdale shown in Fig. 2.7. Only the trend, at low frequency, shows as a clear peak. Compare with Fig. 2.8.

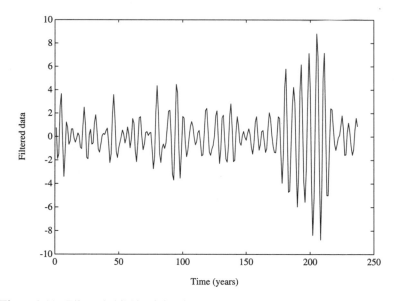

Figure 2.10. Filtered child burial series at Thornton-in-Lonsdale to show the short wavelength oscillation which has been detected by spectral analysis. Filter window = 4 to 10 years. Note emergence of regular mortality crises after 1750 (year 175). Compare with the unfiltered series in Fig. 2.6.

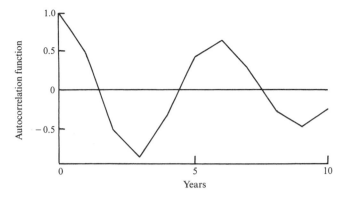

Figure 2.11. Autocorrelation function (acf) of the filtered child burials series at Thornton-in-Lonsdale, 1576–1812. Note maximum peak (0.64) at a wavelength of 6 years with a subsidiary peak at 5 years (see the text).

number of burials about the mean after filtering is shown on the ordinate; years are shown on the abscissa. The filtered data are fed into the auto-correlation program (acf) and the child burials series shows a clear peak at 6 years (read off the abscissa; Fig. 2.11), as predicted by spectral analysis (Fig. 2.8), with a good acf value of 0.64 (the value of the first peak read off the ordinate). However, the acf of adult burials reveals a peak at 5 years but with a poor value of 0.3, suggesting that it should be accepted with caution.

Inspection of Fig. 2.10 suggests that the 6-year oscillation developed most strongly after 1750 and it will be shown in section 13.8 that these peaks in child burials with a 6-year periodicity reflect the epidemics of smallpox at Thornton-in-Lonsdale. The child burials series for the earlier years (1576–1650) was therefore studied by spectral analysis and the power spectrum now shows a 5-year peak during this period and we may provi-sionally conclude that there was a 5-year oscillation in child deaths which became converted into a 6-year cycle associated with smallpox epidemics in the later years.

It is possible, therefore, also to compare the two data series by the coher-ence program specifically for the earlier period, 1576 to 1650, and the results are given in Fig. 2.12, which shows the wavelength on the abscissa and the statistical significance (the level of the probability) of the coherence on the ordinate and it is evident that the adult burial series and the child burial series at Thornton-in-Lonsdale were strongly coherent in the fol-lowing wavebands: 32 years ($P < 0.001$); 3–5 years and 2.5 years ($P < 0.01$). There is good statistical evidence, therefore, suggesting that during these early years, the two data series are strongly interrelated.

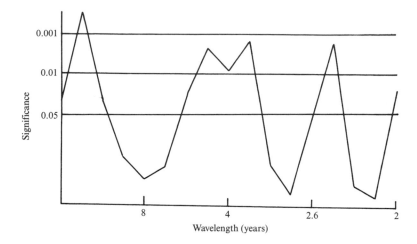

Figure 2.12. Coherence, adult burials versus child burials, Thornton-in-Lonsdale, 1576–1650. Wavelength (years) is shown as the abscissa and the significance of the individual wavebands can be determined from the ordinate.

The two filtered series for this earlier period (1576–1650) may be compared by the cross-correlation function program (ccf; see Fig. 2.13), which shows a clear peak and correspondence at zero years lag (ccf = 0.47), i.e. the oscillations in child and adult burials are synchronous. Figure 2.13 also has peaks at +5 years and −5 years, suggesting that it is the 5-year oscillations in the two series that are synchronising.

Thus, it may be concluded from this example of the use of time-series analysis that in the earlier years under study at Thornton-in-Lonsdale, in spite of the very noisy data series and the lack of synchrony between the major mortality peaks, there was an underlying 5-year oscillation in both series that cross-correlated directly and it may be suggested that adults and children were sensitive to the same driving environmental or economic forces. After 1700, the 5-year oscillation in adult deaths probably continued but this cycle in child burials was replaced with a 6-year oscillation which reflected the 6-year epidemics in smallpox.

In this way it is possible to work with very noisy data series and to extract information on the cycles within them, to predict the statistical significance and confidence limits of the results and so draw tentative conclusions therefrom. This example of the use of times-series analysis on the burials register from Thornton-in-Lonsdale illustrates how phenomena that might not have been obvious using conventional methods of analysis may be revealed.

In conclusion, plots against time of the total of baptisms, of marriages or of burials in parish records often reveal considerable variation and it

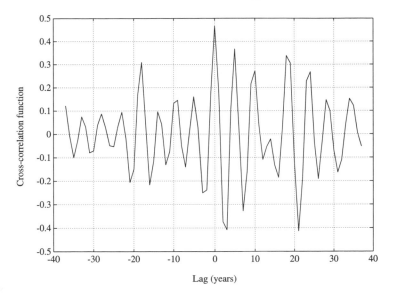

Figure 2.13. Cross-correlation function (ccf), filtered child versus adult burials, Thornton-in-Lonsdale, 1576–1650. Maximum ccf (+0.47) at zero lag showing that the two cycles are synchronous.

is natural to assume that these variations in events reflect variations in the underlying vital rates, and to look for social, economic and meteorological explanations. Conventional time-series analysis is a valuable technique in this search because it allows the investigation of continuous data in real and model populations over time – identifying dominant cycles, isolating oscillations and permitting comparisons between series. The chapters that follow illustrate the value of this technique as a tool, both for the historical demographer in the investigation of population oscillations and their possible causes, and in the study of historical epidemiology. Parish register series are inevitably incomplete because of under registration, missing records and errors and omissions by parish clerks but these shortcomings are of less importance when time-series analysis is used because this technique detects the periodicity and timing of the oscillations in a data series and the absolute values for each year are of secondary importance.

2.3 Matrix modelling of human populations

Matrix population models were developed by Bernardelli (1941), Lewis (1942) and Leslie (1945, 1948) and, of this work, Leslie's papers were the most influential although population ecologists were slow to adopt this type of modelling.

A Leslie matrix model of the population of an English parish, using the data derived from aggregative analysis and family reconstitution and demonstrating the dynamics determined by time-series analysis, is developed in Chapter 4 and represents the evolution of the population with time. The effective reproductive life is assumed to be 50 years. In brief, the model is based on a vector, $x(t)$, which describes the state of the population. It is 50 elements long, arranged in a column and each element contains the number of individuals in that age group at time, t.

The state vector, $x(t)$ is then moved from time t to time $t + 1$, where

$$x(t + 1) = Ax(t) \qquad (2.1)$$

The A matrix comprises the survival and fertility functions for the population which have been derived from the family reconstitution study. Thus, the survival function defines the proportion in each age group at time t that survive to the next age group at time $t + 1$. The survival function is given in the diagonal that lies immediately below the central diagonal that runs from the top left-hand corner to the bottom right-hand corner of the 50×50 matrix (see section 4.1).

The fertility function represents the probability of a woman having a child in each year of her life and this is entered in the top row of the matrix. This is zero outside the child-bearing age.

The eigenvalues (sometimes referred to as 'latent roots' or 'characteristic values') of a square matrix play a fundamental role in the solution of linear systems of difference or differential equations. They provide complete dynamic information from the solution to a set of static, algebraic equations (Caswell, 1989). Since matrix population models are based on a set of matrix difference equations given in Equation 2.1, eigenvalues and eigenvectors are the basis on which most of demographic analysis rests; the eigenvalue is the characteristic gain of the matrix and determines the behaviour of the model which has a 'stable' age distribution (Kailath, 1980), namely the eigenvector associated with the principal eigenvalue of the A matrix (i.e. the eigenvalue with the greatest magnitude). If the principal eigenvalue of A is 1 and if, at any time, the state of the system $x(t)$, is such that

$$x(t) = \alpha n_s(t) \qquad (2.2)$$

where α is a constant scaling factor, then, in the absence of any external disturbances, $x(t)$ will continue to be equal to $\alpha n_s(t)$ at all times in the future.

If the principal eigenvalue is less than or equal to unity, then whatever the initial state of the system, the population will tend to the stable age distribution (Pielou, 1969; Kailath, 1980).

In Chapter 4 we show how a matrix model of a population that was struck by a major mortality crisis can be developed and, provided that the real part of the eigenvalue of largest magnitude is not equal to zero, the response to a disturbance will be oscillatory. The mortality crisis can be regarded as an impulsive disturbance and the A matrix in this model has a maximum eigenvalue exactly equal to 1.0 and the system is marginally stable. We show that the response of the system in this special case is an oscillation of constant amplitude.

Caswell (1989) provided a comprehensive review of matrix population models and he concluded:

The construction, analysis, and biological interpretation of models go hand-in-hand. A model must be constructed before it can be analysed. Model construction requires not only knowledge of the analytical tools that will eventually be applied to the model, but also a concern for the necessary data and for the manipulations needed to transform the data to the required form. Once constructed, a model must be analysed to derive its conclusions. Here mathematical tools, from numerical simulation to more sophisticated analytical approaches, become important. Once a model has been constructed, its consequences are there for the taking. Many published studies have barely scratched the surface of the consequences implied by their demographic models. This is particularly unfortunate as demographic data are not easy to collect. Data of such value should be analysed in as much detail as possible.

We attempt to respond to this challenge in Chapters 4 and 5 where a simple matrix model of the population of a rural town is made and it is shown that it does not adequately represent either the demographic characteristics determined by family reconstitution, or the population dynamics which have been derived by time-series analysis. These deficiencies in the matrix model can be overcome by adding an additional, feedback vector and now the contribution of migration and the factors that determine the wavelength of the endogenous oscillations can be explored.

3

Identification of population oscillations: a case study

3.1 Marginal farming conditions in northwest England

The counties of Cumberland and Westmorland have been described as backward and impoverished (Appleby, 1975), and the area 'remote from large industrial and trading centres; much of it was inaccessible to travellers, and all of it regarded with repulsion by outsiders' (Thirsk, 1967). In addition, Cumberland and Westmorland were left almost untouched by the various agricultural revolutions that spread across the rest of the country during the 16th and 17th centuries. This was mainly the result of the inefficient feudal form of production that persisted long after it had been replaced by the capitalist mode elsewhere; by the end of the 18th century, the Cumbrian peasantry were still firmly entrenched and retained control over a third of the land in the region compared with a national figure of 15% (Searle, 1983). Thus, the far northwest of England was an economically retarded area for much of the 16th, 17th and 18th centuries and experienced periods of growth of population which it supported with increasing difficulty. In 1587, 1597 and 1623, the region suffered very high mortality, which Appleby attributed to famine crises; he thought it unlikely that Cumberland suffered famine in the first half of the 16th century, but admitted that parish records were too few and too unreliable for analysis before 1570. However, the parish registers of Greystoke in the Eden Valley in Cumberland in 1623 where people were described as dying from food shortages provided convincing evidence that the pastoral upland area of the northwest was vulnerable to famines which were, he argued, Malthusian checks operating when the growth of the population outstripped the available food supply (Appleby, 1973).

After deciding that famine was a reality in the 16th and 17th centuries, Appleby extended his analysis to suggest the concept of two Englands, the south subject to trade depressions and harvest failure but able to avoid widespread starvation, whereas the north was pushed past the edge of subsistence by the same dislocations (Appleby, 1978). The economy of the north was more like that of Scotland (where mortality crises and harvest failures persisted up to 1690), Ireland and parts of the Continent, rather than lowland England. Local studies of crisis mortality have provided evidence that there may have been ecological differences between regions that experienced subsistence crises and those that did not and the reasons behind these differences are discussed in Chapter 8. Subsistence crises were more likely in upland areas where the soil and climate were hostile to arable agriculture, and a clear contrast between crisis-free lowlands and crisis-prone upland areas has been found in Lancashire in 1623 (Rogers, 1975), and in Devon and Essex over a longer period (Slack, 1979). Local ecologies of corn-poor and remote pastoral highland communities may have exposed some areas to the threat of famine in a society where markets were less well integrated and lacked later forms of market intervention or provision for ensuring collective welfare. It has been argued that when population growth was negligible there may have been some retreat from arable cultivation in areas of marginal productivity.

Appleby's study of the northwest pointed to the subdivision of holdings and the establishment of a large number of cottagers with minute amounts of land as being the factors that exacerbated the effects of scarcity. In Cumberland, there existed a distinctive form of customary land tenure called tenant right. Kerridge saw the prime feature of this practice as the obligation placed on tenants to do border service against Scotland (Kerridge, 1969), but a further distinction was the frequency of fining. Tenants had the right to inherit the tenement from one generation to the next and a fine was paid to the lord both on the change of tenant (whether by death or alienation) and on the change of the lord. This form of tenancy was called copyhold tenure, by which the tenant held a copy of the entry in the rolls of the manorial court baron and by the 16th century the services had generally been converted into money payments.. Thus, it gave the tenant-right lord more opportunities to take fines than the lord of a copyholding manor could expect. The custom of tenant right was certainly widespread in both Cumberland and Westmorland and, although it gave the tenant the secure inheritance of his tenement, it also gave the landlords the opportunity of charging fines more frequently and at considerably greater amounts.

There are various estimates of the numbers of tenants. One suggests about 10 000 customary tenants in Cumberland in 1766 (*Gentleman's Magazine*, 1766) and by the 1790s two-thirds of the land was occupied by customary tenants (Bailey & Culley, 1794). The tenant farmer existed on holdings of land that were extremely small and so, consequently, was the size of his income. Inheritance customs favoured each son having a piece of their father's holding, but this extreme parcelization of land over generations eventually provided too small a living and increased the number of poor. It has been suggested that, by the early 16th century, partible inheritance was dying out, except along the northern border and in some parts of Westmorland (Thirsk, 1967). The persistence of this extreme subdivision of holdings and the general rise in population at this time appears to have caused some crowding in the valleys with their sparse resources of arable land and there was an effort during Elizabeth's reign to discontinue further division of customary holdings on Crown lands. The outcome was that, according to surveys, many individual holdings were small; the average size of holding was 15.7 acres and the largest 104 (Beckett, 1982). Farm size imposes definite limits on economies of scale so that holders of farms below 10 acres might possess a cow and a few sheep and rely on wage labour for at least part of their income. For areas specialising in beef cattle production and fattening, the demand for labour is likely to have been limited to the seasonal periods of hay-making and to have been concentrated on farms which, because they overwintered large numbers of cattle, had to produce considerable quantities of hay (Gregson, 1989).

Furthermore, with expanding population, holdings often consisted of land enclosed from the marginal lands of the common pasture, usually not good arable, which would have to be returned to grass after they became exhausted. Population growth during the 16th century outran the productive capacity of the arable lands and brought a continued conversion of pasture land to arable to make up the deficit. This type of enclosure by encroachment created numerous marginal holdings that contributed to the overpopulation and resulted in hardship and possibly starvation.

Landlords gradually increased the entry fines demanded of their tenants during the 16th century and, in 1794, William Hutchinson wrote that 'the miserable tenant, who is going to pay an arbitrary fine and a heriot, is perpetually impoverished' and added 'those customary tenures are a national grievance. From this tenure is chiefly to be attributed the vast and dreary wastes that are found in Cumberland'. The stark exploitation of the northwestern tenantry occurred in the 17th century and rent exploitation offered the best return for landlords that could be extracted from such an isolated, largely upland region with limited agricultural potential (Hutchinson, 1794). As late as 1794, the small size of the holdings and the general state of poverty was still apparent: 'There are probably few counties, where property in land is divided into such small parcels as in Cumberland; and those small properties so universally occupied by the owners; by far the greatest part of which are held under the lords of the manors, by a species of vassalage, called customary tenure; subject to the payment of fines and heriots, on alienation, death of the lord or death of tenant' (Bailey & Culley, 1794).

The Eden Valley runs southeast from Carlisle towards Appleby, and sandstones and Magnesian Limestone predominate. The area is mostly protected from the harshest winds and since rainfall at 35–40 inches per annum is less than half that of the exposed Lakeland Fells, mixed farming was feasible (Thirsk, 1984). The characteristic settlement on the fells was the hamlet or single farm and not the village. The arable land was restricted to a few closes near the farmstead or, in larger settlements, lay in scattered parcels in one or more fields which were commonable after harvest. The main business of the upland farmer was the breeding of cattle (which were sold on into more southerly counties) and the keeping of sheep which were pastured on the hills and kept mainly for their wool. The communities of the valley supported a different system of husbandry and a different type of society: villages were more usual than hamlets and the husbandry was mixed; the common fields were larger and played a more important part in the farming system. The main crops grown in the Northern Province were barley (or bigg, a poorer and hardier variety of barley) and oats, the two crops varying in relative importance in different districts. In Cumberland, barley seems to have taken first place and the bread was made of barley flour, whereas oats seem to have been the larger crop in Westmorland and were ground into flour for oat clap bread and malted for the making of beer. March-sown wheat and rye were grown in places scattered all over the Province (Thirsk, 1967).

The parish of Penrith is situated in the valley of the River Eden; it extends about six miles from north to south and four miles from east to west and covers an area of 7586 acres; it is 17 miles southeast of Carlisle and 23 miles from the Scottish border. Penrith had a market as early as 1123, and movement tended to be to, and through, the town. Geographically, however, the parish was semi-isolated, being situated in a valley that was bounded by the Pennines to the east, the Lake District to the west and the Westmorland fells to the south. These factors must, at the time, have provided significant natural barriers that largely confined migration to within the Eden Valley. Penrith was chosen for this case study because, as described above, this area of northwestern England was backward, with marginal farming conditions and with the inhabitants frequently existing under near-famine conditions. It was hoped that such a community would

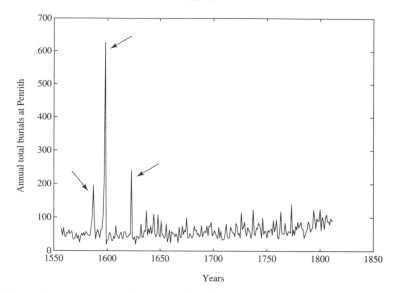

Figure 3.1. Annual total burials at Penrith, 1557–1812. The series is dominated by the mortality crises in 1587, 1596–1598 and 1623 (arrows), which obscure any underlying oscillations. Data source: Haswell (1938).

be living under density-dependent constraints and would display the most interesting demographic cycles of births and deaths in response to these conditions. A full family reconstitution has been constructed from the parish registers of Penrith, but in this chapter only the initial results from simple aggregative analysis are presented.

3.2 Annual burials in the parish register series of Penrith, 1557–1812

The series of total burials (adults plus children) over some 250 years is shown in Fig. 3.1 and it is obvious that it is completely dominated by the enormous mortality of the plague which struck Penrith in 1597–8, when 836 individuals died over this 2-year period (see sections 3.6 and 15.3). There was an earlier plague at Penrith, in 1554 before the parish registers began. Two further mortality crises which occurred in 1587 and 1623 are also evident and these are described and discussed in detail in Chapter 8. A second feature that is discernible by eye is that the mean number of burials from 1557 to 1750 remained constant (about 60 per annum) and the population was in steady-state over this 200-year period. Low-amplitude oscillations are hidden because of the magnitude of the mortality in the plague and Fig. 3.2 shows the data replotted with the peaks of the crises

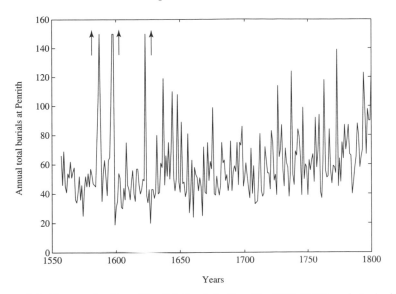

Figure 3.2. Data series from Fig. 3.1 (burials, Penrith, 1557–1800) replotted with the peaks of the mortality crises trimmed (indicated by arrows) so that long wavelength oscillations are now discernible by eye.

trimmed. Longer wavelength oscillations and the rising trend after 1750 are now evident. Spectral analysis of the whole 250-year period reveals three dominant peaks of equal power at the following wavelengths: (a) 5 years, (b) 44 years, and (c) the rising trend after 1750. When the analysis is confined to the period 1557–1750 (omitting the rising trend), only the 5- and 44-year oscillations remain and show clearly. Further analysis shows that the 5-year, short wavelength oscillation persists throughout the 250-year period, whereas the 44-year oscillation disappears after 1750.

The burial series can now be filtered to reveal these separate oscillations and Fig. 3.3 shows the short wavelength oscillation which fluctuated in amplitude throughout the period 1557–1800; its wavelength is 5 years. The long wavelength oscillation is clearly revealed when the series for 1557–1750 is filtered with a broad-band filter; its wavelength is 44 years. This filtered long wavelength oscillation for the steady-state period 1600–1750 is shown in Fig. 3.4, wherein three cycles of the oscillation can be seen.

3.3 Annual baptisms in the parish register series of Penrith, 1557–1812

The unfiltered baptism series is shown in Fig. 3.5 and two features are immediately apparent. Firstly, there was a marked rise in the trend after

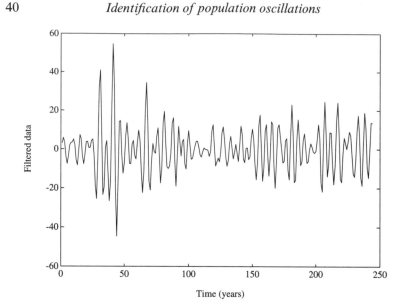

Figure 3.3. Series shown in Fig. 3.2 (burials, Penrith, 1557–1800), filtered to reveal short wavelength oscillations (filter window = 4 to 10 years).

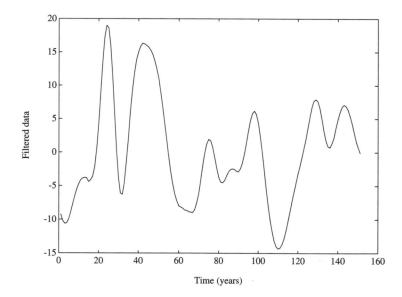

Figure 3.4. Total burials at Penrith, 1600–1750, filtered to reveal the long wavelength oscillations during the steady-state period (filter window = 20 to 100 years).

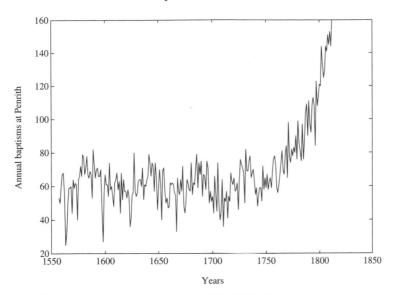

Figure 3.5. Annual baptisms at Penrith, 1557–1812. Three cycles of the long wave-length oscillation during the steady-state period and the marked rising trend after 1750 can be seen. Data source: Haswell (1938).

1750 which was associated with the population boom at that time and was more pronounced than the corresponding rise in burials (compare Fig. 3.2). The mean annual number of baptisms remained constant before 1750, confirming that the population was in steady-state at this time. Secondly, a long wavelength oscillation is detectable by eye during the 200-year period before the boom in 1750.

Spectral analysis of the annual baptisms shows that the dominant oscillations were at (a) 44 years, (b) about 30 years, (c) 8 years, and (d) 5 to 5.6 years, suggesting that the series shown in Fig. 3.5 is complex and is compounded of several different cycles. The data series can now be filtered and the short wavelength oscillation (which persists throughout the 250-year period) is shown in Fig. 3.6 (filter window = 4 to 10 years, covering both the 5- and 8-year cycles). It is non-stationary and its period varies from 5–6 to 8 years.

The long wavelength oscillation revealed after filtering is shown in Fig. 3.7; spectral analysis shows that after the plague in 1597/8, during the period of steady-state, its period is 44 years (comparable with the corresponding oscillation in burials) and, between the plagues, a single cycle is detectable during this 55-year period. This long wavelength oscillation in baptisms is more regular than the corresponding oscillation in burials.

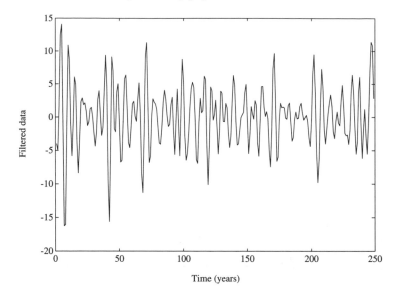

Figure 3.6. Baptisms at Penrith, 1557–1806, filtered to reveal the short wavelength oscillation (filter window = 4 to 10 years).

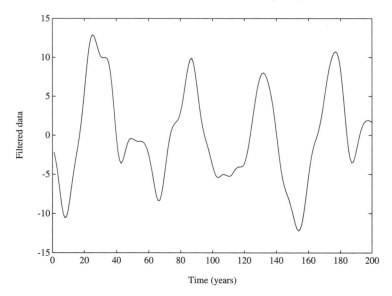

Figure 3.7. Baptisms at Penrith, 1557–1757, during the steady-state period, filtered to reveal the long wavelength oscillation (filter window = 20 to 100 years).

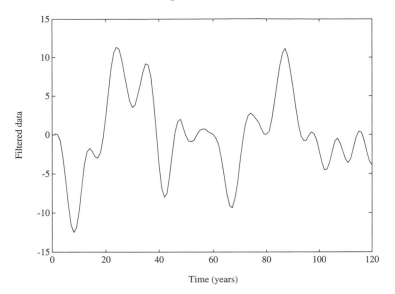

Figure 3.8. Baptisms at Penrith, 1557–1677, filtered to reveal the underlying 30-year oscillation.

The 30-year oscillation seen in the baptism series by spectral analysis is of considerably lower power than the 44-year oscillation and is masked by it. However, it can be seen during the period 1557–1677 by using appropriate filtering (see Fig. 3.8). If the same linear filtering and spectral analysis are carried out for the period 1557–1750, the 30-year peak is markedly reduced, showing that this oscillation decays after 1677 (i.e. 80 years after the plague of 1597/8). Spectral analysis for years 1655–1750 showed no evidence of a 30-year oscillation, confirming that it had then died out.

3.4 Cross-correlations between the burial and baptism series

It is evident from the foregoing that comparable long and short wavelength oscillations can be detected and displayed in the burial and baptism series at Penrith. Do these oscillations cross-correlate?

The short wavelength oscillation persists in both series throughout the 250-year period and Fig. 3.9 shows the negative cross-correlation between them at zero lag, with a good value for the ccf of -0.8, during the first 80 years. This means that in years when the total burials were at a maximum, the number of baptisms was at a minimum (i.e. the oscillations were 180° out of phase). This negative correlation between the two oscillations continued during the period of study, but the value of the ccf weakened progressively.

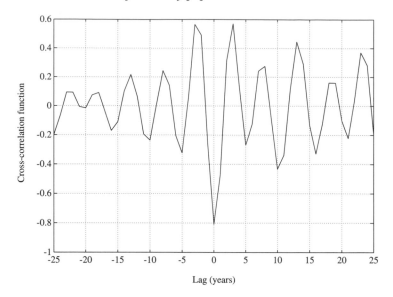

Figure 3.9. Cross-correlation, baptisms versus total burials at Penrith, 1578–1657 (filter window = 4 to 10 years). Minimum value of ccf (−0.8) at zero lag, showing that the two series are 180° out of phase.

The 44-year, long wavelength oscillation in both baptisms and burials was strongly developed after the plague of 1597/8 during the steady-state conditions before 1750. The cross-correlation between these oscillations in the two series is shown in Fig. 3.10; the time between the peaks of the ccf confirms that the wavelength was 44 years and there is strong positive cross-correlation (ccf = +0.74) at virtually zero lag. This means that the long wavelength oscillations in burials and baptisms that followed the plague at Penrith were synchronous, i.e. in contrast with the short wavelength cycles.

3.5 Endogenous versus exogenous oscillations

The family reconstitution study revealed, as would be expected, that the baptism series is not a complete listing of the births in the parish because of underregistration. It is known that the average interval between birth and baptism increased substantially between the 16th and 19th centuries and with it the danger that a young child would die before baptism (Wrigley, 1977). Analysis of the burials recorded in the registers at Penrith when there was no record of a baptism on the family reconstitution forms suggests that mean underregistration at Penrith during 1557–1812 was some 4%. However, in time-series analysis we are more concerned with the

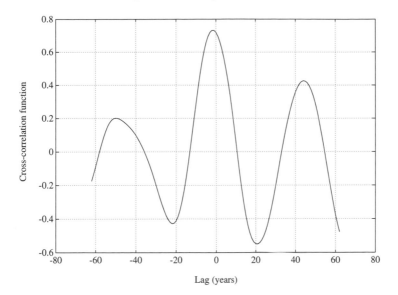

Figure 3.10. Cross-correlation, baptisms versus total burials at Penrith, 1625–1750, in the long waveband (filter window = 40 to 50 years). Maximum ccf value (+0.74) virtually at zero lag showing that these long wavelength oscillations were in synchrony.

relative number of events in successive years and with the timing and periodicity of the oscillations rather than with the absolute values, and the baptism series is regarded as an index of the number of births in the modelling that follows. The burial series is complex, comprising infant, child and adult deaths, each of which has a different sensitivity to external factors, as we show in Chapter 7.

A note in the Penrith parish registers says 'Plauge was in Penreth and Kendall 1554' but there are no further details, although plague was reported in many parts of England as well as in Europe at that time (Barnes, 1889). This first plague was followed by a single cycle (which shows most clearly in the baptism series, Fig. 3.7) before the second plague in 1597/8 with its heavy mortality, which is shown dramatically in Fig. 3.1. This was also followed by clear synchronous 44-year oscillations in both baptisms (Fig. 3.7) and burials (Fig. 3.4). This oscillation again shows more clearly in the baptism series; the filtered picture for burials is obscured by the mortality crises. These findings might suggest that the heavy mortality of the plagues at Penrith may have triggered the long wavelength population oscillations which then persisted for 150 years until the boom began in 1750.

A second feature of the demography of Penrith is the relative constancy in the *mean* annual number of both recorded baptisms and burials throughout the period 1557 to 1750, in spite of the underlying oscillations. Mean annual baptisms ($\pm$SD) were: (1557–1600) 60.9 ($\pm$12.32), and (1600–1750) 60.0 ($\pm$9.77); the overall slope was 0.0047 and this low value suggests that the system is in steady-state. Mean annual burials for 1557–1750 were 59.7 ($\pm$48.78) with a slope of -0.024. The large value for the SD reflects the mortality caused by the plague and these statistics show that recorded baptisms are evenly matched with deaths. Although baptisms fell sharply during the plague (not surprisingly), apart from this brief perturbation, the course of the baptism series is unaffected by the second plague or by the other mortality crises. Equally remarkable is the observation that, in spite of the massive mortality in 1597–1599 and, presumably, the consequent smaller number of breeding adults, the annual number of baptisms (and burials) rapidly recovers to its pre-crisis level, i.e. the steady-state level after the plague is the same as that before. Our preliminary conclusion is that the population remained in steady-state for some 200 years, being contained within upper and lower limits by density-dependent constraints. Steady-state conditions ceased in 1750 when a population boom began, as is clearly shown in Fig. 3.5. Both the 44-year and the 30-year oscillations ceased when the population escaped from the density-dependent constraints in 1750 and did not continue under the boom conditions. In contrast, the short wavelength cycle in both baptisms and burials continued throughout the 250-year period (see Figs. 3.3 and 3.6) and was independent of steady-state conditions.

Two types of oscillation in the population dynamics of Penrith can be distinguished: endogenous and exogenous. Endogenous oscillations are dependent on the properties of the system (fertility, generation length, population size) and are triggered by a single perturbation; they are analysed and discussed in the following sections and in the next chapter. Exogenous oscillations are driven directly by cyclical external factors, although they may have an endogenous component, as in the build-up of a pool of susceptible young children by new births in the genesis of smallpox epidemics. Exogenous oscillations and their interactions are described in detail in Chapters 7 and 8.

These population oscillations at Penrith, determined by time-series analysis above, may be classified as follows:

(1) Endogenous oscillations; these were triggered initially by the combined severe mortality of the famine of 1596 and the plague of 1597–1598 but were self-maintaining thereafter:

(i) Long wavelength oscillations in births and deaths which were in synchrony and which had a period of 44 years. These oscillations persisted as long as the community existed in steady-state but disappeared with the population boom after 1750.

(ii) Medium wavelength, 30-year oscillation in births. This decayed progressively and had disappeared *before* 1750.

(2) Exogenous oscillations; these were of short wavelength, typically 5 to 6 years, but tended to be variable because they were sensitive to, and driven by, external cyclical factors. These exogenous oscillations were detected in both births and deaths (see above) but they were negatively cross-correlated, i.e. the cycles were 180° out of phase. The short wavelength oscillations were detected during both steady-state conditions and the boom. The hypothesis that one of the most important factors that drove the exogenous oscillations was a cycle of malnutrition associated with raised grain prices is advanced in Chapter 7.

3.6 Anatomy of a mortality crisis: the plague at Penrith

As we have seen, the plague that hit Penrith in 1597/8 is an example of an infectious disease that had profound effects on the demography of the community and a summary of its consequences is given in section 15.3. Using the family reconstitution study, we have been able to trace the spread of the disease through individual families and have described its basic biology. The etiology remains unknown, but we suggest that it was not bubonic plague (Scott *et al.*, 1996).

What proportion of the population died in the plague? An inscription in the church at Penrith suggests that the mortality from the plague in the parish was 2260. Although parish registers are liable to understate the extent of mortality during epidemics and to record burials in the churchyard rather than deaths in the parish, it is still generally regarded that these figures would be well in excess of the population at that time (Walker, 1860). Table 3.1 provides estimates of the size of the population at Penrith from different sources. The population size in 1597 (immediately before the plague) and in 1613 has been estimated from the family reconstitution study: the calculated values are 1350 in 1597 and 1150 in 1613. The population estimates for 1596 and 1587 (Table 3.1) are derived from the value for 1597; these results must be regarded as underestimates. Of those dying of the plague, 485 have been identified from the reconstitution study as belonging to 242 families whilst a further 74 families appear unaffected. Sixty-five families appeared in Penrith in the

Table 3.1. *Population estimates for the parish of Penrith*

Year	Estimate	Source
1554		First plague at Penrith
1587	1700	200 deaths, probably largely because of typhus
1596	1500	153 deaths of people native to Penrith, probably because of famine
1597	1350	Before start of plague. Estimated from family reconstitution study
1598		Second plague at Penrith
1599	858	485 deaths of the plague of people native to Penrith
1610	1134	Appearance of 65 new families during 1600–1610
1613	1150	Estimated from family reconstitution study
1623		Mortality crisis (241 deaths recorded in parish register); probably severe famine
1642	1233	Protestation returns for parish; 411 × 3
1673	1147	Hearth tax for township; 270 × 4.25
1676	1365	Compton census for parish
1688	1147	Denton's survey for parish

Note:
Data for 1642, 1673, 1676 and 1688 are taken from Clark *et al.* (1989). Other estimates are from the parish registers and the family reconstitution study.

12 years following the plague, producing a population estimate of 1134 in 1610, a value that agrees well with the estimate of 1150 in 1613 derived from the family reconstitution study and with the estimates derived from the Hearth Tax and other assessments. It is concluded that the population at Penrith was some 1700 before the typhus, famine and plague during the period 1587–1598, and some 1200 in the early 17th century when the community was again settling into steady-state. Assuming that the population was about 1400 at the time of the plague, it is concluded that approximately 40% died of the disease; the value of 30% mortality was chosen for the matrix modelling in Chapter 4, well within this estimate.

Did the plague hit the population at Penrith indiscriminately? The plague in 1597 occurred only 40 years after the parish registers began so that there are few records for the older members of the community. However, an age-specific mortality curve for women dying in the plague has been estimated (Fig. 3.11,

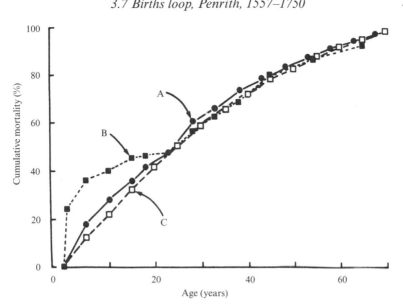

Figure 3.11. Female age-specific mortality in the plague at Penrith, 1597/8. Line A: estimated percentage age-specific mortality of plague victims (closed circles). Line B: cumulative female mortality curve at Penrith, 1600–1649 (closed squares). Line C: theoretical age structure, level 4, Model West, Coale & Demeny, 1966 (open squares). Note the close correspondence between lines A and C.

line A) and this differed from the general, cumulative female mortality curve determined from the family reconstitution data base for 1600–1649 in the age groups 0–20 years (Fig. 3.11, line B) but agrees closely with the theoretical age structure for women, level 4, Model West (Fig. 3.11, line C; Coale & Demeny, 1966), with an expectation of life at birth of 27.5 years. In order to derive an estimate of the age-specific incidence of plague mortality at Penrith that can be compared with other studies, the method described by Schofield (1977) has been used: briefly, the age incidence of mortality during the plague period is compared with the pattern prevailing b ▸ore the crisis. No age group was markedly affected, although those aged over 45 years had a lower than expected mortality and the infection appeared to be random (Scott *et al.*, 1996). Consequently, in the matrix modelling described in Chapter 4, the mortality of the plague is assumed to be indiscriminate.

3.7 The births loop at Penrith during the period 1557–1750

Since baptisms (and burials) remained constant at Penrith during 1557–1750, they can be represented by a simple loop with an overall gain

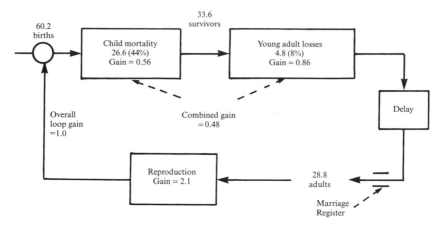

Figure 3.12. Diagram to illustrate the births loop at Penrith, 1557–1750. The mean annual births remained constant during this time. The child and preadult mortality (total gain = 0.48) is followed by the long delay before reproduction which can be measured by inspection of the marriage register. Reproduction is estimated as 2.1 children/woman. Such a system with an overall loop gain of 1.0 and a long delay is inherently unstable and will oscillate in response to a perturbation.

of 1.0 (Fig. 3.12) in which child mortality is followed by a long delay during maturation (characteristic of the human life cycle) and then by reproduction which exactly balances deaths. Preliminary aggregative analysis allows the overall gain to be divided between the different components of the loop. Mean annual child burials, 1557–1750, was 26.6 (i.e. 44% of those born died; gain = 0.56). The marriage register provides an index of the number of births that survive to age approximately 25 years. The mean annual number of marriages, 1557–1750, was 15.6 (± 6.33) with a slope of only -0.022, showing that marriages were also constant. It has been estimated that, during the last part of the 16th century at Penrith, at least 15% of these were remarriages thereby reducing the mean number of marriages to 14.4. Therefore the mean number of young adults who survived and reproduced is calculated to have been 28.8. The number of young adult 'losses' (e.g. not marrying) equals the survivors from childhood mortality (33.6) minus those that married (28.8), i.e. 4.8 or 8% of baptisms. Child and young adult losses totalled 52% of baptisms or, equivalently, a gain of 0.48. The 28.8 adults produced a mean 2.1 births each (i.e. a mean of 4.2 children born per woman). The gain of the birth loop is dominated by the high childhood mortality and, since the system had an overall gain of 1.0 over 200 years, it is suggested that this apparently stable population is regulated in steady-state by a homeostatic mechanism.

A population which has a births loop with a gain of 1.0 (illustrated in Fig. 3.12) will be marginally stable and will tend to oscillate readily if perturbed because, in particular, of the substantial delay introduced by the long period of maturation. It will also oscillate in response to any cyclical changes in the gain of the system; in this respect fluctuations in childhood mortality would be predicted to generate corresponding oscillations in births.

Thus, Fig. 3.12 illustrates the reasons underlying the endogenous oscillations at Penrith; the population dynamics are inherently unstable because the births loop has a gain of 1.0 and so a perturbation such as the massive mortality of the plague will generate population cycles. The results presented in sections 3.2 and 3.3 suggest that outbreaks of the plague in 1554 (of which we have no details) and 1597/8 generated long wavelength oscillations (probably with slightly different periods). A mortality crisis will also generate a medium wavelength oscillation in births in this unstable system; its wavelength (30 years) is equal to the delay in the system, i.e. the mean age at which a women has her median child. Unlike the 44-year endogenous oscillation, it is not maintained and decays (see section 3.3 and Fig. 3.8).

3.8 Are endogenous oscillations detectable in other communities?

Similar endogenous oscillations with a wavelength of about 44 years may have been present in other communities but they are not readily detectable. If, as suggested above, they were triggered by a major perturbation, they would be confined to an identified, single population that suffered a major mortality crisis. Did they occur only in populations maintained in steady-state by some form of density-dependent control? Were such endogenous cycles dependent on population size?

We describe studies of other parishes in Chapter 8, but inspection of their registers shows that the burials and baptisms series do not show long wavelength oscillations. Theoretical considerations suggest that these would follow only after a mortality crisis and so would not be of common occurrence. Three communities of very different sizes which suffered from a plague are presented here as examples where endogenous oscillations may be detected by time-series analysis.

A preliminary study of the city of York (which is described in more detail in sections 8.10 and 10.4) in the 17th century shows that it suffered severely from an outbreak of the plague in 1604 (7 years after Penrith) and 1800 people died there, estimated as between one-quarter to one-third of the population. Mean annual burials rose only slightly during the 17th century

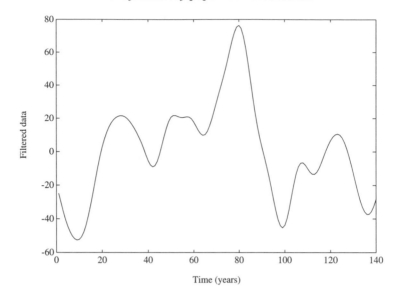

Figure 3.13. Baptisms at York, 1561–1700, filtered to reveal the long wavelength oscillations (filter window = 33 to 50 years).

whereas recorded baptisms increased significantly and the population was rising. Nevertheless, spectral analysis and linear filtering clearly reveal long wavelength oscillations in baptisms (see Fig. 3.13) and burials, with a period of 46 years, that follow the plague and which cross-correlate at zero lag (corresponding with the dynamics of Penrith following the plague of 1598), with a high ccf value of +0.8. The population numbers were controlled by quite extensive immigration/emigration which, in turn, was regulated by the availability of employment in the city (Galley, 1994). Large-scale migration certainly occurred after major mortality crises and, after the 1604 plague, the number of baptisms at York had recovered to the pre-plague level by 1606 (Fig. 3.13).

Kirkoswald was a small town in the Eden Valley, Cumbria, some eight miles north of Penrith, and it is suggested that the population numbered 303 in the Diocesan survey of 1563, 561 in the Protestation Returns of 1642, 450 in the Compton Census of 1676 and 527 in 1688 (Clark *et al.*, 1989). It is reputed to have been visited by the plague, with 42 dying in 1597 and no less than 583 in 1598 which must surely have depopulated the parish. However, there are no accounts to substantiate this in the parish register, but there were other mortality crises in 1587, 1623 and 1649. Unfortunately, the records are not complete and there are few entries for the period 1660–1685, which makes analysis difficult. However, there is a

44-year oscillation detectable in baptisms for the period 1680–1812 and, although a comparable cycle in burials is weak, they cross-correlate very significantly at zero lag (ccf = +0.93). The constancy of recorded events over a long period suggests the existence of a steady-state population maintained by feedback. The population recovered rapidly after the plague to oscillate about the original, pre-plague level as described at Penrith; if there were no feedback, a Leslie matrix model (see Chapter 4) predicts that the population would not recover and would oscillate at a lower level than that before the mortality peak. It is noteworthy that the period of apparent steady-state and the long wavelength oscillations persist after 1750, a period when Penrith was experiencing a population boom and the oscillations disappeared. Kirkoswald is presented as an example of a very small community in which the 44-year oscillation is apparently triggered by a mortality crisis.

The Great Plague of London in 1665, with its devastating mortality, generated long wavelength oscillations in both burials and births which had profound effects on the dynamics of smallpox infections (see section 9.11), an interesting example of the interaction between population demography and lethal diseases. Spectral analysis of the unfiltered data shows that the wavelength of this oscillation in London is 44 years, but it is superimposed on a steadily rising population, swollen by new births and immigrants.

3.9 Conclusions

The community at Penrith remained in steady state for 200 years before the boom began in 1750 and time-series analysis shows that endogenous and exogenous oscillations in both baptisms and burials were superimposed on these conditions. The long wavelength, endogenous oscillations in baptisms and burials were synchronous and were triggered by the two plagues; they did not decay until the population boom began. Furthermore, the steady-state levels of both baptisms and burials rapidly recovered to their pre-plague levels.

Endogenous oscillations (which show more clearly in births than in deaths) can be detected in a range of communities: a very small parish (Kirkoswald), a market town (Penrith), an important city and trading centre (York) and in the metropolis. They were all apparently initiated by a major mortality crisis and had approximately the same wavelength of 44 years. The steady-state conditions of Penrith and Kirkoswald are not a prerequisite for the generation of these endogenous cycles which were also found in the rising populations in the much larger conurbations of York and London.

The short wavelength, exogenous oscillations in baptisms and burials at Penrith, in contrast, are negatively correlated; they are driven by external factors and persist, even during boom conditions. They are considered in greater detail in Chapter 7.

4

Density-dependent control and feedback

In this chapter, we present models for the population at Penrith during the steady-state period, 1600–1750, and compare the predictions from the modelling with the actual population dynamics described in Chapter 3. The constancy of the mean number of births per annum over 200 years strongly suggests that a feedback mechanism drives the system towards a given steady-state.

4.1 Use of a Leslie matrix to model the endogenous oscillations

A conventional Leslie matrix can be used to model the population (see section 2.3) and to describe some of the features of the oscillations observed. The basis of the initial model is a state vector $(x(t))$ with 50 entries which describes the number of women in each age group (i.e. 0–1, 1–2, . . . 49–50) for each year.

$$x(t) = \begin{bmatrix} x_1(t) \\ x_2(t) \\ . \\ . \\ . \\ x_{50}(t) \end{bmatrix}$$

where $x_1(t)$ is the number of people of age 0–1 at time t. This vector characterises the state of the population at time t. There are two factors, mortality and fertility, that will influence the movement from $x(t)$ to $x(t + 1)$. Proceeding from t to $t + 1$, the 0–1 year olds will become 1–2 year olds, except for those that die. This means that

$$x_2(t + 1) = p_1 x_1(t)$$

55

where p_1 is the fraction of 0–1 year olds surviving to become 1–2 year olds. Similarly,

$$x_3(t + 1) = p_2 x_2(t)$$
$$x_4(t + 1) = p_3 x_3(t)$$

and so on. The number of births in year t and hence the number of 0–1 year olds in year $t + 1$ is equal to

$$f_1 x_1(t) + f_2 x_2(t) + \ldots + f_{50} x_{50}(t)$$

where $f_1, f_2 \ldots f_{50}$ represent the fertility for each age group, i.e. the probability that a woman in that age group will give birth. Fertility will equal zero for the young (pre-puberty) and the old (post-menopause).

Then the state vector at time $t + 1$, $x(t + 1)$, is given by

$$
\begin{bmatrix}
x_1(t + 1) \\
x_2(t + 1) \\
x_3(t + 1) \\
\cdot \\
\cdot \\
\cdot \\
x_{50}(t + 1)
\end{bmatrix}
=
\begin{bmatrix}
f_1 & f_2 & f_3 & \cdots & f_{50} \\
p_1 & 0 & 0 & & 0 \\
0 & p_2 & 0 & & 0 \\
 & & & & \cdot \\
 & & & & \cdot \\
 & & & & \cdot \\
0 & 0 & \cdots & p_{49} & 0
\end{bmatrix}
\begin{bmatrix}
x_1(t) \\
x_2(t) \\
x_3(t) \\
\cdot \\
\cdot \\
\cdot \\
x_{50}(t)
\end{bmatrix}
$$

where f_i (for $i = 1$ to 50) = the probability of a woman of that age giving birth and p_i = probability of a woman of age i surviving to age $i + 1$ (Pielou, 1969). Therefore the state vector at time $t + 1$, $x(t + 1)$, is calculated by multiplying the state vector at time t, $x(t)$ by a matrix, which is denoted by A. Since the matrix A describes the evolution of the system from the state at time t to the state at time $t + 1$, it is referred to as the state evolution matrix and

$$x(t + 1) = Ax(t)$$

where $x(t)$ and $x(t + 1)$ are vectors with 50 elements and A is a 50 by 50 matrix. The A matrix is a linear model of what is almost certainly a non-linear process.

Given the state of the system, i.e. the profile of the population at any time, t_0, then the model can predict the female population at all future times, $t > t_0$, by repeated application of this equation. The total female population at time t, $s(t)$, is given by

$$s(t) = \sum_{i=1}^{50} x_i(t)$$

and the number of births, $b(t)$, in year t, is given by

$$b(t) = x_1(t)$$

The number of deaths, $d(t)$, in year t can be calculated from

$$d(t) = s(t + 1) - s(t) - b(t)$$

It is a well-known result of linear systems theory that the behaviour of this model is determined by the eigenvalues of the A matrix (Kailath, 1980). In particular, there will be a 'stable' age distribution, which is the eigenvector, $n_s(t)$, associated with the principal eigenvalue of the A matrix (i.e. the eigenvalue with the greatest magnitude). If the principal eigenvalue of A is 1 and if, at any time, the state of the system, $x(t)$, is such that

$$x(t) = \alpha n_s(t)$$

where α is a constant scaling factor, then, in the absence of any external disturbances, $x(t)$ will continue to be equal to $\alpha n_s(t)$ at all times in the future. It is also readily shown that, if the principal eigenvalue is less than or equal to unity, then whatever the initial state of the system, the population will tend to the stable age distribution (Pielou, 1969).

This approach of evolving the state of the system from an initial point can reveal a great deal about its behaviour. For example, in the absence of any noise or external effects (which is, of course, unrealistic) one of three conditions will dominate:

(1) The system is unstable and the population grows exponentially to infinity.
(2) The system is stable and the population fades exponentially to zero.
(3) The system is marginally stable and after initial fluctuations the population settles at a steady level.

Whether the system is unstable, stable or marginally stable (see Fig. 5.1, p. 76) depends upon the state evolution matrix, A, and in particular upon its maximum eigenvalue. If the maximum eigenvalue is greater than 1, then the system is unstable; if it is less than 1, then it is stable; but it is only if the maximum eigenvalue is exactly equal to 1 that the system is marginally stable and settles down to a steady level. For modelling the population dynamics at Penrith revealed by time-series analysis and described in Chapter 3, therefore, it is important to scale the fecundity to ensure that this is the case.

The A matrix in the model for the baptism series during the period 1557–1750 has a maximum eigenvalue exactly equal to 1.0 and the system is marginally stable. If the system has reached steady-state and the population profile (i.e. the number in each age group) has reached its steady shape then, if a mortality crisis indiscriminately wipes out (say) 30% of the population, the system reaches another steady-state level after a transient period and there will be the following consequences:

(1) The shape of the population profile will be the same as before but the amplitude will be lower. The mean, annual number of baptisms will not recover to its former, pre-crisis level.
(2) The form of the transient response following a mortality crisis is determined by the eigenvalues of A and will be the same whatever the magnitude of the plague.

In summary, time-series analysis of the baptism records at Penrith (section 3.3) reveals the following consequences of the plague in 1597/8: (a) the level of baptisms quickly recovers to the pre-plague level, (b) there is a conspicuous, persistent 44-year oscillation in baptisms from 1600 to 1750, (c) once the transient effect of the plague on the level of births had died away, the mean, annual baptisms remained steady for the next 150 years, (d) there is evidence of a decaying 30-year oscillation in baptisms which follows the plague, and (e) the long wavelength oscillations disappear when the density-dependent constraints on the system are lifted after 1750. As will be shown below, the basic matrix model is consistent with observations (c), (d) and (e), but observations (a) and (b) cannot readily be explained or reproduced by such a model. The constancy of the annual mean number of baptisms over 200 years (1557–1750) and the rapid recovery after the second plague to this level (observation (a)) strongly suggest that a feedback mechanism drives the system towards a given steady-state level and this recovery was probably assisted by immigration into the stricken community. Consequently, the basic matrix model needs to be augmented by a feedback mechanism that drives the system to a 'target' value that equals the optimum level of population that is sustainable with the resources available.

4.2 The 30-year cycle in baptisms

Figure 4.1 illustrates the results of running the model *without the inclusion of feedback* for 43 years, when it is hit by a 'plague' that kills 20% of the female population indiscriminately (section 3.6). The survival function chosen for the model is shown in Fig. 4.1A. The fertility function was based on the assumption that the period of child-bearing lasted 10 years and was centred on an age of 30 years in the women.

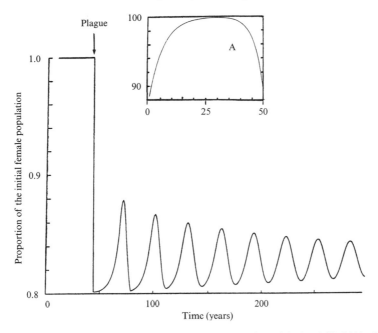

Figure 4.1. Model of annual births following a mortality crisis that kills 20% of the population in year 43. No feedback in the model. Note the generation of a decaying 30-year oscillation; the population fails to return to its earlier steady-state level being maintained at 0.8. Ordinate: proportion of the initial female population. Inset A: percentage of age group surviving 1 year (ordinate) plotted against age (abscissa).

The 20% indiscriminate mortality has two important effects on the model (Fig. 4.1). Firstly, it is followed by a decaying oscillation with a period of 30 years, which shows clearly on spectral analysis; the wavelength of this natural oscillation of the system is, of course, the same as that introduced by the fertility function. Secondly, the system does not return to its pre-plague, steady-state level but oscillates at around 84% of its original value; this is in contrast with the observed events at Penrith, where both baptisms and burials rapidly recovered to their mean, pre-plague, steady-state level. However, the model (without feedback) explains the appearance of the 30-year decaying oscillation in the Penrith baptism series following a plague. It is the consequence of the delay in the loop associated with development to child-bearing age in a system that is marginally stable, with a maximum eigenvalue equal to 1.0 (Fig. 3.12 and section 3.7). The model and events at Penrith (section 3.5) correspond in that the oscillation is triggered by a major mortality crisis and then decays.

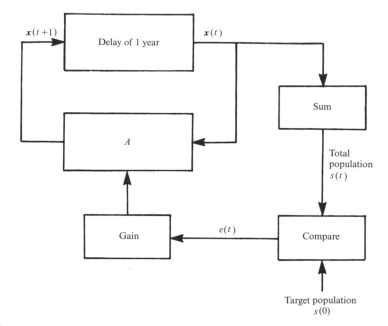

Figure 4.2. Diagram to illustrate the feedback mechanism that is added to the matrix model so that the system is driven to its 'target value', $s(0)$.

4.3 Feedback: model no. 2

As explained above, the first model is not an adequate description of events at Penrith. For the plague to generate the 44-year oscillations that do not decay during the period 1600–1750 and for the number of baptisms to return to its earlier steady-state level, it is necessary to introduce a feedback mechanism into the model (see Fig. 4.2) which drives the system to a 'target' value which equates with the optimum level of the population that is sustainable with the resources available. If this 'target' value is denoted as $s(0)$ then, at each time step in the model calculation, the current level of the population, $s(t)$, is compared with the 'target' value to generate a fractional discrepancy, $e(t)$, which is given by

$$e(t) = \frac{s(t) - s(0)}{s(0)}$$

This discrepancy is multiplied by the gain and is used to adjust the A matrix (see Fig. 4.2).

If there are no external influences, adjustments can be made to only two properties of the system in order to drive the birth rate back to a fixed level, namely fertility and mortality. The results of the family reconstitution study suggest that there were no major changes in fertility during years 1557–1750 (see section 4.5); furthermore the 30-year oscillation is present both before and after the second plague of 1597/8 and thus it is unlikely that there were any major changes to the fertility function as a consequence of the plague (i.e. women were not having children earlier in life). It is therefore probable that changes in mortality and not fertility are the basis of the feedback mechanism that drives the birth rate to its fixed, pre-crisis level.

The feedback mechanism is incorporated into the model by making the mortality function, denoted by m_i (where the probability of survival $(p_i) = 1 - m_i$, for $i = 1$ to 50), time-varying and adjusting it on the basis of the fractional discrepancy $e(t)$ between the 'target' total population, $s(0)$, and the current level of the population, $s(t)$, according to

$$m_i(t) = m_i(0)[1 + ge(t)]$$

where $m_i(t)$ is the probability of a woman of age i dying before she reaches age $i + 1$ in year t, $m_i(0)$ is the probability of death between the ages i and $i + 1$ for the stable age distribution, $n_s(t)$, and g is the gain. The gain is the size of the correction in response to a given discrepancy between the current level of the population and its target level and is defined such that, when g is 10, a 1% fractional discrepancy results in a 10% increase in mortality.

Model no. 2 has been run with different gains on the feedback and different mortality functions for the population and has been subjected to two plagues 44 years apart (as at Penrith) in which 30% of the population were indiscriminately killed. The gain was adjusted to give between the plagues a single oscillation of wavelength 55 years and after the second plague oscillations of wavelength 44 years, thereby corresponding with events at Penrith. The mortality function was initially defined as

$$m_i(0) = e^{-(i + 6.5)/5} + e^{-(57 - i)/5}$$

which gave the profile of the stable population corresponding to the eigenvector of the A matrix, $n_s(t)$; it is illustrated by line A in Fig. 4.3 and produced the decaying oscillation in the number of births per annum shown in Fig. 4.4A, demonstrating that the model does not adequately describe the nondecaying 44-year oscillation at Penrith. However, with the introduction of feedback into the model the mean level of births now returns to the original steady-state value before the plague and thereby corresponds in this respect to the situation at Penrith.

When the mortality function is changed to

$$m_i(0) = e^{-(i + 4.5)/5} + e^{-(57 - i)/5}$$

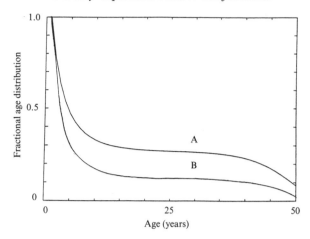

Figure 4.3. Profile of the stable population used in the model with feedback (see Fig. 4.2) and generating the oscillations shown in Figs. 4.4 and 4.5. Ordinate: fraction of population in each age group. Mortality functions: (line A) $e^{-(i+6.5)/5} + e^{-(57-i)/5}$ (line B) $e^{-(i+4.5)/5} + e^{-(57-i)/5}$.

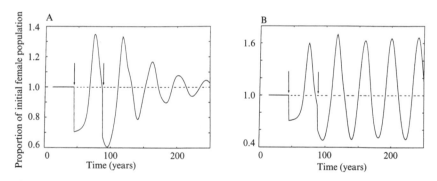

Figure 4.4. Annual births expressed as a proportion of the initial female population (ordinate) following two mortality crises, 43 years apart (arrows). (A) Mortality function used is that shown by line A in Fig. 4.3. Note population returns to its original steady-state level but the oscillation decays. (B) Mortality function used is that given by line B in Fig. 4.3. Oscillation does not decay.

the profile of the stable population is altered to that shown by line B in Fig. 4.3 and the modelling of the number of births per annum after the second plague now shows a persistent and constant oscillation of period 44 years and the mean number of births returns to the steady-state, pre-plague level. The effect of two '30% indiscriminate plagues' and the resultant 55– and 44-year cycles generated by the model is illustrated in Fig. 4.4B and may be compared with events at Penrith shown in Fig. 3.7.

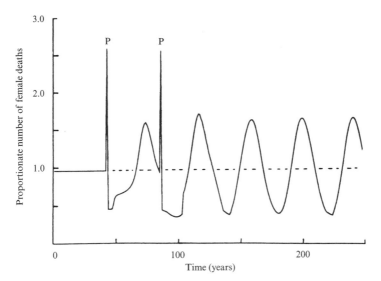

Figure 4.5. Number of deaths per annum (ordinate) predicted by the model using the same conditions as Fig. 4.4B. The oscillations synchronise with the births of Fig. 4.4B. The mortality crises are indicated by P.

The number of deaths per annum following each of the two plagues can also be predicted by the model using the mortality function of line B in Fig. 4.3 and is shown in Fig. 4.5; there is, again, a persistent, non-decaying oscillation following the second plague of period 44 years which corresponds closely to the predicted oscillations in the birth series (Fig. 4.4B). More importantly, the amplitude of the 44-year oscillations in births and deaths generated by the model are of the same magnitude, and the cross-correlation coefficient of births and deaths shows zero lag, i.e. 44-year cycles in deaths are also generated by the model and these synchronise with the predicted 44-year oscillations in the births.

These simulations by the model may be compared with the baptism and burial series from the Penrith registers shown after linear filtering in Figs. 3.4 and 3.7. The cross-correlation function between the two register series, using the same filter, shows excellent correspondence between the two oscillations, with a ccf of +0.7 at virtually zero lag and, furthermore, the amplitudes of the two oscillations during 1600–1750 are of approximately the same magnitude. These observations might suggest that the model no. 2 is valid, i.e. that a heavy and indiscriminate mortality hitting a stable population, which has a 'target' (or steady-state) level and a feedback mechanism, initiates persistent, synchronised oscillations in both the subsequent births and deaths.

4.4 Homeostasis and density-dependent constraints in a single human population

Homeostasis has had a less dominant role in the study of human demography than in animal population studies mainly because, although human population dynamics have probably been governed by homeostasis, it was considered that the control was weak and that the effects are easily masked (Lee, 1987). In addition, previous studies have been complicated by combining and averaging data from many parishes, a process that may conceal individual oscillations in some populations (Lee, 1985, and Chapter 15).

It has been shown in Chapter 3 how the characteristic oscillations can be extracted from the records of a single parish, and matrix modelling and computer simulation have demonstrated how these oscillations reflect the intrinsic properties of the population dynamics, including the role of a feedback component. The two types of endogenous oscillation observed at Penrith have different causes and are dependent on different underlying conditions. The 30-year, decaying cycle in births results from the response of the population to a mortality crisis that causes oscillations with a period equal to the mean time from birth to the middle of the child-bearing age of women, and exemplifies a 'transient' oscillation (Lee, 1974, 1987). The 44-year oscillation, on the other hand, fits the characteristics of a 'control' cycle, and the requirement of a feedback component is indicative of a population that is subject to homeostatic constraint (Wachter & Lee, 1989). Childhood mortality has the overriding influence on the population dynamics and governs the rate of decay of the oscillations; the rate of childhood mortality, therefore, is predicted to have remained constant throughout the steady-state period. See section 7.4, wherein it is shown that improving infant mortality was counterbalanced by rising child mortality because of smallpox.

To simulate the conditions at Penrith a number of assumptions have been made and it is now necessary to assess how well the observed demographic characteristics of Penrith correspond with the theoretical assumptions and predictions of the model. This has been undertaken by a full family reconstitution study of the population and an investigation of the role of migration in maintaining the population in homeostasis.

4.5 Use of the family reconstitution study to validate the model

The family reconstitution study of the community at Penrith has been used to validate the fertility and mortality functions chosen for the modelling; in particular, the population profile (shown in Fig. 4.3) necessary to generate

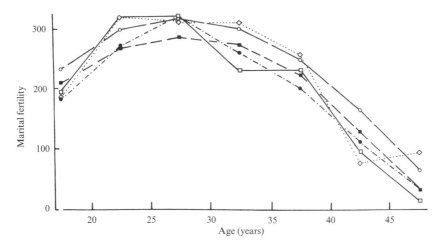

Figure 4.6. Age-specific marital fertility at Penrith (children born per thousand women-years lived) derived from the family reconstitution study (ordinate). Open diamonds: 1557–1599. Closed circles: 1600–1649. Open squares: 1650–1699. Open circles: 1700 1749. Closed squares: 1750–1812.

a non-decaying oscillation seems to require an artificially high level of mortality.

For the period 1600–1700, when the 30-year cycles in baptisms were found, the age of a woman having her median child was found to be 30.9 years (mean age = 31.2 years). This agrees well with the median age predicted by the 30-year oscillation.

The methods by which age-specific marital fertility (the number of children born in relation to a women's age) is calculated was described by Scott & Duncan (1996); the rate is the number of children born per thousand woman-years lived. The calculated, age-specific marital fertility at Penrith, 1557–1812, agrees broadly with that chosen in the model, where it was assumed that child-bearing lasted 10 years and was centred on age 30 years, although the actual marital fertility was found to extend from ages 15 to 45 years. This pattern of marital fertility was virtually unchanged throughout the 250-year period of study, as shown in Fig. 4.6, and a noticeable feature is the lower fertility rates for women aged below 25 years.

Although no human population approaches the potential biological maximum, since such factors as prolonged breastfeeding, periods of abstinence or separation, disease, conception difficulties and abortion can all exert a repressing influence, one group of people has been studied in which some of these factors are eliminated. The Hutterite communities of North America are an Anabaptist sect whose beliefs prohibit extramarital coitus, contraception and abortion, and whose diet and standards of medical care produce high fertility rates. Early marriage is not usual among the Hutterites and the degree of fertility is high in the third decade but the number of births per thousand women falls rapidly once the fourth decade is reached, with a rapid increase in the percentage of sterile couples from 33% at ages 35–39 to 100% a decade later. The total marital fertility ratio for the Hutterite women aged 20–49 for 1921–1930 is shown by line A in Fig. 4.7 and it can be seen that this group exhibits rates well in excess of the other groups depicted. Striking regional variations have been found for some European populations and in Germany, for instance, there were considerable differences in fertility rates between villages; the total marital fertility ratio for four Waldeck parishes for 1662–1849 was 8.3, shown by line B, Fig. 4.7 (Wilson, 1984)

Fertility rates have previously been calculated for 14 reconstituted English parishes and it has been suggested that the resultant patterns of fertility were broadly representative of pre-industrial England (Wrigley & Schofield, 1983). The fertility values found were mostly at the lower end of the range when compared with other historical populations and the average is shown by line C in Fig. 4.7.

Marital fertility at Penrith is shown by line E in Fig. 4.7 and it can be seen that it was much lower than that for these other studies, particularly during the earlier years of child-bearing. The marital fertility rate was well below comparable market towns and may be best compared to the fertility rates found in Third World areas today. The age-specific marital fertility rates for both Nepal, 1977 (line D, Fig. 4.7) and Bengal, 1945–1946, and the shapes of the curves are very similar to that seen at Penrith, particularly regarding the lower fertility rates for women aged below 25 years (Wilson, 1984). The marked subfecundity for these women is the distinguishing characteristic of fertility for Penrith and this pattern is also apparent for populations from Third World countries.

Thus, the marital fertility rates for women at Penrith were amongst the lowest found for any reconstituted population before the widespread use of contraception practices. We have examined the evidence elsewhere (Scott & Duncan, 1996) and conclude that the population was not practising family limitation. What could account for a marital fertility that was markedly lower than that seen for other historical populations but mirrored closely that seen in contemporary developing countries? We conclude from our study of the demography of the parish (Scott, 1995; Scott & Duncan, 1996) that undernutrition is the explanation, wholly or in part, for the low fertility at Penrith, confirming the view advanced in section 3.1 that this might

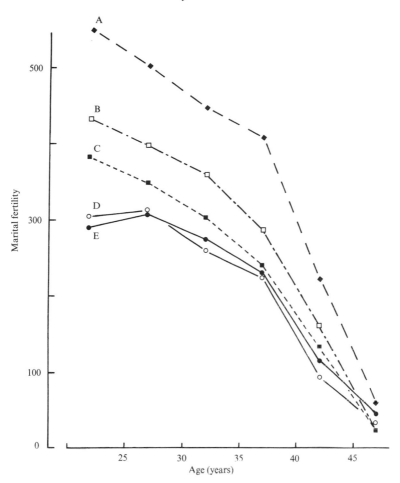

Figure 4.7. Age-specific marital fertility (ordinate) for five populations (children born per thousand women-years lived). Line A (closed diamonds): Hutterites, 1921–1930. Line B (open squares): average of four Waldeck villages of pre-industrial Germany, 1662–1849. Line C (closed squares): average of 14 reconstituted English parishes, 1550–1849. Line D (open circles): Nepal, 1977. Line E (closed circles): Penrith, 1557–1812. Data sources: Wrigley & Schofield (1983) and Wilson(1984).

be the consequence of the far northwest of England being an economically retarded area for much of the 16th, 17th and 18th centuries.

The calculated survival curve for women for 1600–1649 at Penrith (during the period when the synchronous long wavelength oscillations in births and deaths were initiated and maintained) is shown in Fig. 4.8, line A. The mortality was severe and the curve follows level 5 of the Models of

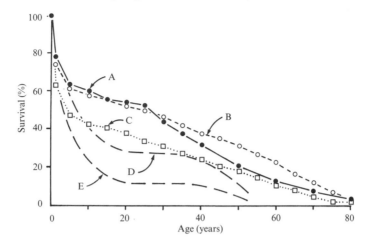

Figure 4.8. Female survival curve at Penrith, 1600–1649 (Line A, closed circles). Line B (open circles): female survival, level 5, Model West, $\overset{o}{e}_0 = 30$ years. Line C (open squares): female survival, level 1, Model West, $\overset{o}{e}_0 = 20$ years (Coale & Demeny, 1966). Line D: theoretical female survival curve that generates a decaying oscillation in the matrix model. Line E: theoretical female survival curve that generates a non-decaying oscillation in the matrix model.

Stable Populations (Model West; life expectancy at birth, $\overset{o}{e}_0 = 30$ years; Coale & Demeny, 1966) for ages 0 to 30 years (Fig. 4.8, line B), but approaches level 1 ($\overset{o}{e}_0 = 20$ years) at ages over 50 years (Fig. 4.8, line C).

The model was then re-run using the true mortality and fertility functions calculated above: the standard 30% indiscriminate mortality crisis generated long wavelength oscillations, but these decayed. Obviously, the actual female mortality was not as severe as that assumed in the original matrix model for the population. If the theoretical female survival curve shown in line D in Fig. 4.8 is used in the modelling, the impact of a 'plague' mortality generates a long wavelength oscillation in births and deaths, but this is again a decaying oscillation. The true survival curve of females at Penrith (line A, Fig. 4.8) only approaches line D in the ages after child-bearing. To generate a non-decaying oscillation in the matrix model, it was necessary to apply the very severe mortality of line E. The true female survival curve at Penrith (line A) falls progressively with the age of the woman, but is certainly not as severe as that shown by line E.

It is concluded that although the model illustrates many of the features of the dynamics of the population at Penrith, including the decaying 30-year oscillation, it is not a complete description of the dynamics that underlie the longer wavelength cycles. Evidently, the population at Penrith was not closed and a number of factors could contribute to a modification of the model: women remaining unmarried or the emigration and immigration of women. The curve shown by line E in Fig. 4.8, which was applied to the model, strictly represents the survival of women who marry and have children; women who remain unmarried, or who leave the parish will, in effect, contribute to changing line D towards line E. The possible importance of these factors will be assessed in the next section.

4.6 The role of migration

Is there evidence that unmarried women contributed to the 'losses' of the female breeding population at Penrith? It is difficult to identify unmarried women, but female deaths (i.e. presumably unmarried) formed 27.5% of the total for 1576–1650 and 26% for 1700–1800. These values are probably overestimates of the effects of unmarried women on the population dynamics, but suggest that a substantial proportion of the women were 'lost' from the breeding population by remaining unmarried and that they made a major contribution to converting, in effect, line D into line E (Fig. 4.8). Wrigley & Schofield (1981) estimated that the proportions of people in England who never married were 21.9% and 19.7% for those born 1600–1650 and 1650–1700 respectively. There is good correspondence between these estimates and if an additional 'loss' of 20% were added to the middle section of line A in Fig. 4.8 (age 15–40 years) the resulting 'survival curve' would be markedly more severe and the loss of women from the effective breeding population is greater than that derived by simple aggregative analysis.

It was assumed in the initial model that the population was closed (i.e. a community not subject to significant migration), but this is a naive assumption and the amount of migration in periods of demographic transition could be substantial, witness the influx of migrants after the plague. It is difficult to obtain quantitative evidence on emigration and immigration accurately by family reconstitution, particularly before 1730, when the registers provided little additional information, but an estimate of the cycles of movement of people into the parish can be derived from the reconstituted family forms. For example, the appearance of a family in the registers where there is no previous record of either partner at Penrith was scored as two immigrants; when one partner at marriage came from another parish, it was scored as one immigrant. The recovery of the parish population

Density-dependent control and feedback

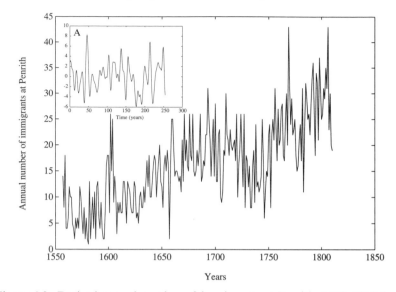

Figure 4.9. Derived annual number of immigrants at Penrith, 1557–1810 (ordinate). Inset A: data series for immigrants, 1557–1810, filtered to show a medium wavelength oscillation (filter window = 10 to 30 years).

clearly required immigration on a scale capable of replacing the deficit and permitting further growth. The most important immigrations would be the influx of married couples following a mortality crisis (such as the plague or severe famine) to fill available 'spaces' in the community and 65 new families appeared in Penrith during the first few years of the 17th century, and a rise in the number of immigrants continued until the middle of the century. Between 1650 and 1750 there is a slight decrease in immigration, and the slope of the line is −0.04. Immigration rises again after 1750. Overall, the mean annual number of immigrants for 1600–1750 was 15.4 (slope = 0.045; Fig. 4.9).

An estimate of the scale of emigration is more difficult. Although it is obvious that families did leave the parish, it is not known when this occurred. However, it is assumed that a couple left the parish after marriage when there were no further events, and the native-born bride and/or groom were scored as emigrants. There is a rise in the number of people leaving the parish at marriage from 1600–1620 on this analysis, after which there is a slight decrease until 1750. The mean annual number of 'emigrants' for 1600–1750 is 3.95 (slope = −0.003).

Time-series analysis revealed that the immigration index was not static but contained oscillations which spectral analysis revealed were of wavelengths 16 and 5–6 years. The filtered 16-year oscillation over the whole period under study (1557–1810) is illustrated in Fig. 4.9A. Between 1650 and 1750, these cycles cross-correlated with adult mortality with a lag of 1 or 2 years (ccf $=+0.5$).

From 1735 to 1812 information is given in the marriage registers of Penrith of the parish of both partners. An annual index of the percentage of partners coming from outside the parish has been calculated as

$$\frac{\text{Number of partners from outside the parish} \times 100}{\text{Number of marriages} \times 2}$$

Spectral analysis of this percentage immigration index at marriage (1735–1812) shows the major peak at 5 years and this 5-year oscillation is synchronous (i.e. cross-correlates at zero lag) with a corresponding oscillation in adult deaths (ccf $= +0.4$). There is evidence, therefore, of population movement at Penrith that is cyclical and tends to respond to increased adult mortality. Prior to 1750 there was more movement from upland areas than from the parishes in the Eden Valley, and from the west rather than the east which may reflect the difficulty in subsistence farming on marginal lands (Scott, 1995). We conclude that Penrith was not a closed population and that there is evidence of losses to the breeding population at Penrith by women who did not marry and by movements out of and into the community and that they are additional to the female mortality which is described by the survival curve shown in Fig. 4.8.

4.7 A migratory feedback vector for the matrix model

The Leslie Matrix (*A* matrix) generates the number of individual women in each age group (up to 50 years of age) at each time step. For each year, the 50 numbers are summed to obtain the total actual population (section 4.1). The new model, presented now, incorporates a migration feedback (or *b*) vector. The total actual population is compared with a nominal 'target' population to generate an error at each time step, i.e.

$$\text{error} = \text{nominal population} - \text{actual population}$$

The error is then multiplied by the feedback vector to obtain 50 numbers which represent the net gains/losses to the female population in each age group. The feedback, which was an integral component of the previous matrix model (section 4.3), is not introduced into the new model that is shown in Fig. 4.10.

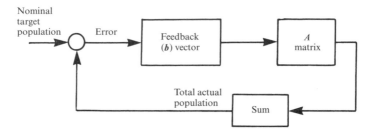

Figure 4.10. Diagram to show the incorporation of the feedback **b** vector into the model.

The oscillations of the system in the absence of feedback depend upon the location in the complex plane of the roots of the characteristic polynomial associated with the Leslie matrix,

$$a(z) = \det(zI - A)$$

where det(.) is the determinant of a matrix; A is the Leslie matrix; I is the identity matrix and z is the complex variable, $z = x + iy$ with $i = \sqrt{-1}$. The period of the oscillations following the impact of the plague are determined by the pair of complex conjugate roots that are closest to the unit circle in the complex plane, defined by $|z| = 1$. The mortality function chosen is that which represents the true female survival curve (line A, Fig. 4.8); Ackerman's pole placement technique (Kailath, 1980) is then used to determine the feedback vector that moves this dominant pair of roots to

$$z = \cos\frac{2\pi}{40} \pm i\sin\frac{2\pi}{40}$$

The calculated feedback vector is shown in Fig. 4.11 and the model (Fig. 4.10) now generates 40-year oscillations in response to the effect of the mortality of the plague. The **b** vector represents the net gains/losses of females to the population, classified by age group; the most important group are aged 15–30 years and positive values here represent a net gain of females in the child-bearing age group. The feedback vector effectively converts the true survival curve (line A, Fig. 4.8) into line E, the theoretically required 'mortality' (or losses of females) to generate non-decaying long wavelength oscillations in births and deaths. The 40-year oscillation in births generated in the model by the **b** vector is shown in Fig. 4.12.

When the error is positive (i.e. the population numbers are low so that the target population exceeds the actual population) the feedback (**b**) vector (Fig. 4.11) implies that there is a net efflux of children, a net influx of young

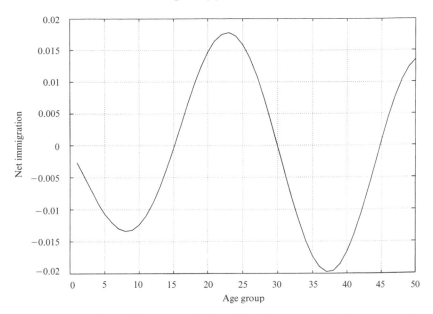

Figure 4.11. Feedback (**b**) vector calculated by Akermans pole placement technique to maintain a 40-year oscillation in the matrix model with female survival represented by line A in Fig. 4.8. Ordinate: net gains/losses to the female population in each age group (abscissa) when the error = +1.

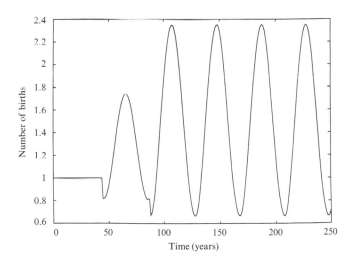

Figure 4.12. A 40-year, non-decaying oscillation in births generated by the model illustrated in Fig. 4.10, using the feedback **b** vector shown in Fig. 4.11. Ordinate: annual number of births relative to a steady-state condition of 1.0.

women and an efflux of older (mostly non-breeding) women. The movement of women is described by the integral of the curve in Fig. 4.11 over a period of 50 years, i.e. if the target population exceeds the actual population by one woman, there is a movement of $+0.015$ women aged 20 and -0.01 of age 5. For example, to a first approximation, we might expect the movement (both inwards and outwards) of 50 women for an error of $+100$ women.

When the error is negative (i.e. population numbers are high) the reverse situation obtains: a net influx of children, a net efflux of young women and an influx of older women. The *b* vector is an example of classic linear feedback. Line E in Fig. 4.8 represents the theoretical curve for the effective breeding female population whereas line A is the actual female survival curve determined at Penrith.

4.8 Conclusions

The characteristic endogenous oscillations and the population dynamics at Penrith during the steady-state period following the crisis mortality of the plague (1600–1750) described in Chapter 3 can be simulated by a Leslie matrix model. However, to replicate the essential features of the dynamics, namely non-decaying endogenous oscillations and a rapid return to the pre-plague level of births and deaths, it is necessary to incorporate feedback into the model, suggesting that Penrith at this time was a population maintained in homeostasis by density-dependent constraints. However, the family reconstitution study shows that although the fertility function corresponds to that used in the model, the level of female mortality at Penrith was not as severe as that required by the model to generate non-decaying oscillations.

But females can be 'lost' from the population by means other than mortality, for example by emigration or by not marrying. The feedback *b* vector summarises the net losses (and gains) by migration but does not distinguish between them. It also illustrates that the original application of the mortality curve to the matrix model is too simplistic and it is evident that density-dependent constraints (particularly the effects of malnutrition) maintained the population at Penrith in steady-state, causing longer wavelength cycles of births, deaths and migration.

5

Modelling the endogenous oscillations and predictions from time-series analysis

The endogenous oscillations in baptisms and burials in the population at Penrith described in Chapter 3 were apparently triggered by the impact of the mortality of the plague. It can be predicted that any population that is also maintained in steady-state and which suffers a major mortality crisis would display similar oscillations (see section 3.8). These oscillations may not be readily detectable in other communities; they may decay rapidly and be obscured by the noise. The response of a discrete population in steady-state to a mortality crisis will depend on the gain of the feedback and can be classified as follows in order of increasing feedback gain.

(1) Overdamped (Fig. 5.1A); when the gain is low, the birth rate recovers slowly to the pre-plague level without any oscillations.
(2) Just underdamped (Fig. 5.1B); with increased gain, the system recovers more rapidly and a low amplitude oscillation develops but is damped out.
(3) Very underdamped (Fig. 5.1C); with more gain and little damping the response decays slowly so that there are a number of periods of the oscillation. In general the period of the oscillation will be less than in type (2).
(4) Marginally stable (Fig. 5.1D); there is a further increase in gain of the feedback and the oscillation does not decay.
(5) Unstable (Fig. 5.1E); the amplitude of the oscillations increases progressively with the very high gain.

The long wavelength cycles in baptisms and burials at Penrith during the steady-state period, 1550–1750, are believed to be of type (4), with no decay in the oscillation. We suggest that where such oscillations in births are found in other communities there would be corresponding cycles in the deaths (with zero lag in the cross-correlation function). However, other

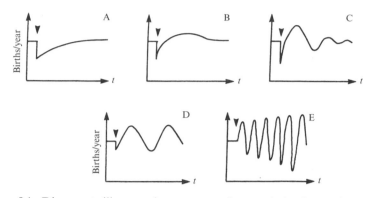

Figure 5.1. Diagram to illustrate the responses of a population in steady-state to a mortality crisis (arrowheads). (A) Overdamped, (B) just underdamped, (C) very underdamped, (D) marginally stable, (E) unstable.

English parishes of this time may be maintained in steady-state with feedback (as shown by a recovery in the annual birth rate to the level before a mortality crisis) but with a low gain, so that the responses would be of types (2) or (3) and would therefore be difficult to detect. If long wavelength cycles, superimposed on steady-state conditions in baptisms and burials, are detected in a parish register series, we may predict that the population was living under density-dependent constraints which either imposed severe pre-adult mortality or caused substantial migratory movements. It is hoped that the foregoing suggestions would be of use to historical demographers in analysing the population dynamics of any rural community.

The foregoing is applicable only to discrete populations but long wavelength cycles are evident in London and are superimposed on a rising trend (section 3.8). This conurbation is not a homogeneous population and Champion (1993) has pointed out that there was a clear difference between the poor populous suburban parishes with a high crisis mortality ratio and the wealthy, intramural parishes. Landers (1993) also suggested that different parts of London would have displayed different levels of mortality and forms of instability; areas containing large numbers of recent immigrants would have had distinctive epidemiological characteristics and the 18th century saw the emergence of a recognisably healthy district in the west of London and a zone of unusually severe mortality around the northern edge of the intramural parishes. London should therefore be regarded as an aggregation of subpopulations, each with its own characteristic demography, and the series of annual births probably represents the summation of the records from areas in steady-state and in boom.

It is necessary to undertake the laborious and time-consuming task of family reconstitution in order to determine many of the demographic features of the communities in English parishes. In the theoretical sections that follow we suggest how historical demographers and those interested in the theory of population dynamics may estimate some of the population parameters by applying conventional time-series analysis to the simple aggregative, annual totals in a parish register series.

5.1 30-year cycles

The births loop (Fig. 3.12), with pre-adult mortality and fecundity each contributing to the gain of the system, has a long delay which is associated with the time taken for maturation; this would make the system unstable and the loop would tend to oscillate at its resonant (or natural) frequency (see section 2.2) in response to a perturbation. Such conclusions are applicable to any community: we expect a major mortality crisis to generate cycles in births that have a wavelength equal to the mean age of the mother at the birth of her median child. These cycles may be difficult to detect because they may decay quickly and may be partially obscured if the child-bearing age is spread over a number of years. Thus, if these cycles can be revealed in a parish register series it would be possible to predict patterns of child-bearing in a community without the labour of family reconstitution. The population at Penrith serves as an example; the plague triggered a decaying oscillation in the baptisms of wavelength 30 years at the resonant frequency of the births loop. Such a finding suggests that the mean age of the mother when having her median child at Penrith during the 17th century was 30 years. This value corresponds to data quoted by Wrigley & Schofield (1981), who estimated from reconstitution studies that the mean age at maternity was 32 years for early modern England as a whole, with a fluctuation of about 2 years between its maximum and minimum levels. The family reconstitution study for the population at Penrith shows that the mean age of a woman having her median child for the period 1600–1700 was 30.9 years (section 4.5) and such a finding confirms the theoretical predictions.

5.2 Estimations of the fertility function

The Leslie matrix model (section 4.1) includes the term f_i which equals the probability of a women of age i giving birth. If the fertility function is narrow (i.e. all women have their children tightly bunched together at the same age), it would be expected that the oscillation associated with the delay in the births

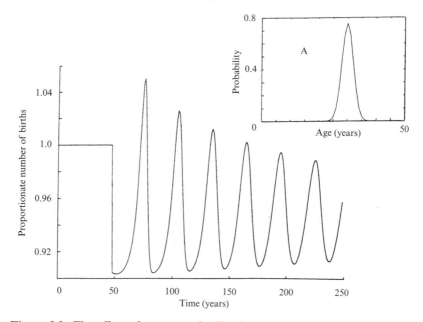

Figure 5.2. The effect of a narrow fertility function on the oscillation in births generated by the matrix model *without feedback* following a mortality crisis that kills 10% of the population indiscriminately. Oscillation slowly decays. Ordinate: proportionate number of births per year. Inset A: fertility function used, with SD = 2.5 years centred on the age of the mother of 30 years. Ordinate: the probability of a woman giving birth in each age group. Abscissa: age of the woman in years.

loop would die out only slowly. Conversely, if the child-bearing age in the population is well spread, the oscillation should die out rapidly. These conclusions can be illustrated by using the matrix model without feedback, including different fertility functions and then inspecting the oscillations generated by a mortality crisis that kills (say) 10% of the population indiscriminately. In the absence of feedback, the dynamics of the population are determined by the dominant eigenvalues of the Leslie matrix. Initially, a narrow fertility function with a standard deviation of 2.5 years (Fig. 5.2A) was chosen. For this case, the magnitude of the dominant eigenvalues are close to unity, so that the oscillations die out slowly (Fig. 5.2), as shown by the amplitude (0.8) of the first peak of the acf of births. The magnitude of the acf oscillation obeys

$$acf = e^{-t/\theta}$$

where t represents lag and θ is the time constant of the decay. An amplitude of 0.8 of the first peak corresponds to a decay with a time constant of 134 years. When the fertility function is wider, with a standard deviation of 6

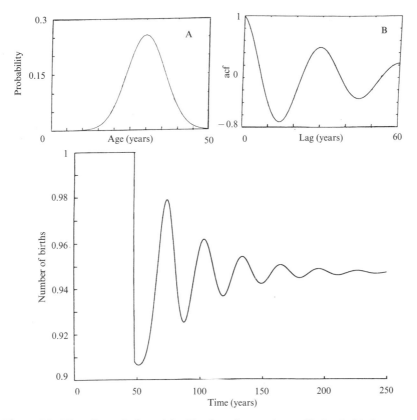

Figure 5.3. The effect of a broad fertility function on the oscillation in births gener-ated by the matrix model *without feedback* following a 10% mortality crisis. Oscillation decays rapidly (compare with Fig. 5.2). Ordinate: proportionate number of births per year. Inset A: fertility function used, with SD − 6 years centred on the age of the mother of 30 years. Ordinate: the probability of a woman giving birth in each age group (abscissa). Inset B: autocorrelation function (ordinate) with the amplitude of the first peak = 0.5; abscissa = lag in years.

years (Fig. 5.3A), the magnitude of the dominant eigenvalues are less, the amplitude of the first peak of the acf of births is smaller than with a narrow fertility function (Fig. 5.3B) and the oscillations die out more rapidly (Fig. 5.3), with a decay rate of 43 years.

Figure 5.4 shows the rate of decay of the oscillation generated by matrix modelling, as measured by the amplitude of the first peak of the acf, plotted against the standard deviation of the fertility function; as expected, the rate of decay increased with the width of the fertility function. The results from modelling shown in Fig. 5.4 were almost independent of any changes in childhood mortality introduced in the model.

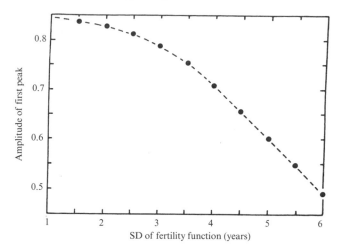

Figure 5.4. Relationship between the amplitude of the first peak of the auto-correlation function of births (ordinate) and the SD of the fertility function in years (abscissa). Data taken from the matrix model without feedback; see Figs. 5.2 and 5.3.

Assuming (probably not unreasonably) that the fertility function approx-imates to a normal distribution, we should like to predict, optimistically, that it may be possible to estimate the pattern of child-bearing by deter-mining the appropriate oscillation by time-series analysis and then com-paring the value of the acf with Fig. 5.4 and so determine the standard deviation of the fertility function. In practice, it is difficult to extract the cycles (of wavelength about 30 years) by linear filtering because of its decay and because of the noise in the records, particularly when any other long wavelength cycles are also present. These oscillations in response to a mortality crisis may show more clearly in parishes that were not in steady-state conditions determined by feedback.

5.3 Mean age at marriage

The marriage registers of a parish are an essential tool for family reconstitution but, so far in this book, we have made little use of them in the time-series analyses. Is it possible for historical demographers to esti-mate the mean age at marriage directly from aggregative analysis without family reconstitution? The population at Penrith is given as an example. Time-series analysis with appropriate linear filtering of the marriage series shows long wavelength cycles that are similar to those found in the baptism series, but these are less clear and of small amplitude. Nevertheless, the cross-correlation function of long wavelength cycles of baptisms versus marriages has a lag of -29 years. We tentatively conclude that the mean age at marriage at Penrith may have been 29 years. When the mean age of *first* marriage at Penrith during the period 1600–1750 was determined by family reconstitution, it was found to be 27.1 years. However, a considerable proportion of the marriages recorded at Penrith were remarriages (particularly after the mortality crises) which will have the effect of raising the mean age at marriage. Family reconstitution studies show that the proportion of marriages that were remarriages in the different cohorts were as follows: (1600–1649) 26%; (1650–1699) 18%; (1700–1749) 16%. We conclude that 29 years probably represents a good estimate of the overall mean age of the partners at marriage at Penrith.

This value compares with 27.8 and 26.5 years for the age of males and females respectively at *first* marriage quoted by Wrigley & Schofield (1981) as the means of 12 reconstitution studies. We suggest that, where long wavelength oscillations can be detected in the births and marriages series recorded in the parish registers, it may be possible to use time-series analysis to predict the mean age at marriage.

5.4 Estimations of the mortality function of a population by time-series analysis

The mortality function of the stable population before the plague, $m_i(0)$, incorporated in the matrix model was defined as

$$m_i(0) = e^{-(i + 6.5)/\tau} + e^{-(57 - i)/5}$$

where i is the age and τ is the 'rate of child mortality'. When the model *without feedback* was hit by a plague, oscillations in the births were generated, the wavelength of which equalled the delay in the births loop; in addition, corresponding oscillations were also generated in the deaths, although these were not necessarily synchronous. It was noticed that as τ was changed, the lag in the main peak of the cross-correlation function between births and deaths also changed. This is illustrated in Fig. 5.5A and B. When $\tau = 3.5$ (low child mortality), the plot of the stable population shows that about 65% of children are surviving to adulthood and the cross-correlation function is offset by about 9 years (Fig. 5.5A). In contrast, when $\tau = 5.5$ and only 20% of children survive to adulthood, the offset was reduced to 2 years (Fig. 5.5B). These cycles of wavelength approximately 30 years differ, therefore, from the long wavelength cycles (44 years) in feedback-controlled populations, where zero lag in the cross-correlation function is predicted (section 3.4).

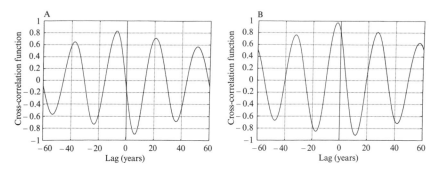

Figure 5.5. Cross-correlation function of births versus deaths produced by the model without feedback following a mortality crisis. (A) $\tau = 3.5$ (low child mortality); offset by about 9 years. (B) $\tau = 5.5$ (high child mortality); offset reduced to 2 years.

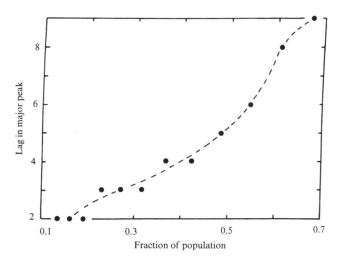

Figure 5.6. Plot to show the lag in the major peak of the births/deaths ccf predicted by the model (ordinate) versus the fraction of the population surviving to age 25 years (abscissa).

Figure 5.6 is a plot that shows how the lag in the major peak of the births/deaths cross-correlation function predicted by the model is dependent on the fraction of the population surviving to age 25 years. We cautiously suggest that, where cycles associated with the delay in the births loop can be filtered out in a parish register series, it may be possible to obtain an estimate of the pre-adult mortality by determining the cross-correlation function and applying it to Fig. 5.6.

This hypothesis has been checked from the registers at Penrith. It was difficult to extract a clear 30-year cycle from the burial series; nevertheless, after linear filtering of both series with conventional techniques over the years 1557–1677, the cross-correlation function of baptisms and burials was found to be offset by 6 years. When more sophisticated filtering techniques, based on the approach of Kalman (described by Goodwin *et al.* (1986)), were used, a lag of 6 years in the cross-correlation function was again found, suggesting that the fraction of the population that survived to age 25 years was 0.54 (see Fig. 5.6).

The female survival curve for Penrith for 1600–1649 derived by family reconstitution studies (see Fig. 4.8) confirms that 54% of the females survived to age 25 years, and we suggest that this theoretical technique would be worth testing on other communities.

5.5 Why is the wavelength of endogenous oscillations approximately 43 years?

It has been suggested that some human populations have been maintained in homeostasis and examples of control by density-dependent checks include the long-run stationarity of hunter–gatherer populations, recovery from demographic crises and the association of fertility with size of land holding (Lee, 1987). Long wavelength oscillations have been detected in population size, fertility and real wages (Lee, 1974, 1987; Herlihy, 1977; Wrigley & Schofield, 1981). The cycles in the fertility of the USA have a periodicity of about 44 years, although the years covered, 1900–1984, allow for only two oscillations (Lee, 1974). A 43-year cycle has been found in deaths in the city of Florence from 1275 to 1500 (Herlihy, 1977) and a 55-year oscillation in the birth series of 19th century France (Lee, 1974). Demographers have suggested theoretical models of a steady-state population in which the oscillations may be driven by feedback (Easterlin, 1980; Wachter, 1991) and changes in fertility and birth rate have been advanced as the most probable underlying mechanism (Lee, 1974),

It is difficult to present a synthesis of these studies because they include both exogenous and endogenous oscillations, they are largely concerned with metapopulations rather than with single communities, little is known of the underlying population dynamics and it is not clear what initiated the oscillations. We have suggested (Chapter 3) that the synchronous, endogenous oscillations in baptisms and burials at Penrith were triggered by a major mortality crisis and are characteristic of a population under density-dependent constraints maintained by feedback. Comparable endogenous oscillations can be detected in other communities ranging in size from small parishes to large populations (section 3.8) and their wavelength seems to be similar, namely 43 or 44 years. We have used the matrix model with feed-back that was developed in section 4.3, varying the different parameters to resolve which are the major factors that determine the wavelength of these synchronous endogenous oscillations in births and deaths.

The most important variables studied were (a) the gain of the feedback (defined in section 4.3), (b) the characteristics of the female survival curve (see Fig. 4.8), and (c) the mean and standard deviation of the fertility dis-tribution. The wavelength of the synchronous oscillations in births and deaths triggered by a mortality crisis in the model proved to be a function of the feedback and the mean of the fertility distribution. As before (section 4.2), if there was no gain in the feedback, the steady-state level of births and deaths did *not* recover to the pre-crisis level and the *decaying*, synchronous oscillations in births and deaths had a wavelength equal to the mean of the fertility distribution (i.e. the mean age at which the women have their median child).

(1) *Effect of varying the mean of the fertility distribution.* Figure 5.7A shows the results of varying the value of the mean of the fertility distribution with the gain on the feedback set at 7; 43-year, stable synchronous oscillations in births and deaths were generated after a mortality crisis when the mean of the fertility function was 30 years. Raising the mean age at which women had their median child increased the wavelength of these non-decaying oscillations whereas reducing the mean of the fertility function decreased the wavelength of oscillations.

(2) *Effect of varying the gain.* With the mean of the fertility function set at 30 years, non-decaying, synchronous, 43-year oscillations were gener-ated with a gain of 7; reducing the gain over the range 7 to 2 produced a progressively increasing decay, although the wavelength remained at 43 years (Fig. 5.7B). In real life, once the system was oscillating at its resonant frequency, these decaying oscillations would be 'pumped-up' and maintained by noise and mortality crises (see Chapters 9 and 10) and a gain of 2–3 would probably be adequate to replicate the endoge-nous, 43-year oscillations at Penrith. Below a gain of 2, as the level of feedback was reduced, the oscillations decayed more rapidly and their wavelength fell sharply to 30 years (the mean of the fecundity func-tion) at a gain of 0.5, i.e. when there was no effective feedback in the system.

Non-decaying, synchronous, 43-year oscillations were still produced at gains of 8 or 9, but a secondary, 5-year, oscillation was superimposed on the cycle of deaths.

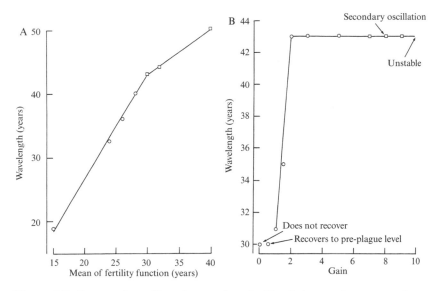

Figure 5.7. Factors that affect the wavelength (λ) of the synchronous endogenous oscillations in births and deaths predicted by the matrix model (ordinate). (A) Effect of varying the mean of the fertility function (years; abscissa); SD = 3; gain = 7; open circles = decaying oscillations; open squares = non-decaying oscillations. (B) Effect of varying the gain (abscissa); mean of the fertility function = 30 years; open circles = decaying oscillation; open squares = non-decaying oscillation; 43-year oscillations generated with a gain in the range 2 to 7.

(3) *Effect of variation of the standard deviation of the fertility function.* In the modelling described above, the standard deviation of the fertility function was set at 3, giving a child-bearing age from 20 to 40 years. Changing this value of the standard deviation over the range 2 to 3.5 has little effect on the oscillations generated by the model. At values of the standard deviation of 4 and 5 the wavelength remains at 43 years but the oscillations decay very slowly; 5-year secondary oscillations are superimposed with a standard deviation below 1 (i.e. a very short span of child-bearing). We conclude that it is the mean and not the standard deviation of the fertility function that is of most importance in determining the wavelength of the endogenous oscillations.

(4) *Effect of ameliorating the mortality function.* If the fraction of the population that survives to age 20 is raised from 0.14 to 0.3, the wavelength of the oscillations generated by the model is slightly reduced from 43 to 41 years but, as would be expected, the oscillations now decay rapidly.

To conclude, matrix modelling suggests that the synchronous, endogenous oscillations in births and deaths that can be discerned in single populations living under density-dependent constraints during the 17th century were triggered by a mortality crisis. If the dynamics were not governed by feedback, the oscillations would have a wavelength equal to the mean of the fertility function and would decay. However, if the gain of the feedback is raised above 2, the wavelength is increased so that, with a mean of the fertility function of 28–30 years, the predicted wavelength of the synchronous cycles in birth and deaths is 40–43 years. These observed long wavelength, endogenous cycles reflect the interaction of the demographic parameters and the dynamics of the population (i.e. the fertility function and the gain of the feedback).

6

Cycles in the grain price series

Short wavelength mortality cycles, with a period of about 5 to 6 years, were described in Chapter 3; in this and succeeding chapters we consider them in more detail and show that they occurred commonly in a variety of different communities (see section 15.1) and that, in some instances, lethal infectious epidemics were superimposed on the peaks of the oscillations. What external factors drove these exogenous mortality cycles? One thesis, developed further in Chapters 7 and 8, is that mortality, particularly among children and infants, is sensitive to the subtle effects of fluctuating malnutrition. Obviously, outright famine caused deaths, as described in the parish registers of Greystoke in Cumberland in 1623, but disasters on this scale seem to have been rare, even in the marginal economies of the north-west. Rather, we have used time-series analysis and other statistical techniques to show that an inadequate diet, perhaps lacking in nutritive value, vitamins or trace elements had serious, and hitherto undetected, direct and indirect effects on pregnancy, neonatal, post-neonatal and childhood mortality, and susceptibility to disease.

It is suggested that the annual grain prices provide a good measure of the fluctuations in nutritive levels, particularly among the poorer sections of a community and that, in certain circumstances, the annual price of grains interacted with the price of other commodities to produce years of particular hardship (see Chapter 8). Communities living under marginal farming conditions would be particularly susceptible in such hardship years.

Grain prices in past centuries were subject to violent fluctuations from one year to another, although some regularity in the longer-term movement of prices has been discerned. The prime cause of these annual fluctuations has been ascribed to the weather, which, in the short run, largely determined the supply of agricultural produce and this dependence on the weather meant that agricultural prices fluctuated more markedly than other prices. Modern economic systems are provided with a number of built-in stabilizing influences but these conditions were largely absent in England in the 16th and 17th centuries and the dramatic fluctuations in grain prices had to be endured as one of the penalties of a backward economic system, in particular the consequence of the inelasticity in demand and supply conditions which distinguished arable agriculture from most other economic activities. Drought was normally advantageous to the wheat harvest in England and, unless prolonged, was seldom a cause of failure among the other cereal crops because of the predominance of heavy moisture-retaining clay land over lighter sandy soils. The main danger to cereal crops is believed to have been prolonged rainfall in summer accompanied by an almost total absence of sunshine, when crops failed to ripen and yields were poor. An excessively cold winter and spring were also said to be harmful to the wheat harvest but had little effect on spring-sown barley, oats and pulses (Thirsk, 1967).

Any study of the fluctuations in grain prices is dependent on the pioneering work of Hoskins, who provided an analysis, decade by decade, from 1480 to 1759. He suggested that really bad harvests came 1 year in 6, agreeing closely with the popular belief in the 16th century that a bad harvest came once every 7 years. His examination of harvest sequences revealed no discoverable rhythm and he suggested that good or bad runs were not basically because of weather cycles and, although short term climatic fluctuations may well have been implicated, he believed that the underlying factor was that of yield ratios in an agrarian economy that worked normally on a very fine margin between sufficiency and shortage (Hoskins, 1964). Hoskins concluded that for the vast majority of the population these short-term fluctuations in the cost of food 'were infinitely more important than the long-term movements to which economic historians have always paid such assiduous attention' (Hoskins, 1968).

Pfister (1988) studied the significance of meteorological variables in determining grain prices in Europe for the period between the mid-16th and mid-19th centuries using a model based on monthly estimated measurements of temperature and precipitation, and distinguished between weather and non-weather effects. Subsistence crises were found to be triggered by the combination of a cold spring and a rainy midsummer whereas, in the long run, grain prices were more closely related to the intensity and duration of trade cycles. Spectral analysis and autoregressive models of agricultural prices in pre-19th century Europe have shown that the prices of all cereals and potatoes rose simultaneously in subsistence crises and that regional fluctuations in the prices of cereals existed in Germany because of differences in production, commercialisation and consumption practices (Roehner, 1991).

The existence of long wavelength cycles, with a period greater than 30 years, in the prices of cereals in Europe from the 16th to the 20th century has been studied (Bos *et al.*, 1986); such cycles are clearly different from the short run fluctuations described by Hoskins. Only weak indications of such long waves were found although there was strong evidence of cycles with 10 to 13- or 15-year periods which seemed to be caused by clusters of unfavourable events in population, climate, structures of production or modes of behaviour. There was no evidence of a relation, as had been suggested, between these medium wavelength oscillations and sunspot activity.

Two theories have been advanced to explain the fluctuations of grain prices: firstly, that demand remains constant but rigid and cannot adapt itself to fluctuations in the harvest and, secondly, that the amount of grain offered to the market is subject to fluctuations by producers who consume a certain amount of their own harvest. Subsistence farming and the instabilities of supply and demand must be included in these models of the grain market. During good harvests, subsistence-farmers reduce their purchases in the market and increase the amount of grain they offer to it; during bad harvests, they increase their purchases in the market and reduce the amount of grain offered.

In this chapter we consider the underlying causes of the grain price cycles in England and have determined (a) the origins of the short wavelength oscillations in the wheat, oats and barley series, (b) the interaction between the cycles in the different grain series, and (c) the effect of weather and other factors in driving these cycles. We show that both short wavelength and medium wavelength oscillations can be detected by conventional time-series analysis in the national wheat price index, but only the medium wavelength oscillation correlates significantly with weather conditions and we suggest that other factors may contribute to the short wavelength oscillation.

6.1 Sources for the data series

Seasonal mean temperatures in central England (°C) for 1659–1812 were taken from Manley (1974), and seasonal rainfall at Kew from 1697 to 1812 (expressed as percentages of the 1916–1950 averages) were taken from Wales-Smith (1971); winters include the month of December from

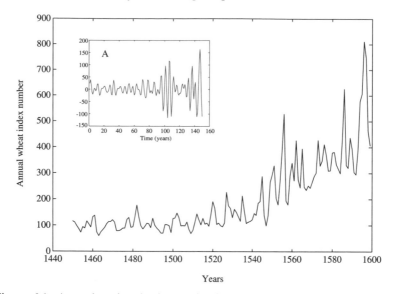

Figure 6.1. Annual national wheat price index (ordinate) for the early years, 1450–1599. Note rising trend and the emergence of a short wavelength oscillation after 1550. Inset A: wheat price index, 1450–1599, filtered to reveal the short wavelength oscillation (filter window = 4 to 10 years). Data source: Bowden (1967).

the previous year. The national grain price indices, 1450–1749 (wheat, barley and oats) were taken from Bowden (1967, 1985); the baseline for 1450–1649 was the mean grain price for 1450–1499; the baseline for 1650–1749 was the mean value over these years. Absolute wheat prices (shillings) 1600–1812, were taken from Stratton (1970). Details of further statistical tests concerning possible problems of non-stationarity in the grain price series are given in section 6.12.

6.2 Cycles in the wheat price index

The national wheat price index for the early years, 1450–1599, is shown in Fig. 6.1 and the genesis of the oscillations can be seen clearly. Before 1550 the cycles were of low amplitude and spectral analysis of this period shows a dominant oscillation with a wavelength of 8 years. This low amplitude, short wavelength oscillation is shown after filtering in Fig. 6.1A. A weak, medium wavelength oscillation in the wheat price index for these early years before 1550 is also detectable; its wavelength is 10 years. After 1550 the earlier stability is lost, the index shows a clear rising trend (Fig. 6.1) and the oscillations emerge at relatively greater amplitude: spectral analysis of the

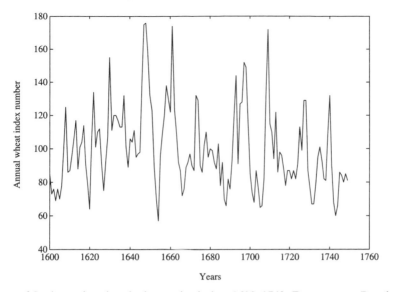

Figure 6.2. Annual national wheat price index, 1600–1749. Data source: Bowden (1985).

period 1550–1600 shows a short wavelength oscillation and a weaker medium wavelength oscillation with a periodicity of 10 years. The emergent short wavelength oscillation after 1550 has a wavelength of 5–6 years and is shown after filtering in Fig. 6.1A. In summary, the low amplitude, short wavelength oscillation with a period of 8 years during the period 1450–1550, changed sharply after 1550 into a 5–6-year oscillation with a much greater amplitude which was superimposed on a rising trend, as is clearly shown in Figs. 6.1 and 6.1A.

This rising trend levelled out and the two types of oscillation in the wheat price index (short and medium wavelength) became more regular and were well established after 1600 (Fig. 6.2). Spectral analysis for the period 1600–1749 shows the short wavelength (6 years; $P < 0.005$) and the medium wavelength (fluctuating periodicity, predominantly 12-year wavelength but changing to a strong 16-year cycle developing after 1660; $P < 0.005$) cycles. The short wavelength oscillation during this period is shown in Fig. 6.3 after filtering; a more detailed analysis of the series shows that the wavelength was predominantly 8 years during the early years but stabilized thereafter at 6 years. The strong medium wavelength cycle also found during 1600–1749 and continuing until 1812 is described in greater detail below and these different oscillations in the wheat index are summarised in Table 6.1.

Table 6.1. *Characteristics of the cycles in the wheat index, 1450–1749*

	Wavelength (yr)		
Cohort	1450–1550	1550–1599	1600–1749
Short wavelength	8	5–6	6
Medium wavelength	10	10	12 and 16

Note:
Periodicity of different cycles determined by spectral analysis of the unfiltered and filtered data series.

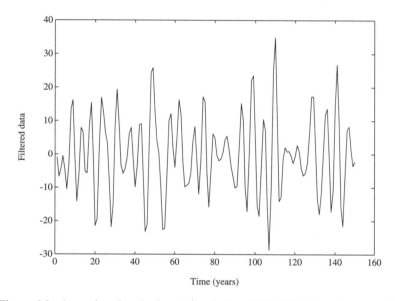

Figure 6.3. Annual national wheat price index, 1600–1749, filtered to reveal the short wavelength oscillation (filter window = 4 to 10 years).

6.3 Oats and barley price indices

The national indices for oats and barley prices for the period 1450–1749 are quoted by Bowden (1967) and the trends and their pattern of oscillation correspond closely with that of the wheat prices and with each other. Thus, the indices of both barley (Fig. 6.4) and oats (Fig. 6.5) also remained steady for the first 100 years (1450–1550) with short wavelength oscillations of very low amplitude; after 1550 the indices also showed a rising trend with the short wavelength oscillations superimposed (period = 5 years for barley

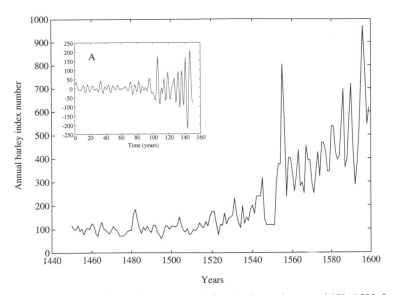

Figure 6.4. Annual national barley price index for the early years, 1450–1599. Inset A: barley index, 1450–1599, filtered to reveal the short wavelength oscillation (filter window = 4 to 10 years). Data source: Bowden (1967).

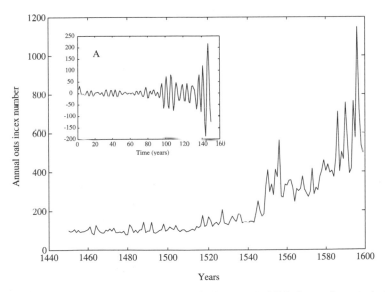

Figure 6.5. Annual national oats price index, 1450–1599. Inset A: oats index, 1450–1599, filtered to reveal the short wavelength oscillation (filter window = 4 to 10 years). Data source: Bowden (1967).

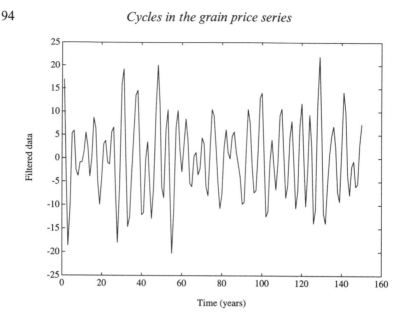

Figure 6.6. Annual national oats price index, 1600–1749, filtered to reveal the short wavelength oscillation (filter window = 4 to 10 years). Data source: Bowden (1985).

and 6 years for oats) which developed strongly over the next 50 years, corresponding to the pattern in wheat prices. Filtered series are shown in the insets of Figs. 6.4 and 6.5. A medium wavelength oscillation with a period of 12–13 years was detectable during 1450–1550 in the barley index and this period changed to 10 years during 1550–1600. No significant medium wavelength oscillation was detected in the oats index (see Table 6.2).

During the following period, 1600–1749, the short wavelength oscillations became firmly established in both the barley and oats indices and are clearly seen after filtering (see Fig. 6.6). The wavelength of the oscillation in the barley index was 6 years during 1600–1680, which changed to 5.5 years thereafter. Oats showed a 5-year periodicity throughout. A strong, medium wavelength oscillation with a periodicity of 12 years ($P < 0.05$) was clearly shown by spectral analysis in both the barley and oats indices.

6.4 Correspondence between the grain price indices

The apparent correspondence between the different grain price indices was tested on the raw data by the coherence program, and the cross-correlation functions were determined from the filtered series. The results are summarised in Table 6.2, which shows that both the oats and barley indices synchronize closely with the wheat series; both are strongly coherent in the

Table 6.2. *Synchrony of short and medium wavelength oscillations in grain prices indices*

	Wavelength (yr)											
	1450–1550				1550–1599				1600–1749			
Cohort ccf with wheat:	Periodicity (yr)	Lag (yr)	ccf	P	Periodicity (yr)	Lag (yr)	ccf	P	Periodicity (yr)	Lag (yr)	ccf	P
Barley – short	6	0	0.6	0.001	5	0	0.7	0.001	6→5.5	0	0.8	0.001
Oats – short	(4–6)	0	0.8	0.001	6	0	0.8	0.001	5	0	0.6	0.001
Barley – medium	12→13	0	0.7	0.01	10	0	0.7	0.01	12	0	0.9	0.001
Oats – medium	ND	0	0.6	0.001	ND	0	0.8	0.001	12	0	0.9	0.001

Note:
Table shows cross-correlation and coherence between wheat versus oats or barley indices. Note high significance of coherence in both the short and medium wavelength oscillations. Arrow indicates progressive change of wavelength during the 150-year cohort. ccf, cross-correlation function. ND (oats) indicates that no medium wavelength oscillations were detectable by linear filtering, although good ccf and *P* values were obtained between the two series.

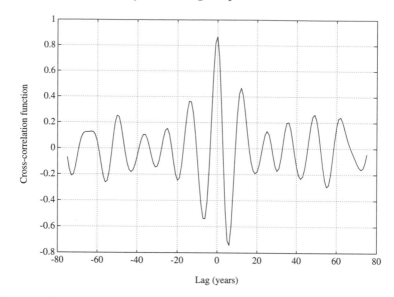

Figure 6.7. Cross-correlation function, wheat index versus barley index, 1600–1749. Filtered data (filter window = 8 to 20 years). Maximum peak of ccf (+0.87) is at zero lag.

short and the medium wavebands ($P \leq 0.01$) over a period of 300 years. The filtered series synchronise at zero lag in both the short and medium wavelengths, see Table 6.2; the cross-correlation function values confirm the significance of the correspondence. An example of the cross-correlation function, wheat series versus barley series, 1600–1749, is shown in Fig. 6.7. A similar analysis showed that the barley and oats series are also significantly and strongly cross-correlated throughout the period 1450–1749. We conclude that the annual price indices of the three grains are strongly interdependent and oscillate together in both the short and medium wavebands.

This finding confirms previous accounts. Bowden (1967) concluded that the short-term movements in the prices of wheat, barley, oats and rye were broadly similar because each grain was in some degree a substitute for the others, while any extremes of climate in spring or summer affected the yield of all; the graph of the prices of wheat, beans, peas and oats at Lincoln, 1543–1620, shows that these commodities moved in close sympathy with each other (Hoskins, 1964).

Since the prices of the different grains were so closely linked, we have used annual wheat prices as a measure of the fluctuating levels of nutrition in the following chapters and in the next section we explore the different factors that may have caused the clearly defined cycles in the price of this grain.

6.5 The effect of seasonal temperature on wheat prices

The weather and British agriculture are both such varied quantities that the interplay between them is certain to be complex. There is a range of interactions stemming from the diversity of the weather and, except for extremes, the temperature and rainfall requirements of agricultural crops are seldom the same so that the conditions which are ideal for one may be far from so for another (Bowden, 1985). Extreme weather events tend to cluster and the recurrence of clustered years of meteorological extremes appears to be the outstanding feature of 1200–1850. There were three main epochs of rise in grain prices in Europe, i.e. 1300, 1600 and 1800, and the biggest of these changes was a many-fold increase between 1550 and 1650, a phenomenon too widespread to be attributable to any of the wars of the period. The price rise in 1800 was largely because of the influence of the Napoleonic War, but it also coincided with the latest period of advance of the glaciers and of the Arctic sea ice surrounding Iceland. Although it has been concluded that the changes in prices around 1300 and 1600 were largely climate induced (Lamb, 1978), the rising trend of wheat prices between 1550 and 1650 and between 1731 and 1811 were also times when the population of England almost doubled and, for each period, the rising demand caused an increase in the price index that outstripped the rise in population.

The period 1550–1700 was also characterised by variability of temperature; the mid-16th century saw the start of a period of cooling and there were persistent cold intervals particularly during 1605–1615, 1674–1682 and 1695–1698. Severe winters were experienced in the 1560s and 1600s, and wet, cool summers occurred in 1570, the 1590s and 1620s (Lamb, 1978). The first half of the 18th century was relatively warm, although 1709 and 1740 were cold over most of the northern hemisphere. From 1770 onwards, there was a fairly steady drop in temperatures until 1820 (Landsberg, 1981). The milder climatic circumstances of 1652 and 1654 afforded a brief respite from periods of high prices during 1645–1651 and 1656–1663. However the weather conditions up to 1691 were conducive to the production of grain and this period was noted for a number of warm, dry summers culminating in a drought in 1684. Unusual cold and exceptional rainfall in the 1690s led to crop failures in 1692–1699 and high prices.

These changes in mean temperature are summarised in Table 6.3 and it can be seen that there was a rise in temperature from the 17th to the 18th century. A degree or half a degree does not sound impressive but small changes in the mean temperature may reflect significant differences in the frequency of occurrence of extreme values. In Iceland, a decrease of annual temperature of 1 deg.C reduces the growing days by 27%, illustrating that

Table 6.3. *Average temperatures for England, 1659–1812*

Cohort	Average	Winter	Spring	Summer	Autumn
1659–1699	8.6	2.9	7.5	14.9	9.1
	(−0.027)	(−0.021)	(−0.028)	(−0.026)	(−0.034)
1700–1749	9.2	3.7	8.0	15.4	9.8
	(0.003)	(0.004)	(0.0004)	(0.0003)	(0.01)
1750–1812	9.1	3.3	8.1	15.5	9.4
	(0.003)	(−0.004)	(0.001)	(0.002)	(0.002)

Note:
Seasonal temperature data taken from Manley (1974). Figures in brackets are the slopes of the line during the cohort.

small fluctuations may be critical in marginal areas (Bryson & Padoch, 1981). There is little doubt that harvest yields in the period under study reacted more sensitively to weather fluctuations before the advent of hybrid seed, artificial fertilizer, mechanized harvesting and the other agricultural advances of the last century (DeVries, 1981).

The weather affects cereal crops in several different ways, some of which are closely linked to the season of the year or the stage of growth. In 1880, Lawes & Gilbert examined the history of a long run of seasons and concluded that the most abundant wheat harvests had been preceded by above-average temperatures during most of the winter and early spring. Most of these years had low winter and spring rainfall and slightly less than average summer rainfall. In contrast, the seasons of lowest wheat production had been characterized by severe, or at least changeable, conditions in the winter and spring with, at the same time, above average rainfall (Lawes & Gilbert, 1880). However, the most powerful determinant of the condition of the cereal harvest was believed to be the state of the weather at sowing because the cereal suffered if the weather was cold and backward; hard wind, frosts and cold rain could damage young shoots (Holderness, 1989).

In this section, we show that only the medium wavelength oscillation in wheat prices correlates significantly with weather conditions, in contrast with the short wavelength oscillation where the association was weak.

The possibility that wheat yields and hence prices were influenced by weather conditions during the growing and harvesting seasons has been explored by conventional multivariate regression analysis; data series for seasonal temperature are known from 1659 and for seasonal rainfall from 1697. The wheat price series (taken from Stratton, 1970) rather than the wheat index has been used for this analysis because comparisons with oats and barley indices are not necessary here. Analysis of seasonal temperatures (winter, spring, summer and autumn) versus wheat prices for the complete period 1659–1812 shows that it is only winter temperatures ($P = 0.046$) that had a significant effect; i.e. low winter temperatures are associated with high wheat prices. When this effect of temperature is studied in different periods, the importance and significance of the effect of winter temperature rises: 1659–1780, $P < 0.01$ and in 1700–1750, $P < 0.002$. Additionally, a large negative coefficient was obtained from the analysis for summer temperature, suggesting that low temperatures in this season may affect wheat prices. Multivariate analysis for the period 1659–1780 of winter and summer temperatures shows that both have a significant effect on wheat prices (winter temperatures, $P = 0.01$; summer temperatures, $P = 0.005$). Seasonal rainfall had a smaller effect, as described in greater detail in the Appendix, section 6.12.3. These findings have been confirmed by time-series analysis and, in particular, the correlation with seasonal temperatures in the different wavelength oscillations has been further explored in the following sections.

6.5.1 *Effect of winter temperatures*

Spectral analysis of the winter temperature data series for the period 1659–1812 shows a dominant medium wavelength oscillation that has a period of 12–13 years. The winter temperature and wheat price series cross-correlate negatively at zero lag when they are filtered to reveal medium wavelength oscillations, i.e. low winter temperatures are associated with high wheat prices in the same year.

6.5.2 *Effect of summer temperatures*

Spectral analysis of the annual summer temperature series shows a peak in the medium waveband at 14 years. The coherence program, which tests the significance of the correlation between summer temperatures and wheat prices, shows that the two series correspond negatively, i.e. low summer temperatures are associated with high wheat prices in the medium wavelength oscillation. The association is significant throughout the period 1659–1812 ($P < 0.05$) but this significance is particularly evident during the earlier years, 1659–1780 ($P < 0.01$). Figure 6.8 shows the wheat price series (1659–1812) filtered to reveal the medium wavelength cycle (λ is predominantly 16.7 years; $P < 0.005$); it cross-correlates negatively with the filtered summer temperatures series (see Fig. 6.9), confirming the results from the coherence program.

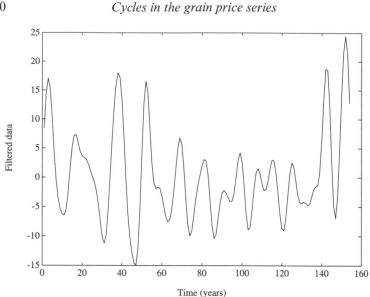

Figure 6.8. Annual national wheat price series (shillings), 1659–1812, filtered to reveal the medium wavelength oscillation (filter window = 8 to 20 years). Data source: Stratton (1970).

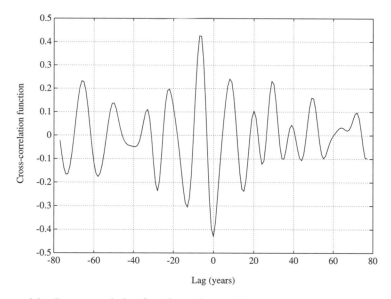

Figure 6.9. Cross-correlation function, wheat prices versus mean summer temperatures, 1659–1812, filter window = 8 to 20 years. Minimum ccf (−0.43) at zero lag. Data sources: Stratton (1970) and Manley (1974).

We conclude tentatively that these results suggest that, in the medium waveband, both low winter and low summer temperatures are associated with poor yields and high wheat prices, with summer temperatures probably having a more significant effect.

6.5.3 Principal component analysis of the seasonal temperatures

Low temperatures in winter may well affect subsequent spring and summer temperatures, so producing a generally cold growing and harvest season and this possible interactive climatic effect has been explored by principal component analysis and the results of this statistical technique are described in more detail in the Appendix, section 6.12.2. In brief, the spring temperature series during the period 1659–1812 was found to be significantly correlated with the mean temperature in the preceding winter. Likewise, summer temperatures were also significantly correlated with those of the preceding winter, whereas there was no correlation with autumn temperatures. This study suggests, therefore, that the annual wheat price was correlated with the weather conditions from winter to summer in that year. Multivariate analysis confirms that low winter and low summer temperatures have the dominant effect, but the analysis described in the Appendix, section 6.12.2, indicates that low winter temperatures may also be acting indirectly by causing low summer temperatures. Low summer temperatures probably affect harvest yield directly by causing adverse growing conditions. Thus, the results of time-series analysis suggest that these effects of seasonal temperature are detectable in the medium wavelength oscillations of the wheat price series (period about 12–16 years; see Fig. 6.8) but are less strongly associated in the short wavelength oscillations.

6.6 The effect of rainfall on wheat prices

The multivariate regression analysis program was then re-run including the data on seasonal rainfall as well as temperature over the period 1697–1812, but, again, only low winter temperatures showed significance ($P = 0.016$). When the analysis is restricted to the early years, 1697–1781, the overall analysis of variance shows that the regression is significant ($P = 0.005$), the significance of winter temperature is increased ($P = 0.001$) and the effect of winter rainfall now becomes significant ($P < 0.05$). However, the coherence program with winter rain as input and wheat prices as output shows no significance in the medium and short wavebands, although there is correspondence ($P = 0.025$) at high frequencies. We conclude that winter rainfall did not have a cyclical effect and acted only on a simple annual basis.

Wigley & Atkinson (1977) have suggested that it is not the level of precipitation, but the soil moisture deficit that may have the greater effect on plant growth. A dry soil and a continuing high level of evapotranspiration prevent the crop from withdrawing water from the soil, leading to stunted growth and even wilting of the plants. Their data series for mean soil moisture deficits during the growing season (May–August) at Kew, 1698–1812, was tested by time-series analysis and, as would be expected, high spring or summer rainfall correlated with low water deficits at zero lag. There is cross-correlation and coherence between wheat prices and moisture deficits, both overall and in the filtered medium waveband, but at a 1-year lag and with the two series being negatively correlated, i.e. most surprisingly, low wheat prices (and presumably good yields) were associated with drought conditions, the converse of the expectations of Wigley & Atkinson. We conclude that this analysis confirms that rainfall and soil moisture deficit had only limited effects on the medium wavelength oscillation in wheat prices.

6.7 Wheat prices and short wavelength temperature cycles

Spectral analysis of the data series for winter or summer temperatures also reveals smaller, secondary peaks of wavelength 5 years in both. These short wavelength cycles also cross-correlate negatively with the corresponding cycle in wheat prices (shown in Fig. 6.3), i.e. again low temperatures synchronize with high wheat prices. This finding was confirmed by analysis with the coherence program and we conclude that the short wavelength cycle in wheat prices correlates with these low seasonal temperatures but the effect is less marked than in the medium wavelength cycles.

Spectral analysis of the data series for mean soil moisture deficits, 1698–1812 (Wigley & Atkinson, 1977), described above, reveals major peaks at wavelengths of 3 and 5 years, and the 5-year oscillation shows weak cross-correlation and coherence at 1-year lag with wheat prices but, paradoxically, a good growing season (reflected in low wheat prices) was again apparently correlated with drought conditions. We conclude that rainfall and moisture deficits in the soil are of only limited significance on wheat prices in the short wavebands.

6.8 Use of a predicted wheat price series: distinction between the medium and short wavelength oscillations in the wheat price series

Multivariate analysis has shown that certain seasonal weather conditions had strong effects on the annual wheat price, and time-series analysis has confirmed that the medium wavelength cycles were particularly sensitive. Using this analysis it is possible to construct, as shown in the Appendix, section 6.12.3, a regression equation which predicts, theoretically, the wheat price in any year, based on the seasonal climatic conditions for that year, if it were influenced only by weather. Thus, a *predicted* annual wheat price during the period 1697–1812, if it were influenced only by weather, can be calculated from the following equation, which uses the coefficients given in the multivariate analysis.

Wheat price (shillings) =
  79.9 + (0.027 × summer rain) + (0.0262 × autumn rain)
  + (0.0783 × winter rain) − (2.05 × summer temperature)
  − (0.48 × autumn temperature) − (3.61 × winter temperature)

Note the high coefficients for summer and winter temperature, indicating their dominant influence on prices. Spectral analysis of this theoretical wheat price series shows the medium wavelength oscillation, confirming that this cycle in wheat prices can be explained as the consequence of weather conditions. However, spectral analysis of this predicted price series also shows a wide variety of oscillations in the short and medium wavebands, but the 6-yearly, short wavelength cycle which is characteristic of the actual wheat price series (see Fig. 6.3 and Table 6.1) is of very low power. This confirms the suggestion that the short wavelength cycle may not have been *directly* linked to climatic conditions and that there were other factors producing this oscillation in the wheat price series. This hypothesis was tested by comparing the predicted and actual wheat price series as described in the Appendix, section 6.12.3. When the predicted annual wheat prices are deducted from the real prices, the resulting data series (the residuals) should represent those components that were less related to the climatic factors on which the predicted price series was solely based. Spectral analysis of this recalculated series now shows that the only oscillation in the short waveband was of wavelength 5.3 years, confirming that the short wavelength cycle in wheat prices was not strongly driven by weather conditions.

One possibility is that wheat prices in the *short term* were influenced for economic and agricultural reasons by the prices declared in the preceding year, the so-called autoregressive effects. This hypothesis was confirmed by re-running the multiple regression of the wheat price series, winter and summer temperatures versus wheat prices in the preceding year. The temperatures now have reduced significance whereas the autoregressive term is significant at $P = 0.0005$, indicating the 'carry-over' effect of prices into the subsequent year (see section 6.9).

There are therefore two different types of cycle in the national wheat price series, medium wavelength (12–16 years) and short wavelength (5–6 years); it is the former that is most closely affected by weather conditions (particularly low winter and summer temperatures) whereas the short wavelength cycle in grain prices is primarily driven by other factors.

6.9 What drove the different cycles in wheat prices?

It has been shown that the colder the winter the greater the month-to-month temperature variability (Tromp, 1980). Bergthorsson (1985) also found a strong relationship between hay yield and winter temperatures in Iceland between 1901 and 1975, and noted that cold winters were more effective than cold summers in restricting grass growth. Similarly Eckstein and co-workers (1985) found that the annual Swedish harvest index was significantly related to annual winter temperatures from 1756 to 1869, but no significant correlations were found between the quality of the harvest and spring, summer or autumn temperatures or annual rainfall. DeVries (1981) found a significant negative correlation between the annual price of rye and annual winter temperatures in Netherlands during 1635–1839. He also found that a critical factor influencing the level of arable crop yields in northwestern Europe was the amount of precipitation, particularly in winter; high rainfall levels between November and March delayed spring planting.

However, we have shown that the use of a combination of statistical techniques can integrate these reports; the results of multiple regression and principal component analysis suggest that weather had a significant effect on prices in the *medium* waveband, probably via an effect on crop yields. Low winter and low summer temperatures are significantly associated with high wheat prices and, presumably, with poor crop yields. Principal component analysis indicates that the effect of winter temperatures may be mainly indirect, i.e. a cold winter establishes a cold growing and harvesting season during spring and summer. The significant association of high wheat prices with low summer temperatures in England in the 17th and 18th centuries described in this chapter is probably direct. The effect of seasonal rainfall appears to be of secondary importance and is effective only on a simple annual basis, i.e. heavy rain at a specific period in summer could ruin a harvest. Analysis shows that these effects of weather operate mainly on the medium wavelength oscillation in English wheat prices, whereas the short wavelength oscillation is less significantly related to weather conditions. Comparison of the real annual wheat price index with that predicted from the equation derived from multivariate analysis confirms that the medium wavelength oscillation, but not the short wavelength oscillation, is driven by weather conditions.

What then are the other causes of the short wavelength cycles in wheat prices? An index of prices is partly artificial and is driven by economic factors as well as by grain yields in the fields at harvest time. Cycles in oats, barley and wheat prices were synchronous and oscillated together; if one grain was in poor supply the prices of the others were driven up also. The poor were prevented from substituting cheaper grains and the failure of the crops had a ripple effect that was felt throughout the economy. Appleby (1979) also noted that all grains rose symmetrically in price, preventing the labouring poor from switching from their usual bread grains to cheaper grains and thereby staying alive. Harrison (1971) recognised that all prices rose in years of high prices, although not to the same extent. Obviously, major transient (non-cyclical) weather events can contribute to a bad harvest in any one year (e.g. scorching of the oats crop in Lancashire in 1762). Hoskins (1968) suggested that the cyclical disposition of grain prices was not basically because of weather cycles but was related to the underlying factor of yield ratios.

One bad harvest, by reducing the yield ratio to dangerously low levels, tended to generate another because of the scarcity of seed-corn, and it has been suggested that this effect was cumulative until a change in the weather pattern broke the sequence and restored the normal balance between bread-corn and seed-corn (Hoskins, 1968; Bowden, 1967). Wrigley (1989) noted the relationship between grain prices and the size of the harvest and suggested that fluctuations in price may reflect the level of grain stocks carried over, varying with the abundance of the harvest, and not on the runs of deficient and abundant harvests.

These are so-called autoregressive effects in which the grain price is strongly influenced by the price in the preceding 1 or even 2 years. An autoregressive term included in the multiple regression in the present study is highly significant ($P = 0.0005$) and a second autoregressive term is also significant ($P = 0.012$), showing that the wheat prices in the two preceding years have detectable effects.

The closer the farmer operates at subsistence level, the larger the number of years in which he will have no surplus to sell and must therefore enter the market as a buyer at high prices. For the 16th and 17th centuries, the English agrarian economy operated on a very fine margin between sufficiency and shortage and, where a society consumed almost all of its annual output within a year, any fluctuation in the harvest must have had overriding economic significance. Such economic factors could have made a major contribution to the clear short wavelength oscillation in grain prices that emerged strongly at the end of the 16th century, but it seems that other regulatory mechanisms were probably implicated in generating such a regular oscillation, as described in the next section.

6.10 Rust and other parasitic infestations of grain crops

'To the farmer of this period pests and diseases were rather like the poor: he had them with him always. It was almost certain that he would lose some part of his crops to an attack by some fungus or insect. How much he lost is not told' (Brown & Beecham, 1989). Fungal diseases, such as mildew, loose bunt and rust were the major scourge of cereals that frequently destroyed whole crops. Rust diseases of cereals were the most damaging and, periodically, severe epidemics have plagued humankind.

Could these fungal diseases be a contributory factor to the short wavelength oscillations observed in grains prices? It is now known that rust had two alternative life cycles in one of which the fungus existed and underwent sexual reproduction during the winter on the barberry (*Berberis vulgaris*), which was found in woods and used in field hedges and boundaries and hence, once this fact was known, barberry bushes were destroyed in the late 19th century.

Rust has the ability to cycle between these alternate hosts and, like other fungal diseases, can display endemic and epidemic conditions; for instance, a fungal parasite can be endemic with a long interdependent association with the plant host(s) when disease levels are low and vary little over time. Thus, as shown in Fig. 6.10, because rust had two life cycles, only one of which existed on the barberry, the eventual destruction of the bushes did not eradicate the disease completely because the alternate life cycle of the inner loop of asexual reproduction on the wheat alone would be sufficient for the infestation to continue.

Two kinds of rust have been identified: Orange Leaf-Rust caused by *Puccinia rubigo-vera* and Black Stem Rust caused by *Puccinia graminis*. The former did not grow on the barberry at all, and the distinction between the two was important since Orange Leaf-Rust depleted the wheat plant during the early stages of growth whereas the Black Stem variety was more serious

Spring   Summer

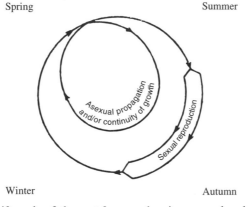

Winter   Autumn

Figure 6.10. Life cycle of the rust fungus, showing asexual and sexual cycles.

since it drained the plants later in their growth. These parasitic fungi grow on a range of host plants, including wheat, oats and barley. With the exception of the rust on wheat which did infect barley, rust on one cereal could not infect the others. There was not one *Puccinia graminis* but several. *Puccinia graminis* sp. f. *avenae* was found in oats, *Puccinia graminis* sp. f. *tritici* on wheat and barley and a few of the other grasses, and *Puccinia graminis* sp. f. *secalis* on rye (Large, 1958).

The epidemic state of rust describes explosive outbreaks associated with an increase of intensity as well as of extensity, and a progressive epidemic occurs when the disease spreads to new regions and, after having reached a high level of severity during the early years of conquest, settles once again to endemic status. If the disease develops explosively, affecting a large number of individuals, it may spread to a new region where it will have the character once again of a progressive epidemic. Yellow Rust on wheat, endemic in the Netherlands, sometimes follows this pattern, becoming progressive whenever a new physiological form of the disease appears. A description of a rust epidemic is as follows. Population bursts of fungi occur when diseased seeds are planted, or the fungus that has invaded the alternate host emerges. Shoots become diseased and the fungus spreads throughout the field from these primary diseased shoots; the fungus must increase about a billion-fold in order to destroy all the fields in the vicinity. Conditions that favour infection are susceptible host plants, a virulent pathogen, and suitable weather conditions conducive to the disease. A lower than usual rate of infection suggests that some condition is adverse, i.e. there are more resistant than susceptible host plants, or that the weather is too dry for a disease that needs moisture. The epidemic will recede when

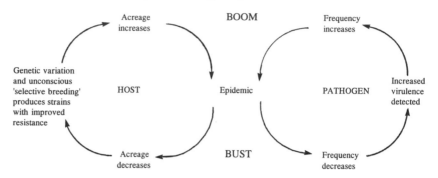

Figure 6.11. Diagram showing the boom-and-bust cycles of rust diseases.

less healthy tissue is available for infection or, more often, because the crops ripens. If conditions do not change from year to year, the epidemic will settle down and the infection rate will remain constant but any departure from uniformity, whatever the source, could cause an increase in infectivity and the threat of an epidemic. For instance, depleted stocks of seed corn following a deficient harvest would decrease the amount of plant host that is available to the pathogen during the next season. Each year without an epidemic would increase the proportion of seed corn available for planting and consequently the number of susceptible host plants would rise until conditions were suitable for an explosive epidemic, resulting in a much reduced crop yield. In this way, the process would be self-perpetuating and these 'boom-and-bust' cycles (Fig. 6.11) account for many of the most damaging epidemics of cereal diseases (Priestley, 1978).

Even during the early periods of agriculture of the 17th and 18th centuries, the outbred wheat would show wide genetic variability, with differing degrees of susceptibility to fungal attack; one of the major ways of developing this protection is by the development of a thickened cuticle in the host plant to prevent fungal entry. The farmer would, unconsciously, use a form of selective breeding in that the seed corn from a harvest during a severe fungal attack would, inevitably, tend to come from the resistant varieties of wheat plants that had survived to maturity. Consequently, a greater proportion of resistant grains would be sown and resistant plants would be harvested in the following year. However, the fungus which is producing astronomical numbers of spores would, in turn, have been developing more active penetrant strains and so the boom-and-bust cycle of fungal epidemics would tend to develop (Fig. 6.11). This cycling process is further complicated because at times when no significant rust infestations were present, the rust-resistant strain might be at a selective disadvantage to the non-resistant strains (the resistant gene would be at an advantage only when there is a major fungal infestation), so promoting the latter and exacerbating the development of another rust epidemic. Consequently, a 'technological arms race' between wheat and fungus develops in which successive resistant strains are overcome by more potent fungal strains which succeed in overwhelming the defences of the host plant, an example of how living systems are continually evolving at all levels. More recently, even after the eradication of the barberry and with highly developed selective plant breeding, epidemic outbreaks of rust continue to appear at intervals, causing widespread destruction of grain crops. Severe rust epidemics would be less likely to recur the year following an outbreak in the same way that it is unlikely that there would be smallpox epidemics in successive years (see Chapter 13) and they would have an inherent periodicity dependent upon the time taken to build up a sufficient number and density of susceptible host plants.

We suggest, therefore, that the regular short wavelength cycle in grain prices was not greatly affected by cycles in the weather (unlike the medium wavelength oscillation) and that the peaks of the oscillations were sharpened by economic and autoregressive factors and possibly by regular epidemics of fungal diseases.

6.11 Conclusions

Conventional time-series analysis of the English wheat price series, 1450–1812, reveals a short wavelength (period 6 years) cycle and a medium wavelength (period 12–16 years) cycle throughout this time, although they developed strongly only at the end of the 16th century. The comparable cycles revealed in the series of oats and barley prices are strongly coherent with wheat prices, i.e. the different grain prices moved in synchrony and consequently the wheat price series has been used in the following chapters as an index of nutritive levels. The factors driving the cycles in wheat prices are summarised in Fig. 7.10: the medium wavelength oscillation in wheat prices correlates with weather conditions; low winter and summer temperatures are the most significant factors. Both may have a direct effect on the growth and harvesting of the crop, but cold winters may also have indirect effects by establishing a generally cold spring and summer. High winter rainfall is of secondary importance. However, the short wavelength cycle in wheat prices is not significantly correlated with weather and it is suggested that it is driven by economic factors, the short-term effects of a good or bad harvest (autoregressive effects), and possibly regulated by regular epidemics of fungal pathogens of grain. The effects of this oscillation in grain prices in driving exogenous population cycles is considered in Chapters 7 and 8 and the subliminal (and not readily detectable) effects of malnutrition on the epidemiology of lethal infectious diseases are discussed in Chapters 9 to 14.

6.12 Appendix: Statistical considerations

6.12.1 Non-stationarity in the wheat price series

Analysis of any data series is complicated if the oscillations contained therein are not stationary. Possible problems with non-stationarity were addressed as follows. For a signal to exhibit weak stationarity it has to satisfy two criteria: (a) the mean remains constant, and (b) the autocorrelation function (acf) remains constant (i.e. they are both independent of time). The programs employed, including the coherence procedure, involve detrending so that the mean is equal to zero. These analyses therefore satisfy criterion (a) above. Where the acf does not remain constant over long periods of time, the data series have been subdivided into cohorts and the short wavelength oscillations were found to have a stable acf and the cross-correlation and coherence tests have been applied to the cohort. Finally, the series have been filtered specifically to remove periodic factors. The wheat price series can be described by the following equation:

$$\text{wheat}(t) =$$
$$\mu - \alpha_1 \text{ winter temp}(t) - \alpha_2 \text{ summer temp}(t) - \alpha_3 \text{ autumn temp}(t)$$
$$+ \alpha_4 \text{ winter rain}(t) + \alpha_5 \text{ summer rain}(t) + \alpha_6 \text{ autumn rain}(t) + \eta(t)$$

where $\eta(t)$ is non-white noise. Analysis of the residuals indicates that they can be modelled by an ARIMA process, driven by white noise

$$\eta(t) = \beta_1 \eta(t - 1) + \beta_2 \eta(t - 2) + e(t) - e(t - 5)$$

where $\beta_1 = 0.72$ and $\beta_2 = -0.006$ and where $e(t)$ is white at the 99.5 % level (Box and Pierce test). We conclude that the major non-stationary term is the periodic component, the short wavelength oscillation.

6.12.2 Principal component analysis of the interaction of seasonal weather conditions

Seasonal weather conditions may influence the temperatures in the succeeding months. For example, the major effect of a cold winter might be to cause a generally cold growing and harvest year, rather than having a direct effect on the crop. This effect can be studied by principal component analysis. When the spring temperature data series (1659–1812) is regressed on the winter temperature series as predictor, the two files are significantly correlated ($P < 0.0005$). The summer temperature series is also significantly correlated with winter temperatures, $P = 0.006$. Autumn temperatures are not correlated with winter temperatures. Thus, the association between high wheat prices and low winter and summer temperatures, shown above, may indicate a sensitivity of the prices to a generally cold year.

This possible interaction of the independent variables has been checked by principal component analysis of the annual data series of the four seasonal temperatures. Only principal component 1 (PC1) had an eigenvalue (variance) > 1 which accounts for 53% of the total variance; the coefficients of PC1 were winter 0.862, spring 0.401, summer 0.232, autumn 0.206. When the component score, calculated from the co-variance matrix, is regressed with the wheat price series, only PC1 is significant ($P = 0.019$). We conclude from principal component analysis that the annual wheat price is correlated with the weather conditions in that year. Multivariate analysis suggests that low winter and summer temperatures have the dominant effect but the coefficients of PC1 indicate that low winter temperatures may also be acting indirectly by causing low summer temperature.

The possible effects of seasonal rainfall have also been checked by principal component analysis. The coefficients of PC1 (which accounts for 32% of the variance) are winter -0.366, spring -0.681, summer -0.627, autumn $+0.097$. When the component score, calculated from the co-variance matrix is regressed with the wheat price series, none of the principal components (PC1 to PC4) shows any significant correlation.

6.12.3 Predicted wheat prices series

Multivariate analysis shows that spring rainfall and spring temperature were completely without significant effect on wheat prices. Consequently, the analysis was run with these two variables omitted; the analysis of variance now shows that the overall regression is significant ($P < 0.001$). The predicted wheat price can be determined from the coefficients of this analysis as follows:

wheat price (shillings) =
  79.9 + (0.027 × summer rain) + (0.0262 × autumn rain)
  + (0.0783 × winter rain) − (2.05 × summer temperature)
  − (0.48 × autumn temperature) − (3.61 × winter temperature)

Note the high coefficients (and relative importance) for summer and winter temperature.

This regression equation can then be used to predict the annual wheat price if it were influenced only by weather, and the predicted annual wheat prices are calculated for the period 1697–1812 from the derived coefficients and the actual mean seasonal temperatures and rainfall for that year. Spectral analysis of this calculated series shows dominant oscillations of 3 years and 14 years, but does not show the 6-year cycle seen in the real price series (Fig. 6.3). The predicted and real wheat price series were coherent in the 8–16-year ($P < 0.025$) and the 3-year waveband ($P < 0.05$), suggesting that these cycles in wheat prices can be explained as the consequence of weather conditions.

When the predicted annual wheat prices are deducted from the real prices, the resulting data (residuals) should represent those factors that were less related to climatic factors. Spectral analysis of this recalculated series now shows a dominant 6-year cycle and it is suggested that this short wavelength cycle in prices was not *directly* linked to climate.

7

Interactions of exogenous cycles: a case study

7.1 Introduction

Human populations often appear to fluctuate in response to cyclic patterns in the economic or natural environment. Short-run variations in grain prices (described in Chapter 6) and real wage levels have been suggested to be responsible for the fluctuations in fertility in England during 1541–1871 (Galloway, 1988) and for mortality cycles in England, Sweden and France (Lee, 1981; Eckstein et al., 1985; Richards, 1983; Bengtsson & Ohlsson, 1984; Weir, 1984). A study of the annual fluctuations in deaths in London (1670–1830) has shown that the epidemic diseases of typhus, fevers and smallpox were strongly associated with price increases (Galloway, 1985), and mortality was also found to be significantly associated with cold winters in England and Sweden (Lee, 1981; Eckstein et al., 1985). Food supply could constitute a dominant density-dependent factor that controls population dynamics, but there are few reliable records on which to base a quantitative analysis of the effects of malnutrition in the past and this has necessitated the use of data such as stature as a proxy for nutrition (Floud, Wachter & Gregory, 1990; Fogel, 1994). Historians and historical demographers have suggested correlations between food intake, disease and the mechanisms that push or pull populations and affect their stability (Rotberg, 1983). Recent research indicates that, in many European nations before the middle of the 19th century, the national production of food was at such low levels that the poorer classes were bound to have been malnourished and this led to a high incidence of disease (Duncan et al., 1994a; Fogel, 1994). In addition, malnutrition in utero may predispose young children to certain epidemic diseases such as whooping cough (section 11.10), measles (section 11.6) and scarlet fever (section 14.7), as well as being of critical importance for the subsequent health of the adult (Barker, 1992a).

The concept of regular, exogenous oscillations in births and deaths in an individual community was introduced in Chapter 3 of which the 5–6-year oscillation had the most profound effects on the population dynamics. Since these exogenous cycles were found under steady-state as well as in boom conditions, it is evident that they were probably not dependent on homeostatic dynamics nor on density-dependent constraints. What external events drove these exogenous oscillations? Was the short wavelength oscillation common to the majority of rural communities? If so, were these oscillations in synchrony (see section 15.1)?

An analysis of infant mortality can be derived only from a family reconstitution study which we have carried out for the parish of Penrith in the Eden Valley, Cumbria, and in this chapter we present an intensive case study of the interactions of the population cycles, building on the matrix modelling described in Chapter 4. The main objective of this study is to show how the methods of time-series analysis can be used to elucidate the population dynamics of a single community and to determine the economic and geographical factors on which they are based. The findings are derived from quantitative data and statistical confidence limits are given. These ideas are developed progressively through this chapter, which reveals the complexity of the interacting factors that regulate the exogenous population cycles (see Fig. 7.10), which, in turn, are superimposed on the endogenous longer wavelength oscillations described in Chapters 3 and 4. The contribution of smallpox epidemics to the childhood mortality cycles at Penrith is described in Chapter 13 and the study of exogenous mortality oscillations is extended to other communities in Chapter 8, wherein it is suggested that the correlation of mortality with different commodity indices reveals the nature of the underlying economics of the population. We believe that this is the first fully integrated, quantitative study of population dynamics in a human community.

7.2 Driving the short wavelength population oscillations at Penrith

The thesis presented in this chapter is that the oscillations in grain prices, described in the preceding chapter, and the corresponding availability of food had profound but subtle effects on the population at Penrith and was one of the major factors in driving the short wavelength oscillations in births and deaths. The national prices for wheat, oats and barley moved in synchrony and, as explained in Chapter 6, the wheat price series has been used as a general index of nutritive levels. No local grain prices are available for Cumbria for the pre-industrial period, but the population cycles correlate well with national grain price indices. The short wavelength cycle in wheat prices did not correlate with weather conditions but was appar-

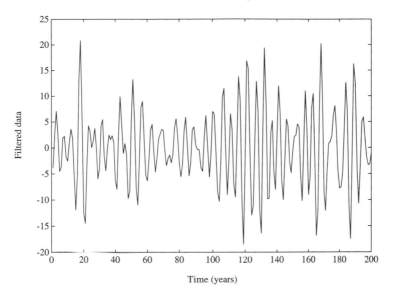

Figure 7.1. Burials of children plus infants at Penrith, 1607–1807, filtered to reveal the short wavelength oscillation (filter window = 4 to 10 years). Data derived from family reconstitution study.

ently driven by economic factors and the short-term effects of a good or bad harvest (autoregressive factors); it was of the most direct importance in driving the mortality cycles at Penrith.

7.3 Short wavelength mortality oscillations in the population dynamics

The total burial series at Penrith for the whole period, 1557–1812, is shown in Fig. 3.1 and spectral analysis reveals a short wavelength cycle in mortality (period≈5 years). However, this series is complex, being compounded of adult, child and infant deaths and, when these series are analysed separately, it is apparent that the periodicity arises predominantly from a persistent 5-year oscillation in child burials (0 to 14 years of age) which is evident by eye in the unfiltered series and is revealed more clearly after filtering in Fig. 7.1. Spectral analysis of the unfiltered and filtered series shows that the wavelength of this oscillation overall was predominantly 5 years, but before 1700 it was non-stationary, changing from 6 to 5 years. During the first 100 years (between 1557 and 1650), when the parish experienced several major mortality crises (see Chapter 8), the oscillations in adult and child burials are synchronous and this cross-correlation is highly significant ($P < 0.001$) with a cross-correlation function (ccf) of $+0.9$.

Are these cycles in child and adult mortality at Penrith exogenous, being a direct response of the population to famine and hardship? As a first step to answering this question, the family reconstitution study of Penrith has been used to divide the total child burial series into infants (0–12 months) and children aged from 1 to 14 years because, as described in section 7.4, infant mortality responded differently to fluctuations in the wheat price series. In brief, child (age 1 to 14 years) and adult burials were both strongly correlated with wheat prices for the first 100 years but after 1650 they responded differently.

7.3.1 *The short wavelength cycle in child burials*

Spectral analysis of the burial series of children aged 1–14 years in the different cohorts shows a 5–6-year oscillation from 1557–1700 which became strongly 5-yearly thereafter. Coherence analysis of the period 1557–1650 shows that child burials were strongly correlated with wheat prices in the short waveband ($P < 0.01$). The cross-correlations of child burials versus wheat prices can be summarised as follows:

1557–1600:	ccf = +0.6	Lag = 2 years, i.e. cycles not synchronous.
1600–1650:	ccf = +0.2	Zero lag.
1650–1700:	ccf = +0.4	Zero lag; see Fig. 7.2.
1700–1750:	ccf = −0.4	Lag at +1 years, i.e. child burials are no longer synchronous with the corresponding oscillation in wheat prices.
1750–1812:	ccf = +0.4	Zero lag, i.e. the two series are again in synchrony.

Thus, a short wavelength oscillation in the child burials series at Penrith emerged in the 16th century with a periodicity of 5–6 years which developed into a clear 5-yearly oscillation after 1700, as can be seen in Fig. 7.1 and is confirmed in the spectral analysis in Fig. 7.3 ($P < 0.05$). This mortality cycle was closely associated with a corresponding oscillation in wheat prices which also appeared at the end of the 16th century (section 6.2), suggesting that a rise in child deaths may have been associated with high wheat prices.

7.3.2 *Smallpox epidemics and the short wavelength oscillation in child mortality*

The short wavelength oscillation in child burials became more regularised after 1650 and spectral analysis for the period 1700–1775 (see Fig. 7.3)

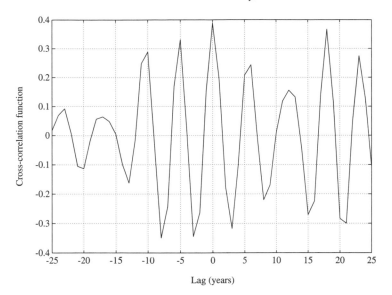

Figure 7.2. Cross-correlation function, burials of children aged 1 to 14 years versus wheat prices, 1650–1700. Filter window = 4 to 10 years. Maximum ccf (+0.4) at zero lag showing that the two series are in synchrony.

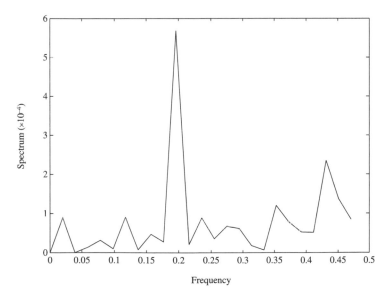

Figure 7.3. Spectral analysis of the child burial series (ages 1 to 14 years) at Penrith, 1700–1750. Unfiltered data. Significant peak ($P < 0.05$) at a wavelength of 5.1 years.

shows that the 5-year oscillation was now strongly established. Are these cycles associated with periodic outbreaks of a lethal epidemic disease? A fatal strain of smallpox appeared in England around 1630 (Razzell, 1977; Corfield, 1987) and, although smallpox is specifically mentioned only twice in the Penrith registers (in 1656 and 1661), it is shown in section 13.1 that there is good evidence for the development of 5-yearly epidemics of small-pox. Regular epidemics of smallpox were established in Penrith and were superimposed on the pre-existing cycles of child mortality which may have been driven by the short wavelength oscillation in wheat prices described above. It is suggested in Chapter 13 that cycles of malnutrition caused by regular high grain prices produced a corresponding oscillation in suscepti-bility that was sufficient to drive the system and trigger the epidemics of smallpox. In this way, the oscillatory tendency for the dynamics of the small-pox epidemics at Penrith would become phase-locked to the driving effects of increased susceptibility associated with high wheat prices, and the pre-existing short wavelength oscillation in child mortality that was established in the 16th century was sharpened and intensified, and the 5-yearly periodic epidemics of childhood smallpox mortality made a dominant contribution to the 5-year oscillations in overall child mortality and smallpox after 1650.

7.3.3 Adult mortality cycles

The adult mortality series (Fig. 7.4) is dominated by the many deaths in the plague during 1596 to 1598 and in the mortality crises of 1587 and 1623. Spectral analysis and filtering (Fig. 7.5) show that the periodicity of the short wavelength oscillation in adult deaths was predominantly 5 years; it was strongly coherent with wheat prices during the first 100 years (1557–1650) and the cross-correlations between adult burials and prices in the different cohorts were:

> 1557–1600: ccf = −0.7   Lag at +1 years, i.e. cycles not synchronous.
> 1600–1650: ccf = +0.35 Zero lag.
> 1650–1700: ccf = +0.2   Zero lag.
> 1700–1750: ccf = −0.2   Lag at +1 years, i.e. cycles asynchronous.
> 1750–1812: ccf = +0.2   Zero lag.

These results correspond closely with those described for child burials above.

Although the 5-year, short wavelength oscillation in adult burials was still correlated with wheat prices after 1650, the coherence was less signifi-cant than that of child burials, and adult burials were found to be more

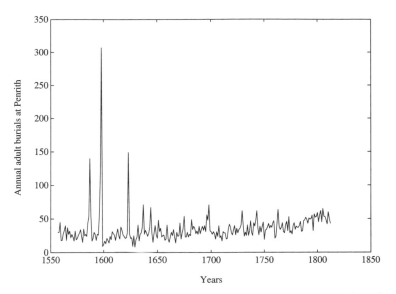

Figure 7.4. Annual adult burials at Penrith, 1557–1812. Note mortality crises in 1587, 1596–1598 and 1623.

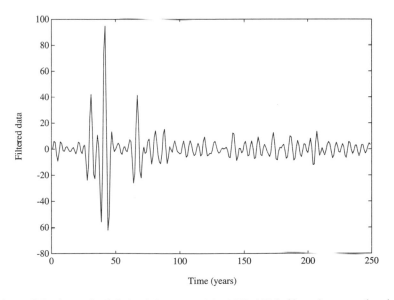

Figure 7.5. Annual adult burials at Penrith, 1557–1806, filtered to reveal a short wavelength oscillation (filter window = 4 to 10 years).

Table 7.1. *Life table burial rates for infants and children at Penrith (sexes combined)*

Age groups (yr)	Cohort					
	1557–1599	1600–1649	1650–1699	1700–1749	1750–1774	1775–1812
0–1	250	248	221	205	163	109
1–4	98	132	141	158	154	119
5–9	53	42	38	53	54	42
10–14	33	21	27	24	26	54
% death rate (0–14 years)	43	44	43	44	40	32

Note:
Burial rates derived from the family reconstitution study. Infant deaths calculated as the first 12 months after baptism. Children aged 1 to 14 years. Burial rates per 1000, expressed as q_x, the probability at age x of dying before reaching age $x + n$.

significantly associated then with climatic conditions in the medium wave-band, as described in section 7.10.

It is suggested, therefore, that the exogenous, short wavelength cycles in both child and adult deaths were driven by periods of malnutrition associated with the peaks of the oscillations in grain prices that emerged and developed in the late 16th century in England. Adults and children responded differently after 1650: child mortality cycles were exacerbated by regular smallpox epidemics, whereas adult burials correlated more significantly with climatic conditions.

7.4 Infant mortality at Penrith

It is fundamental to geographical studies that infant deaths are indicators of adverse circumstances (Robinson, 1992) such as were found in the marginal conditions at Penrith during the 17th and 18th centuries; a high neonatal mortality and a high incidence of low birth weight are believed to be directly associated with poor maternal nutrition (Barker, 1992a; Barker & Osmond, 1986a; Barker & Martyn, 1992). The family reconstitution study, in which infant deaths are calculated as those dying during the first 12 months after baptism, shows that infant mortality at Penrith was high and, until the middle of the 17th century, 25% of children died during the first year of life; mortality fell progressively thereafter. Table 7.1 shows this steady fall in infant mortality at Penrith in the successive cohorts and the corresponding rise in mortality in the 1- to 4-year age group which is the

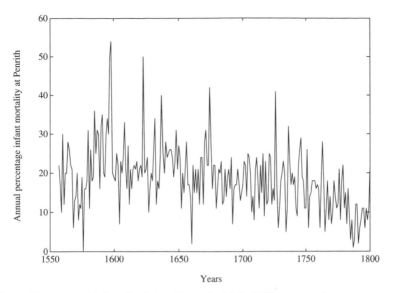

Figure 7.6. Annual infant burials at Penrith, 1557–1800 expressed as a percentage of the baptisms in the year of death. Note the falling trend after 1740. Data derived from family reconstitution study.

result of the establishment of regular lethal smallpox epidemics. Thus, the improvement of infant mortality was counterbalanced by rising childhood mortality until the introduction of inoculation; later, vaccination against smallpox became effective at the end of the 18th century. This amelioration of infant mortality is shown in the downward slope of the unfiltered infant burial series shown in Fig. 7.6. Spectral analysis of the annual infant mortality at Penrith (expressed as a percentage of baptisms in the year of death) reveals a short wavelength oscillation which overall has a 5–6-year periodicity and this is shown for the period 1557–1806 after filtering in Fig. 7.7. Analysis of the characteristics of this oscillation in infant deaths in the different cohorts is summarised in Table 7.2.

Table 7.1 shows that the infant mortality rates at Penrith were high up to the mid-17th century but, by the beginning of the 18th century, the rate had improved to one in five and, by the start of the next century, to one in nine. It has been suggested that an infant mortality rate under 10% (see Table 7.1) for any period before the 20th century is very low and so it might be reasonable to be suspicious of a rate close to this value at Penrith for the last period. This might be a consequence of the underregistration of children who died soon after birth, a phenomenon known to have become increasingly widespread by the 18th century (Schofield & Wrigley, 1979).

Table 7.2. *Characteristics of the short wavelength oscillation in infant deaths at Penrith and its correlation with wheat prices*

Cohort	Wavelength determined by spectral analysis (yr)		Cross-correlation with wheat prices	
	Unfiltered	Filtered	ccf	Lag (yr)
1557–1600	5–6	5–6	0.55	−1
1600–1650	7 (secondary 5)	7 and 5	0.6	0
1650–1700	6	6	0.1	0
1700–1750	5	5	90° out of phase	
1750–1812	5	5	0.5	0

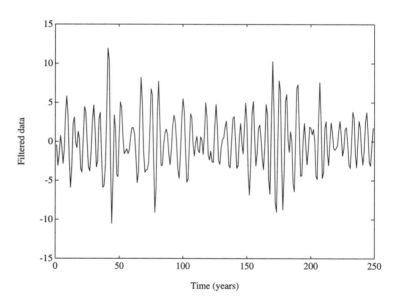

Figure 7.7. Annual infant burials at Penrith, 1557–1806, expressed as a percentage of the baptisms in the year of death filtered to reveal the short wavelength oscillation (filter window = 4 to 10 years).

Comparing the infant mortality rate with the death rates of children aged 1–4 is one way of assessing any discrepancy, since serious underregistration would show low values for infants relative to those for the older group. However, at Penrith, the burial rates for this group also showed a significant fall during the period in question (Table 7.1).

The hypothesis that a rise in wheat prices caused an increase in infant mortality was tested by the coherence program and it was found that the

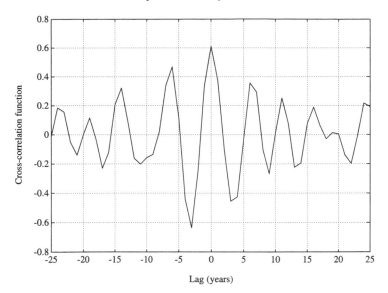

Figure 7.8. Cross-correlation function, wheat price series versus infant burials (expressed as a percentage of the baptisms in the year of death) at Penrith, 1600–1650. Filter window = 4 to 10 years. Maximum ccf (+0.6) at zero lag showing that the two series are in synchrony.

two series were significantly correlated ($P < 0.001$) in the short waveband at zero lag or at a lag of +1 years. The cross-correlation between infant mortality and wheat prices in the different cohorts is summarised in Table 7.2. Again, this synchronous correlation is particularly evident during the first 100 years and the ccf for 1600–1650 is shown in Fig. 7.8. This finding suggests that the complex fluctuation in infant mortality was driven, in part, by periods of hardship and malnutrition to which the population at Penrith was susceptible.

Infant mortality is conventionally subdivided into neonatal deaths in the first 28 days of life and post-neonatal deaths during the first 1 to 12 months of life. Using the family reconstitution study at Penrith, the annual infant burial series was subdivided into neonatal mortality (28 days post-baptism; normally no data are available in the parish registers for the exact day of birth) and post-neonatal mortality (1 to 12 months of life) expressed as a percentage of live births. Both mortality series were strongly coherent with wheat prices in the short wavelength bands ($P < 0.001$). The data series of neonatal and post-neonatal mortality (expressed as a percentage of live births) were then divided into five cohorts and each was run on the coherence program with wheat prices as input and mortality as output. The results are

Interactions of exogenous cycles

Table 7.3. *Coherence between the wheat price index and neonatal or*
post-neonatal mortalities

Cohort (dates)	% Neonatal mortality			% Post-neonatal mortality		
	Lag (yr)	Waveband (yr)	*P*	Lag (yr)	Waveband (yr)	*P*
1557–1599	+1	3–4.5	<0.001	0	3.5–4	<0.01
					5–8	<0.001
					10–30	<0.01
1600–1649	+1	2.5–3	<0.001	+1	2	<0.001
		3–3.5	<0.01		3–3.7	0.001
		5–11	<0.01		4	<0.01
					7–11	<0.001
1650–1699	0	2	<0.001	0	2.5–4	<0.001
		3	0.001			
		7–9	0.01			
1700–1749	+1	3–4	<0.001	0	3	<0.01
		7–11	0.001			
1750–1812	+1/+2	2	<0.01	+1	3	<0.001
		3	0.01		5–6	0.001
		5	0.01			

Note:
Mortality expressed as a percentage of baptisms in the year of death.

summarised in Table 7.3, which shows that both mortality series are strongly coherent with wheat prices ($P < 0.001$) in the short wavebands in every cohort. During the period 1750–1812, when conditions at Penrith ameliorated and the population boom began, the significance of the coherence between wheat prices and neonatal mortality fell, with $P = 0.01$. The lag between the data series (Table 7.3) was 0 or +1 years, with post-neonatal mortality tending towards synchronisation (zero lag) and neonatal mortality showing predominantly a lag of +1 years, i.e. peaks of post-neonatal mortality tended to occur in years of high wheat prices whereas high neonatal mortality tended to occur in the following year (i.e. when the pregnancy occurred during a period of high wheat prices). These findings suggest, therefore, that raised neonatal mortality (which followed high wheat prices by 1 year) was related to the malnutrition of the mother during pregnancy, whereas cycles of post-neonatal mortality (which synchronised with wheat prices) were directly dependent on the food supply during the first year of life, which would have had a direct effect on both lactation and weaning.

7.5 How does malnutrition affect child and infant mortality?

Barker and his colleagues have shown by their studies in historical epidemiology that nutrition before and during pregnancy and in infancy is of critical importance for growth and development of the embryo and also for the subsequent health of the adult. A high neonatal mortality and a high incidence of children with a low birth weight are both directly associated with poor maternal nutrition. Neonatal mortality in the past was high in places where babies were born with low birth weight and is also known to have been associated with high maternal mortality. High rates for both neonatal and maternal mortality were found in places where the physique and health of women were poor (Barker & Osmond, 1986a,b; Barker, 1992a,b; Barker & Martyn, 1992) and infant deaths are indicators of adverse circumstances (Robinson, 1992). Current research has found that the rates of infant mortality, mental retardation and cerebral palsy are many times greater in low birth weight babies, and cot-death cases today have been linked to kidney defects arising from a form of growth retardation that resulted from the deprivation of essential nutrients in the womb (Hinchliffe *et al.*, 1993). A mother's weight, body composition and eating habits in the months before pregnancy appear to be important. Current evidence shows that women contemplating pregnancy should be taking folic acid and vitamin B_{12}, since the nervous system has already been laid down in the developing foetus by the time pregnancy is confirmed (Godfrey *et al.*, 1994) and low levels result in babies born with nervous system abnormalities which include spina bifida.

These studies were developed using data series from the 20th century but unfortunately comparable information is not available for pre-industrial societies. The community at Penrith suffered a major mortality crisis in 1623 (which is described in Chapter 8) triggered, it is suggested, by the synergistic effects of synchronous high wheat and low wool prices. The period 1615–1632 at Penrith (that is, about 10 years before and after the 1623 crisis) has been examined in detail, using the family reconstitution study, to determine the effects of severe malnutrition in pregnancy on mortality during the first month of life and in post-neonates. The fate of the children born in each year has been followed and the results are summarised in Table 7.4 which shows the age-specific mortality of infants and children classified by the year of birth, so that it is possible to trace the fates of children born in each year by following along the respective lines. For example, of the children born in 1615, 21.2% died as infants in that year (column 3) and 11.5% died as 1-year olds in the following year (column 4). A further 7.7% of the children born in 1615 died between 2 and 5 years of age (column 5), i.e. between 1617 and 1620.

Interactions of exogenous cycles

Table 7.4. *Age-specific mortality for children baptised at Penrith during the period 1615–1632*

| Year | No. of baptisms | Age-specific mortality classified by year of baptism (% of baptisms) | | | | | Wheat prices per qtr (sh) | Total deaths |
		Infant	1–2yr	2–5yr	6–14yr	Total 1–14yr		
(1)	(2)	(3)	(4)	(5)	(6)	(7)	(8)	(9)
1615	52	21.2	11.5	7.7	3.8	23.0	39	35
1616	41	22.0	4.9	2.4	7.3	14.6	40	57
1617	62	21.0	0	8.1	4.8	12.9	49	57
1618	48	22.9	4.2	14.6	0	18.8	47	46
1619	51	17.6	3.9	9.8	3.9	17.6	35	40
1620	42	21.4	2.4	11.9	7.1	21.4	30	43
1621	54	22.2	1.9	3.7	1.9	7.5	30	50
1622	48	18.8	16.7	4.2	6.3	27.2	59	49
1623	40	50.0	2.5	0	0	2.5	52	241
1624	40	20.0	2.5	5.0	2.5	10.0	48	39
1625	53	20.8	1.9	7.5	3.8	13.2	52	34
1626	55	23.6	3.6	9.1	3.6	16.3	49	43
1627	68	10.3	5.9	1.5	1.5	8.9	36	20
1628	56	16.1	12.5	1.8	8.9	23.2	28	43
1629	49	20.4	4.1	4.1	2.0	10.2	42	43
1630	50	18.0	2.0	4.0	2.0	8.0	56	37
1631	54	25.9	5.6	5.6	1.9	13.1	68	41
1632	55	34.5	0	12.7	5.4	18.1	53	80
Mean	51						45.2	55.4
SD	7.42						10.96	47.9

Note:
The fate of the children (age at death or surviving) born in each year can be traced along the respective row. qtr, quarter; sh, shillings; SD, standard deviation.

There were 48 births in 1622 (column 2), close to the mean annual value of 51 (derived from family reconstitution studies for that period). Although wheat prices (column 8) rose sharply in that year and were high for 1622/3, infant mortality (18.8%, column 3) remained low. However, infant mortality rose dramatically in the following year and 50% of those born died during the first year of life; none of those who survived the first year of life died in the parish up to age 14 years. The results for 1623 illustrate the deleterious effects of high wheat prices during pregnancy in 1622, which subsequently caused severe infant mortality. High wheat prices also had a direct effect on the mortality of very young children: 16.7% of the children born in 1622 died in their second year of life (column 4), i.e. during the famine of 1623.

Wheat prices were again very high (68 shillings per quarter) in 1631 and total deaths rose to 80 in the following year; 34.5% of those born in 1632 died in infancy (Table 7.4). Conversely, 1627/8 was a period of low wheat prices and the total deaths were very low whereas births and marriages in the parish were at a peak. Infant mortality (expressed as a percentage of baptisms) was particularly low in 1627 and 1628 (Table 7.4, column 3).

Although poor nutrition during pregnancy was apparently associated with markedly increased infant mortality, columns 4–6 and column 7 in Table 7.4 show that the mortality of the surviving children had little correlation with the annual wheat price index in either the year of their birth or the year preceding their birth and it is concluded that Table 7.4 does not provide evidence that famine conditions during pregnancy have indirect and later effects on the subsequent mortality of children over the age of 1 year. However, wheat prices in later years do have a *direct* effect on childhood mortality; note the high mortality of children in 1623 who were born in 1622 before the crisis (Table 7.4, column 4). The higher values of mortality in the age groups 2–5 years (column 5) for the children born in years 1618–1620 illustrate how these children were also directly affected by the famine conditions of 1622/23 and died then.

7.6 Analysis of neonatal and post-neonatal mortality in the crisis of 1623 at Penrith

The possible effects of malnutrition on infant mortality has been assessed further and the records for Penrith for the period 1621–1624 have been divided into 12 overlapping groups, each containing the total conceptions for three consecutive months, and the number of subsequent neonatal and post-neonatal infant deaths for each group are shown in Fig. 7.9. For example, group C contained 15 children who were conceived during the period December 1621 to February 1622 (i.e. pre-famine conceptions and who were born before there was a noticeable rise in mortality); of these, one child died as a neonate and four as post-neonatal infants. Children in groups D, E and F were conceived before the famine but were exposed to malnutrition and famine conditions during the second and third trimesters of pregnancy. Group G was exposed to famine *in utero* and after birth, and groups H, I and J were exposed *in utero* to famine conditions but not after birth. Control groups A, B, C, K and L were either pre-famine conceptions

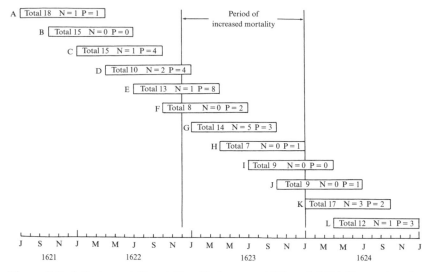

Figure 7.9. Infant mortality at Penrith between 1621 and 1624 illustrating the effects of the famine of 1623. N, neonatal deaths; P, post-neonatal deaths. The births are divided into 9-month cohorts, reflecting whether conception and pregnancy were before, during, or after the period of famine. The month that the infant was conceived is shown on the abscissa. The cohorts are separated by 3 monthly intervals. Thus, groups A, B, C, K, and L are control groups; D, E, and F were infants conceived before, but born during the famine; G infants were conceived and born during the famine; H, I, and J were conceived before, but born after the famine. The results of the χ^2 are tabulated as follows:

Groups	Survivors	Neonate deaths	Post-neonate deaths	Total
ABCKL	61	6	10	77
DEF	14	3	14	31
G	6	5	3	14
HIJ	23	0	2	25
Total	104	14	29	147

$\chi^2 = 32.4$; 6 d.f.; $p < 0.001$.

and births or post-famine conceptions and births. It is evident that the number of baptisms fell considerably during the period of famine. The number in each group is necessarily small but the results provide a good indication of the effects of malnutrition during pregnancy.

Overall, a highly significant departure from random expectation was established ($P < 0.001$) and three main tendencies became apparent (Fig. 7.9). Firstly, groups D, E and F, conceived before the famine but born when food shortages were acute, displayed a large rise in post-neonatal burials whereas neonatal mortality was not raised. Group E infants (exposed during the last trimester of pregnancy and then after birth) were the most vulnerable, with the highest level of post-neonatal mortality. Group D also had a high level of infant mortality with twice as many post-neonates dying as neonates. These foetuses were exposed during the last trimester of pregnancy to conditions that were probably less severe than those experienced by group E. Secondly, equally significant are the increased mortality rates as neonatal infants for those conceived and born during the famine (group G); this group included five neonates who died as unbaptised infants. Thirdly, conversely, the children of the famine (groups H, I and J) showed remarkably low infant mortality and, although the numbers were small, there were no neonatal deaths and only two post-neonatal deaths out of a total of 25.

7.7 Conclusions: the effects of malnutrition on infant mortality

Time-series analysis shows that raised infant mortality at Penrith was significantly correlated with high wheat prices and, it is suggested, with periods of malnutrition. An inadequate diet during and after pregnancy, rather than outright starvation, has subtle but profound effects on the mortality of the infants. Children of the 1623 crisis who survived infancy did not appear to be at special risk and this observation is in accord with a previously published study on the effect of famine conditions which found that these children had a better survival during the first two decades of life (Hart, 1993). The effects can be direct or indirect. Table 7.3 and Fig. 7.9 provide tentative evidence that neonatal mortality was related to malnutrition of the mother during pregnancy (there is a lag of $+1$ years with the wheat prices index), whereas post-neonatal mortality (zero lag with wheat prices) depended directly on food supply during the first year of life, as this affected both lactation and weaning. However, since famine conditions would frequently overlap pregnancy and infancy, a clear separation of the lag period for the two components of infant mortality would not be expected. These conclusions concerning the effects of malnutrition during pregnancy and infancy at Penrith during the 16th, 17th and 18th centuries are, of necessity, based on indirect evidence but they fully support the classical studies in historical epidemiology of the early 20th century by Barker and his colleagues (Barker *et al.*, 1989, 1991; Barker, 1992a). They had access to the admirable and detailed records of Hertfordshire and have demonstrated clearly that nutrition in pregnancy has a profound effect on neonatal mortality, even though this population was not existing at subsistence level as at Penrith.

The crisis at Penrith in 1623 can be compared with the Dutch hunger winter between September 1944 and May 1945, when the West Netherlands under enemy occupation was exposed to severe famine during a particularly harsh winter. The other regions of the Netherlands acted as controls in these studies: the South was liberated before the end of 1944 and the agricultural North escaped the worst of the food shortages. Before 1944, the population of West Netherlands had a daily ration of 1800 calories, which was reduced to 1600 calories by mid-1944 and thereafter it declined progressively to 400 calories in April 1945, although children and expectant and nursing mothers received additional calories. The far-reaching effects of this famine have been documented; for example there was an immediate increase in mortality. The records for the West Netherlands for the period 1943–1947 have been divided into the following groups: (a) pre-famine conception and birth, (b) pre-famine conception but exposed to famine during the second and third trimesters of pregnancy, (c) pre-famine conception, exposed to famine *in utero* but not after birth, (d) conceived and exposed *in utero* to famine conditions, but not after birth, and (e) post-famine conception. The cohort exposed during the last trimester of pregnancy and then after birth were the most vulnerable, with higher levels of neonatal mortality and mortality of liveborn children. Conversely, the children of the famine who survived infancy did not appear to be at special risk and it was found that they had better survival during the first two decades of life. Stein *et al.* (1975) have identified a daily ration of 1500 calories as the threshold that sustained fecundity in West Netherlands; furthermore the nutritional threshold for conception was clearly lower than the nutritional threshold for foetal viability. It was concluded that famine exerts its greatest effect just before, or just after birth, rather than early in the prenatal period. These findings correlate well with the events at Penrith in 1623 (Fig. 7.9). The highest neonatal mortality was recorded in the cohort conceived and born during the famine, whereas the highest post-neonatal mortality was found in cohorts conceived before and born during the famine, particularly those that were exposed to the severest effects of the famine during the last trimester (groups D and E).

It is probably unwise to draw general conclusions from the extreme Dutch hunger winter; some of the potential effects of famine on children may have been mitigated because of the rationing policy that favoured pregnant mothers and young children; the severe famine lasted only 7 months and an adequate supply of food was then rapidly re-established. The continuing marginal conditions at Penrith in the 16th and 17th centuries probably more closely mirror those of communities in the Third World today. It was concluded that there was no evidence in the study of the population of West Netherlands for an unequal impact of prenatal famine exposure on mortality by social class, whereas increases in mortality during periods of famine in Bangladesh in 1974/5 were highest among the poor of the population, probably corresponding to conditions in Penrith.

7.8 The short wavelength oscillation in baptisms at Penrith

The short wavelength oscillation in the baptism series at Penrith is clearly shown after filtering in Fig. 3.6. It has a wavelength that varied between 5 and 8 years, with a dominant 5-year oscillation during 1557–1650, an 8-year oscillation from 1650–1750, and a 6–8-year oscillation thereafter. It cross-correlates well with the oscillation in total burials but is completely out of phase: i.e. high annual burials correspond with low annual baptisms. This negative correlation is particularly significant for the first 100 years (see Fig. 3.9; ccf $= -0.8$) and overall the two series correspond negatively at zero lag with $P < 0.01$ in the 5-year waveband. However, analysis of the different cohorts shows that after 1700 this negative correlation was lost and the two cycles came into synchrony.

The family reconstitution study has shown that age at first marriage, mean family size and marital fertility at Penrith did not change significantly during the period under study (see Scott, 1995, and section 4.5). Age at first marriage was late and marital fertility was low by historical comparison and the possible link between fertility and poor nutrition has been discussed elsewhere (Scott & Duncan, 1996, 1997a). Previous studies have suggested that individuals may anticipate harvest failure and restrict fertility accordingly (Livi-Bacci, 1986), but the results above suggest that the cycle in baptisms was not an immediate response to variations in grain prices but was driven directly by fluctuations in mortality.

7.9 Short wavelength oscillation in immigration at Penrith

The measures of immigration used in this study (see section 4.6) are of necessity imprecise and so the calculated lags between variables are approximations but, nevertheless, the correlations of calculated migratory movements with adult mortality and wheat prices are particularly significant statistically. We have shown in Chapter 4 that migration played an important part in maintaining the steady-state conditions at Penrith during

1557–1750 and computer modelling suggests how the population dynamics of this community could be controlled by migratory movements (section 4.7; Duncan *et al.*, 1994a). Losses amongst adults at times of hardship were quickly (often within 2–3 years) replaced by newcomers, and this positive response is apparent after the major mortality crises of 1598/9 and 1623. We have shown in section 7.3.3 that the peaks in the short wavelength oscillations in wheat prices were associated with rises in adult burials which, in turn, promoted an influx of migrants and a concomitant rise in illegitimacy. The association between immigration and illegitimacy was particularly noticeable after the mortality crises of the late 16th and early 17th centuries and during the boom period of 1750–1812 (Scott & Duncan, 1997a; see also section 15.4).

7.10 Medium wavelength oscillations in adult burials at Penrith

The medium wavelength oscillation that is detectable in wheat prices had a less significant effect on the cycles in mortality: the population responded quickly and more significantly to the sharper changes in hardship and malnutrition that are reflected in the short wavelength oscillations in grain prices and wool prices (see Chapter 8). However, a medium wavelength oscillation in *adult* mortality is detectable by time-series analysis and it was strongly developed in the years between 1660 and 1760; its wavelength during this time was 11 years. Coherence and cross-correlation studies show that this medium wavelength oscillation in mortality cross-correlates directly with low winter temperatures (ccf = −0.65; the cycles cross-correlate negatively, $P < 0.025$).

7.11 Medium wavelength oscillations in migration at Penrith

We have described previously (Scott & Duncan, 1997a) the medium wavelength oscillation in immigration at Penrith that is significantly associated with elevated wheat prices ($P = 0.001$). These migratory movements also correspond with adult mortality: between 1650 and 1750 the medium wavelength cycle in immigration cross-correlates with adult mortality with a lag of 1 or 2 years ($P < 0.05$).

7.12 Interactions between the different oscillations: an overview

The ways in which, it is suggested, the different cycles in the demographic data at Penrith interact and are driven by oscillations in wheat prices and

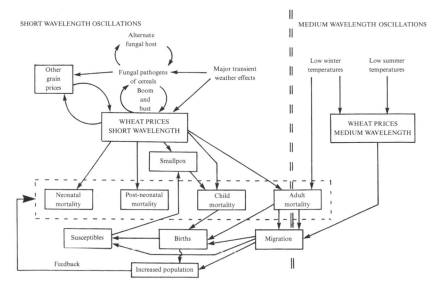

Figure 7.10. Summary diagram of the suggested interaction of exogenous cycles at Penrith. The short and medium wavelength oscillations that have been detected in the wheat prices series by time-series analysis are shown in the upper part of the figure, together with the various factors that may interact with, and serve to drive, them. The short wavelength oscillation in wheat prices is also subject to auto-regressive factors (section 6.9). The distinction between the short and medium wavelength mortality oscillations is shown by the vertical dividing line; where a population response exhibits both types of oscillation, the appropriate box is shown spanning this line. The arrows indicate highly significant correlations and operate at zero lag except for neonatal mortality and migration (each at +1 years) and births which are negatively associated with total mortality. The feedback effects of increased population size on mortality is indicated.

low winter temperatures are shown in summary in Fig. 7.10. The short and medium wavelength cycles in wheat prices that have been identified by time-series analysis (see Chapter 6) are shown in the upper part of the figure and the different demographic oscillations that they drive are shown below, separated by a vertical line into short and medium wavelength cycles. Adult mortality and migration cycles are shown spanning this dividing line because analysis shows that both types of oscillation can be detected therein. The arrows indicate highly significant relationships ($P < 0.01$).

The short wavelength oscillation in wheat prices had the dominant (and statistically significant) effect throughout but this is particularly noticeable during the first 100 years of the study when all the mortality series were strongly associated with fluctuations in wheat prices. Thereafter, adult mortality showed a much less significant response and analysis suggests that low winter temperatures had the dominating effect (Fig. 7.10). In very cold winter months, the population would be more susceptible to respiratory infections, influenza, intestinal disorders and hypothermia. Studies of pre-industrial England, Sweden and Italy have shown that higher mortality correlated with low winter temperature (Eckstein *et al.*, 1985; Galloway, 1985), and recent work has shown that mortality from heart disease in the 20th century is sometimes 70% greater in winter than summer (Wilmshurst, 1994). In addition, rises in adult mortality at Penrith, in both the short and medium terms, resulted in an influx of immigrants to fill the vacated niches in this saturated habitat (section 4.6; Scott & Duncan, 1997a).

From the mid-17th century, however, the results presented in this chapter have suggested that there was a different response between young children and infants to the effects of variations in the quality and quantity of food: the short wavelength cycles in grain prices appeared to drive the oscillations in neonatal (during pregnancy), post-neonatal (directly during the first year of life) and child (via susceptibility to infectious diseases) mortality.

Smallpox has been shown to contribute substantially to the cycles in child mortality (see Fig. 7.10) and it is suggested that the epidemics were triggered by the peaks in the short wavelength oscillation in wheat prices. Initiation of an epidemic is critically dependent on the build-up of a sufficiently large pool of susceptible children by new births (see section 9.2) and by the immigration of families that have not previously been exposed to the disease. Such families would have moved from smaller communities in the surrounding countryside where the density and size of the population was below a critical level for the development of a full smallpox epidemic (Duncan *et al.*, 1994a). Although it is generally inferred that nutritional deficiency had little or no direct responsibility for the effects of the disease (Livi-Bacci, 1991), it is shown in Chapter 9 how a small variation in susceptibility to smallpox caused by cycles of malnutrition could contribute to the initiation of an epidemic. Those on the edge of subsistence would be more directly affected by harvest failure, resulting in an ill-nourished and occasionally starving substratum who would be the first victims; thereafter, the disease would spread rapidly throughout the population. This interaction between wheat prices, smallpox and child mortality, together with the effects of cycles of immigration and births which provided a build-up in the pool of those susceptible to the disease is shown in Fig. 7.10. The next epidemic of smallpox is critically dependent upon the build-up of a sufficient density of susceptibles (section 9.4), thereby completing the loop contained in this figure. In this way, the smallpox epidemics (and consequent child mortality) became locked into the short wavelength oscillation in wheat prices.

Infant mortality fluctuated throughout the period under study and it has been suggested that this oscillation was driven by alternating periods of hardship and plenty; the coherence between infant burials and grain prices is highly significant ($P < 0.001$) throughout. The availability of food and the inadequacy of the diet during hardship had multiple effects on infant mortality; a high proportion of babies with low birth weights would be produced and there would be a rise in neonatal and post-neonatal mortality. Recent research stresses the importance of the habitual diet of the mother prior to, or in the first trimester of, pregnancy; what occurs later in pregnancy is less important. An adequate diet of folic acid and other vitamins during pregnancy would be compromised during periods of malnutrition, so increasing neonatal mortality. In addition, a sharply fluctuating food supply could produce another exacerbating and paradoxical effect on infant mortality, particularly in the poorer classes: a large and potentially beneficial placenta could be built-up early in pregnancy with satisfactory nutrition following a good harvest, but, if this were rapidly followed by a drastic reduction in food supply, the large placenta would deprive the developing foetus of adequate nutrition (D. J. P. Barker, personal communication). This would imply that, under these particular conditions with a large placenta, the foetuses exposed to inadequate nutrition during the second and third trimesters would be more severely disadvantaged than those that were exposed during the first three months *in utero*. Lactation would also be seriously affected by malnutrition, producing unhealthy infants with an impaired resistance to disease and an increased post-neonatal mortality. These effects of cyclical wheat prices and malnutrition during pregnancy were discussed more fully by Scott *et al.* (1995).

The short wavelength oscillation in baptisms at Penrith was significantly and *negatively* correlated with total burials (i.e. the two cycles were 180° out of phase; Fig. 3.9) corresponding exactly with the matrix modelling that was developed in Chapter 4. If an oscillation in mortality is fed into the simple model *without feedback*, it responds with an oscillation in births at the same frequency, but 180° out of phase. Thus, a rise in mortality in these short wavelength oscillations is accompanied by a fall in births which then rise to a peak 2–3 years later. In this way, positive feedback is established: oscillatory peaks in child deaths trigger peaks in births, which then augment the pool of young children susceptible to smallpox and thereby accelerate their rise to threshold density for the initiation of the next epidemic. Once established, the 5-year cycle of epidemics will be self-propagating, driven by the time required to raise the susceptibles to this critical density and requiring only occasional resetting by raised wheat prices. Although it is difficult to separate the role of primary and secondary influences on baptisms, the model suggests that it is fluctuations in mortality that drive the oscillations in baptisms and not an immediate response to high or low grain prices.

During the first 200 years of the period under study (1557–1750), as shown in Chapter 3, the population at Penrith remained in steady-state: mean annual births equalled mean annual deaths and was constant throughout. However, long wavelength oscillations were superimposed on the mean steady-state level by which this community maintained homeostasis: the population dynamics were regulated by feedback in which mortality crises were counterbalanced by rising birth rates and immigration, until saturation of the habitat produced rising mortality and emigration of individuals and families who were unsuccessful in securing a permanent livelihood in the parish. This complex effect of feedback on the population dynamics at Penrith is illustrated in Fig. 7.10, wherein the different types of mortality that have been identified, each with their individual sensitivity to external factors, are shown enclosed within a dashed line. These mortalities drive migration and births which, in turn, not only augment the pool of susceptibles to smallpox but also increase population size. This rise in population size acts as a density-dependent control which increases the pressure on scarce resources in an area where malnutrition and famine were ever-present threats, and is followed by the inevitable increase in mortality (see Duncan *et al.*, 1992).

Adults would tend to respond to population pressure by emigration whereas the effects of density-dependent control in this community were seen most strongly in the mortality of infants and children which, as shown above, were subtly regulated via the complex effects of nutritive levels. Malthus (1798) suggested that improvements in mortality would be short lived since, under steady-state conditions, if deaths from one disease were eliminated they would be replaced by mortality resulting from another malady. Table 7.1 shows the life-table burial rates for infants and children at Penrith. In total, 44% of children died before reaching the age of 15 and this overall level of mortality was constant for over 200 years. The pattern, however, was not identical for all age groups of children: although mortality in the first year diminished steadily, this reduction was balanced by an upturn of mortality in the older age groups because surviving infants encountered new and greater threats in early childhood. The level of child mortality for ages 1–4 years rose steadily until the middle of the 18th century, which was consequent upon the emergence of smallpox as a lethal disease, before improving considerably, perhaps because of the introduction of inoculation during the last quarter of the 18th century (see section 9.7). In contrast, age groups 5–9 and 10–14 showed less dramatic changes, except for a rise of 50% for the latter group during the last 50-year period (after 1750) possibly related to the emergence of consumption.

7.13 Variation in the interaction of exogenous cycles in different cohorts

The interacting oscillations illustrated in Fig. 7.10 represent a generalised overview of events at Penrith throughout the period 1557–1812. Correlating links (arrows) are shown only where good cross-correlation coefficients and statistical probabilities can be demonstrated even though, as would be expected in any human population, the data series are inevitably noisy. However, conditions varied throughout this period and consequently the linkages differ in their strength and importance in different cohorts. For example, the major mortality crises occurred during the first 100 years studied; the population was in steady state until 1750 and boomed thereafter; the lethal form of smallpox did not emerge until about 1630 and before that time the disease was of little importance.

The period under study has, therefore, been divided into four sections (1557–1650, 1650–1699, 1700–1749 and 1750–1812) and, using the family reconstitution study, the significance of the cross-correlations in each cohort was analysed to highlight subtle differences that reflect the detailed changing patterns of the economic history of this community at Penrith.

Years 1557–1650

The end of the 16th and beginning of the 17th centuries were dominated by the following features: an upward trend in grain prices and the emergence of clear short wavelength oscillations therein; major crises of plague, typhus and famine; and less spectacular mortality responses to fluctuating grain prices. The rising population trend would also add greatly to the pressure such that, in the Malthusian sense, the positive check operated by means of increased mortality to moderate the rise in population and to restore the balance with resources. The major mortality crises were spiky and operated as triggers (as for the plague mortality of 1597/8) or as transient perturbations to the population. The long wavelength oscillations, clearly established from 1600 and triggered by the mortality of the plague, were because of the feedback control, of which childhood mortality was a major factor. Smallpox was not evident and so the periodicity of the oscillation in childhood deaths was not geared to a threshold density of susceptibles and therefore the oscillations were non-stationary. Infant mortality rates were particularly sensitive to changes in wheat prices and were at the highest level, with 1 in 4 dying before the age of 1.

Years 1650–1699

Child burials were closely related to barley prices, with respect to the short wavelength cycles during this period. Although mortality was still linked to grain prices, the population had become less sensitive to harvest failure, and vital events fluctuated less significantly. When the worst of the mortality crises of the 16th and first half of the 17th centuries had passed, the smaller mortality peaks were often associated with smallpox outbreaks and the cycles in mortality and baptisms were of a low amplitude, with a fundamental 5-year periodicity. Child and adult burials were no longer in synchrony because they were now driven by different factors: adults had escaped from the overriding restriction of nutritional levels and were more affected by the medium wavelength cycles in low winter temperatures, implying that unfavourable weather conditions, more often than crop failures, initiated deaths. Neonatal and post-neonatal mortality were still significantly affected by fluctuations in grain prices, with post-neonatal mortality displaying the strongest response.

Epidemic outbreaks of smallpox now played an important role in influencing fluctuations in mortality and there was an associated rise in mortality for children in the 1–4 year age group. The small reduction in infant mortality increased the size of the group at risk to smallpox and hastened the time taken to accumulate a sufficient-sized pool of susceptible children.

Baptisms were strongly and negatively associated with adult burials in the 5-year bandwidth ($P < 0.001$) and less significantly with child burials ($P < 0.01$). The fall in baptisms occurred one year after the rise in mortality but recovered by year 2 or 3.

Although not so prone to famine conditions, there was still ample evidence of continuing poverty in this cohort; for example, all tax assessments for this period (1660, 1672 and 1693) placed Cumberland as the lowest in terms of tax assessed per acre. Farm holdings were still small, but the rural population was steadily declining as towns offered more opportunities of economic betterment, and the economic differential acted as a magnet, attracting the rural poor with the lure of employment possibilities.

Years 1700–1749

The demographic data derived from the family reconstitution study for the first part of the 18th century suggests a brief movement away from the subsistence level and an improvement in living standards. Marital fertility was at its highest and approached the level seen for other English parishes. There was a smaller number of spinsters, childless couples and bridal pregnancies and, again, an improvement in infant mortality rates, particularly for those aged 1–5 months. Post-neonatal mortality, which was, as has been demonstrated, particularly sensitive to changes in wheat prices, was now less significantly correlated – a condition seen only during this period (see Table 7.3). More importantly, mortality overall had escaped from the domination of the joint effect of high wheat prices coupled with low real wages, and statistical analysis for this period shows that peaks in both child and adult mortality synchronized with low wheat prices and high wages. Smallpox was the most important disease and the epidemics were more regular.

A major factor in the population dynamics of this period was determined by the migration of workers both in and out of the parish, after which there was a rise in outmigration. When wheat prices were low and wages were high, there was a steady influx of migrants into the community, particularly up to the decade of the 1720s. Immigration was predominantly from outlying (upland) districts and a significant entry of people with their families would contribute on a cyclical basis to a corresponding cyclic rise in the pool of those susceptible to smallpox, probably both adults and children. This period encompassed the so-called agricultural depression of 1730–1750 (which was the result of a long decline in the price of grain) and the changing balance of prosperity between arable and pastoral areas. The fall in grain prices and increased demand for meat and dairy products favoured the Cumbrian livestock farmer and provided some protection against the adverse effects of the depression.

Thus, although feedback dominated the total number of people that could be accommodated within the parish, as witnessed by the very clear persistence of the long wavelength oscillations, 1700–1749 stands out as a period of superficial calm, with mortality unrelated to wheat prices. The falling trends of grain prices pushed wages to the forefront and their cyclical nature prompted the movement in and out of the parish. Fertility rose and mortality was slightly improved, despite the persistent domination of child mortality by smallpox; there was no detectable evidence of vaccination or variolation having significant effects during this period. In fact, analysis of the data suggests that this unusual halcyon period was probably restricted to a mere 20 years, i.e. 1720–1740, and it is interesting that deaths of the immigrants during the early part of this period contributed significantly to the large number of pauper burials when there was a downswing in economic conditions in the 1740s. In spite of this, however, there is no doubt that Cumbrians were prospering by comparison with their contemporaries else-where, and with their predecessors of the previous century.

Years 1750–1812

The major change that occurred after 1750 at Penrith was the disappear-ance of the link between population size and mortality. For 200 years (1550–1750) the population at Penrith had existed under steady-state conditions, when the most interesting oscillations were revealed, but the fol-lowing period (1750–1812) was characterised by a steady increase in the population. During period 1750–1785, the gain on the births loop changed from 1.0 (see Fig. 3.12) to 1.011, and to 1.019 during 1785–1812. The short wavelength oscillations in deaths continued during this period, and these generated corresponding oscillations in births, showing that these cycles still occurred even when the loop gain was greater than 1.0 and when condi-tions were no longer marginally stable. Annual baptisms rose sharply and almost doubled in 50 years (see Fig. 3.5). Annual adult deaths also rose during 1750 to 1800, but less dramatically, and there was a progressive increase in longevity and an improvement in adult mortality which was no longer adversely affected by medium wavelength oscillations in winter tem-peratures.

The effective resources of the community at Penrith prior to 1750 were limited and these determined the maximum size of population that could be sustained. The resources that constituted the most important part of the density-dependent control were food supply and employment niches. The optimal level of population that could be supported rose after 1750; the family reconstitution study shows that fertility did not increase whereas total childhood mortality fell progressively. A sustained period of low mortality, which applied to adults and to children, was the primary cause of the population boom after 1750. This marked change in the population dynamics and the removal of density-dependent controls probably resulted from improvements in agriculture and transport in Cumberland (McKeown, 1983; see also section 15.4). The interaction of the different cycles at Penrith during the boom is summarised in Fig. 7.11.

7.14 Summary of exogenous cycles at Penrith

The findings presented in this chapter illustrate how a family reconstitu-tion study of a single community can be analysed to dissect out the sub-tleties of the interactions between the different exogenous cycles. The

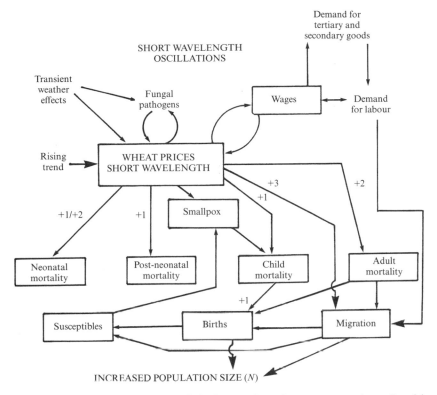

Figure 7.11. Summary diagram of the interaction of exogenous cycles at Penrith during the boom period, 1750–1812. Large arrowheads indicate the dominant effects with a *P* value of <0.001; small arrowheads represent significant associations at *P* < 0.01. The time lags are zero unless indicated. There are no medium wavelength oscillations in wheat prices and feedback is no longer operating during the boom. The effects of economic factors, detectable by time-series analysis, are shown in the upper, right-hand side of the figure.

population at Penrith was living under marginal conditions for the first 200 years and the evidence presented is of a homeostatic regime where malnutrition and epidemic disease acted to regulate the balance between resources and population size. This provides an ideal historical population for an investigation of the subtle direct and indirect effects of malnutrition. Throughout the period studied, a short wavelength oscillation in grain prices was apparently an important external factor that drove exogenous cycles in mortality, birth rate and migration. In particular, the different responses of children to variations in food supply has been emphasized; fluctuations in poor nutrition correlated significantly with the variations in mortality rates for infants (probably indirectly during pregnancy and directly during the first year of life) and for young children (via susceptibility to lethal infectious diseases). Migratory movements contributed to the maintenance of homeostasis in the population dynamics. A medium wavelength cycle in low winter temperatures was associated with adult mortality which, in turn, promoted an influx of migrants into this saturated habitat. A model (Fig. 7.10) incorporating these interacting associations between vital events and exogenous cycles is presented: the importance of grain prices as a density-dependent factor is emphasized; they constituted an important component of the negative feedback of this population and drove the exogenous, short wavelength mortality cycles. Cycles of births and immigration provide a positive feedback for the build-up of susceptibles and the initiation of smallpox epidemics and for increased population size. The interacting and synergistic effects of the prices of other commodities is analysed and described in the next chapter. We believe this to be the first quantitative, integrated study of the population dynamics in a single human community.

7.15 Appendix: Stationarity of the Penrith data series

Possible problems with stationarity of the data series were addressed by following the procedure outlined in section 6.12.1. The marked rises in burials and baptisms during the population boom post-1750 are non-stationary effects and hence the statistical analyses of the data series have been confined to the period 1557–1750.

7.15.1 Penrith child burials

This series can be described by the following equation:

$$x(t) = \mu + \alpha \, \text{wheat}(t - 1) + e(t)$$

where $\mu = 16.1$ and $\alpha = 0.25$ and where $e(t)$ is accepted as white noise, using the Box and Pierce test (Shumway, 1988) at the 99% probability level. We conclude that variations in wheat price act as an exogenous driver for variations in child burials.

7.15.2 Penrith adult burials

ARIMA analysis of this series suggested that an autoregressive term is important. The series can be described by an ARX model (autoregressive with exogenous input) in the following equation:

$$x(t) = \mu + \alpha_1 \text{ wheat}(t - 1) + \alpha_2 x(t - 1) + e(t)$$

where $\mu = 2.4$, $\alpha_1 = 0.62$, and $\alpha_2 = 0.21$. The Box and Pierce statistic shows that the residuals are white noise at the 99.5% probability level.

7.15.3 Penrith infant burials series

Regression of infant burials versus wheat $(t - 1)$ is significant at $P = 0.04$. acf and pacf (partial autocorrelation function; see Shumway, 1988) of the residuals suggest that there are autoregressive and 5-year periodic components:

$$x(t) = \mu + \alpha_1 \text{ wheat}(t - 1) + \alpha_2 x(t - 1) + \eta(t)$$

where $\mu = 13.02$, $\alpha_1 = 0.066$, $\alpha_2 = 0.22$ and where $\eta(t) = $ non-white noise. Analysis of the residuals indicates that they can be modelled,

$$\eta(t) = e(t) - e(t - 5)$$

The acf of the estimate $e(t)$ at all lags lies well below the standard error upper limit of $1.96/\sqrt{n}$, but the Box and Pierce statistic is significant only at the 85% level. We conclude that the infant burial series contains a number of non-stationary terms but that $e(t)$ may be considered as white noise and the major non-stationary term is the short wavelength oscillation.

7.15.4 Penrith baptism series

We have shown (Duncan *et al.*, 1992) that a long wavelength oscillation (of wavelength approximately 44 years) in total burials drives a corresponding oscillation in baptisms with zero lag. Regression of baptisms versus total burials (1557–1750) gives $P = 0.004$. If the regression of baptisms versus total burials $(t - 1)$ is run, no significant result is obtained and we conclude that the long wavelength cycles dominate the baptism series. These long wavelength components are filtered out during a study of the correlation between the short wavelength oscillations. The acf of the residuals shows that the series comprises non-white noise and we conclude that it is coloured by short wavelength oscillations. The baptisms series may be described by the following equation:

$$x(t) = \mu + \alpha_1 \text{ total burials}(t) + \alpha_2 x(t - 1) + e(t) - e(t - 5)$$

where $\mu = 45.2$, $\alpha_1 = -0.038$, $\alpha_2 = 0.29$. The acf of the estimated $e(t)$ at all lags lies well below the standard error upper limit of $1.96/\sqrt{n}$, but the Box and Pierce statistic is significant only at the 70% level. Examination of the acf suggests that there are small periodic components at 10 and 19 years; if these are removed using differencing, the significance of the Box and Pierce statistic increases to the 90% level. Both these cycles were specifically removed by filtering when studying the properties of the short wavelength oscillation.

8

Mortality crises and the effects of the price of wool

8.1 Mortality crises in northwestern England

In addition to visitations of the plague, Cumberland and Westmorland suffered three major mortality crises at the end of the 16th century and the start of the 17th century, in 1587/8, 1596/7 and 1623. Events during the 1623 crisis at Penrith have been described in the preceding chapter. The recurring population crises in England between 1550 and 1640 have long been known to historians, and influenza, typhus and plague have been blamed for the excess deaths. Appleby (1973) has made a careful study of a series of parishes in the northwest and has addressed the problem of whether these crises were the results of disease or starvation. He makes the following point 'we must be able to separate starvation from disease. Confounding the two confuses their causes which can be quite different. A community troubled by recurring famine is either poor or has a grossly inequitable distribution of wealth. A community afflicted with epidemic disease is not necessarily either of these.' He concludes from his study that the crisis of 1587/8 was probably caused by typhus augmented by famine, whereas the mortality in Cumbria in 1596/7 was caused by starvation and not by epidemic disease. The disastrous harvest of 1596 would have led to the excessive mortality in 1597, allowing a short lag as the poor took the desperate measure of selling their few possessions to avert starvation. Famine was again widespread in 1623 and he concludes that it was entirely responsible for the excessive mortality in that year.

We have shown in the preceding chapter that famine and outright starvation are not necessary to promote a rise in mortality; quite small amplitude oscillations in wheat prices are sufficient to cause malnutrition among the poor, with subtle but severe consequences for pregnant women, and causing a rise in infant and child mortality. There remain two further unanswered questions. First, although wheat prices were at a peak of the short wavelength oscillation in 1623, they were not markedly higher than in the preceding or following peaks, raising the question why the crisis occurred in that year. Second, why were these mortality crises confined largely to the northwest when the remainder of England was subject to the same effects of the national grain prices? These questions are addressed in this chapter and the role of other price indices, particularly that of wool, is examined in a range of communities in the Northern Province.

8.2 Other economic factors affecting the population dynamics

As shown in Chapter 6, the prices of wheat, barley and oats moved in synchrony and the wheat price series has been used in Chapter 7 as a common index of fluctuating levels of nutrition at Penrith. However, the main business of the farmer on the fells was the breeding of cattle and the keeping of sheep, whereas, in the Eden Valley where Penrith was situated, the husbandry was more mixed (Thirsk, 1967). In this section we examine the possible effects of wool prices on the population dynamics at Penrith.

The main object of sheep farming in Tudor and Stuart times was the production of wool, the quality of which varied considerably in different parts of the country. Cumberland and Westmorland had always produced short and very coarse wool, which was regarded in 1638 as being among the worst grown in England; these short-staple wools were manufactured into only the most inferior types of woollen cloth (Bowden, 1971).

Among livestock farmers, the adverse effects of a harvest failure were felt with particular severity by the wool growers because clothing was the principal consumer good on which income might be saved in times of food scarcity. Thirsk (1967) compared the statistics relating to cloth exports, wool prices and English and continental grain prices during the 16th and 17th centuries and concluded that good harvests were fundamental to the prosperity of the wool industry both at home and abroad because they led to a buoyant demand for wool. Thus, the sheep-farming industry was sensitive to the level of grain prices because the income-elasticity of demand for clothing was high: a long run of good harvests meant a rising demand for clothing and the need for more wool, so that cloth exports increased, wool prices rose and the sheep-farming industry expanded (Thirsk, 1967).

The unfiltered series of the wool price index for the critical period covering the mortality crises, 1557–1643, is shown (together with the wheat price index) in Fig. 8.1 and two features are detectable by eye. Firstly, there is a strongly rising trend in wool prices over this period which runs in parallel with the corresponding rise in wheat prices. Secondly, there is a clear

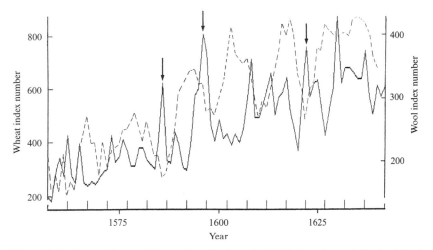

Figure 8.1. Comparison of the series of wheat (solid line) and wool (dashed line) price indices, 1557–1643. Arrows indicate the mortality crises in the northwest in 1586/7, 1596/7 and 1623 when high wheat prices coincided with low wool prices. Data sources: Bowden (1967, 1985).

medium wavelength oscillation in wool prices and spectral analysis (Fig. 8.2) shows that its period is 12 years ($P < 0.005$).

The mortality crises suffered in northwestern England in 1586/7, 1596/7 and 1623 are indicated on Fig. 8.1, a study of which lends support to the thesis advanced by Thirsk (1967; see above) that, in years when high wheat prices synchronised with low wool prices, as in the crisis years indicated, economic conditions were hard and mortality was high. With a 5–6-year oscillation in wheat prices and a 12-year oscillation in wool prices, there is potential for a synergistic interaction leading to a mortality crisis every 12 years. This possible interacting effect between the 5–6-year oscillation in wheat prices and the 12-year oscillation in wool prices is illustrated in Fig. 8.3, where the two series, appropriately filtered, are linked together and the years of potential mortality crises (very low wool prices coupled with high wheat prices) are indicated.

8.3 The effect of wool prices on the mortality cycles at Penrith, 1587–1643

This interaction between the indices of these two commodities and its impact on mortality at Penrith has been studied by simple regression in which the effect of wheat and wool are analysed separately, and then by multiple regression in which the effects of the two commodities are combined. The effects on adult, child and infant mortality at Penrith during

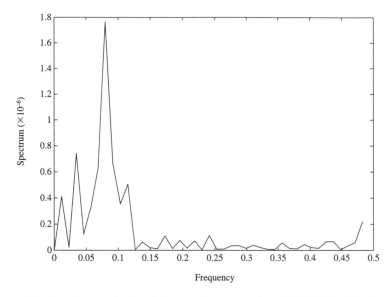

Figure 8.2. Spectral analysis of the wool price index, 1557–1643. Significant ($P < 0.005$) peak at wavelength of 12 years.

1587–1643 are compared in Table 8.1 and the results are confirmed by an analysis of the coherence between the mortality cycles and the wool price index. Simple regression confirms the findings of Chapter 7; mortality in the three categories was significantly correlated with the wheat prices, with adults and infants showing the strongest association. Only adult mortality was significantly correlated with the wool price index on simple regression analysis. However, a different picture emerges with multiple regression; the significance of the correlation with wheat is increased and the mortality series of adults, children and infants are now significantly correlated with low wool index numbers and with the overall regression. The three mortality series are also significantly coherent with the wool index (Table 8.1).

These completely opposite effects of wool and wheat prices on the economy at Penrith are further illustrated Fig. 8.4A and B which shows the cross-correlation functions of infant mortality versus the two series separately during the period 1587–1643. Infant mortality was chosen as the most sensitive indicator of economic conditions and, as can be seen, it was strongly associated with both high wheat prices (ccf = +0.72; lag = −1 year) and low wool prices (ccf = −0.63; lag = +1 year, see summary in Fig. 8.5.

The period analysed, 1587–1643, includes the plague of 1597/8 but precedes the major impact of smallpox mortality in children, and this study illustrates how the exogenous short wavelength mortality cycles

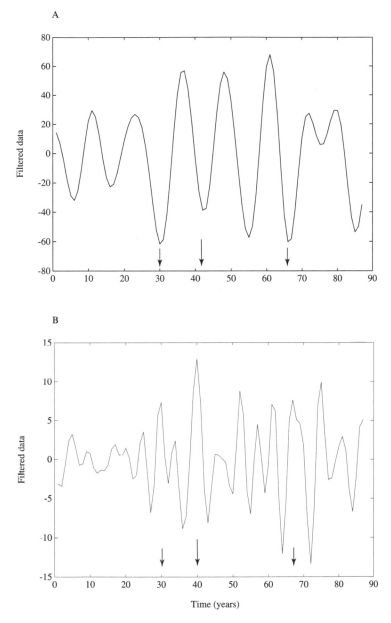

Figure 8.3. Filtered series of the wheat and wool price indices, 1557–1643. Arrows indicate the years of potential mortality crises when low wool prices could interact synergistically with high wheat prices, culminating in the actual mortality crises in the northwest 1 or 2 years later. (A) Wool index; filter window = 10 to 16 years to show the 12-year oscillation (see Fig. 8.2). (B) Wheat index; filter window = 4 to 10 years to show characteristic short wavelength oscillation.

Mortality crises and wool prices

Table 8.1. *Regression analysis of mortality at Penrith versus wheat and wool price indices during the period 1587–1643*

	Mortality (P)		
Analysis	Adult	Child	Infant
Simple regression			
High wheat index no.	0.002	0.025	0.009
Low wool index no.	0.017	NS	NS
Multiple regression			
High wheat index no.	<0.001	0.004	0.001
Low wool index no.	<0.001	0.018	0.004
Overall regression	<0.001	0.005	<0.001
Coherence with wool index	0.01	0.001	0.001
(Wavebands, yr)	(8)	(11)	(16)

Note:
Child mortality = children + infants. NS, not significant.

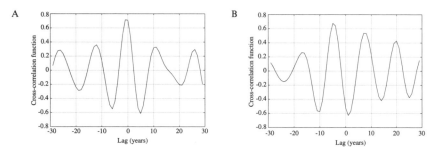

Figure 8.4. Cross-correlation functions of infant mortality at Penrith versus wheat and wool indices, 1587–1643. Filter window = 10 to 16 years. (A) Versus wheat, maximum ccf (+0.72) at a lag of −1 to 0 years. (B) Versus wool, *minimum* ccf (−0.63) at a lag of +1 year.

at Penrith (period of 5–6 years) that are driven by wheat prices and described in Chapter 7 are clearly modulated by wool prices. The three severe mortality crises experienced at Penrith in 1586/7, 1596/7 and 1623 were not solely because of high wheat prices and famine in these years, but the hardship was exacerbated by sharply falling wool prices. In 1630, when the price of corn rose to an excessive level and there was an extraordinary dearth in England (Hoskins, 1968), the price of wool dipped only slightly (Fig. 8.1) and there was no accompanying rise in mortality in the northwest. In conclusion, the mortality oscillations and population dynamics at Penrith are more complex than the inter-

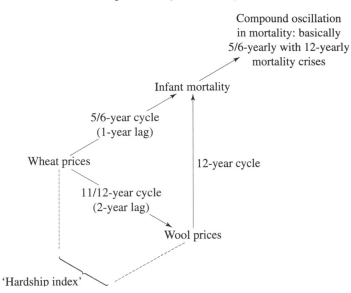

Figure 8.5. Diagram to illustrate the suggested interaction of the effects of wheat and wool prices on infant mortality at Penrith during the period 1557–1650. It is suggested that high wheat prices drove down wool prices and that the two commodities interacted synergistically to generate a medium wavelength oscillation (12 yearly) of mortality crises in vulnerable communities.

actions illustrated in Fig. 7.10; these exogenous cycles are clearly sensitive to, and modulated by, wool prices.

8.4 Computation of a 'hardship index'

Since economic hardship was associated with both high wheat and low wool prices, an index of annual potential hardship can be constructed by subtracting the wool price from the wheat price for each year and this series is plotted in Fig. 8.6. The series calculated for 1557–1643 changes in character around 1585, when the amplitude of the peaks increases sharply, coincident with the start of the mortality crises. The years of the mortality crises in northwestern England are indicated and these coincide with the major peaks in this derived index. Spectral analysis (Fig. 8.7) of the whole period 1557–1643 shows that the dominant wavelength is 12 years ($P < 0.005$). The 12-year oscillation was probably present before 1580, demonstrating the underlying contribution of wool prices, but the peaks of the hardship index were of smaller amplitude, probably because wheat prices exhibited only a low amplitude oscillation at this time, see Fig. 8.6. This 'hardship index' has been computed from national commodity indices and

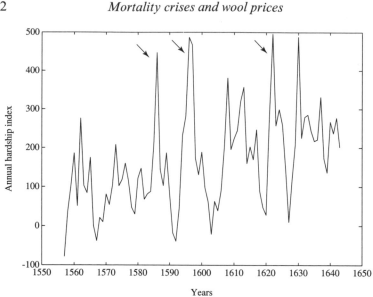

Figure 8.6. Calculated hardship index (ordinate), 1557–1643, calculated as the annual wheat price minus the wool price. Note the years of high hardship level and potential mortality crises. Arrows indicate the mortality crises in the northwest in 1587, 1597, 1623.

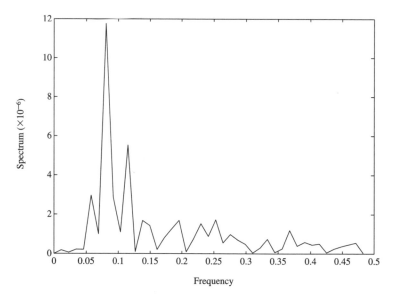

Figure 8.7. Spectral analysis of the hardship index, 1557–1643. Significant peak ($P < 0.005$) at wavelength of 12 years.

Table 8.2. *Correlation of mortality at Penrith during 1557–1643 with the 'hardship index'*

	Mortality		
Analysis	Adult	Child	Infant
Regression (*P*)	0.0001	0.001	0.0001
Coherence (1557–1643)	11–16 (0.001)	11 (0.001)	8–11 (0.001)
Wavebands (*P*)	5 (0.001)	5 (0.001)	5 (0.001)
Coherence (1580–1632)	11–16 (0.001)	11–16 (0.001)	8–11 (0.01)
Wavebands (*P*)	5 (0.001)	5 (0.001)	5–6 (0.001)

Note:
Correlation tested by simple regression or coherence analysis against the 'hardship index' calculated from the wool and wheat price indices, as described in the text.

so would be applicable to the study of the dynamics of any identified community in England. An index could be calculated for a parish that was appropriate for the dominant, local economic factors; for example, mortality cycles may be driven by wheat and cattle prices in lowland farming areas and also in upland, northwestern areas after 1650.

The wheat/wool 'hardship index' has been tested against adult, child and infant mortality during the period 1557–1643 in the case study of the population dynamics at Penrith and the results of simple regression and coherence analysis are presented in Table 8.2: mortality in all three burial series is significantly correlated with the computed hardship index. Each mortality series was also strongly coherent with the index in the wavebands around 11 years (reflecting the contribution of wool prices) and 5 years (reflecting the dominant influence of wheat prices), both when the whole period was analysed and during its later years, 1580–1643, when the oscillations in the wheat prices and hardship indices were firmly established.

8.5 Did wheat prices drive wool prices during the period before 1650?

It is generally accepted by agricultural historians that, because the income-elasticity of demand for clothing was high, a marked rise in wheat prices severely depressed wool prices (Thirsk, 1967). This inverse correlation during the critical period 1550–1650 is detectable by eye in the unfiltered indices compared in Fig. 8.1 and in the filtered series shown in Fig. 8.3; the

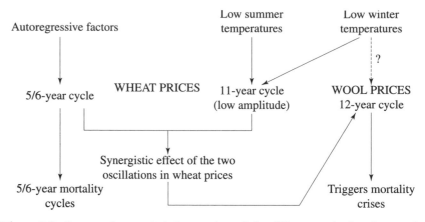

Figure 8.8. Suggested synergistic interaction of the different cycles in wheat and wool prices to produce the mortality crises in the northwest during the late 16th and early 17th centuries.

latter figure shows the 5–6-year oscillation in high wheat prices corresponding to the troughs in the 12-year oscillation in wool prices. If high wheat prices were driving down wool prices, why did only alternate peaks in wheat prices drive down wool prices?

The answer to this question seems to lie in the analysis of the wheat price series presented in Chapter 6; in addition to the dominant short wavelength oscillation (probably driven by economic and autoregressive factors) there is a secondary, medium wavelength oscillation (period = 11 years) that correlated with low seasonal temperatures (see section 6.5). When the two indices are filtered, these two medium wavelength oscillations in wool and wheat prices are seen to be completely out of phase, with a lag of 1 year; i.e. the peak of high wheat prices was followed one year later by the trough in wool prices.

The suggested pattern of events is shown in Fig. 8.8; in years when the peaks in the two (probably independent) oscillations in wheat prices coincided, food was scarce with no money to spare for clothing and consequently wool prices fell sharply, producing a double blow for communities that were dependent on sheep farming. In these years, one of the severe mortality crises suffered in Cumbria in the late 16th and early 17th centuries could readily be triggered. We conclude that the three major mortality crises were triggered in northwestern England in those communities where the economy was dependent on rearing sheep and growing grain in years when wheat prices were particularly high (i.e. when both the short and medium wavelength oscillations in prices were in synchrony)

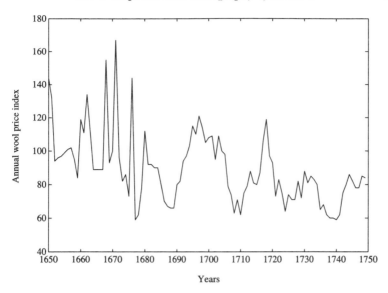

Figure 8.9. Wool price index (ordinate), 1650–1749, showing the falling trend and a change in pattern after 1680.

and wool prices were low, the two commodities interacting synergistically. Appleby (1973) also noted that the economy in Cumbria was squeezed by a depression in the clothing industry and a collapse in the demand for raw wool in 1623 and he concluded that the resulting loss of income appears to have been even more catastrophic than the elevated food prices of the 1590s.

8.6 Effects of wool prices on the economy and demography of Penrith after 1650

No major mortality crises were experienced at Penrith or in northwestern England after 1650 and the wool price index for the next 100 years shows a steadily falling trend (see Fig. 8.9) with a clear change in its character around 1680. Before that time, the series shows pronounced, but irregular, oscillations which are followed after 1680 by a low amplitude, medium wavelength oscillation. Spectral analysis of the wool price index during this later period (1680–1750) shows a strong peak covering the 17–25-year waveband ($P < 0.005$). Spectral analysis for the whole period 1650–1749 shows major peaks at wavelengths of 25 and 17 years ($P < 0.05$).

A hardship index for the period 1655–1749 (computed from the wheat and wool price indices) is shown in Fig. 8.10; again the medium wavelength

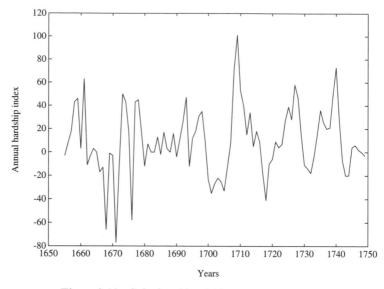

Figure 8.10. Calculated hardship index, 1655–1749.

oscillation is evident after about 1680 (reflecting the contribution of wool prices) and spectral analysis shows a strong peak at 14 years ($P < 0.005$).

The adult, child and infant burial series at Penrith do not cross-correlate with either the wool price index or the hardship index in the medium waveband during the 100-year period (1650–1749). This is in complete contrast with the previous 100 years described above. However, the oscillations in all three mortality cycles at Penrith correlated significantly ($P < 0.001$) in the short wavebands, both with the hardship index and with the wool price index during the early years of this period, 1655–1685, suggesting the continuation of the 5-year mortality cycles begun in the preceding century.

The falling trend in wool prices, shown in Fig. 8.9, reflects a period of severe depression in the wool industry, and some farmers in the northwest reduced the size of their flocks or ceased their involvement altogether (Bowden, 1971). By the end of the 17th century, the Cumberland and Westmorland farmer had moved towards more cattle and fewer sheep, and Marshall (1980), in his analysis of inventories, found that, between 1667 and 1750, cattle were the largest single item of possession and of more value than the sheep. This is supported by an analysis of mortality at Penrith during later periods, 1650–1750; although high wheat prices still exerted a marked effect on mortality, wool prices were less important and, instead, high beef prices were now significantly associated with burials of infants ($P = 0.029$) and adults ($P = 0.037$). Therefore, the synergistic interaction of low wool and high wheat prices no longer affected mortality so dramatically and famine crises, such as occurred in 1623, were never again experienced in the northwest of England.

8.7 The mortality crisis of 1623 in northwestern England

The child and infant mortality at Penrith during the crisis of 1623 is described in detail in sections 7.5 and 7.6; this mortality crisis was confined mainly to the north and northwest of England, with only a few scattered outbreaks elsewhere in the country (Wrigley & Schofield, 1981); in this section we present the results of a survey of a range of communities in the northwest. Was the mortality experienced at Penrith typical of neighbouring parishes? An analysis of over 80 parishes in Lancashire showed that burials in 1623 were more than twice the average of the decade (Rogers, 1975) and a study of Stockport, a large Cheshire parish of 14 townships, also revealed a substantial increase (Millward, 1983). The crisis was widespread in Cumberland and Westmorland and was also severe in Scotland, where losses were estimated to be in excess of 10% of the total population for Dumfries and over 20% for Dunfermline, which is considerably more than the 5% calculated for Lancashire (Appleby, 1973; Rogers, 1975; Flinn, 1977). Only average, or slightly above average, burials, however, were found for some West Yorkshire and mid-Wharfedale areas (Drake, 1962; Long & Pickles, 1986).

However, the communities in northwest England were not affected with equal severity in 1623. An aggregative analysis of 25 parishes between 1613 and 1624 has been undertaken; they were chosen because they represent a reasonable cross-section: Penrith, Cartmel, Lancaster, Poulton-le-Fylde, Whalley, Brough and Kendal were all market towns (Everitt, 1967), Newbiggin and Cliburn were small parishes, and Greystoke represents a large, but scattered community. North Meols is situated on the coast, and Ingleton and Thornton-in-Lonsdale are in the uplands, on the western side of the Pennines. The infant mortality rate has been calculated from the aggregative analysis data as the number of burials occurring within a year of baptism and expressed as a percentage of live births; this will underestimate the true rate because it does not take into account the deaths of infants who migrated from the parish during the first year of life or those who died before christening. The crisis mortality ratios (CMRs) were calculated as the number of burials in 1623 as a ratio of the mean for the preceding decade and the results are shown in Table 8.3. The parishes in Cumberland and Westmorland suffered most severely: Bridekirk and

Table 8.3. *Comparison of events in 1623 with events in the preceding decade in 25 parishes in northwestern England*

| Parish | County | Average no. of events p.a. for decade preceding 1623 | | | Events in 1623 | | | | | | |
		Bapts	% Infant mort.[a]	Adult:child ratio	CMR Total	CMR Adult	CMR Child	% fall in baps	% rise in infant mort.	Adult:child ratio	Change in Adult:child ratio
Bridekirk	Cumb.	31	13	3.5	6.2	5.9	6.8	45	300	1.7	0.5
Greystoke	Cumb.	44	21	1.6	3.9	5.1	2.6	54	120	2.6	1.6
Penrith	Cumb.	57	20	3.6	5.1	5.4	4.6	33	230	2.2	0.6
Crosthwaite	Cumb.	92	10	5.2	6.9	6.2	8.8	44	320	1.8	0.4
Newbiggin	West.	5	9	2.3	3.4	3.0	4.2	60	730[b]	1.4	0.6
Cliburn	West.	4	7	5.4	4.1	3.9	4.7	25	0	3.2	0.6
Morland	West.	32	9	4.3	4.4	4.4	4.4	41	67	2.7	0.6
Lowther	West.	14	5	7.6	3.8	3.8	4.0	43	120	4.6	0.6
Warcop	West.	21	10	2.0	4.1	5.9	1.7	53	170	9.0	4.5
Brough	West.	39	13	3.3	4.2	5.1	2.9	44	100	2.7	0.8
Crosby Ravensworth	West.	32	10	2.5	4.1	4.2	4.8	35	100	1.5	0.6
Kendal	West.	257	21	2.4	3.1	3.7	2.5	40	52	2.2	0.9
Ingleton	W. Yorks.	29	17	2.4	1.8	1.7	2.1	28	29	1.4	0.6
Cartmel	Lancs.	75	19	2.5	2.8	3.8	1.5	50	32	3.9	1.6
Urswick	Lancs.	17	18	4.9	4.3	3.8	3.3	0	0	3.1	0.6
Thornton-in-Lonsdale	Lancs.	13	15	1.9	1.1	1.5	0.6	27	39	3.9	1.6
Caton	Lancs.	19	16	4.4	3.0	3.5	2.1	37	56	2.8	0.6
Lancaster	Lancs.	101	10	2.6	3.1	3.2	3.2	26	40	2.0	0.6
Cockerton	Lancs.	52	10	2.3	4.5	4.7	4.2	52	168	1.9	0.8
Poulton-le-Fylde	Lancs.	77	18	1.4	3.4	4.3	2.8	53	89	1.4	0.0
Whalley	Lancs.	52	21	3.4	2.3	2.7	1.7	17	80	3.5	1.5
North Meols	Lancs.	21	8	3.1	1.9	2.3	1.1	47	125	6.3	2.0
Prestwich	Lancs.	48	15	2.8	3.1	3.5	2.5	25	62	2.9	1.0

Sefton	Lancs.	53	21	2.3	1.5	1.4	1.5	58	114	1.6	0.7
Walton-on-the-Hill	Lancs.	42	14	3 4	1.3	1.6	1.0	43	122	5.9	1.7
Mean			14.0	3.2	3.5	3.8	3.2	39.2	130.6	3.0	1.0
SD			5.0	1.4	1.4	1.4	1.9	14.1	149.3	1.8	0.9

Notes:

[a] Infant mortality expressed as percentage of live births in that year.

[b] Rise in infant mortality occurred in 1624.

CMR, crisis mortality ratio; SD, standard deviation. Cumb., Cumberland. West., Westmorland. Yorks., Yorkshire. Lancs., Lancashire.

Data Sources: Brierley, 1908, 1923, 1931, 1952; MacLean, 1911; Chippindall, 1931; Haswell, 1927, 1932, 1937, 1938; Smith & Dickinson, 1951.

Crosthwaite experienced a rise in mortality that was six to seven times greater than that for the previous decade, whereas five parishes (the upland settlements of Thornton-in-Lonsdale and Ingleton and three south Lancashire communities) appeared to have escaped relatively unscathed.

The adult to child burial ratio showed that adult burials usually exceeded child burials in the decade preceding the crisis period. But there was a change to this pattern in 1623 and, particularly for the northern parishes in the study, the proportion of children dying increased markedly. Two determining factors that have been suggested to explain the occurrence of crisis mortality were, firstly, the density of settlement, with market towns and the adjacent parishes experiencing higher than average incidence and, secondly, altitude because lower crisis rates were found in parishes more than 300 ft above sea level (Wrigley & Schofield, 1981). However, regression analysis shows that there was no significant difference between the estimated size of the parish and its CMR in the present study, nor was there any correlation with altitude, a finding that supports the work of Long & Pickles (1986), who found that parishes of high altitude in Yorkshire at this time did not suffer particularly high mortality.

As the two northern-most counties displayed particularly high mortality, the CMR for total burials was also analysed with latitude and, although there was a positive significant association between all parishes and the degree of latitude ($P = 0.04$), it was evident that there was a dividing line, located approximately between southern Westmorland and northern Lancashire, north of which the relationship with latitude was particularly significant (total burials CMR, $P = 0.002$; adult CMR, $P = 0.004$; child CMR, $P = 0.006$). In addition, the percentage fall in baptisms during the crisis experienced by these northern parishes also showed the same positive response ($P = 0.035$). On the other hand, there was no significant correlation between the mortality ratios and baptisms and latitude for the parishes of Lancashire, nor was there any relationship between latitude and the change in the ratio of adult to child burials.

Of most interest, perhaps, is the infant mortality rate which showed that (surprisingly), for the decade preceding the crisis year, Lancashire parishes experienced higher rates than the communities in Cumberland and Westmorland, i.e. 15.4% versus 12.3% respectively. This is supported by regression analysis: infant mortality was negatively associated with latitude ($P = 0.017$) but, again, this relationship was most noticeable for the communities of Cumberland and Westmorland, i.e. the survival rate for infants in *normal* years significantly improved as one moved northwards from south Westmorland to northern Cumberland ($P = 0.003$). In 1623, however, a complete reversal of this trend is apparent and the risks to infants living in the same region now *increased* from south to north ($P = 0.04$).

8.8 Wheat versus wool: factors determining mortality in six northwestern parishes, 1587–1643

Could the synergistic interaction between high wheat prices and low wool prices account for the varying severity of the crisis, with changes in the pattern of infant mortality depending on the basic economy of the community? An aggregative analysis was made for six parishes (including Penrith, described above) whose records are extant for the period 1587–1643, so encompassing the three major mortality crises. Table 8.4 shows the parishes listed in order of latitude and, consequently, in order of severity of crisis in 1623; it also gives the results of simple and multiple regression analysis for adult and child mortality, corresponding to Table 8.1.

For the upland parishes of Crosthwaite in Cumberland and Crosby Ravensworth in Westmorland, low wool prices had the most important influence but, like Penrith, the combined effect with high wheat prices is very marked (Table 8.4). Crosthwaite suffered major mortality crises in 1587 and 1623 and Crosby Ravensworth suffered in all three crisis years, 1587, 1597 and 1623, suggesting the synergistic effect of wheat and wool prices. The evidence from these studies suggests, therefore, that the economy of these farming communities on the fells was strongly dependent on sheep rearing, as suggested by Thirsk (1967).

However, only adult mortality showed a significant response at Cartmel (Lancashire) and Thornton-in-Lonsdale (Lancashire–Yorkshire borders) – the former to both wheat and wool prices, the latter only to wheat prices – whereas children at Walton-on-the-Hill (Lancashire) were adversely affected by the price movements of both commodities. Further regression analysis (data not shown) has revealed that adult burials at Thornton-in-Lonsdale were also significantly associated with variations in cattle prices ($P = 0.013$) and all mortalities at Walton-on-the-Hill were linked to the prices of hides (adults $P = 0.006$; children $P < 0.001$). These factors were not significantly associated with mortality at Penrith, Cartmel, Crosthwaite or Crosby Ravensworth. The parishes of Cartmel, Walton-on-the-Hill and Thornton-in-Lonsdale, lying to the south of Cumbria, did not suffer from the mortality crises of 1587, 1597 or 1623, again suggesting that the economy of these parishes was less sensitive to wool prices, although Cartmel was a market town specialising in sheep and corn (Everitt, 1967).

Table 8.4. *Regression analysis of wheat and wool index numbers with mortality in northwestern England*

	Simple Regression		Multiple Regression		
Parish	High wheat index nos. *P*	Low wool index nos. *P*	High wheat index nos. *P*	Low wool index nos. *P*	Overall *P*
Penrith, Cumberland, 1587–1643					
Adult mortality	0.002	0.017	<0.001	<0.001	<0.001
Total child mortality	0.025	NS	0.004	0.018	0.005
Infant mortality	0.009	NS	0.001	0.004	<0.001
Crosthwaite, Cumberland, 1587–1643					
Adult mortality	NS	0.011	0.008	0.002	0.001
Total child mortality	NS	0.007	NS	0.002	0.005
Crosby Ravensworth, Westmorland, 1587–1643					
Adult mortality	NS	0.008	0.019	0.002	0.002
Total child mortality	NS	0.009	0.019	0.002	0.002
Cartmel, Lancashire, 1592–1643					
Adult mortality	0.028	0.013	0.010	0.004	0.002
Total child mortality	NS	NS	NS	NS	NS
Thornton-in-Lonsdale, West Yorkshire, 1587–1643					
Adult mortality	0.007	NS	0.003	NS	0.009
Total child mortality	NS	NS	NS	NS	NS
Walton-on-the-Hill, Lancashire, 1587–1641					
Adult mortality	NS	NS	NS	NS	NS
Total child mortality	0.007	0.002	0.05	0.015	0.001

Notes:
NS, not significant.
Data series calculated from the following sources: Crosthwaite, Brierley (1931); Crosby Ravensworth, Haswell (1937); Penrith, Haswell (1938); Thornton-in-Lonsdale, Chippindall (1931); Cartmel, Brierley & Dickinson (1907); Walton-on-the-Hill, Smith & Dickinson (1951).

This type of analysis is a valuable one for historical demographers; by correlating the mortality series with the range of commodity indices in multiple regression analysis, it is possible to suggest which synergistically interacting factors governed the economy of an identified community.

In summary, therefore, this analysis of parishes in the northwest has shown that the severity of the mortality in the late 16th and early 17th centuries was linked to the relative dependence of the community on wool production. Small farmers and husbandmen were numerous amongst the wool growers and they often existed at the margin of subsistence, requiring an adequate price for their wool to purchase grain on the market, to pay rents and to meet normal everyday expenses (Bowden, 1967). For such regions, specialising predominantly in wool production, periods of high wool and low wheat prices (as during the decade 1613–1622 preceding the 1623 mortality crisis; see Table 8.3) were times of relative plenty, and infant mortality for Cumberland and Westmorland was at a *lower* level than for the communities further south in Lancashire. In 1623, however, the double impact of high grain and low wool prices proved disastrous, resulting in chronic food shortages, malnutrition and even famine, with the inevitable rise in mortality. In Lancashire, the principal occupation was cattle rearing and fattening and fewer farmers kept flocks of sheep (Thirsk, 1967). Consequently, the farmers there may not have experienced the comparative halcyon periods when wheat prices were low and wool prices high, but neither did they suffer so grievously when the reverse scenario occurred.

We have shown how an analysis of the interactions between the effects of the prices of different commodities can reveal the dominant factors affecting mortality in smaller-sized communities in the northwest. We now analyse two other communities. Firstly, Lancaster, a market town larger than Penrith, in north Lancashire and, secondly, York, a major city in northern England. Both populations have economic features of interest.

8.9 Interaction of the economic factors that affect the population dynamics at Lancaster, 1600–1785

In the Middle Ages, Lancaster owed its importance primarily to its strategic position as a border fortress defending against the frequent Scottish raids. However, during 1550–1750, a considerable change took place: Lancaster's military significance disappeared following the unification of the Crowns in 1603 and there followed the economic development of Lancaster as a market town serving the surrounding areas that were devoted to dairy, sheep, arable and poultry farming, and as a port and by the beginning of the 18th century it had considerable trade with the West Indies, South America, the Baltic and other British ports.

The parish registers for Lancaster are not available before 1600 and so they have been studied by time-series analysis only during the period 1600–1785. Inspection of the baptism series shows a steady and pronounced rise from 1705; mean annual baptisms were 80 for 1600–1700 and 128 for 1700–1785 and so the population size was some 1.3 times that of Penrith during its steady-state period. Child burials also rose after 1705 and

Table 8.5. *Significance of the correlation between the burial series at Lancaster and wheat and wool prices in different cohorts*

Cohort	Burial series	Simple		Multiple		
		Wheat	Wool	Wheat	Wool	Overall
1600–1643	Child	<0.001	NS	<0.001	NS	NS
	Adult	NS	0.01	NS	0.007	0.018
1650–1685	Child	NS	NS	NS	NS	NS
	Adult	NS	NS	NS	NS	NS
1685–1750	Child	NS	0.006	(0.055)	0.003	0.004
	Adult	NS	NS	NS	NS	NS
1750–1785	Child	NS	0.014	NS	NS	NS
	Adult	(0.06)	NS	NS	NS	NS

Notes:
NS, not significant.
Results (values of *P*) for high wheat and low wool prices by simple and multiple regression. Prices lagged by 1 year. Lancaster data series calculated from Brierley (1908).

adult burials after 1740, and the population boom began in Lancaster some 40 years before that in Penrith. The community at Lancaster suffered the severe mortality crisis of 1623, with a total of 269 deaths compared with 114 in the preceding year. This mortality crisis suggests that the economy of Lancaster at this time may have been dependent on both wool and wheat.

Spectral analysis reveals short wavelength oscillations in the mortality series with the following characteristics:

> Child burials: wavelength = 5 years, 1600–1750, changing to 4–5 years post-1750 during the smallpox epidemics (see Fig. 13.14 and section 13.10). This oscillation was coherent with wheat prices in the 6-year waveband from 1600–1750 and in the 4–5-year waveband from 1750–1785.
>
> Adult burials: wavelengths = 11 to 12 years and varying between 4 and 6 years during 1600–1785; the latter oscillation was coherent with wheat prices.

The results for regression analysis are summarised in Table 8.5. During the critical period 1600–1643, which included the mortality crisis of 1623, child burials were sensitive to wheat prices (it will be remembered that no 11-year cycle was detected in child burials), whereas adult burials were sensitive to wool prices, probably reflecting the 11-year cycle shown by this mortality series. During the short period 1650–1685, when wool prices displayed sharp oscillations (see Fig. 8.9), mortality was not related to either commodity. After 1685, the sensitivity was reversed, with child burials now being correlated with wool prices; the significance was increased when wheat prices were included.

In conclusion, there is evidence that the economy at Lancaster was dependent on both wheat and wool (although children and adults displayed differential sensitivity to the two commodities) and so experienced the mortality crisis of 1623 that was typical of northwest England. As a developing port and market town, Lancaster probably had other economic factors that provided protection against the extreme vagaries of the market, although both child and adult mortalities remained largely coherent with wheat prices. However, after 1685, child burials were significantly correlated with low wool prices, perhaps because Lancaster became the major port for the importation of wool (Bowden, 1971).

8.10 Paradoxical effect of wool prices on infant mortality at York

York was a major city in northern England in the 17th century and the mortality of the 13 parishes contained within the city walls has been carefully studied by Galley (1994, 1995). York suffered a severe mortality crisis in 1604 when there was an outbreak of plague, but escaped completely from the mortality crises of 1586/7, 1596/7 and 1623 that are characteristic of northwest England and described above. Infant mortality is regarded as a sensitive index of malnutrition and hardship but, of course, the details are available for the 17th century only from family reconstitution studies. We are indebted to Dr Chris Galley, University of Liverpool, who provided us with the infant mortality series for the City of York which we have expressed as a percentage of the baptisms in each year, during the period 1571–1643. Spectral analysis reveals a primary 4-year oscillation and a secondary 11-year oscillation that show more strongly when the period analysed is restricted to 1591–1643. These two oscillations are clearly revealed after filtering (Fig. 8.11A and B).

The infant mortality series cross-correlates clearly with the 11-year cycle in wool prices after 1591 (see Fig. 8.12; ccf = +0.54), a finding that is confirmed by multivariate analysis ($P = 0.004$) and coherence studies ($P < 0.001$) in the 11-year band. However, the surprising result from this analysis is that the correlation is *positive*, i.e. high infant mortality is associated with high wool prices, in complete contrast with the conditions in

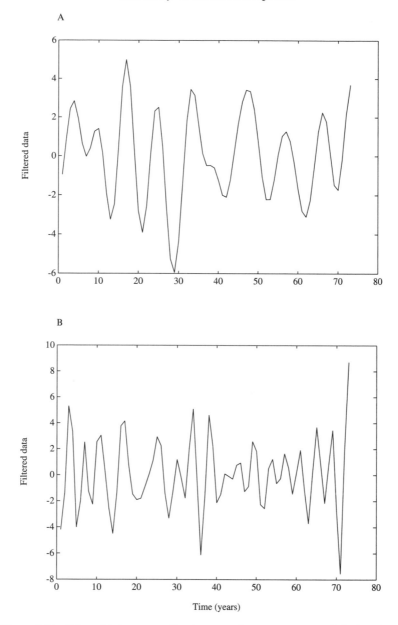

Figure 8.11. Filtered infant mortality (expressed as a percentage of the baptisms in each year) at York, 1571–1643. (A) Filter window = 6.7 to 20 years. (B) Filter window = 3 to 8 years. Data source: C. Galley, personal communication.

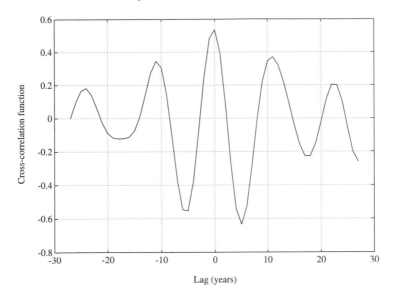

Figure 8.12. Cross-correlation function, wool index versus infant mortality at York, 1591–1643. Filter window = 6.7 to 20 years. *Positive* ccf (+0.54) at zero lag.

northwestern communities described above. Infant mortality at York during the early 17th century also correlated with the wheat price series in the short waveband by cross-correlation function and coherence ($P <$ 0.01).

Child (age 1 to 14 years) mortality at York is described in section 10.4 and it is shown that the smallpox epidemics were initially superimposed on the short wavelength mortality cycle that was predominantly sensitive to high wheat prices but also cross correlated positively with wool prices, i.e. again, high child mortality was associated with high wool prices.

The picture that emerges from this study is a city where infant mortality cycles were associated most significantly with wool prices and secondarily with wheat prices. Unexpectedly, the effects of these two commodities did not interact synergistically to produce the three standard mortality crises at York and, apparently, it was high wool prices that were associated with infant mortality. The situation in the early 17th century was evidently different in York from that in northwestern England, perhaps explicable by different economic conditions.

Galley (1995) has shown that York at this time was a trading centre serving a rural hinterland that was experiencing a population increase and was also an important administrative centre. The King's Council in the North, which acted as the northern parliament, was based in York from

1561 to 1641, the period of the study in this section, and this administrative role stimulated the economy of the city, and the inns and victualling trades were important in catering for numerous visitors. It was a large market centre, with butchers, cordwainers, bakers and tailors dominating the occupational structure. International trade was also important, and wealthy merchants exported cloth and other merchandise down the Ouse and on to the Continent. We suggest that, although infant and child mortalities were sensitive to the synergistic effects of wheat and wool prices, the prosperous community at York was largely protected during the three mortality crises of 1586, 1597 and 1623 because of its diversified trading interests. Mortality was exacerbated by cycles of high (rather than low) wool prices presumably because York was a buying and exporting market rather than a selling and producing market that was characteristic of the farms and communities in the fells of Cumbria.

To conclude, time-series analysis of the mortality crises at the end of the 16th century and the start of the 17th century, described by Appleby as characteristic of the northwest, shows that they occurred only in years when the hardship and malnutrition caused by fluctuations in two commodity indices synchronised and interacted synergistically. Examination of the statistical intercorrelation between the mortality cycles (both child and adult) in a population and the different commodity prices allows the historical demographer to explore the underlying economic factors that were of most importance in controlling the dynamics of the exogenous cycles in a community.

9

Modelling epidemics for the demographer: the dynamics of smallpox in London

It was shown in Chapter 7 that infant deaths made a major contribution to the overall mortality at Penrith. It is possible to determine infant mortality in the 16th and 17th centuries only by family reconstitution techniques, and such studies are necessarily confined to relatively small populations. Life-table burial series for the community at Penrith in successive cohorts are shown in Table 7.1 and it can be seen that infant mortality declined progressively in the 17th and 18th centuries, but child (age 1 to 14 years) mortality correspondingly increased. This was because of the spread of a lethal, infectious disease, smallpox, as suggested in section 7.3.2, and we show in this chapter that it was a major factor in determining mortality patterns and the demography of England in the 17th, 18th and 19th centuries.

There are reasons to believe that smallpox as a human disease was of great antiquity; lesions on the mummified face of Rameses V, dated 1160 BC, suggest that he died of smallpox (Dixon, 1962) and the disease is first clearly described by the Persian physician, Rhazes, in about AD 900 (Kahn, 1963). It was spread through Europe by the Saracen invaders and by the returning Crusaders. The Spaniards took smallpox with them to the West Indies in 1507 and to Mexico in 1520, decimating the Indian population (Cliff & Haggett, 1988).

Smallpox was apparently rarely lethal in England until the 1630s (Appleby, 1981), and many accounts suggest that a particularly virulent strain began to afflict people at that time (Corfield, 1987) with a gradual but significant increase in the case fatality rate (Razzell, 1977). It was feared in England from the final visitation of plague in 1665 until the end of the 19th century when it ceased to be endemic because of variolation, inoculation and vaccination (Smith, 1987). In the 17th and 18th centuries it became the most devastating affliction of the Western world and most people in areas where smallpox was endemic generally contracted the disease before the age of ten. In 1707, some 18 000 of the total population of 50 000 of Iceland died from the disease in a single year. In the New World, Boston experienced eight epidemics during the 18th century with attack rates as high as 52% of the population (Downie, 1970). Survivors from an epidemic became immune, so that susceptibles in the population were mostly children who had not yet been exposed to the virus.

Smallpox was an acute infectious disease caused by a brick-shaped virus, *Orthopoxvirus*, a genus that also includes cowpox, monkeypox and vaccinia viruses. In individuals not protected by vaccination, the case fatality was said to be 15–25% overall, rising to 40–50% in the very young and the very old. There was a characteristic pustular rash, which left facial pockmarks on most survivors. It was transmitted through oropharyngeal secretions by direct face-to-face contact between a susceptible person and a patient with a rash. Occasionally airborne spread occurred over longer distances and infection could also occur via inanimate objects, such as patient's bedding (Cliff & Haggett, 1988). It was one of the most frightening and ugly diseases imaginable; the rash developed into pustules filled with fluid which were extremely painful, and patients were afraid to move in case their lesions started bleeding. Photographs of victims in the 20th century do not convey the dreadful smell associated with the disease.

Since smallpox was eradicated, research with the stocks of the virus on the elucidation of its DNA sequence has continued which has shown that it is uniquely adapted to humans. The gene sequence shows 'hits' with the human immune system and smallpox has 50–100 genes that interact with human defence mechanisms. Within these genes are instructions that seem to have been stolen from the host's immuno-inflammatory response, i.e. the smallpox virus is mimicking its host and thereby reaching a new level of complexity. When a cell is infected or invaded by a virus it sends out SOS signals (protein molecules) that leave the infected cell and bind to receptors on the surfaces of nearby healthy cells and so issue a warning to them to create fever or inflammation, thus enabling the immune system to kill the virus. Pox viruses have copied from humans the genetic information for making receptors and, using these stolen genes, they make decoy receptors which hijack the human messenger molecules, so that as the warning SOS protein signals attempt to home in on healthy cells they are trapped by the fake receptors of the virus and the warning never gets through. In this way, the pox viruses can regulate fever and the inflammatory response of the host and can sabotage the human immune system. The smallpox virus is another example of how living systems are continually evolving at all levels.

Razzell (1977) in the introduction to his book on the *Conquest of Smallpox* recorded a letter to the *Gentleman's Magazine* in 1803 about the rise in the population of England in the late 18th century: 'One very great cause of increasing population may be ascribed to the success of inoculation for smallpox. One in four or five . . . usually died of this loathsome disorder in the natural way of infection . . . so that this saving of lives alone would account for our increasing number, without perplexing ourselves for any other causes'. It can be seen from Razzell's careful documentation and analysis of the evidence that smallpox deaths in the 17th and 18th centuries and its progressive elimination after the introduction of variolation in 1721 had a major impact on population dynamics in Britain. This interaction between the biology of smallpox epidemics and overall population dynamics is considered further in this and succeeding chapters.

9.1 Smallpox mortality in London, 1650–1900

In this section we look at smallpox deaths in London and show how time-series analysis can be used to elucidate the dynamics of the disease and to trace the evolution of the epidemics in the metropolis. There is no attempt to summarise the wealth of data on smallpox given in the seminal works of Creighton (1894) and Razzell (1977) to which reference may be made for background information; rather, a completely different approach to historical epidemiology is attempted by analysing data series to elicit quantitative information concerning the occurrence and biology of the epidemics and comparing the findings with mathematical models of the epidemiology of the disease. In this way, we try to bridge the gap between historical studies of infectious diseases and the current interest in the mathematical modelling of epidemics in the 20th century (where excellent and complete data series are available), which is exemplified by the work of Bartlett (1957, 1960), Anderson & May (1991) and Grenfell (1992).

Annual smallpox deaths in London over some 250 years, 1647–1893, were taken from the Bills of Mortality (Creighton, 1894), which are not complete (Landers, 1993), but Appleby (1975) concluded that the data contained therein are probably more complete and more accurate than any available in England at that time. As described in Chapter 2, perfect data series, although desirable, are not essential for the statistical tool of time-series analysis which is more concerned with the timing and synchronization of the peaks and troughs of the cycles than with absolute values. The data for smallpox deaths in London are displayed in Fig. 9.1, which shows the fluctuations in the basic endemic level, on which are superimposed clear epidemics of the disease in

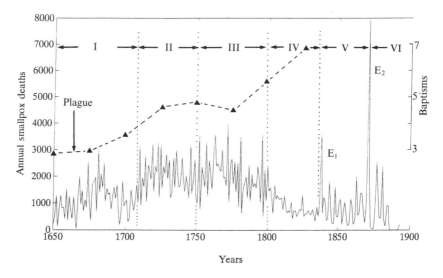

Figure 9.1. Annual smallpox deaths (ordinate) in London over some 250 years, 1647–1893, divided into cohorts: I = 1647–1707; II = 1708–1750; III = 1751–1800; IV = 1801–1835; V = 1836–1870; VI = 1871–1893. The plague in 1665 and the major smallpox epidemics of 1838 (E_1) and 1871 (E_2) are indicated. The dashed line (solid triangles) gives the cumulative number of baptisms in the preceding 25 years (thousands), right-hand ordinate. Data sources: Bills of Mortality (Creighton, 1894) and Wrigley & Schofield (1981).

years when there was a sharp rise in mortality. The important features illustrated by this figure are as follows: (a) The severe mortality of the Great Plague in London in 1665 (indicated on Fig. 9.1) which had an effect on the population dynamics and is discussed in section 9.11. (b) Inoculation against smallpox was more widely administered after about 1750 and vaccination was introduced in 1796 and became compulsory for infants in 1853; these practices clearly modified the pattern of the epidemics after 1800 and eventually led to the disappearance of the disease at the end of the 19th century. (c) The late outbreaks of smallpox in the mid-19th century (shown as E_1 and E_2 on Figs. 9.1 and 9.2), particularly the epidemic in 1871 that followed the Franco-Prussian War, which triggered *decaying* epidemics and showed that the underlying dynamics of the disease had now changed.

It is obvious from Fig. 9.1 that not only did the endemic level fluctuate but the pattern of the disease and the frequency of the epidemics changed throughout the 250-year period. This changing pattern of the epidemics has been studied by time-series analysis, using spectral analysis to determine their frequency in the different cohorts. Figure 9.1 can be divided into separate periods (cohorts), each having a characteristic interepidemic interval (T):

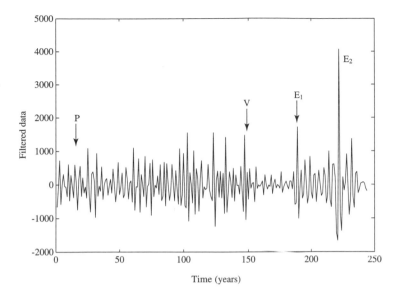

Figure 9.2. Filtered smallpox deaths in London, 1647–1893; filter window = 2 to 5.3 years. There is a clear change in the pattern of epidemics after 1800 when vaccination (V) became effective. The major epidemics of 1838 (E$_1$) and 1871 (E$_2$) triggered decaying oscillations indicative of SEIR dynamics. P = plague of 1665.

(I)   1647–1707: T changing from 4 years to predominantly 3 years.

(II)   1708–1750: endemic level rising, T changing from 3 to 2 years.

(III)   1751–1800: T firmly established at 2 years.

(IV)   1801–1835: endemic level falling steadily; epidemics greatly reduced in amplitude; T = 2–3 years.

(V)   1836–1870: epidemics re-initiated following a major outbreak in 1838; endemic level continuing to fall; T = 4 years.

(VI)   1871–1893: a major epidemic in 1871 (the biggest during the 250-year period) triggered three further decaying epidemics before smallpox ceased to be a serious disease.

The epidemics revealed after filtering are shown in Fig. 9.2 and the major events that influenced the epidemiology of the disease are indicated.

9.2 Modelling the smallpox epidemics

Can the epidemiology of smallpox epidemics in London be modelled and so explain this changing pattern in the biology of the disease? The theory of the epidemics of infectious diseases has been widely studied (see

Anderson & May, 1982, 1985, 1991; Olsen & Schaffer, 1990; Bolker & Grenfell, 1993, 1995; Tidd, Olsen & Schaffer, 1993, for detailed accounts) and basic models are presented which cover the spread of the virus in a population, a proportion of which is made up of non-immune, and hence susceptible, individuals who may be exposed to the disease and so become infected. Of these, a proportion will die but the majority will recover and will then be immune. These are termed SEIR (susceptibles-exposed-infectives-recovered) models and can be summarised as follows. The population, N, is assumed to remain constant where the net input of susceptibles (new births) equals the net mortality, μN (where μ = the overall death rate of the population, and hence the life expectancy of the population = $1/\mu$). The population is divided into susceptibles (X), latents (infected, not yet infectious, H), infectious (Y) and recovered (and hence immune, Z). Thus, $N = X + H + Y + Z$. It is assumed that the net rate at which infections occur is proportional to the number of encounters between susceptibles and infectives, βXY (where β is a transmission coefficient). Individuals move from latent to infectious at a *per capita* rate, σ, and recover, so becoming immune, at rate γ. The dynamics of the infection as it spreads through these classes are then described (see Anderson & May, 1982) by the following equations:

$$dX/dt = \mu N - \mu X - \beta XY \qquad (9.1)$$
$$dH/dt = \beta XY - (\mu + \sigma)H \qquad (9.2)$$
$$dY/dt = \sigma H - (\mu + \gamma)Y \qquad (9.3)$$
$$dZ/dt = \gamma Y - \mu Z \qquad (9.4)$$

The disease will maintain itself within the population provided that the 'reproductive rate' of the infection, R, is the expected number of secondary cases produced by an infectious individual in a population of X susceptibles. For the system defined by Equations 9.1 to 9.4:

$$R = \frac{\sigma \beta X}{(\sigma + \mu)(\gamma + \mu)} \qquad (9.5)$$

The criterion $R > 1$ for the establishment of the disease can be expressed as the requirement that the population of susceptibles exceeds a 'threshold density', $X > N_T$ where:

$$N_T = (\gamma + \mu)(\sigma + \mu)\beta\sigma \qquad (9.6)$$

A linearised model of the epidemics is developed in the next section but readers who do not enjoy the mathematics can proceed directly to section 9.4 wherein the important conclusions are summarised.

9.3 Theory of the dynamics of infectious diseases

The equations describing the dynamics of infectious diseases represent a nonlinear system but a linearised model is described below. The dynamics are described by a standard SIR (susceptibles–infectives–recovered) model (Bolker & Grenfell, 1995) which is driven by periodic variations in susceptibility (Rand & Wilson, 1991; Duncan *et al.*, 1994a; Bolker & Grenfell, 1995). This has the form:

$$\frac{dx}{dt} = \mu - \mu x - N\beta xy (1 + \delta\beta \sin \omega t) \tag{9.7}$$

$$\frac{dy}{dt} = N\beta xy (1 + \delta\beta \sin \omega t) - (\mu + \nu)y \tag{9.8}$$

where N = number in the population
     x = number of susceptibles expressed as a fraction of N
     y = number of infectives expressed as a fraction of N
     μ = death rate = 1/life expectancy $(\overset{o}{e}_0) = 0.04$ years^{-1}
     β = transmission coefficient (susceptibility to disease)
     $\delta\beta$ = fractional variation in susceptibility
     ν = rate of recovery from disease = 1/infectious period (12 days) = 30 years^{-1}
     ω = angular frequency of oscillation in susceptibility = 2π/period of oscillation

This model ignores both the latent period of the infection and the mortality resulting from the disease. These factors can be included in the model, but they do not substantially alter the results (see also section 12.5.1).

In the absence of variations in susceptibility ($\delta\beta = 0$), the steady-state values for the proportion of susceptibles and infectives are (Anderson & May, 1991):

$$x_0 = \frac{\mu + \nu}{N\beta} \tag{9.9}$$

$$y_0 = \frac{\mu}{\mu + \nu}(1 - x_0) \tag{9.10}$$

When $\delta\beta > 0$ is small, Equations 9.7 and 9.8 can be approximated by a linearised model, by defining:

$$x = x_0 + x_1 \tag{9.11}$$
$$y = y_0 + y_1 \tag{9.12}$$

where x_1 and y_1 represent the variations in x and y from their steady-state values. Substituting Equations 9.11 and 9.12 into Equations 9.7 and 9.8 (using Equations 9.9 and 9.10) and ignoring higher order terms gives:

$$\frac{dx_1}{dt} \approx -(N\beta y_0 + \mu)x_1 - (\mu + \nu)y_1 - (\mu + \nu)y_0 \, \delta\beta \sin\omega t \qquad (9.13)$$

$$\frac{dy_1}{dt} \approx N\beta y_0 x_1 + (\mu + \nu)y_0 \, \delta\beta \sin\omega t \qquad (9.14)$$

These equations describe a forced second-order linear system where the forcing function is the periodic driving term $(\mu + \nu)y_0 \, \delta\beta \sin\omega t$, i.e. oscillations in susceptibility or the transmission coefficient $(\delta\beta)$ can act as a driver for the system (Olsen & Schaffer, 1990; Rand & Wilson, 1991; Tidd *et al.*, 1993). The system can be characterised by its natural, undamped frequency, ω_n, and by its damping factor, ζ, which is a dimensionless ratio in the range 0 to 1 and is a measure of the degree of damping within the system, i.e. the attenuation of the amplitude of the oscillation at its resonant frequency. The damping factor is given by

$$\zeta = \frac{N\beta}{2(\mu + \nu)} \sqrt{\frac{\mu}{N\beta - (\mu + \nu)}} \qquad (9.15)$$

For the values of μ, ν and $N\beta$ used to describe the smallpox epidemics in London, ζ is small (much less than 1) indicating that the system is lightly damped. Since ζ is small, the system will amplify a driving term that has a frequency at the resonant frequency ω_r, where

$$\omega_r = \sqrt{1-\zeta^2}\, \omega_n \approx \omega_n \qquad (9.16)$$

and

$$\omega_n = \sqrt{\mu[N\beta - (\mu + \nu)]} \qquad (9.17)$$

If the driving term for the system is $\delta\beta \sin\omega t$, the linear response of the fraction of the population is simply a scaled and phase-shifted version of the input signal, i.e. a sinusoid at the same frequency, but with a different amplitude and phase. Thus the output becomes

$$\delta\beta A(\omega) \sin[\omega t + \phi(\omega)]$$

where:

$$A(\omega) = \frac{1}{N\beta} \sqrt{\frac{\omega^2 + \mu^2}{\left(1 - \frac{\omega^2}{\omega_n^2}\right)^2 + \frac{4\zeta^2\omega^2}{\omega_n^2}}}$$

and:

$$\phi(\omega) = \tan^{-1}\left(\frac{\omega}{\mu}\right) - \tan^{-1}\left(\frac{2\zeta\omega\omega_n}{\omega_n^2 - \omega^2}\right)$$

For any frequency of driver ω, the amplitude and relative phase shift of the oscillation in infectives can be calculated. An interesting consequence is that if ω is less than the driving frequency (i.e. for low frequency drivers) the infectives *lead* the driving term but for high frequency drivers, the infectives *lag* the driving term.

Because ζ is small, the frequency response of the system is very sharp, so that the amplification will be limited to driving terms that have a frequency close to this resonant frequency (Franklin, Powell & Emani-Naeini, 1994). As a result, the oscillations in x_1 and y_1 will be dominated by frequency components close to ω_r. The period of the resonant frequency is

$$T = \frac{2\pi}{\sqrt{\mu[N\beta - (\mu + \nu)]}} \tag{9.18}$$

Thus, the interepidemic interval is determined by $N\beta$. Since $\mu \ll \nu$, this expression is equivalent to that given by Anderson & May (1991).

$$T = 2\pi\sqrt{(AD)} \tag{9.19}$$

where A = average age of contracting the disease; D = length of infectious period.

In addition to its dominant effect on ω_r, $N\beta$ also affects the amplitude of the periodic driving term. Substituting Equations 9.9 and 9.10 into $(\mu + \nu)y_0\delta\beta \sin\omega t$ gives the periodic driving term $\mu\left[1 - \dfrac{\mu + \nu}{N\beta}\right]\delta\beta \sin\omega t$, where the amplitude is defined by $\mu\left[1 - \dfrac{\mu + \nu}{N\beta}\right]\delta\beta$.

Thus, an increase in N (e.g. population size/density) will amplify the effect of the oscillations in susceptibility ($\delta\beta$), i.e. the more crowded the population, the bigger the effect of a standard oscillation in $\delta\beta$.

Strictly, Equations 9.7 and 9.8 require that N, the total population, remains constant, but if N varies more slowly than the resonant frequency of the system, then Equations 9.13 and 9.14 are still valid approximations to the dynamics of the underlying system (see also section 12.5.2).

9.4 Conclusions from the linearised model of infectious diseases

Equations 9.1 to 9.4 describe an SEIR model in which, if the disease is introduced into the population, it responds with epidemics at regular intervals (T) but these would gradually decay and the annual number of those infected would settle at a steady, endemic level. Clearly this is not the case with smallpox in London where the major epidemics persisted for 150 years (periods I–III, Fig. 9.1) and extensive studies have sought to explain how such a system could be driven (or 'pumped up', Anderson & May, 1991) by stochastic effects or by seasonal forcing so that the epidemics were maintained. In particular, the study of non-linear dynamics of measles epidemics has allowed the development of elegant deterministic (Olsen & Schaffer, 1990) and stochastic (Bartlett, 1957, 1960) models, incorporating spatial dynamics, seasonal forcing and age structure to account for the striking pattern of these epidemics and it has been suggested that measles dynamics in developed countries may exhibit low dimensional chaos (Olsen & Schaffer, 1990; Rand & Wilson, 1991; Grenfell, 1992; Tidd *et al.*, 1993; Bolker & Grenfell, 1995).

However, the modelling presented in section 9.3 shows that, theoretically, the system could be driven and the epidemics maintained by a periodic variation in susceptibility (β) to the disease. Strictly, β is defined as the transmission coefficient. In this chapter we use time-series analysis to examine whether cyclical external factors could act to generate an oscillation in susceptibility ($\delta\beta$) and so maintain the smallpox epidemics in London shown in Fig. 9.1.

It is evident from Figs. 9.1 and 9.2 that the interepidemic interval of smallpox in London did not remain constant over the 250 years, but varied from 2 to 4 years in the different cohorts (see Table 9.1). Mathematical modelling (section 9.3) shows that the system would oscillate readily (i.e. regular epidemics would be generated) if driven by an oscillation in susceptibility ($\delta\beta$). The system will oscillate at its 'preferred or natural frequency' or resonant frequency (ω_r) in the same way that a tuning fork oscillates at its natural frequency when struck. Epidemics occur at ω_r which is determined by the number in the population (N), the susceptibility to the disease (β), the death rate (μ) and the rate of recovery from the disease (ν), see Equation 9.17.

Since μ and ν are generally constant for a particular disease, the resonant frequency of the system (ω_r, i.e. the natural frequency of the epidemics), will be determined by the product $N\beta$. Although N is most conveniently measured by the size of the population, its density will probably have an additional effect; a greater density will exacerbate the spread of the disease. Thus, Equation 9.17 predicts that changes either in the population size or in overall susceptibility to the disease will be reflected in changes in the periodicity of smallpox epidemics. This period of the resonant frequency is given by Equation 9.18 from which, knowing the observed interepidemic interval for any cohort, the relative value of $N\beta$ can be derived.

An increase in N (i.e. the size and/or density of the population) will also

Table 9.1. *Characteristics of the smallpox epidemics in London in different cohorts*

Cohort	Observed T (yr)	Mean predicted age (yr)	Predicted $N\beta$	Seasonal driver	Correlation with driver Coherence waveband (yr)	P	ccf (at 0 lag)	Smallpox mortality vs. wheat prices in 5–6 year waveband at 0 lag ccf	Coherence P
I. 1659–1707[a]	4→3	12→7	91→139	(i) Low winter temp	3.6	0.001	−0.51	+0.57	<0.001
II. 1708–1750	3→2	7→3	139→276	(i) Low autumn rain	2.9	0.001	−0.31	+0.61	0.001
				(ii) Low winter temp	2.5	0.001	−0.33		
III. 1751–1800	2	3	276	(i) Low autumn rain	2.5	<0.001	−0.18	+0.35	NS
				(ii) Low spring rain	2	0.001	−0.21		
IV. 1801–1835	2→3	3→7	276→139	(i) Low winter rain	2.3	<0.001	−0.33	+0.76	<0.001
V. 1835–1870	4	12	91	NS	—	NS	—	—	NS

Notes:
NS, not significant.
[a] No rainfall data available. T determined by spectral analysis. Predicted mean age of contracting the disease determined from Equation 9.19, assuming $D = 12$ days. Predicted relative $N\beta$ for each value of T derived from Equation 9.18.

amplify the driving effect of an oscillation in susceptibility, i.e. the more crowded the population, the greater the effect of a standard oscillation in $\delta\beta$.

The system is also characterised by its damping factor, ζ (see Equation 9.15) which determines the rate of decay of the epidemics. It is a dimensional ratio in the range 0 to 1 which is a measure of the degree of damping within the system, i.e. the attenuation of the amplitude of the oscillations (i.e. the epidemics) at its resonant frequency. For the values of death rate (μ) and rate of recovery from smallpox (ν) used in the modelling of the London epidemics, ζ is low (0.058). Because the system is so lightly damped, it will oscillate readily, producing regular epidemics of the disease; large amplitude epidemics will be maintained, in response to an oscillation in susceptibility ($\delta\beta$) of only very small amplitude *if this oscillation in $\delta\beta$ is at the resonant frequency of the system*. Because ζ is small, the frequency response is very sharp so that the system can be driven only by an oscillation in $\delta\beta$, the frequency of which is very close to the resonant frequency.

Equation 9.19 shows that the average age of catching an infectious disease is related to the frequency of the epidemics; the shorter the interepidemic interval, the lower the mean age of contracting the disease.

Finally, an important conclusion can be drawn from Equation 9.6: an epidemic will not explode unless the pool of susceptibles (usually produced by new births, but sometimes augmented by the immigration of non-immune families from the surrounding countryside) reaches a critical density. This, as is described in Chapter 13, is the major factor in determining whether an epidemic could be generated in a rural town.

9.5 Changes in the interepidemic interval

The interepidemic interval (T) for smallpox in London changed progressively in the different cohorts, and Table 9.1 shows the predicted relative values of $N\beta$ calculated from Equation 9.18 for each value of T, and the dynamics of the disease can be interpreted on the basis of the mathematical theory developed in sections 9.3 and 9.4 as follows. The frequency of the epidemics is determined by the product $N\beta$ and over the 150-year period 1647–1800, when the smallpox epidemics were firmly established in London, the dynamics of the disease were clearly different from the period post-1800 (see Figs. 9.1 and 9.2). The cumulative total births in London for each preceding 25-year period is plotted in Fig. 9.1 and this provides a relative measure of population size (N) in terms of susceptibles. During 1647–1750 (cohorts I and II), N rose steadily and, concomitantly, T fell from varying between 4 and 3 years (1647–1707) to varying between 3 and 2 years (1708–1750).

However, after 1750, when T clearly changed to 2 years (suggesting a rise in $N\beta$), the number of baptisms was stationary and did not begin to rise again until the end of the 18th century, suggesting that the population was not expanding markedly. We have shown in Chapters 6 to 8 that the annual wheat prices provide a good measure of the fluctuating levels of nutrition in England in earlier centuries; mortality cycles were directly correlated with a short wavelength oscillation in wheat prices, and inadequate nutrition in pregnancy is known to cause low birth weight in infants, with a greater susceptibility to infectious diseases (Berman, 1991). The annual wheat price series shows a falling trend from 1650 to 1750, but had a rising trend after 1750 until 1815. The latter was a period of high food prices and hardship in England, particularly among the poorer classes (Walter & Schofield, 1989) and we suggest that malnutrition caused an overall increase in susceptibility (β) to smallpox and consequently a rise in $N\beta$ and a fall in T to 2 years after 1750. In summary, the interepidemic interval was reduced in 1647–1750 mainly because of rising N, and in 1750–1800 mainly because of rising β.

9.6 Driving the epidemics, 1647–1800

The smallpox epidemics do not decay during the first three cohorts and the interepidemic interval was reduced, and theoretical considerations (Equations 9.13 and 9.14) show that oscillations in susceptibility ($\delta\beta$), even of low amplitude, would be sufficient to drive the system. An increase in N will amplify the effect of an oscillation in $\delta\beta$ (see section 9.3).

Were there oscillations in seasonal weather conditions during the 18th century that could have produced regular cycles of susceptibility which, in turn, might have driven the dynamics? The data series for annual seasonal temperatures (1659–1893) and rainfall (1697–1893) (see section 6.1) were studied by spectral analysis in each of the cohorts to determine the existence of any major oscillations, in particular those with the same wavelength as the smallpox epidemics. Cross-correlation functions with seasonal temperatures or rainfall were also tested by coherence and, where significant association was found in these wavebands, the results were further checked by multivariate analysis.

The findings are summarised in Table 9.1, which shows the characteristics of the smallpox epidemics in each of the cohorts. No rainfall data are available for the first cohort, but throughout the 18th century (cohorts II and III), the smallpox epidemics were significantly associated with low autumn rainfall. In the third cohort, 1751–1800, the epidemics were also secondarily associated with low spring rainfall, and in the period 1708–1750 the epidemics correlated with low rainfall in all four seasons, with autumn rain having the most significant effect. We conclude that the spread of smallpox was favoured by dry conditions which could act as the driver for the regular epidemics of the disease.

During the first cohort, 1659–1707 (the period of 3–4-year epidemics), the dynamics may also have been driven by dry conditions but the lack of rainfall data prevents confirmation; nevertheless the epidemics were strongly correlated with low winter temperatures during this period. This correlation continued in the next cohort (1708–1750), with cold winters acting as a secondary driver (see Table 9.1).

The smallpox virus is known to do better in conditions of relatively low temperature and humidity and, as a result, the disease is seasonal (Sarkar, Ray & Manji, 1970). In Bangladesh the seasonality was so marked that the Bengali word for the spring of the year, *bashunto*, is the word for smallpox. In the Punjab there was a distinct winter peak (November to February), with very few cases between June and September (Benenson, 1989). Henderson (1974) gives data on 27 introductions of smallpox into Europe between 1961 and 1973. Twenty introductions in the period from December to May spawned 483 subsequent cases (an average of 4.025 per introduction per month); seven introductions between June and November produced only 11 subsequent cases (0.262 per introduction per month). Landers (1986) also noted a significant association between smallpox mortality in London and low annual rainfall (1675–1750); low winter temperatures, particularly in February, were also significant at the 95% confidence level during this period. In moist tropical heat the smallpox virus seems less able to survive, and experiments to test its viability in bales of cotton showed that its survival time was doubled for a reduction in relative humidity from 84% to 73% (Christie, 1980). Spread of the disease via the dried crusts would be enhanced in dry conditions (K. McCarthy, personal communication). Field data also suggest enhanced transmission of droplet infections in dry weather (Harper, 1961), perhaps because the nasopharyngeal mucosa dries more rapidly in these conditions, thereby lowering resistance to the disease (Waddy, 1952).

Where smallpox epidemics are occurring at the resonant frequency of the system, ω_r, only a small amplitude oscillation in $\delta\beta$ would be necessary to drive the system (Duncan *et al.*, 1994a). It is suggested that oscillations in seasonal dry conditions, which were occurring at the same frequency as ω_r

for the system, acted to generate an oscillation in $\delta\beta$ and so, in turn, drive the epidemics.

As recorded above, no seasonal rainfall data are available for the period 1647–1707, but the 3–4-year epidemics which are characteristic of this cohort were significantly associated with low winter temperatures, an effect that persisted into the next cohort. It is suggested that during this earlier period when the resonant frequency, determined by a low $N\beta$ (low population size/density), was 3–4 years, there was probably no prevailing oscillation at this wavelength in seasonal dry conditions and the system was probably directly driven at its resonant frequency (ω_r) by an oscillation in cold winter temperatures with which it was significantly coherent in the 3–4-year waveband.

9.7 The effects of vaccination (cohorts IV and V)

The introduction of variolation (or inoculation) and, more particularly, vaccination in 1796 had a dramatic effect on the dynamics of smallpox. Razzell (1977) has provided the following helpful summary of the differences between these preventive measures:

Inoculation is the injection of smallpox virus taken from a pustule of a person suffering from smallpox, whereas vaccination is the injection of virus taken originally from a cow suffering from cowpox. The two injections are distinguished by the symptoms and results that they produce: inoculation usually produces pustular eruptions around the body, typical of a mild form of smallpox, and is consequently infectious in that it spreads the disease to an unprotected population; vaccination produces only a local vesicle at the site of injection, which is not infectious. Both injections protect from future attacks of smallpox by eliciting the manufacture of antibodies. . . . Vaccination, unlike inoculation, is a safe injection, both for the person injected and the unprotected population exposed to him, and this was the reason why inoculation was replaced by vaccination. I have challenged this conventional medical view . . . arguing that the vaccines used in Jenner's lifetime were in fact derived from smallpox virus, and that early vaccination was a form of inoculation. This conclusion undermines the polarisation of vaccination and inoculation, with the one being viewed as safe and effective, the other as dangerous and demographically damaging; it also raises the question as to the actual historical contribution of inoculation in reducing smallpox mortality. No-one has queried the prophylactic power of inoculation to protect against attacks of smallpox and it is generally agreed that being severer in its effects than vaccination, it produced a larger amount of anti-body and a much longer period of immunity (usually for lifetime).

The marked reduction in the size of the pool of susceptibles in London as progressively more young children were vaccinated caused a steady fall in the endemic level, a marked reduction in the amplitude of the epidemics (see Fig. 9.1) and an extension of the interepidemic interval (Table 9.1). These small epidemics in cohort IV were now most significantly correlated with low winter rainfall, although multivariate analysis suggests ($P = 0.02$) that the modest outbreaks of smallpox were associated with dry conditions in all four seasons in 1800–1835.

9.8 Change to SEIR dynamics in cohorts V and VI

However, against this background of the gradual disappearance of the disease in cohort IV, there was a severe outbreak of smallpox in 1838 (Fig. 9.1; E_1) which was followed by nine clear epidemics of large amplitude superimposed on a continuing falling trend. The epidemics progressively decreased in amplitude. The interepidemic interval in cohort V was now 4 years, reflecting the much smaller pool of susceptibles during this period when widespread vaccination was practised; it would take 4 years of new births before the susceptibles built up to a level that was adequate for the initiation of the next epidemic.

The epidemics during 1835–1870 (cohort V) were not significantly correlated with seasonal climatic variables and it is concluded that during this period the dynamics of the disease can be described by Equations 9.1 to 9.4 and by a standard SEIR model, i.e. the system is not driven, and the epidemics slowly decayed following the major outbreak in 1838, as predicted by theory and shown in Fig. 9.1. These SEIR, non-driven dynamics continued and are particularly well illustrated after 1870 in cohort VI. The biggest outbreak of smallpox recorded in London occurred dramatically in 1871 (see Fig. 9.1, E_2) at a time when the disease had almost ceased to be endemic, and this epidemic was followed by major, but sharply decaying epidemics (i.e. the system was not driven and the epidemics were not maintained) and smallpox was virtually eliminated by the end of the 19th century.

9.9 Age of catching smallpox

The average age of catching the disease can be predicted from Equation 9.19, assuming $D = 12$ days (Anderson & May, 1991). As T in London changed from 4 to 3 to 2 years, so the average age of catching smallpox fell correspondingly from 12 to 7 to 3 years, i.e. in the 17th century there would be quite a wide spread in the age of young people catching the disease, whereas in the late 18th century, when the interepidemic interval was firmly established at 2 years, it would be largely confined to young children; see Table 9.1 which summarises the changing biology of smallpox and its underlying effects on the demography of the city.

9.10 Is there an underlying 5-year oscillation in smallpox epidemics?

Smallpox epidemics occurred at 5-yearly intervals in small rural towns in England in the 17th and 18th centuries, with no outbreaks of the disease in the interepidemic years. It is suggested in Chapter 13 that these epidemics were driven by an oscillation in wheat prices which caused periodic malnutrition and associated susceptibility to the disease (Duncan *et al.*, 1994a). The short wavelength oscillation in the annual national wheat price series was discussed in Chapter 6 and shown in Fig. 6.3. Smallpox mortality in London in each cohort was analysed to determine whether a secondary oscillation, which correlated with the wheat price series, is detectable and the results are shown in Table 9.1. There is evidence for a subsidiary, low amplitude, 5–6-year cycle in smallpox mortality from 1659 to 1835 which is coherent with the wheat price series at zero lag in the 5–6-year waveband for the first two cohorts, 1659–1750 ($P < 0.001$). However, the correlation between the two series was of limited significance during the period 1750–1800 (when $T = 2$ years) but was again highly significant at zero lag in the 5–6-year waveband during 1800–1835 (see the cross-correlation function shown in Fig. 9.3; ccf $= +0.8$), when the epidemics declined markedly in amplitude. There was no correlation with the wheat price series after 1835.

This secondary, 5-year oscillation in smallpox mortality, which is detectable throughout cohorts I–IV (1659–1835), is therefore most significantly correlated with wheat prices during 1800–1835, when the endemic level was falling and the epidemics were of small amplitude. An oscillation of malnutrition may have augmented an oscillation in susceptibility ($\delta\beta$) and so have contributed to driving the system in cohort IV.

The 5-year oscillation in mortality was also significantly associated with the wheat price series during cohorts I and II, 1659–1750, but the major epidemics were strongly linked with seasonal, particularly dry, conditions and it is suggested that cycles of malnutrition would have only marginal effects in directly driving the epidemics via an oscillation in $\delta\beta$. However, Landers (1986) has suggested that rises in bread prices promoted an immigration of the rural population into London and there is evidence (see Chapter 13) to support the view that substantial numbers of small-town dwellers had not contracted the disease before adulthood and were, therefore, susceptible.

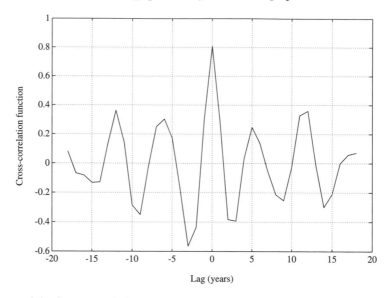

Figure 9.3. Cross-correlation function, wheat prices versus London smallpox deaths, 1800–1835. Filter window = 4 to 10 years. Maximum ccf (+0.8) at zero lag.

An oscillation in wheat prices would cause a cyclical, 5-yearly influx of immigrants to swell the pool of susceptibles and cause a corresponding subsidiary cycle in the basal, endemic level of smallpox. In this way, smallpox epidemics became integrated into the general population dynamics of the metropolis. In conclusion, it is suggested that malnutrition probably had subtle effects on the dynamics of smallpox epidemics in London which are not readily detectable without time-series analysis: it caused a general rise in susceptibility and consequently contributed to an increased $N\beta$ and a reduction in T during 1750–1800 (section 9.5); it may have contributed to a 5-year oscillation in susceptibility in very young children and so have acted as a driver for the low amplitude, 5-yearly epidemics during 1800–1835; and it may have contributed to a 5-year cycle in susceptible immigrants and so generated a secondary (and very much less important) cycle of epidemics.

9.11 Long wavelength oscillations in smallpox mortality

London was stricken by the enormous mortality of the Great Plague in 1665. The identity of the disease is not known for certain; it may have been bubonic plague, as is popularly supposed, when the causative organism, a coccobacillus, *Yersinia pestis*, is carried by the flea of the Black Rat, but

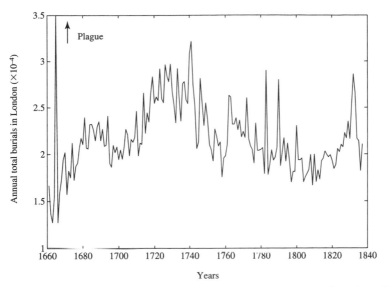

Figure 9.4. Total annual deaths in London, 1660–1837. Long wavelength oscillation detectable by eye. Data source: Bills of Mortality (Creighton, 1894).

Twigg (1984) has presented a carefully argued and detailed case in which he
suggests that some other infective agent may have been responsible.

This exceptionally severe mortality in 1665 had profound consequences on
the population dynamics in London. As the community recovered with a rise in
immigrants and in births, a long wavelength oscillation in total deaths was generated during the period 1660–1837, which is shown in Fig. 9.4 (data taken from
the London Bills of Mortality; Creighton, 1894) and spectral analysis reveals
that the wavelength is 44 years ($P < 0.05$). This long wavelength oscillation,
which is generated by a mortality crisis, corresponds with the oscillations in baptisms and burials that were detected by time-series analysis in the community at
Penrith and which were triggered by the outbreak of a plague there and persisted
for 150 years (Duncan *et al.*, 1992; Scott *et al.*, 1996; see section 3.8).

Although there is only a short run of smallpox data before 1665, the
mean annual mortality from smallpox was almost constant during this
period. After the plague, the trend in smallpox mortality rose steadily, with
a clear, long wavelength oscillation superimposed. This oscillation is detectable by eye in Fig. 9.1 and may be compared with total London deaths in
Fig. 9.4. These two series cross-correlate (1667–1808; ccf = +0.6), and it is
suggested that the long wavelength oscillation in the endemic level of smallpox mortality reflects the underlying fluctuating population level and
consequently the size of the pool of susceptibles.

9.12 Conclusions

We have shown in this chapter how the techniques of time-series analysis can be used to elucidate the details of the epidemiology of a lethal, infectious disease. It must be emphasised that the original data series (taken from the Bills of Mortality) was for deaths and not cases of smallpox which may give biased results. However, these are the only data available for this historic period. A linearised mathematical model for infectious diseases is presented in section 9.3 and the findings of time-series analysis are consistent with a model system that is driven (i.e. the epidemics are maintained and do not decay) by an oscillation in susceptibility ($\delta\beta$) caused by seasonal conditions up to 1835. The interepidemic interval changed progressively in successive cohorts; this was caused initially by a rise in population size/density (N) and later by an increased susceptibility (β) related to malnutrition. It is concluded that the evidence from time-series analysis suggests that the epidemics of smallpox in London were not maintained by stochastic effects but were directly driven by a low amplitude oscillation in susceptibility caused by regular seasonal weather conditions.

The importance of fluctuating wheat prices and malnutrition in affecting the biology of infectious diseases is further emphasised in later chapters. Vaccination had a profound effect on the dynamics of smallpox and the biology changed after 1835 and the results during this period are consistent with an undriven SEIR model in which severe outbreaks of the disease are followed by decaying epidemics. These changes in the biology and epidemiology of smallpox are summarised in Table 9.1.

The dynamics of smallpox have also been integrated into the population dynamics of the city: mortality from the disease was related to population cycles following the plague and also to immigration resulting from famine and hardship in the country.

In the following chapters the dynamics of other, lethal, infectious diseases, elucidated by the techniques of time-series analysis, are described and their basic biology is interpreted on the basis of the mathematics presented in section 9.3. However, this is a linearised model of what is clearly a non-linear system and a full non-linear model of infectious diseases is developed in the next chapter and compared with the linearised model.

10

Non-linear modelling of the 2-yearly epidemics of smallpox: the genesis of chaos?

The changing dynamics of smallpox in London was traced in Chapter 9; it emerged there as an endemic, lethal disease by 1647 and the interepidemic interval gradually fell from 4 to 3 to 2 years, linked to a progressive rise in $N\beta$ (the product of population size and susceptibility). Major 2-yearly epidemics were developed during 1750 to 1800, but thereafter the effects of vaccination became established and both the endemic level and the amplitude of the epidemics were sharply reduced, as shown in Fig. 9.1. Was smallpox characterised by 2-yearly epidemics elsewhere in England before vaccination modified the biology of the disease? In this chapter, the pattern of smallpox epidemics is first studied in large cities outside London, using the data that is available for the 18th century. Secondly, the linearised model of infectious diseases developed in Chapter 9 is compared with a full non-linearised model which is described in section 10.5 and, finally, the existence of chaos in the dynamics of infectious diseases is discussed.

10.1 Deaths in smallpox epidemics in Scotland

There is little direct evidence for the status of smallpox in the 17th and 18th centuries in large cities other than London, although there have been a number of suggestions that the disease was endemic in such cities as Nottingham, Chester, Northampton, Norwich and Manchester after 1725 and before it was brought under control first by inoculation and then by vaccination (Mercer, 1985).

However, some quantitative data are available for Scotland. During the last two decades of the 18th century, smallpox killed over 36 000 people in Glasgow, which constituted nearly a fifth of all deaths in that period. The overwhelming majority of smallpox victims were young children, since nearly all surviving adults were immune (Hopkins, 1983). Statistics for

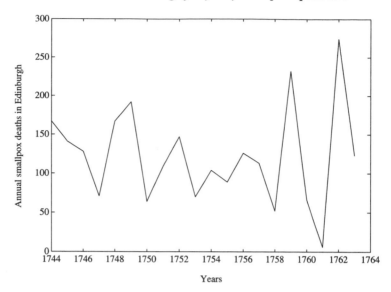

Figure 10.1. Annual smallpox deaths (ordinate) at St Cuthbert, Edinburgh, 1744–1763. Data source: Creighton (1894).

annual smallpox deaths have been recorded (Creighton, 1894) over short periods in St Cuthbert, Edinburgh (1744–1763) and Glasgow (1783–1812), where the disease was clearly endemic by these times (Mercer, 1985).

The data series for Edinburgh are plotted in Fig. 10.1 and the 2- and 3-year oscillations show clearly on spectral analysis. The data series for Glasgow are plotted in Fig. 10.2 and spectral analysis reveals the 2-year oscillation; it is evident that at the end of the 18th century, when the disease was at its height (associated with a high $N\beta$), smallpox epidemics were established in Glasgow and Edinburgh with the characteristic 2-yearly pattern. There was a falling trend in the endemic level of smallpox deaths at Glasgow after 1800 which corresponds with the biology of smallpox in London at the beginning of the 19th century (see Fig. 9.1 and section 9.7) when the effects of widespread vaccination became apparent.

10.2 Smallpox epidemics at Chester

Chester, with a population of 14 700, had 1385 cases of smallpox in 1774, with 202 deaths, 180 of them being children under 5 years of age (Creighton, 1894). The burial series of the parish registers of Holy Trinity Church (one of ten parishes in Chester) have been analysed by time-series analysis to determine, by indirect means, quantitative evidence for the incidence of

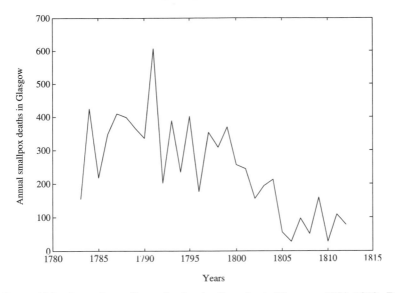

Figure 10.2. Annual smallpox deaths (ordinate) at Glasgow, 1783–1812. Data source: Creighton (1894).

smallpox in the city. Many historical reports (Creighton, 1894; Razzell, 1977; Mercer, 1985) show that (a) the disease was largely confined to children who formed the bulk of susceptibles in endemic or epidemic situations and the mean age at death has been calculated as 2.6 years (Razzell, 1977) and 4.5 years (Scott & Duncan, 1993), (b) an epidemic of smallpox exploded suddenly but quickly burnt out, and (c) major outbreaks tended to be confined to certain months of the year. The burial series of Holy Trinity, Chester, has therefore been divided into adult and child burials and spectral analysis of the child burials over the whole period, 1598–1812, shows that oscillations of periods 2 and 4.4 years were strongest among the short wavelength cycles. When the child burials series was divided into three sections, spectral analysis revealed the following short wavelength cycles:

(1) 1598–1670: only weak 7.5-, 2- and 5-year oscillations.
(2) 1670–1740: strong 4-, 2- and 3-year oscillations suggesting that an oscillation was becoming established but that the wavelength varied from 2 to 4 years.
(3) 1740–1812: a dominant 2-year cycle with a secondary 3-year oscillation.

The child burial series, 1600–1812, was then filtered and these short wavelength cycles of mortality are shown in Fig. 10.3.

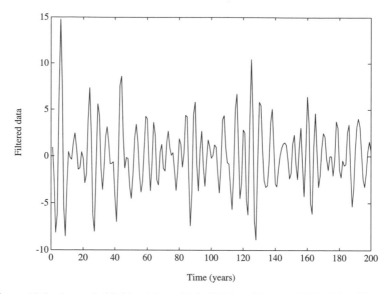

Figure 10.3. Annual child burials at Holy Trinity, Chester, 1600–1800, filtered to reveal a short wavelength oscillation. Filter window = 4 to 10 years. Data source: Farrall (1914).

Inspection of the child burial series at Holy Trinity, Chester, shows periodic aggregations of child deaths with high mortality for 10–12 weeks (i.e. the epidemic apparently burnt out quickly). The series has therefore been analysed further by determining the largest total of child deaths for three consecutive months in each year. Spectral analysis of this derived series (1598–1812) shows a major oscillation at a wavelength of 3 years, with a secondary cycle peak at 2 years. Filtered data are shown in Fig. 10.4, which shows this short wavelength oscillation, and they can be directly compared with Fig. 10.3; the 3-year oscillation became much more significant statistically after 1750.

Because smallpox deaths were confined to a few months in 1 year (i.e. the epidemics burnt out quickly), the child burials at Chester (Holy Trinity) have also been scored on a monthly basis and divided into three cohorts using spectral analysis and linear filtering. The cycles revealed by linear filtering are shown in Fig. 10.5 and the results from this study may be summarised as follows:

(1) 1598–1656: spectral analysis shows weak peaks in the power spectrum at 32 and 25 months (i.e. 2–3 years). Oscillations are irregular and of small amplitude; the cycle in child burials is only weakly developed (Fig. 10.5A).

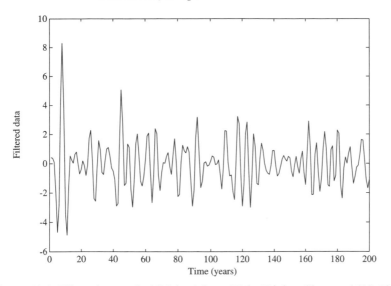

Figure 10.4. Filtered annual child burials at Holy Trinity, Chester, 1600–1800, plotted as the highest total for three consecutive months in each year. Filter window = 4 to 10 years.

(2) 1657–1729: spectral analysis shows a peak at 50 months (= 4 years). Oscillations during this cohort are therefore more regular and of consistently greater amplitude (Fig. 10.5B).

(3) 1730–1812: spectral analysis shows a peak at 41 months (= 4 years; $P < 0.005$). The oscillation has now become more firmly established and analysis of the last 20 years (1792–1812) shows that the wavelength has shortened to 2 years (Fig. 10.5C).

The foregoing presents novel ways of analysing parish register series and provides quantitative evidence, therefore, of a basic short wavelength oscillation in child mortality at Chester which became progressively established during the period 1600 to 1800 (see Fig. 10.3). The wavelength was approximately 3–4 years in the 17th century and 2–3 years in the 18th century. It is suggested that the methods of analysis employed (the results of which are shown in Figs. 10.4 and 10.5) reveal mortality that is related to smallpox; i.e. this child mortality had a strong seasonality (Fig. 10.5) and the duration was confined largely to three months (Fig. 10.4), circumstantial evidence for smallpox which was a fatal, highly infectious disease of children with explosive, but short-lived, epidemics which had a seasonal basis; the interepidemic period was 2–3 years when firmly established. Figure 10.5A to C illustrates how these suggested smallpox epidemics were progressively established on the pre-existing cycles of child mortality

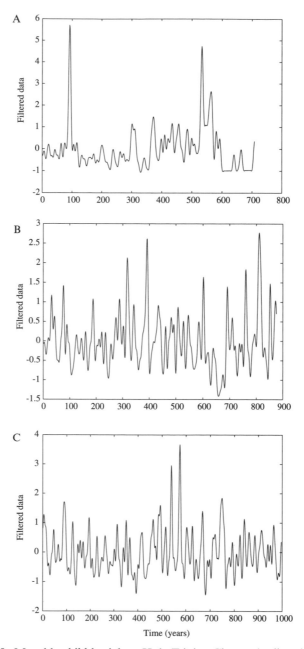

Figure 10.5. Monthly child burials at Holy Trinity, Chester (ordinate), filtered to reveal the short wavelength oscillation. Filter window = 20 to 64 months. Abscissa: time (months). (A) 1598–1656 (some missing data at the end of series); (B) 1657–1729; (C) 1730–1812.

shown in Fig. 10.3. Figure 10.5 shows that the epidemics became more regular, of progressively greater amplitude, and that the inter epidemic period was gradually reduced.

Obviously the evidence is indirect and is concerned only with fatalities and not with the number of cases of smallpox. It is suggested that: (a) the changes between Fig. 10.5A and B reflect the increase in the virulence and case fatality rate of smallpox that emerged in the mid-17th century; and (b) the change in pattern from a 4-year oscillation in 1657–1729 (Fig. 10.5B) to a 2–3 year oscillation in 1730–1812 (Fig. 10.5C) reflects the growth of the population at Chester (i.e. the progressive rise in $N\beta$, the product of population size/density and susceptibility to smallpox, see section 9.4) and the change from the conditions of a rural town, described in Chapter 13, to a sufficiently large conurbation for the disease to become endemic with the characteristic 2–3-year epidemics super-imposed.

The parish registers of Holy Trinity, Chester, specifically record deaths from smallpox during the short period from 1787 to 1810 and the peaks (maximum = 10 deaths in 1788) correspond with the epidemics shown in Fig. 10.4, but people died of smallpox in every year during this 23-year period, confirming that it was endemic at Chester at the end of the 18th century. The causes of death were also recorded in detail in the two decades around 1800 in the burials register for St John's, a parish on the east side of Chester, and smallpox epidemics corresponding to the epidemics at Holy Trinity (Fig. 10.4) are clearly evident, confirming that the disease was also endemic with superimposed 2-yearly epidemics in this parish. The number recorded as dying of smallpox at Holy Trinity in the epidemic years was higher, with a maximum of 37.

10.3 Drivers for the smallpox epidemics at Chester

Spectral analysis and the autocorrelation function of the annual child mortality series determined as the largest total of child burials in three consecutive months confirms the findings from the monthly burials series and shows that the interepidemic interval (T) at Chester changed progressively from 4 years to 3 years to 3–2 years at the end of the 18th century (see summary in Table 10.1). This data series has been studied by multiple regression analysis, and coherence and cross-correlation function to search for possible seasonal drivers for the epidemics which might generate an oscillation in susceptibility ($\delta\beta$). The results can be summarised as follows:

Table 10.1. *Comparison of the suggested drivers for the smallpox epidemics at London and Chester associated with different interepidemic periods*

	London		Chester	
T (yr)	Period	Driver	Period	Driver
4	1659–1707	Low winter temperatures	1657–1729	Low winter temperatures (Low winter rainfall[a])
3	1708–1750	Low autumn rainfall	1730–1790	Low winter rainfall up to 1760
		Low winter temperatures		Low winter temperatures
2	1751–1800	Low autumn rainfall	1790–1812	Low winter rainfall
		Low spring rainfall		

Notes:
London data of deaths from smallpox from the Bills of Mortality; Chester data = annual child deaths calculated as the largest total of child deaths in three consecutive months. Seasonal temperature data available from 1659.
[a] Seasonal rainfall data available only from 1700.

(1) During the period 1659–1795, when T changed from 4 to 3 years, child mortality was significantly associated with low winter temperatures ($P < 0.001$).
(2) Seasonal rainfall data are available from 1700 and child mortality correlated significantly with low winter rainfall from 1701–1760 ($P < 0.001$), when $T = 4$–3 years and then again from 1790–1812 ($P < 0.001$) when $T = 3$–2 years.
(3) Thus, low winter temperatures could act as a driver for smallpox at Chester from 1659–1790, being followed by low winter rainfall thereafter. However, low winter rainfall probably acted synergistically with low winter temperatures to produce an oscillation in susceptibility from 1700 (and perhaps before that time when rainfall records began) until 1760.

These suggested drivers are summarised in Table 10.1, where a direct comparison with smallpox epidemics in London is made. The probable seasonal drivers in the two cities are compared on the basis of T; the epidemics evolved more rapidly to the 2-yearly pattern in London because of the faster rise in $N\beta$ there. The correspondence between the suggested seasonal conditions revealed in Table 10.1 before the start of the effects of inoculation and vaccination is striking, with low winter temperatures interacting with low winter (Chester) or low autumn (London) rainfall to produce a driving oscillation in $\delta\beta$. The data series for London is taken from the Bills of Mortality of actual smallpox deaths whereas the series for Chester is of child burials, the peaks of which are believed to represent deaths from this disease. The excellent correspondence between London and Chester provides circumstantial evidence that the oscillation in child deaths in the latter city shown in Fig. 10.5C does represent smallpox epidemics. It is also suggested that there was a common seasonal factor driving smallpox epidemics in large cities where the disease was endemic, namely cold, dry conditions in winter and/or autumn.

10.4 Smallpox at York

York was one of the half-dozen leading provincial cities in England; its population grew steadily from about 8 500 in 1561 to perhaps 11 000 by 1600 and for much of the 17th century it remained at about 12 000 (Galley, 1995). The mortality of the 13 parishes contained within the old city walls has been the subject of a very careful study by Galley (1994), who recorded peaks of crisis mortality among children in the early 17th century, with particularly severe child mortality in 1639. A series of lesser peaks is evident from the mid-17th century, suggesting a succession of epidemics, although there was no indication in the parish registers of the cause of death. Are these smallpox epidemics? Galley (1994) quoted a study by Laycock (1844), who was working from an account by Dr Wintringham of the weather and epidemics in York between 1715 and 1735.

Smallpox appeared at three or four intervals during the 20 years over which his observations extend. In 1715 they assumed the confluent form, and a malignant type; in the subsequent year their virulence was diminished, and in the winter of 1717 they disappeared altogether. In April 1721 the measles were epidemic, and in the spring of 1723 the confluent small-pox re-appeared, accompanied in some instances with petechiae. In September, 1725, the measles of a mild character became epidemic, and continued through the winter, and in the summer of 1726 the small-pox took their place, also in a milder form than in 1723. In the autumn of 1729, the distinct kind accompanied an epidemic influenza, and in the following year were associated with measles and other exanthemata. In the winter of 1731, they became more malignant in character, but disappeared almost entirely as summer advanced. In the spring of 1732, they re-appeared in the neighbourhood, were confluent, and in the summer were prevalent in the city, but in a milder form. In the winter of 1733, the influenza which extended over Europe was prevalent in York, and there was with it a few cases of small-pox: in autumn the latter were more frequent, but of a milder kind, and maintained that character through the winter and spring of 1734: in the autumn of that year they became confluent.

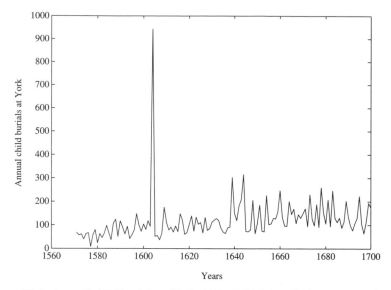

Figure 10.6. Annual child burials at York, 1571–1700. Note the heavy mortality of the plague in 1604. Data source: C. Galley, personal communication.

We are indebted to Dr Chris Galley, who provided us with his valuable data series for York for the period 1571–1700. The unfiltered child burial series (see Fig. 10.6) shows an obvious change in its characteristics after 1635 and spectral analysis of the period 1571–1635 shows strong short wavelength oscillations at 4, 5 and 6 years, whereas spectral analysis of the later period, 1635–1700, shows strong cycles at 5 and 2.5 years. Spectral analysis of the whole period (1571–1700) shows the strongest oscillations at 5 and 2.3 years and these findings suggest initially that before 1635 there was a basic short wavelength oscillation in child mortality of about 5 years periodicity, which may have persisted through the 17th century. However, after 1635, 2- to 3-yearly lethal epidemics were superimposed which have the hallmarks of endemic smallpox. This working hypothesis is tested as follows.

York suffered from an outbreak of plague in 1604 which killed between a quarter and a third of the population and the child burial series has therefore been filtered for the period after this, 1610 to 1700, and is shown in Fig. 10.7; the results are consistent with a low amplitude 5-year cycle up to 1635, followed by high amplitude 3-yearly epidemics which develop into 2-yearly epidemics during the last 30 years of the century. These suggested 2–3-yearly epidemics during 1635–1700 are shown more clearly after filtering in Fig. 10.8.

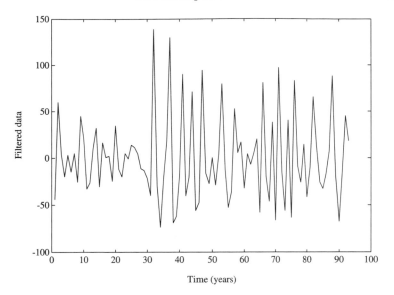

Figure 10.7. Annual child burials at York, 1610–1700, filtered to reveal the short wavelength oscillation which emerged strongly after 1640 (year 30). Filter window = 2 to 7 years.

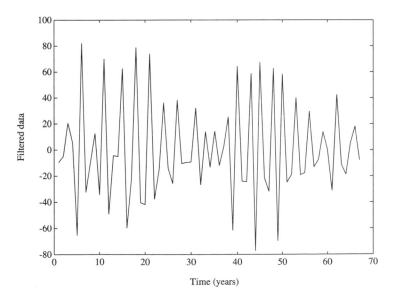

Figure 10.8. Filtered annual child burials at York, 1635–1700. Filter window = 2 to 4 years.

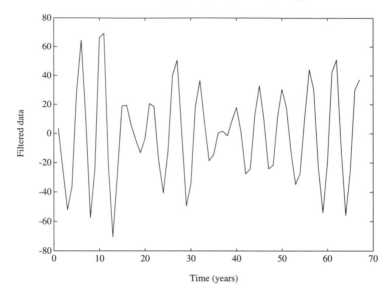

Figure 10.9. Filtered annual child burials at York, 1635–1700. Filter window = 4 to
10 years.

A 5-year oscillation is detectable, persisting after 1635 and underlying the suggested dominant epidemics and is shown after filtering in Fig. 10.9. There is evidence that this 5-year oscillation in child burials correlated with the corresponding short wavelength oscillation in wheat prices: the wheat prices and child burials series are coherent in the 5-year waveband for the whole period, 1571–1700, $P < 0.025$ (see Fig. 10.10), and more significantly for the earlier period, 1571–1650, $P < 0.01$. Child mortality during this time before the establishment of the epidemics was also sensitive to *high* wool prices, as shown by the cross-correlation function and coherence studies and discussed in section 8.10.

In conclusion, the child burials series at York displayed a 5-year oscillation from 1571 which was probably driven by malnutrition and hardship caused by oscillations in the prices of commodities. This compares with a similar, basic 5-year oscillation in child mortality, driven by wheat prices that is described in a rural market town, Penrith, in Chapter 7. Epidemics became established at York after 1635, with the arrival of the virulent and lethal form of smallpox. At Penrith, smallpox developed, with 5-yearly epidemics superimposed on the pre-existing child mortality cycle (section 7.3.2), but because York was a very much larger conurbation of high density the smallpox epidemics there were immediately established on a 3-yearly basis which evolved later into 2-yearly epidemics because of a rising

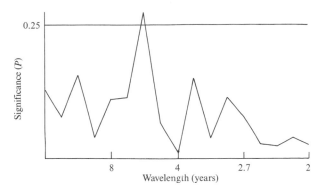

Figure 10.10. Coherence, wheat prices versus child burials at York, 1571–1700. The two series are coherent ($P < 0.025$; ordinate) for the whole period. Abscissa: wavelength (years).

$N\beta$ (the number of annual baptisms at York were increasing at this time). This evolution of the epidemics is comparable to the situation at London and Chester and it is probable that the disease was endemic at York almost immediately after 1635.

Thus, in large cities in the 18th century in England and Scotland, smallpox had evolved into a lethal endemic disease, climaxing with the characteristic 2-yearly epidemics.

10.5 Linear versus non-linear models of the 2-yearly smallpox epidemics

Equations 9.1 to 9.4 (section 9.2) describing the epidemics of infectious diseases constitute (as will be shown below) a non-linear system, and a linearised model thereof has been developed in section 9.3 which represents a good approximation of the underlying system. A full, non-linear model is presented in the following sections and this will be compared with the linearised model used earlier. Readers who do not welcome the derivation of the equations on which the non-linear model is based can proceed directly to section 10.6, wherein the major conclusions are summarised.

The basic equations (Equations 9.1 to 9.4) concerning the theory of viral epidemics (Anderson & May, 1991) can be summarised as follows. The population, N, is assumed to remain constant where the net input of susceptibles (births) equals the net mortality, μN (where μ = death rate, and life expectancy = $1/\mu$). The population is divided into susceptibles (X), latents (H), infectives (Y) and recovered and hence immune (Z). It is assumed that the net rate at which infections occur is proportional to the number of encounters between susceptibles and infectives, βXY (where β is a transmission coefficient). Individuals move from latent to infectives at a *per capita* rate, σ, and recover, so becoming immune, at rate γ.

Three changes have been applied to these equations:

(1) The latent stage of the infection is ignored and the latents are incorporated into infectives.
(2) The death rate from smallpox, α, is included in the equations.
(3) The variables X, Y and Z give the absolute numbers in each class but, using the approach described in Anderson & May (1991), the equations are written in terms of the fraction of the population in each class by defining three new variables,

$$x = \frac{X}{N}; \quad y = \frac{Y}{N}; \quad z = \frac{Z}{N}$$

Incorporation of these changes reduces the basic equations to

$$\frac{dx}{dt} = \mu - \mu x - N\beta xy \tag{10.1}$$

$$\frac{dy}{dt} = N\beta xy - (\mu + \alpha + \gamma)y \tag{10.2}$$

Note that it is necessary to solve only two equations because the fraction of the population that is immune, Z, can be deduced from the fact that $x + y + z = 1$.

Equations 10.1 and 10.2 describe the response of a non-linear equation in terms of a pair of coupled first-order differential equations. Because this system can be described by only two differential equations, it is not possible for the system to display chaotic behaviour. However, it is proposed that the model is driven by periodic variations in the susceptibility to infection, as suggested in section 9.3 and developed further in this and subsequent chapters. This variation is represented by

$$\beta(t) = \beta \left[1 + \delta\beta \sin\frac{(2\pi t)}{\lambda} \right] \tag{10.3}$$

where λ is the wavelength of the periodic variation and β is the nominal or steady-state value of the transmission coefficient or susceptibility. The amplitude of the variation is determined by $\delta\beta$, which represents the change in susceptibility expressed as a fraction of β.

An alternative description of the dynamic response of the system can be obtained by defining

$$\Phi = \frac{2\pi t}{\lambda} \tag{10.4}$$

and Equation 10.3 can then be written as

$$\beta(t) = \beta(1 + \delta\beta \sin\Phi) \tag{10.5}$$

and Equations 10.1, 10.2 and 10.5 can be rearranged to give

$$\frac{dx}{dt} = \mu - \mu x - N\beta xy(1 + \delta\beta \sin\Phi) \tag{10.6}$$

$$\frac{dy}{dt} = N\beta xy(1 + \delta\beta \sin\Phi) - (\mu + \alpha + \gamma)y \tag{10.7}$$

$$\frac{d\Phi}{dt} = \frac{2\pi}{\lambda} \tag{10.8}$$

In this form it can be seen that the response of the system, which is driven by periodic variations in susceptibility, can be described by three coupled, first-order, non-linear differential equations. Because there are three equations, the dynamics of this system can exhibit a chaotic response, as will be shown below.

Further insight into the response of the model can be obtained by considering Equations 10.6 and 10.7 as consisting of the sum of a linear component and the non-linear term, $N\beta xy(1 + \delta\beta \sin\Phi)$. The amplitude of the variation in the force of the infection, $\delta\beta$, determines whether the linear or non-linear term dominates.

If a linear system is driven by a sinusoidal variation, the output in both the number of susceptibles and the number of infectives is sinusoidal where:

(1) The frequency of the output variation is the same as the frequency of the driving variation.
(2) The amplitude of the output variation will be different from that of the amplitude of the driving term.
(3) The output variation will be phase-shifted relative to the driving variation.

For given values of death rate (μ), smallpox death rate (α) and recovery rate (γ), the natural frequency of the system is determined by the value of $N\beta$ (where N is the population size and β is the steady-state value of susceptibility or transmission coefficient before any oscillations are applied), as described in the linearised model detailed in section 9.3.

In this chapter, the dynamics of smallpox in large cities are considered, where $N\beta$ is high and, as we have seen, the epidemics are driven at the characteristic 2-year intervals. In Chapter 13 the smallpox epidemics in rural towns are discussed and the interepidemic interval (T) is shown to be 5 years. The natural resonant frequency (ω_r) of these two types of population can be characterised using frequency response plots (or Bode diagrams) of the linear portion of the systems. Figure 10.11A and B illustrates the response of the linear portion where $N\beta = 270$ (conditions in London); Fig. 10.11A plots the amplitude of the output variation generated by a unit input variation against frequency. The maximum output amplitude is generated by an input frequency of 0.5 (i.e. period $= 2$ years; Fig. 10.11A). Fig. 10.11B shows the corresponding phase shift in degrees; for frequencies below 0.5 the output leads the input and for frequencies above 0.5 the output lags the input. Figure 10.11C (magnitude of response) and D (phase shift) illustrates the corresponding responses where $N\beta = 65$ (conditions in medium-sized rural towns). The system has a natural frequency of 0.2 (period $= 5$ years).

The foregoing applies to the linear element of the system. The response is approximately linear for small amplitudes of the variation ($\delta\beta$), so that for a sinusoidal variation in $\delta\beta$ the output is sinusoidal at the same frequency, but different in amplitude and phase. As $\delta\beta$ is increased, the non-linear effects begin to become significant (see below).

A fourth-order Runge–Kutta–Fehlberg method is used to integrate the differential equations using the SIMULINK module in the PRO-MATLAB package. However, the integration procedure proved to be susceptible to numerical errors when using Equations 10.6 to 10.8 in the form given, particularly in regions where the number of infectives is small (i.e. between epidemics). The robustness of the integration procedure can be improved by transforming Equations 10.6 and 10.7 using the substitutions

$$u = \ln x$$
$$v = \ln y$$

so that

$$\frac{du}{dx} = \frac{1}{x}$$

$$\frac{dv}{dy} = \frac{1}{y}$$

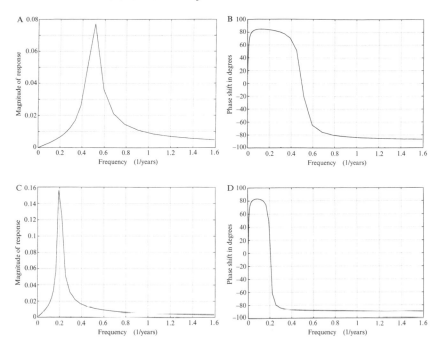

Figure 10.11. Bode diagrams to illustrate the frequency response plots of the linear portion of the systems. (A and C) Amplitude of the response of model systems plotted against the frequency of the input. (B and D) Phase shift in degrees (ordinate) plotted against input frequency. (A and B) $N\beta = 270$ ('London model'), maximum output amplitude generated at a frequency of 0.5 (wavelength = 2 years). (C and D) $N\beta = 65$ ('Penrith model'), natural frequency = 0.2 (wavelength = 5 years).

This leads to

$$\frac{du}{dt} = \mu e^{-u} - \mu - N\beta(1 + \delta\beta\sin\Phi)e^{v} \qquad (10.9)$$

$$\frac{dv}{dt} = N\beta(1 + \delta\beta\sin\Phi)e^{u-} (\mu + \alpha + \gamma) \qquad (10.10)$$

Compared with the effects of variations in the transmission coefficient, $\delta\beta$, when driving the epidemics the model system is markedly less sensitive to fluctuations in the disease-induced death rate, α, and in the non-diseased induced mortality rate, μ, suggesting that a periodic fluctuation in susceptibility will have the dominant effect on driving the epidemics.

10.6 Conclusions from the non-linear model

The dynamics of the non-linear model system are again defined by $N\beta$ (the product of population size/density and susceptibility to the disease, see section 9.4) and in a large city, such as London or Chester, the relative $N\beta$ is calculated to be 270 (see Fig. 10.11A and B). The non-linear model is also used for rural towns in Chapter 13, where the dynamics are very different, and $N\beta = 65$ (see Fig. 10.11C and D). The driving force for the non-linear system is again a cyclical (sinusoidal; Fig. 2.1) variation in susceptibility ($\delta\beta$), and the model responds readily to a low amplitude oscillation in $\delta\beta$ which could be produced by seasonal drivers *operating at the same frequency* as the resonant frequency of the system (ω_r) as described in section 9.6. When the model is run with a low amplitude $\delta\beta$, the period of variation of which is 2 years, 2-yearly epidemics are produced, superimposed on an endemic level. We conclude that the non-linear model satisfactorily describes an epidemic system that is driven by a regular oscillation in susceptibility, the frequency of which is at, or close to, the resonant frequency of the system.

Such driving inputs have been identified and used in analysing and modelling the epidemics of smallpox, measles and whooping cough in subsequent chapters, but first we explore whether this full, non-linear model could be driven and maintained (i.e. the epidemics would not decay as they would in an SEIR model) by stochastic and other effects. Thus, the effects of driving the system with an oscillation in susceptibility ($\delta\beta$), the frequency of which is *not* at ω_r, are described in sections 10.7 and 10.8.

The input to the system is (a) white noise, see section 10.7; (b) an annual (i.e. 1-year) cycle, as has been suggested for driving the biennial measles epidemics (Dietz, 1976; Aron & Schwartz, 1984), see section 10.8; or (c) a 5-year cycle associated with grain prices (which is described in Chapter 6), see section 10.8.

The dynamics are simulated assuming $\mu = 0.04$ (i.e. the average age at death, $\overset{\circ}{e}_0$, = 25 years), α (the death rate from smallpox) = 4.0, γ (the survival or recovery rate) = 20.0, the latent plus infectious periods = 15 days (= 0.04 year), i.e.

$$\alpha + \gamma = 24 \text{ (death rate + survival rate)}$$

(i.e. if 1 in 6 of those infected die of the disease, see Scott & Duncan, 1993, $\alpha = 24/6 = 4$, and $\gamma = 24 - 4 = 20$).

Modelling was developed using the SIMULINK module in the PRO-MATLAB package and run on a Sun Workstation. The model is run for a 250-year period and the figures show the results for the last 20 years (in the figures of the fraction of population infected or fraction of population susceptible) or the last 50 years (in the phase diagrams).

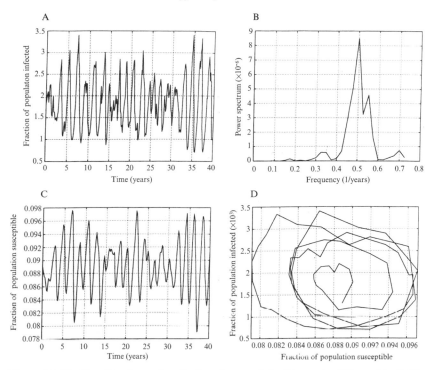

Figure 10.12. Results of running the London model with a noisy $\delta\beta$ equal to 0.05. $N\beta = 270$. (A) Fraction of the population infected; smallpox is endemic. (B) Power spectrum of the fraction of the population infected; peak at a wavelength of 2 years. (C) Fraction of the population susceptible. (D) Phase diagram of infectives versus susceptibles.

10.7 Can white noise pump up the smallpox epidemics?

Anderson & May (1991) have suggested that stochastic effects can perpetu-ate an oscillation and in this section, before modelling the effects of peri-odic variations in susceptibility, the possibility is explored that the introduction of a noisy signal to β may be sufficient to pump up the decay-ing oscillation that, it is predicted, would be generated by Equations 9.1 to 9.4. Olsen & Schaffer (1990), for example, suggest that for large popula-tions, temporal changes in chickenpox incidence are best explained as a noisy annual cycle. Broad-band noise was produced from a random noise generator with zero mean. The variation in susceptibility ($\delta\beta$) was defined as the standard deviation of the noise.

Figure 10.12 shows the results of running the London model ($N\beta = 270$) with a noisy $\delta\beta$ equal to 0.05 (i.e. peak-to-peak amplitude = 0.3). This large variation in susceptibility (30% peak-to-peak) produces epidemics

(Fig. 10.12A) with a periodicity of 2 years (see power spectrum, Fig. 10.12B) that are superimposed on an endemic infection. Figure 10.12C illustrates the fraction of the population that is susceptible and, as would be expected with a noisy input, the phase diagram of infectives versus susceptibles (Fig. 10.12D) is noisy. It is concluded that an input of random noise in $\delta\beta$ of *large amplitude* would serve to drive the London model at its natural frequency of 2-yearly epidemics; thus, the non-linear model shows that 2-yearly epidemics could be driven simply by random noise (Bartlett, 1957, 1960) without incorporating spatial dynamics or seasonal forcing.

10.8 Examples of modelling the London smallpox epidemics: can the system be driven by an oscillation in $\delta\beta$ that is not at the resonant frequency?

Example 1

The system is driven with a 1-yearly (annual) sinusoidal input of susceptibility which might reflect annual changes in β associated with the usual seasonal changes of temperature and weather.

Definitions: $\delta\beta = 0.08$.   Period of sinusoidal input = 1 year. $N\beta = 270$

The results of modelling are shown in Fig. 10.13 which shows conventional graphs of the fraction of the population infected or susceptible against time and also a three-dimensional phase diagram in which is plotted the change in $\delta\beta$ versus the fraction of population infected versus the fraction of population susceptible. As will be shown below, phase diagrams are particularly helpful in detecting chaotic responses in the model. The 8% annual fractional change in β generates a clear 2-year oscillation in the fraction of the population infected although there is evidence of the effects of the annual input in the interepidemic years. The number of infectives does not drop to zero in the interepidemic periods, showing that the disease is endemic (Fig. 10.13A and C), although the ratio of the number infected in the epidemic years to the number infected in the interepidemic years (the endemic level) is artificially high and does not correspond to the actual smallpox mortality shown in Fig. 9.1. The progressive rise in the number of susceptibles, which crashes at the epidemic, is shown in Fig. 10.13B. The phase plane of susceptibles versus infectives versus the fractional change in $\delta\beta$ after the system has stabilized is shown in Fig. 10.13C; the phase diagram is simply the result of driving a non-linear system with a sinusoidal input. We conclude that a simple (8%) annual variation in β is sufficient to pump up the system, so that it oscillates at its

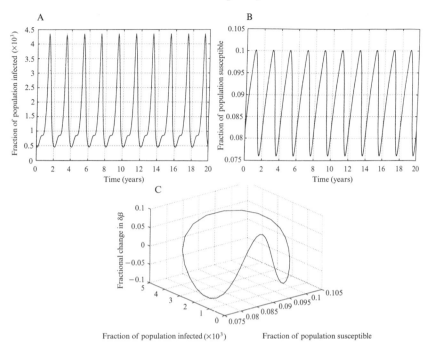

Figure 10.13. Response of the modelling of smallpox in London. $N\beta = 270$; $\delta\beta = 0.08$; period of sinusoidal input = 1 year. (A) The fraction of the population infected; dominant 2-year oscillation; smallpox is endemic. (B) The fraction of population susceptible. Abscissa: time (years). (C) Phase diagram of the fraction of population susceptible versus the fraction of population infected versus the fractional change in $\delta\beta$.

natural frequency, ω_r (2 years) which has been determined by the chosen $N\beta$; i.e. a 1-year input will generate a 2-year output. Thus, the non-linear model shows that the 2-yearly epidemics do not necessarily need a driver oscillating at ω_r to maintain them; the system would oscillate if driven by an annual variation in susceptibility, *provided that the amplitude of $\delta\beta$ is sufficiently high.*

Example 2

The sinusoidal, driving input in susceptibility is complex, comprising a simple 1-year cycle and a 5-year cycle, i.e. the annual cycle of Example 1 is modified by the addition of a small component of the wheat price cycle. Analysis of smallpox deaths in London shows that there is a secondary, low amplitude 5-year oscillation during 1659–1835 which correlates with the wheat price series (see section 9.10) and the objective of this modelling is to

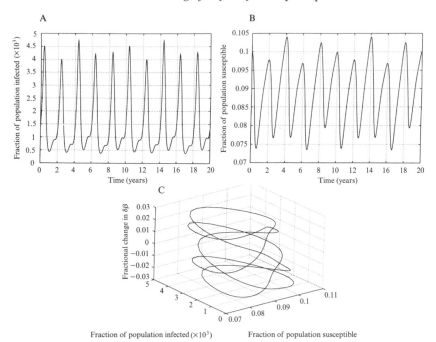

Figure 10.14. London model driven by a compound input of 75% 1-year cycle and 25% 5-year cycle; $\delta\beta = 0.11$, $N\beta = 270$. (A) The fraction of the population infected; smallpox is endemic. (B) The fraction of population susceptible. Abscissa: time (years). (C) Phase diagram of the fraction of population infected versus the fraction of population susceptible versus the fractional change in $\delta\beta$.

investigate whether the addition of a 5-year oscillation to the 1-year input would make the system respond more readily with 2-yearly epidemics.

Definitions: sinusoidal $\delta\beta = 0.11$.   Input compounded of 75% 1-year cycle, 25% 5-year cycle. $N\beta = 270$.

The change in the fraction of the population infected is shown in Fig. 10.14A and the change in the fraction of the population susceptible to smallpox is shown in Fig. 10.14B. Again, the number of infectives does not drop to zero in the interepidemic periods. The oscillation generated is less regular than that shown in Fig. 10.13A and, superficially, more closely resembles the London smallpox epidemics that have been determined by filtering the Bills of Mortality series (see Fig. 9.2). This is illustrated by the phase diagram (fraction of the population infected plotted versus fraction susceptible versus $\delta\beta$) in Fig. 10.14C; this does not touch the *x*-axis, confirming that smallpox was endemic.

Table 10.2. *Regions of response of the London system to a variation in δβ*
(Nβ = 270; period of sinusoidal input = 1 year)

Range of amplitude of δβ	Behaviour	Figure
0–0.055	Regular 1-year cycle	10.15A
0.055–0.25	Regular 2-year cycle (with 1-year component detectable)	10.13
0.25–0.285	1st bifurcation; regular 4-year pattern repeat, although 2-year spikes dominate	10.15B
0.285–0.293	2nd bifurcation; regular 8-year pattern repeat	10.15C
0.293–0.297	3rd bifurcation; 16-year pattern repeat	
0.3–0.434	Chaotic	10.15D
0.435–0.62	Regular 4-year pattern – true epidemics with "zero" infectives between outbreaks (not endemic)	10.15E
0.63	1st bifurcation; 8-year pattern repeat	10.15F
0.64	2nd bifurcation; 16-year pattern repeat	
0.66	Chaos (although 4-year peaks are still discernible)	10.15G

10.9 The response of the non-linear model to a progressive increase in δβ

Equations 10.6 and 10.7 describe a non-linear system that is defined by the value of $N\beta$ (see also section 9.4 for the role of $N\beta$ in the linearised model); populations with differing values of $N\beta$ have different fundamental characteristics, including the period of their natural (resonant) frequency. The system has two components, a basic linear element, with the remainder of the system being non-linear (see section 10.5). As $\delta\beta$ (which is the amplitude of the variation that drives the system) is increased, the non-linear effects become more significant. This effect of progressively raising $\delta\beta$ has been studied in the London model ($N\beta = 270$) when it is driven by a sinusoidal 1-year (annual) input, i.e. the system is not being driven by a seasonal driver operating at its resonant frequency. The results are summarised in Table 10.2. At low levels of $\delta\beta$ (<0.055), the 1-year input generates a regular, simple 1-year output cycle (Fig. 10.15A), but at $\delta\beta = 0.055$ the response of the system changes and, within the broad range of $\delta\beta = 0.055$ to 0.25, a regular 2-year cycle is generated. At the lower end of this range (e.g. $\delta\beta = 0.059$), the 1-year component of the output is clearly evident;

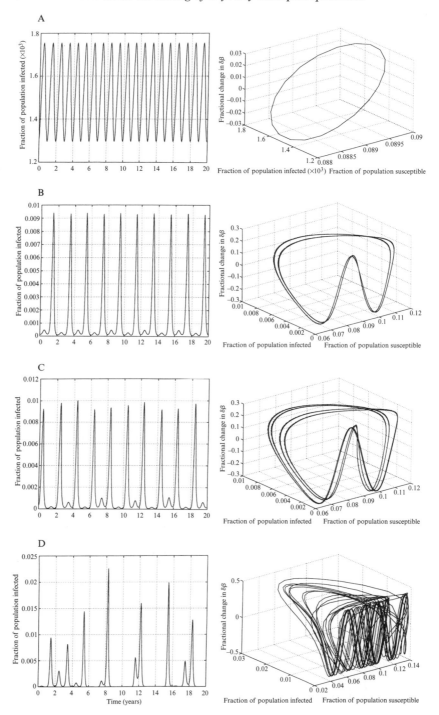

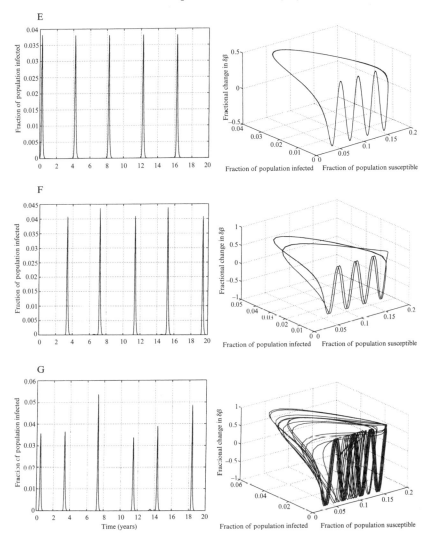

Figure 10.15. Different steady-state responses of a non-linear system (the London model) to a progressive increase in $\delta\beta$. $N\beta = 270$. Period of sinusoidal input = 1 year. Figures illustrate the fraction of the population infected when the system has settled after the introduction of the oscillation in $\delta\beta$ (left-hand column; abscissa = time in years) and the corresponding phase diagram of the fraction infected versus the fraction susceptible versus the fractional change in $\delta\beta$ (right-hand column). Values for $\delta\beta$: (A) 0.03; (B) 0.26; (C) 0.292; (D) 0.434; (E) 0.435; (F) 0.63; (G) 0.8.

however at values of $\delta\beta > 0.065$ the 1-year component is of little importance (see Fig. 10.13; $\delta\beta = 0.08$). As $\delta\beta$ is increased to around 0.25 there is
a bifurcation (revealed on the phase diagram), so that the pattern repeats
every 4 years although the dominant oscillation remains at 2 years (Fig.
10.15B). Further bifurcations occur at $\delta\beta = 0.285$ (Fig. 10.15C) and at $\delta\beta$
$= 0.293$ (note the very narrow ranges of $\delta\beta$ in Table 10.2 for these marked
changes in the response of the system to occur).

The system becomes chaotic (see discussion below, section 10.10) at
$\delta\beta = 0.3$ (Fig. 10.15D) and remains so until, at $\delta\beta = 0.435$, it abruptly
switches back to a condition of steady 4-year epidemics with virtually
no infectives between the outbreaks, i.e. smallpox is no longer endemic.
This abrupt transition is clearly illustrated by comparing Fig. 10.15D
($\delta\beta = 0.434$) and 10.15E ($\delta\beta = 0.435$) where there is only a very small
change (0.23%) in $\delta\beta$. It seems that chaos in the model system is related
to the transition from the endemic to the epidemic condition. As $\delta\beta$
increases further (>0.63), bifurcations again occur, see Fig. 10.15F
(note the narrow ranges of $\delta\beta$ for changes in the character of the
response of the system, Table 10.2), and the system becomes chaotic
once more, although the underlying 4-year oscillation remains visible
(Fig. 10.15G).

We conclude from this modelling that (a) if $N\beta = 270$ is accepted as a
description of the conditions in London (see Fig. 10.11), the annual variation in susceptibility that would trigger the 2-yearly epidemics lies in the
range $\delta\beta = 5\%$ to 25% (these are relatively large values of $\delta\beta$ when compared with an oscillation of $\delta\beta$ which is at the resonant frequency of the
system); and (b) chaos may be associated with the transition from the
disease being endemic, with major superimposed epidemics, to the condition of regular epidemics with virtually no infectives in the interepidemic
years.

10.10 Chaos and epidemics of infectious diseases

Biologists and epidemiologists have become interested in recent years in the
possibility of the existence of chaos in the systems that they study. Until a
few years ago, it was generally believed that biological dynamics are inherently simple and observed deviations from regular behaviour were viewed
as evidence for stochastic perturbations from without. With the discovery
of deterministic chaos in simple models in fields ranging from biochemistry
to population biology, there are an increasing number of reports of con-
crete evidence of chaotic fluctuations (Olsen, Truty & Schaffer, 1988).

A variety of ecological models exhibit chaotic dynamics because of non-linearities in population growth and in interspecific interactions (Pascual, 1993); the use of non-linear dynamics is now common in the field of population biology, and chaos theory has been introduced in ecology to explain the fluctuations of animal populations over time and in economics to interpret the day-to-day variation in economic cycles.

Measles epidemics in the UK and USA in the 20th century are among the best documented of human diseases in terms of epidemiology and population dynamics (Bolker & Grenfell, 1993; Fine, 1993) and it is in these data series that the majority of studies have concentrated in seeking evidence of chaos. The persistent, seemingly irregular, but non-random pattern of measles epidemics arises, it is suggested, simply from changing the contact rates regularly over the course of each year (Aron, 1990). This sort of pattern is called chaos and chaotic systems can perhaps best be characterised by saying that they exhibit a phenomenon called sensitivity to initial conditions. That is, given knowledge of the initial state to finite precision, one cannot predict the *long-term* behaviour of the system. In this sense, chaos resembles random motion but, at the same time, it is generally true that certain statistical quantities (fractal dimensions, Lyapunov exponents, metric entropy) are invariant under chaotic flows and by computing these quantities it is often possible to distinguish chaos from noise. For example, low-dimensional chaotic systems may exhibit distinctive geometries when viewed in phase space (Olsen *et al.*, 1988; see Fig. 10.15). In terms of measles epidemiology, this characteristic sensitivity to initial conditions means that very small changes in the number of infectives or susceptibles can make large differences in the behaviour of the system a few weeks later. Chaos produces complicated patterns that do not follow any sort of simple cycle (although the basic 2-yearly epidemic pattern is preserved in the seasonal SIR model), but are nevertheless not random; given the exact number of cases and susceptibles in a chaotic system today, we can predict the number tomorrow (Bolker & Grenfell, 1992).

In Fig. 10.15A the number of infectives in a non-linear model is plotted against time, giving a conventional picture of the predicted epidemics from an annual driver, and alongside is plotted a three-dimensional phase diagram, which is a graph of the number of infectives versus the number of susceptibles versus the fractional change in $\delta\beta$. The time co-ordinate is lost in the latter graph but it is possible to get a better idea of the changing relationship between the variables. The line followed by an epidemic through time on a phase diagram is called an attractor and, irrespective of the numbers of infectives and susceptibles at the start, the epidemic eventually comes to travel along the attractor. In the phase diagrams shown in Figs. 10.13, 10.14 and 10.15 the smallpox model is run for 250 years but the results for only the last 50 years are shown in the plots.

The attractor of the driven non-linear model starts as a simple oval at small $\delta\beta$ (Fig. 10.15A) and the system goes once round this oval in a year, but when the amplitude of $\delta\beta$ increases enough to produce a 2-year cycle, the attractor folds over (Fig. 10.15B), reflecting the different patterns in even and odd years. Chaos in epidemic systems (particularly measles and chickenpox) has been studied by many workers including Grenfell (1992), Bolker & Grenfell (1993), Tidd *et al.* (1993) and Rand & Wilson (1991), who argue that the best explanation of the observed unpredictability is that it is a manifestation of what they term chaotic stochasticity. Such chaos is driven and made permanent by the fluctuations from the mean field encountered in epidemics, or by extrinsic stochastic noise, and is dependent upon the existence of chaotic repellors in the mean field dynamics. For such systems, chaotic stochasticity is suggested to be far more ubiquitous than the presence of deterministic chaotic attractors. The paper by Bolker & Grenfell (1992) is a good introduction to this controversial topic of chaos in the epidemics of infectious diseases.

10.11 Chaos and the modelling of smallpox epidemics

Table 10.2 shows that if the amplitude of $\delta\beta$ is raised progressively above 0.25 in the non-linear model of smallpox in London, the dynamics alter dramatically, with bifurcations and chaos; the system then switches sharply again at $\delta\beta = 0.435$ to a pattern of *4-yearly* epidemics (i.e. a 1-year input and a 4-year output) with virtually no infectives between outbreaks. This theoretical finding suggests that chaos may be associated with the transition from the endemic condition to the strictly epidemic condition. The modelling shows that the system exhibits a chaotic response if the amplitude of the variations in susceptibility ($\delta\beta$) is sufficiently high. However, the presence of the variation in susceptibility (the driver) is a sufficient condition for inducing this chaos; an undriven system which is defined solely by Equations 10.1 and 10.2 cannot become chaotic. Such chaotic conditions are probably of only theoretical interest, since presumably $\delta\beta$ will not normally be at such high levels and the London smallpox mortality (Fig. 9.1) series confirms that the disease was endemic throughout the period of study.

10.12 Do the theoretical models of chaos in epidemic systems have any basis in reality?

A satisfactory model of an epidemic system has to reproduce the observed patterns of the epidemiology of the disease and it must fit the data better than any alternative model that can be constructed (Bolker & Grenfell, 1992). Olsen *et al.* (1988) suggested that the question is not whether biological chaos exists, but whether it is ubiquitous and important in the overall functioning of living systems. There is general agreement that the data series for measles in the 20th century represents the most probable source for detecting chaotic systems; various workers have derived Lyapunov exponents and fractal dimensions for their data and for their models and have shown them to be equivalent (Olsen *et al.*, 1988; Olsen & Schaffer, 1990; Tidd *et al.*, 1993), although this does not prove that measles epidemics are chaotic. The practical problem when working directly from the data becomes the distinction between chaos and noisy periodicity (Pool, 1989; Olsen & Schaffer, 1990; Ellner, 1993). Very long data sets are needed for most techniques when searching for chaos, but non-linear forecasting has been used successfully as a way of distinguishing chaos from measurement error in time-series (Sugihara & May, 1990) and it has been concluded that measles exhibits low dimensional chaos in New York City and in seven large cities in England, whereas on a larger, country-wide scale (i.e. a metapopulation, see Chapter 15) the dynamics appear as a noisy 2-year cycle (Sugihara, Grenfell & May, 1990). Again, therefore, it is important to examine the dynamics of individual populations separately; pooling the results may obscure underlying differences. Olsen *et al.* (1988) studied childhood diseases in Copenhagen, Denmark, and concluded that the dynamics of measles, mumps and rubella show low dimensional chaos, whereas outbreaks of chickenpox conform to an annual cycle with noise superimposed.

However, most of the models of measles epidemics described in the foregoing incorporate seasonal forcing (see Bolker & Grenfell, 1993); the modelling is comparable to driving the non-linear model for smallpox with an annual driver, as illustrated in Fig. 10.15, which shows that chaos occurs only under special conditions, with a high amplitude driver. When the system is driven by a *very low amplitude* oscillation in $\delta\beta$, the frequency of which is *at the resonant frequency* (ω_r) of the system, epidemics are readily generated at ω_r. Provided such a suitable environmental driver is available to produce an oscillation in $\delta\beta$, it is not necessary to postulate a chaotic system in an infectious disease in an identified population (see the dynamics of measles epidemics described in Chapter 11). When metapopulations are considered (as in England and Wales) with different dynamics in the constituent populations (see Chapter 15) the overall data series will probably appear confused.

10.13 Theoretical considerations of the effects of population size and density

Both the linearised and the non-linear modelling show that the biology of the epidemics and, in particular, the interepidemic interval (T), is determined by the product of population size and susceptibility ($N\beta$). Figure 9.1 and Table 9.1 show how the dynamics of smallpox in London changed progressively with time; T was reduced during the 17th and 18th centuries largely because of increased population size but probably also linked to an increased sensitivity to the disease after 1785 (section 9.5).

The theoretical effect of changing $N\beta$ in the non-linear model is considered in this section; in practice, this modelling will be applicable to a comparison of the dynamics of the disease in different-sized communities (or to a community that is growing) because susceptibility (β) is assumed to remain constant for this analysis. N is probably not simply the number in the population, although this is usually the only convenient measure available, but is also related to the density of the population, because crowding will promote the spread of the disease. Indeed, as shown in Chapter 13, scattered communities do not appear to have suffered from smallpox epidemics. The effects produced when either a 1-year or a 5-year sinusoidal driver is applied to a population with a progressive increase in $N\beta$ are briefly considered in this section. The 5-year driver is included because (unlike for London and other large cities described in this chapter), the smallpox epidemics have been shown to be 5-yearly in medium-sized rural towns (Duncan *et al.*, 1993; see Chapter 13). The amplitude of $\delta\beta$ is arbitrarily fixed at 0.1, which is within the range that generates a 2-year cycle in the London model (Table 10.2) and a 5-year cycle in the rural town model. The results for a range of $N\beta$ from 65 to 600 are shown in Table 10.3.

The 1-year sinusoidal input produces an endemic response throughout the range of $N\beta$ but, with $\delta\beta = 10\%$, the 2-yearly epidemics characteristic of London are found only over a finite range of $N\beta$: $250 < N\beta < 330$. The characteristic 2-yearly epidemics superimposed on an endemic condition for London are shown at $N\beta = 270$; interestingly, the system reverts to 1-year oscillations above $N\beta = 330$.

Table 10.3. *Responses shown by the non-linear model to a progressive increase in Nβ with a 1 yearly or 5 yearly sinusoidal change in δβ*

Wavelength of driver	Nβ						
	65	130	200	270	330	350	600
1 year	1 yr Endemic	1 yr Endemic	1yr Endemic	2 yr Endemic	2 yr Endemic	1 yr Endemic	1 yr Endemic
5 year	5 yr Epidemic	5 yr Epidemic	5 yr^a Endemic	5 yr Endemic	5 yr Endemic	5yr Endemic	5 yr Endemic

Notes:
$δβ = 0.1$.
^{a} Intermediate, small oscillations seen two years after each 5-yearly epidemic.

The model responds to a 5-year driver with 5-yearly epidemics and with no infectives during the interepidemic years at values of $Nβ$ over the range 65 to 130; this epidemic pattern is characteristic of medium-sized rural towns (Chapter 13). At a value of $Nβ$ around 180, the response of the model to a 5-year driver switches from the epidemic to the endemic condition, as shown in Table 10.3. The results summarised in Table 10.3 are applicable only to the value of $δβ$ chosen (10%); different responses may be obtained if markedly different values of $δβ$ are used (see Table 10.2). Nevertheless, these responses illustrate the fundamental difference between medium-sized rural towns ($Nβ < 180$) and cities and larger conurbations ($Nβ > 250$).

10.14 Comparison of the linearised and non-linear models of infectious diseases

Does the linearised model developed in section 9.3 and used as the basis for the analysis of the epidemics described in Chapter 9 represent a satisfactory model when considering a system that is driven by an oscillation in $δβ$, the frequency of which is at, or close to, its resonant frequency? The two models are compared in this section using the same parameters, and the results are shown in Fig. 10.16, where $Nβ$ is set at 60.5 to give a resonant frequency for the system of 5 years (Equation 10.16), simulating the dynamics of scarlet fever epidemics described in Chapter 14. The other variables used in the modelling are, $μ = 0.04$ year^{-1}, $ν = 21$ year^{-1} and

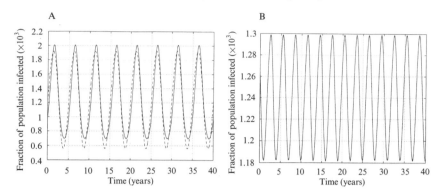

Figure 10.16. Comparison of linearised and full, non-linear models where $N\beta = 60.5$, $\mu = 0.04$ year^{-1}, $\nu = 21$ year^{-1}, $\omega_r = 5$ years, $\delta\beta = 0.003$. Solid line = non-linear model; dashed line = linearised model. (A) Wavelength of input ($\delta\beta$) = 5 years; i.e. at ω_r. (B) Wavelength of input ($\delta\beta$) = 3 years, i.e. not at ω_r. The non-linear and the linearised models give almost identical results in (A) and (B). The amplitude of the epidemics in (B) is reduced when compared with (A) (note scales on the ordinate) because the system is not oscillating at ω_r. Abscissa: years.

$\delta\beta = 0.003$ (a very low amplitude). The solid lines in Fig. 10.16 represent the output from the full non-linear model and the dashed lines the output from the linearised model. The period of the driver ($\delta\beta$) in Fig. 10.16A is 5 years (i.e. at the ω_r of the system) and it can be seen that the two outputs are very similar, differing only slightly in the amplitude of the epidemics. It is therefore reasonable to use a linearised model for describing the oscillations in endemic systems where the magnitude of these oscillations is significantly smaller than the endemic level of the disease.

Fig. 10.16B illustrates the linear and non-linear models with the same characteristics, but the period of the driver is 3 years, i.e. it is not at the ω_r of the system. The responses of the linearised and non-linear models are identical and we conclude that the former constitutes a satisfactory working model. Figure 10.16B shows that in both models, although ω_r remains at 5 years ($N\beta$ is unaltered), the system oscillates at the frequency of the driver (3 years). Furthermore, the amplitude of the epidemics is reduced because the system is not now oscillating at ω_r.

It is noteworthy in Fig. 10.16A that large amplitude epidemics are produced in response to a very small $\delta\beta$ (0.003), i.e. only a very low amplitude oscillation in susceptibility is necessary to maintain the epidemics. This is an important point; the low value of $\delta\beta$ (0.3%) that is sufficient to maintain the epidemics is in contrast with the very much larger amplitude of $\delta\beta$ required to drive the system by white noise (5%; section 10.7) or by a 1-year variation in susceptibility (8%; section 10.8). These theoretical findings illustrate the great sensitivity of the system even to a very low amplitude oscillation in $\delta\beta$, provided that it is at, or close to, the resonant frequency. Stochastic or annual drivers would need to be at least ten-fold greater to drive the system whereas, in practice, it can be predicted, that the epidemics would respond to any appropriate seasonal driver at a frequency of ω_r.

11

Measles and whooping cough in London

In addition to smallpox, measles and whooping cough were also serious lethal diseases in earlier centuries in the UK. Although these are now conquered in the developed world they remain a serious threat to life in Third World countries where, it has been estimated, 17 million people die annually from infectious diseases. Conditions there, with poor nutrition and inadequate medical services approximate to life in England in the 17th and 18th centuries, where fatality rates fell only towards the end of the 19th century. Thus, in many underdeveloped countries today, malnutrition and infectious diseases can occur in the same unfortunate children and together they play a major role in causing high child mortality and morbidity rates (James, 1972; Glasziou & Mackerras, 1993). In particular, measles remains as a significant threat to life in those regions of Africa and Asia where nutrition is inadequate (Fraser & Martin, 1978).

The dynamics of measles and whooping cough in London are studied by time-series analysis in this chapter and the possible effects of seasonal driving and malnutrition are correlated with the mathematical modelling presented in section 9.3.

11.1 Measles epidemics in London, 1630–1837

Bolker & Grenfell (1992) wrote of measles epidemics:

Most humans who have lived since the time of Babylon have caught the measles virus. Measles is so infectious that in small isolated human populations the infection burns itself out . . . measles has probably evolved since the first densely settled human civilization (Bartlett, 1957; Black, 1966). Improved communications now mean that few communities are isolated, and almost everyone in the world is exposed to measles. In the 1960s mass vaccination programmes began around the world. Everyone still experiences measles in some form, though; 95 per cent of adults have measles antibodies in their blood, either from catching measles or from receiving measles vaccine. Despite this ubiquity, and despite upwards of a million deaths a year from measles in developing countries (McLean, 1986), the details of measles population dynamics . . . are still not completely clear.

Measles epidemics in the UK and USA in the 20th century are among the best documented of human diseases in terms of epidemiology and population dynamics (Bolker & Grenfell, 1993; Fine, 1993). The comparative simplicity of infection and immunity (Black, 1966) allows the construction of epidemiological models; the measles virus has no reservoir other than the human host and, since permanent immunity follows infection, persistence of the virus depends on a continuous supply of susceptibles, which is provided by new births. The study of measles epidemiology has allowed the development of elegant deterministic (Olsen & Schaffer, 1990) and stochastic (Bartlett, 1957, 1960) models incorporating spatial dynamics, seasonal forcing and age structure to account for the striking pattern of these epidemics and it has been suggested that measles dynamics in developed countries may exhibit low dimensional chaos (Olsen & Schaffer, 1990; Rand & Wilson, 1991; Grenfell, 1992; Tidd *et al.*, 1993; Bolker & Grenfell, 1995). Mathematical modelling suggests that about 2500 cases per year is the minimum to prevent breaks in the continuity of disease transmission which compares with data from cities in Britain and America where fadeout was found with fewer than 4000–5000 cases per annum, corresponding to populations of about 250 000 (Bartlett, 1957, 1960; Anderson, Grenfell & May, 1984). Measles was endemic in the UK in this century, with superimposed epidemics, and it is generally agreed that the interepidemic interval was 2–3 years (Anderson & May, 1991).

In London, case mortality from measles (usually because of post-infective pneumonia) was about 14% in 1914 but fell sharply thereafter. This high mortality rate corresponds to that in underdeveloped countries today, where it is accepted as being linked to poor nutrition, low birth weight and vitamin A deficiency. Improved diet and vitamin A supplementation leads to a marked fall in the mortality of the disease (James, 1972; Barclay, Foster & Sommer, 1987; Berman, 1991). Reports from practitioners in England in the 18th century showed that a healthy child rarely died of measles; fatalities occurred in infants of weak constitution, particularly in members of the working class in the most populous centres (Creighton, 1894).

In the following sections, the origin and evolution of measles epidemics in London in earlier centuries (1629–1837) are traced using the annual deaths from the Bills of Mortality (Creighton, 1894). Measles became established as an endemic disease in London after about 1700, with superimposed epidemics. Far from being constant, the interepidemic interval

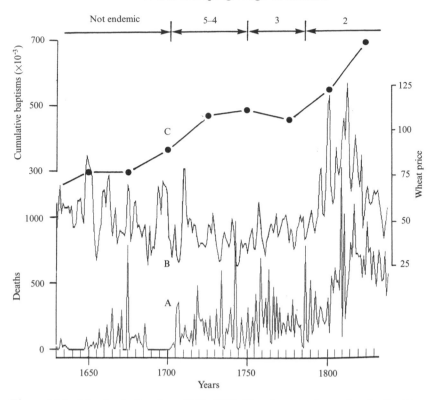

Figure 11.1. Measles in London, 1630–1837. Line A: annual measles deaths. Line B: annual wheat prices (shillings). Line C: cumulative number of baptisms in the preceding 25 years (thousands). Above: division into different interepidemic intervals. Data sources: Creighton (1894), Stratton (1970) and Wrigley & Schofield (1981).

changed progressively from 1700 to 1800. The disease had a high mortality rate and the numbers of deaths from measles rose sharply after 1785 associated, it is suggested, with a rising trend in wheat prices at that time, with consequent malnutrition and hardship.

11.2 Annual measles deaths in London

Annual deaths from measles in London from 1630 to 1837 are plotted in Fig. 11.1A and, although there are missing data points at the end of the 17th century, it can be seen that the disease was probably not truly endemic then, but became endemic in London after 1700, with a substantial number of deaths in each year and, during the period 1700–1785, the trend in measles mortality rose steadily. This trend (the endemic level) then rose sharply after 1785 (suggesting an increased susceptibility) but clearly fell again after 1812 (Fig. 11.1A). The annual wheat price series for this period is plotted in Fig. 11.1B and it can be seen that its trend after 1700 corresponds closely to that of the measles deaths series, with the same marked rise after 1785 and a fall after 1812. The trends in the two series cross-correlate ($P < 0.001$). This correspondence suggests that the rising trend in measles mortality may have been associated with an increased susceptibility which resulted from poorer nutritional standards. About 50% of food expenditure in England during the first half of the 18th century went on grain in the form of bread flour and ale but this proportion rose after 1785 during the period of high food prices and population pressure, particularly among the poorer classes (Walter & Schofield, 1989) and we conclude that the marked rise in the trend in measles mortality (and probably in susceptibility also) after 1785 (see Fig. 11.1A) was probably directly linked to the malnutrition of the poorer classes which stemmed from the rising grain prices (see Fig. 11.1B).

11.3 The interepidemic interval

Spectral analysis of the measles deaths series in the different periods shows that the wavelength of the oscillations (i.e. the interepidemic interval, T) changed progressively through the 18th century from 5–4 years, when the disease first became endemic, to 3 years and then to 2 years after 1785 (see Table 11.1 and Fig. 11.1). The epidemics are illustrated in the filtered deaths series in Fig. 11.2. Thus, the 2-yearly measles epidemics that were characteristic of developed countries in the early 20th century were firmly established in London by the end of the 18th century.

11.4 Effects of population size and density on the biology of measles epidemics

Equation 9.18 demonstrates theoretically how the periodicity of measles epidemics is dependent on the relative value of $N\beta$, i.e. the product of population size/density (N) and susceptibility to the disease (β). The predicted relative values of $N\beta$ calculated from Equation 9.18 for the different interepidemic intervals in the four cohorts is shown in Table 11.1 and the dynamics of the disease can be interpreted on this basis as follows. The cumulative total baptisms in London for each preceding 25-year period is plotted in Fig. 11.1, line C and this provides a relative measure of population size (N) in terms of susceptibles. During the period 1630–1700, measles

Table 11.1. *Measles epidemics at London. Interepidemic period, predicted mean age of contracting the disease and predicted Nβ in different periods. Coherence between measles epidemics and annual wheat prices or mean annual autumn temperatures are shown for the different short wavebands*

Cohort	T (yr)	Predicted age (yr)	Predicted Nβ	High wheat prices coherence Wavebands (yr)	Lag (yr)	Low autumn temperatures coherence Wavebands (yr)	Lag (yr)
I. 1700–1720	5/4	15/10	64	4–6***	2	4–6***; 3***	0
II. 1720–1750	4	10	85	5***	2	5**; 2–3***	0
III. 1750–1785	3	5	133	5***	2	3***	0
IV. 1785–1837	2	2	270	5***	2→3	5**; 3***; 2***	0

Notes:
** $P < 0.01$; *** $P < 0.001$.

T is the interepidemic period (determined by spectral analysis). Predicted mean age of contracting the disease derived from Equation 9.15. Predicted $N\beta$ derived from Equation 9.18, assuming $D = 15$ days.

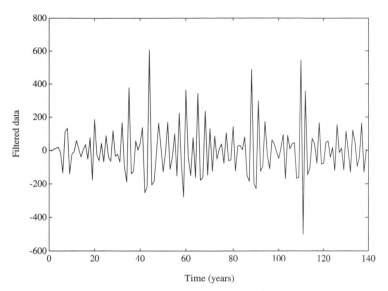

Figure 11.2. Annual measles deaths in London, 1700–1837 (the period when the disease was endemic) filtered to show the epidemics. Filter window = 2 to 6 years.

was not truly endemic; N and β were both low. The epidemics were irregular, but filtering and spectral analysis suggests that they were basically 3-yearly and cross-correlation tests suggest that they were probably triggered directly by fluctuating wheat prices. After 1700, as the population size (N) increased (indicated by the rising trend in Fig. 11.1, line C), measles became established as an endemic disease, initially with 5-yearly epidemics during cohort I (1700–1720) but changing to a pattern of stable 4-year epidemic intervals during cohort II (1725–1750), when relative $N\beta$ is calculated to be 85 (Table 11.1).

In cohort III (1750–1785), T shortened to 3 years, associated with a rising population size in London (Fig. 11.1, line C). Relative $N\beta$ for the 3-yearly epidemics in this cohort is calculated as 133 (Table 11.1); i.e. compared with the preceding period, calculated $N\beta$ rose 1.5 times whilst N rose only 1.1 times. We conclude that the rising population size at this time was not sufficient to account for the change in T and that the small rising trend in wheat prices (Fig. 11.1, line B) produced an increased susceptibility to the disease which contributed to the rise in $N\beta$ and the establishment of the 3-year period of the epidemics.

After 1785, 2-yearly measles epidemics became firmly established in London (Table 11.1), superimposed on the sharply-rising endemic death rate from the disease (Fig. 11.1, line A). The value of $N\beta$ for 2-yearly epidemics is calculated as 270, representing a doubling from the calculated $N\beta$ during the 3-yearly epidemics of the preceding period. Although the population was rising sharply after 1785 (Fig. 11.1, line C), the increase was only some 1.2–fold during the transition from 3- to 2-yearly epidemics. However, this was the period during which there was a marked rise in the trend of wheat prices (Fig. 11.1, line C), with associated hardship and malnutrition, and we conclude that this caused a marked increase in general susceptibility (β) which now made a major contribution to the rise in $N\beta$.

Thus, a progressive change in $N\beta$ in London during the 18th century would account for the observed change in the interepidemic period. Equation 9.19 predicts that as the periodicity of the epidemics fell, the average age of contracting the disease fell (see Table 11.1), so that in the first half of the 18th century the average age was probably 10–15 years, whereas this predicted value had fallen to just over 2 years after 1785. This conclusion is in agreement with the observation that the average age at death from measles declined over the 18th century and that most deaths from measles in the late 18th and in the 19th centuries were in children aged from 6 months to 3 years (Creighton, 1894). In the early years of the 18th century, with 5- to 4-yearly epidemics, even adults would be contracting measles, but as $N\beta$ rose, so the disease would be progressively confined to children as the adults became immune and eventually, after 1785, only very young children would remain as susceptibles.

11.5 Were the measles epidemics driven?

What drove the measles epidemics in London that are clearly seen in Fig. 11.2? Because the system is lightly damped (damping factor, $\zeta \approx 0.05$; Equation 9.15), the epidemics would decay only slowly and oscillations in susceptibility of only small amplitude would be necessary to drive such a system at its resonant frequency, ω_n, which is determined by $N\beta$ (Equation 9.17).

The cross-correlation between the measles and wheat prices series has been tested by coherence, cross-correlation function and by multiple regression in the different periods and the results are summarised in Table 11.1 in which the years 1700–1837 are divided into four cohorts identified by their different interepidemic periods (T). The two series are strongly and significantly ($P < 0.001$) correlated in the short wavebands but it was noteworthy that there was a 2-year lag in the coherence which changed to a 3-year lag after 1800, i.e. an oscillation in high wheat prices was followed by a measles epidemic with high mortality 2 or 3 years later.

The possible cross-correlation between the epidemics of measles mortality and mean annual seasonal temperatures was similarly tested, but only low mean autumn temperatures were consistently and significantly ($P <$ 0.001) correlated with the epidemics of the disease. The results are given in Table 11.1 and measles mortality and low autumn temperatures are strongly coherent in the short wavebands at zero lag, i.e. low autumn temperatures were directly associated with measles epidemics and mortality. However, in cohort IV (1785–1837) the epidemics became progressively more firmly established at 2-yearly intervals and the significance of their correlation with low autumn temperatures was reduced. Instead, after 1800, the epidemics correlated more closely with low spring temperatures ($P < 0.001$) in the 2-year waveband at zero lag. Spectral analysis of the seasonal temperature series during the years of the last cohort shows that it is only in spring temperatures that a 2-year oscillation is found; the other seasons show a 3-year oscillation (i.e. they were not at ω_r).

Thus, it is suggested that, during the 18th century, oscillations in autumn temperatures constituted an input of a seasonal fluctuation in susceptibility ($\delta\beta$) that directly drove the system at its resonant frequency. After 1800, the 2-year epidemics also cross-correlated with low spring temperature, the only season to show a 2-year periodicity by spectral analysis. At this time, with a rising population in London and high $N\beta$, the system was probably strongly geared to its 2-year resonant frequency and any seasonal drop in temperature was probably sufficient to produce a change in $\delta\beta$ that would trigger epidemics provided that it oscillated with a periodicity of 2 years.

These findings may be compared with the monthly notifications of measles (note, not deaths) in the USA and UK in the 20th century, which show a marked rise in incidence between September and December in both epidemic and non-epidemic years. Originally this was attributed to congregation at the start of the autumn term at school, but is more usually explained as a weather-related effect (Fine & Clarkson, 1982). The present study suggests that the effects of lowered temperatures in autumn in triggering epidemics at the resonant frequency of the system may date back to the start of measles as an endemic disease in a large population centre, nearly 300 years ago.

11.6 Effects of malnutrition during pregnancy on measles epidemics

The measles epidemics also cross-correlated with wheat prices ($P < 0.001$, Table 11.1; see above), although at a 2-year lag (and with a 3-year lag after 1800). Sharp, oscillatory rises in wheat prices in England during the 17th and 18th centuries led to a rise in neonatal mortality and subsequent impaired resistance to disease in very young children (Scott *et al.*, 1995; see also Chapter 7). It is suggested that the measles epidemics were also *indirectly* geared to oscillations in wheat prices: malnutrition in pregnancy produced a greater susceptibility (β) to measles in the very young progeny and hence a rise in the number of children dying in the next epidemic. Consequently, oscillations of malnutrition during pregnancy combined synergistically with lowered autumn temperatures to provide an oscillation in susceptibility ($\delta\beta$) of low amplitude which was sufficient to act as an input to drive the system at its resonant frequency of epidemics which was determined by $N\beta$. The frequency response of the system is very sharp because ζ is small, so that the epidemics would be driven preferentially by oscillations in $\delta\beta$ close to the resonant frequency.

Thus, the progressive rise in $N\beta$ determined the evolution of the measles epidemics in London during the 18th century from initially at 5-year intervals to finally at 2-year intervals which persisted into the 20th century until an extensive vaccination programme was promoted. Concomitantly, the mean age of contracting the disease fell progressively. With its dependence on population size/density, its sensitivity to inadequate nutrition and variations in susceptibility, measles in London in the 18th century would have had features in common with the dynamics of the disease in underdeveloped countries today (Editorial, *Lancet*, 1968; Bamgboye & Familusi 1990; Berman, 1991; Caldwell, 1996), where, with poor nutrition and inadequate medical services, measles is still a killing disease: pneumonia is the dreaded complication and mortality may be 25% or more (Christie, 1980). In the contemporary Third World and in historic Europe, famine or malnutrition often results in deaths from measles (Foster, 1984; Caldwell, 1996); infectious diseases (even those that the modern West regards as fairly innocuous) have been the greatest killer of children and the records for Sweden for the century following 1775 show both measles and whooping cough to have been major killers (Nelson, 1994). Malnutrition may interfere with the immune response to the measles virus: giant cells persist in nasal secretions and the illness is prolonged. Protein deficiency seems to be associated with a much higher incidence of complications, especially bronchopneumonia (Christie, 1980). Our results with the lagged effect of wheat prices suggests that the diet in pregnancy may be of particular importance in reducing susceptibility in the progeny. Furthermore, an understanding of the biology and dynamics of the disease would be relevant to any programme aimed at eliminating measles internationally (Fine, 1993); a global crisis is currently facing rich and poor nations and more than 17 million people die from infectious diseases each year, one million of them from measles.

11.7 Whooping cough epidemics in London

Whooping cough has not received the epidemiological attention given to measles (Wright, 1991), although there is general agreement that the inter-epidemic interval (T) in England and Wales in the 20th century was 3 years before mass immunization (Anderson & May, 1991; Howell & Jennings, 1992), in distinction from measles where it was 2 years (Anderson *et al.*, 1984). In this section we describe the origins and evolution of whooping cough epidemics in London in the 18th century, using the Bills of Mortality (Creighton, 1894) as a data source. Like measles, whooping cough was a major factor in infant mortality and we suggest that the pattern of epidemics of this disease in the 18th century is also relevant to conditions in under-developed countries today, where whooping cough remains abundant and is still a major cause of death in malnourished populations (Wright, 1991; Syedabubakar *et al.*, 1995). The risk factors include large family size, crowding, low birth weight, malnutrition and vitamin A deficiency (Berman, 1991).

Susceptibility to whooping cough is shown in the following sections to be governed by fluctuating levels of malnutrition that were directly associated with oscillations in wheat prices. During 1720–1785, the epidemics were maintained by fluctuating seasonal temperatures which interacted with oscillations in wheat prices, but (surprisingly) after 1785 the dynamics of the disease escaped from the pattern predicted by the mathematical theory that has been developed in sections 9.3 and 9.4.

11.8 Annual whooping cough death series in London, 1701–1812

Annual deaths from whooping cough in London, 1701–1812, are plotted in Fig. 11.3A and it can be seen that the disease was not endemic until 1720; thereafter the endemic trend rose progressively with regular epidemics superimposed and much more steeply after 1785. The English annual wheat price series over the same time scale is plotted in Fig. 11.3B and the trend in prices corresponds with the trend of the whooping cough series; the two series cross-correlate ($P < 0.001$). Although correlation does not prove causality, it is suggested that the marked rise in whooping cough mortality (and probably in susceptibility also) after 1785 (Fig. 11.3A) was directly linked to malnutrition (as with other infectious diseases in the 18th century)

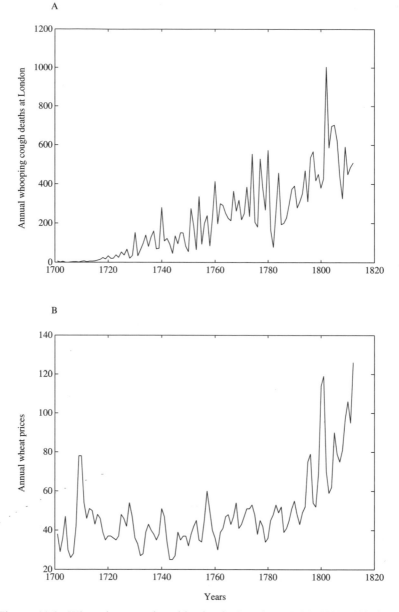

Figure 11.3. Whooping cough epidemics in London, 1701–1812. (A) Annual whooping cough deaths (ordinate). (B) Annual wheat price (shillings, ordinate). Data sources: Bills of Mortality (Creighton, 1894) and Stratton (1970).

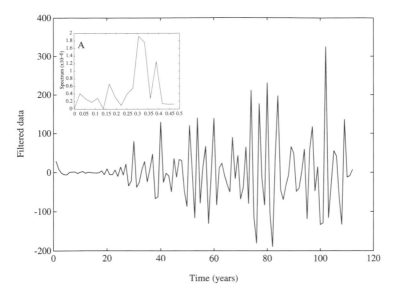

Figure 11.4. Annual whooping cough deaths in London, 1701–1812, filtered to show the emergence of the epidemics. Filter window = 2 to 7 years. Inset A: spectral analysis of the data series, 1750–1785, the period of the 3-yearly epidemics. Ordinate: power of spectrum. Abscissa: frequency.

which stemmed from the rising grain prices at that time (see Fig. 11.3B and section 11.2).

11.9 Periodicity of whooping cough epidemics

Spectral analysis of the whooping cough deaths series shows that the 18th century can be divided into different periods wherein the wavelength of the oscillations (i.e. the interepidemic interval, T) changed progressively. Between 1720 and 1750, as the epidemics emerged and became established, this interval fluctuated around 3 and 5 years, but during 1750–1785 the interepidemic interval changed clearly to 3 years and the amplitude of the epidemics increased (see Figs. 11.3 and 11.4). Spectral analysis for this middle period is shown in Fig. 11.4A. After 1785, associated with a rising endemic trend, the whooping cough epidemics again became less regular, but now with a basic periodicity of about 5 years. The epidemics throughout the whole period, 1701–1812, are shown in the filtered whooping cough deaths series in Fig. 11.4, which illustrates the development of the epidemics and the progressive increase in their amplitude.

The relative predicted values of $N\beta$ (the product of population size/density and susceptibility) for whooping cough calculated from Equation 9.19 are: 123 (for $T = 3$ years); 75 (for $T = 4$ years) and 53 (for $T = 5$ years) and the changing periodicity of the epidemics in London (see Table 11.2) can be interpreted on this basis as follows. The cumulative total baptisms in London for each preceding 25-year period (see Fig. 11.1C) provides a relative measure of population size (N) in terms of susceptibles. During the early years of the 18th century, 1700–1720, whooping cough was not endemic in London and N and β were low, but after 1720, following the population (N) increase, whooping cough became established as an endemic disease, with variable 5-yearly epidemics (1720–1750).

In cohort III, during 1750–1785, T shortened to 3 years and theoretical considerations suggest that $N\beta$ would have risen correspondingly from relative values of about 53 to 123. However, N was not rising markedly at this time and it is suggested that the rising trend in wheat prices (compared with the earlier falling trend during 1700–1740) caused an increase in susceptibility (β) and was a component of the increased $N\beta$ which caused a corresponding change in the resonant frequency of the system (ω_r) and in the interepidemic interval from a variable 5 to 3 years (Equation 9.19; see Table 11.2). This suggested increased sensitivity to whooping cough associated with rising wheat prices after 1785 corresponds with the findings for measles mortality at that time (see section 11.4) and, again, there is evidence for malnutrition having profound but subliminal effects on the population dynamics that are not readily detectable.

Concomitantly, it can be predicted from Equation 9.19 that the average age of catching whooping cough fell to 3 years during the period 1750–1785. In the early years of the century, as the disease became endemic in London and the 5-yearly epidemics evolved, even adults may have been contracting whooping cough, but as N and β rose, so the disease would be progressively confined to children.

11.10 Driving the epidemics

Figures 11.3A and 11.4 show clearly that the whooping cough epidemics did not decay during the 18th century in London; rather, they increased markedly in amplitude and the interepidemic interval was reduced and so it may be concluded that the system must have been driven.

The cross-correlation between whooping cough epidemics and the short wavelength oscillation in annual wheat prices was tested by the time-series techniques of coherence and cross-correlation. The two series are strongly coherent in the 5-year waveband ($P < 0.001$) at zero lag in the period

Table 11.2. *Characteristics of the whooping cough epidemics in London in the different cohorts*

Cohort	Observed T (yr)	Predicted mean age (yr)	Predicted $N\beta$	Estimated relative size of pool of susceptibles (thousands) (N)	Seasonal driver	Correlation with driver at 0 lag Coherence waveband (yr)	P	ccf	Whooping cough mortality vs wheat prices Coherence waveband (yr)	P	ccf	Lag
I. 1700–1720	Not endemic			405								
II. 1720–1750	5(3)	6–9	53	463	(i) Low autumn temp	5	<0.001	−0.22	5	<0.001	0.38	0
					(ii) Low winter temp	5	<0.001	−0.33				
III. 1750–1785	3	3	123	466	(i) High autumn temp	3	<0.001	0.38	3	<0.001	0.2	0
					(ii) Low winter temp	3	<0.001	−0.39				
IV. 1785–1812	5	8–9	53	550			NS		4–5	<0.001	0.41	1

Notes:

NS, not significant.

T was determined by spectral analysis. Predicted mean age of contracting whooping cough was determined from Equation 9.19, assuming $D = 27$ days (Anderson & May, 1991). Predicted relative $N\beta$ for each value of T was derived from Equation 9.18. Relative values of N were derived from the cumulative number of baptisms in London for the preceding 25 years (from Wrigley & Schofield, 1981).

1720–1750 and we conclude that the strong 5-year oscillation in wheat prices (clearly seen in Fig. 11.3B) caused a corresponding oscillation in susceptibility and so directly drove the whooping cough epidemics.

The correlation between the whooping cough epidemics and seasonal temperatures was also tested and strong coherence ($P < 0.001$) was found with both mean low winter and mean low autumn temperatures at zero lag in the 5-year and other short wavebands in cohort II, 1720–1750.

However, in cohort III, 1750–1785 (when the interepidemic interval, T, was 3 years; see Fig. 11.4A), the whooping cough and wheat price series were strongly coherent in the 3-year waveband ($P < 0.001$) at zero lag. The whooping cough series was also strongly coherent with mean low winter ($P < 0.001$) and (surprisingly) with mean *high* autumn temperatures ($P < 0.001$) in the 3-year waveband.

In summary, seasonal temperatures were the dominant factors driving the epidemics during cohorts II and III, but the whooping cough epidemics also cross-correlated directly with the oscillation in the wheat price series and we conclude that oscillations in both seasonal temperatures (in autumn and winter) and in wheat prices acted synergistically to produce the oscillation in susceptibility (transmission coefficient, $\delta\beta$, Equations 9.13 and 9.14) that drove the system, maintaining the epidemics at the resonant frequency, ω_r, of the system which was determined by $N\beta$ (see Table 11.2). Thus, during the period 1750–1785 the whooping cough epidemics in London became established in the pattern that was shown later in the 20th century in England (Anderson & May, 1991).

11.11 Dynamics of whooping cough epidemics after 1785

In cohort IV (when T lengthened again to $\sim$5 years and the amplitude of the epidemics was reduced), seasonal temperatures were found to have no significant driving effects, whereas the whooping cough series was again strongly coherent in the 4–5-year waveband with wheat prices ($P < 0.001$), but now at a lag of 1 year, i.e. high wheat prices were significantly associated with a peak of whooping cough epidemics in the following year. Clearly, the dynamics of the disease changed after 1785, with a rise in T suggesting a fall in $N\beta$ (Equation 9.18), and yet the population size (N), the trend in wheat prices and the endemic level of whooping cough were all rising sharply at this time and it is evident that $N\beta$ would have remained high after 1785 and the resonant frequent of the system would have been unaltered at 3 years (or even reduced to 2 years). Why did the interepidemic period paradoxically lengthen to 5 years after 1785, when theoretical considerations suggest that it should not change? The whooping cough epidemics ceased to be correlated with seasonal temperatures at this time and we conclude that there was no suitable environmental driver at the resonant frequency of the system (3 years). However, the epidemics were now strongly correlated with the 5-year oscillation in wheat prices, although with a 1-year lag. The rising trend in wheat prices (Fig. 11.3B) and in the endemic level of whooping cough (Fig. 11.3A) suggest that malnutrition was causing a marked increase in susceptibility to the disease and was now the dominant factor in generating a 5-year oscillation in β and so driving the epidemics, but not at the resonant frequency of the system. Instead, the epidemics were oscillating at the frequency of a driver that was closest to its resonant frequency (ω_r). Since $N\beta$ was high, the damping factor, ζ, remained high at > 0.09 (equivalent to a predicted, but not actual, inter-epidemic interval of 3 years) instead of 0.06, as would be predicted by $T = 5$ (Equation 9.19), so that the system could be driven at a frequency different from (but close to) its resonant frequency provided that there was a marked rise in the amplitude of the oscillations of β, i.e. the force of the driver would have to be increased. In this way, the system became locked onto the 5-year oscillation in wheat prices which generated the driving oscillation in susceptibility.

In addition to its dominant effect on ω_r, $N\beta$ also affects the amplitude of the periodic driving term. Substituting Equations 9.9 and 9.10 into ($\mu + \nu)y_0 \, \delta\beta \sin \omega t$ gives the periodic driving term $\mu\{1-[(\mu + \nu)/N\beta]\}\delta\beta \sin \omega t$, where the amplitude is defined by $\mu\{1 - [(\mu + \nu)/N\beta]\}\delta\beta$. Thus, an increase in N (e.g. population size/density) will amplify the effect of the oscillations in susceptibility ($\delta\beta$), i.e. the more crowded the population, the bigger the effect of a standard oscillation in $\delta\beta$. Since N in London was rising sharply at this time, the effect of oscillations in susceptibility ($\delta\beta$) will be amplified.

There are two consequences predicted by the theory of linear dynamic systems which support the conclusions above if the whooping cough epidemics were not driven at the resonant frequency, ω_r, during cohort IV (1785–1812). Firstly, the magnitude of the effect will be reduced, i.e. the amplitude of the oscillations (or epidemics) will fall and this is shown during the years 1780–1800 in Fig. 11.3A. Secondly, as the driving frequency is increased, the lag becomes greater (as happens with similar systems such as smallpox; see the frequency response, or Bode, diagrams shown in Fig. 10.11 and Duncan *et al.*, 1994a), which agrees with the observation that the whooping cough epidemics lagged the peaks of the wheat price series by 1 year during 1785–1812.

11.12 Conclusions: whooping cough in underdeveloped countries today

Thus, as we have shown for measles (see above), the evolution of the whooping cough epidemics in London is also consistent with a linearised model, where T is determined by population size and susceptibility to the disease, which is a direct result of malnutrition; the epidemics are driven by an oscillation in susceptibility that is linked to seasonal low temperatures. However, the dynamics of the system appear to escape from the simple application of mathematical modelling after 1785; apparently there was no satisfactory seasonal driver at this time and susceptibility was determined primarily by the 5-year oscillation in wheat prices and the system does not oscillate at its natural frequency (ω_r) determined by $N\beta$.

Once again, therefore, we have an example where malnutrition has a profound, but hidden, effect on population cycles. With its dependence on population and crowding, its sensitivity to inadequate nutrition and variations in susceptibility, whooping cough in the 18th century in London would have had many features in common with the dynamics of the disease in underdeveloped countries today, where severe malnutrition may be seasonal as a result of crop cycles (Keusch, 1991). A major whooping cough epidemic occurred in Cape Town in 1947, before the widespread use of whooping cough vaccine, causing 107 deaths (Strebel *et al.*, 1991). These results suggest that, as well as the extensive use of vaccination, attention should also be paid to the amelioration of malnutrition as a means of controlling the epidemic and endemic lethal levels of whooping cough. Children in the developing world today constitute the largest population with acquired immunodeficiency because of the consequences of malnutrition on the immune system (Keusch, 1991) and mortality from whooping cough in developing countries approaches or exceeds that seen 100 years ago in the industrialised world (Wright, 1991).

11.13 Demographic analysis of the interacting effects of three lethal infectious diseases

The dynamics of measles and whooping cough epidemics have been described in detail in this chapter and the biology and modelling of smallpox epidemics have been presented in Chapters 9 and 10. In this section we present an analysis of the interactions of these three lethal infectious diseases and their impact on the demography of London during 1750 to 1812, the period when the epidemics were at their height and these diseases were responsible for a dreadful mortality among children.

11.13.1 Features of the biology of the three diseases in London

Analysis of the London Bills of Mortality show that smallpox, measles and whooping cough had a number of features in common and the following points can be established:

(1) The lethal effects of the three diseases emerged at about the same time in London – smallpox and measles in the second half of the 17th century although whooping cough was not diagnosed as having a major effect until after 1700.

(2) The mortality from smallpox exceeded that from whooping cough and measles combined by at least 4 to 1.

(3) All three diseases show a progressively rising endemic level through the 18th century linked to rises in the size of the London population and probably to greater susceptibility ($N\beta$), although smallpox mortality stabilized at the end of the century, probably associated with the effects of inoculation.

(4) There is a common pattern in that there was a sharp rise in the endemic level of the three diseases after 1750, apparently linked to the concomitant rise in wheat prices which, it is suggested, caused a rise in susceptibility and an accompanying increase in $N\beta$.

(5) One consequence of a progressively rising $N\beta$ during the 18th century was the evolution of the pattern of epidemics with a progressive shortening of T until the 'climax' was reached at the end of the century with a very short interepidemic interval indeed (2 or 3 years). It was for this reason that the period 1750–1812 was chosen for special study (see below).

(6) Analysis and modelling suggest that the results are consistent with the hypothesis that the epidemics were driven at ω_r by an oscillation in susceptibility, the frequency of which was at, or close to, ω_r (whooping cough around 1800 was an exception, see section 11.11). This oscillation in $\delta\beta$ was linked to seasonal weather conditions.

(7) Rising wheat prices caused rising prices of the staple food in London and consequently the poorer classes suffered from malnutrition. Rising wheat prices and malnutrition had some of their most important (but not immediately obvious) effects on the demography of London via an exacerbation of the mortality of children from these infectious diseases. Malnutrition affected the dynamics of these diseases in London in two quite different ways. Firstly, it changed the overall susceptibility and so amplified $N\beta$ and, secondly, the short wavelength oscillation in wheat prices could have contributed synergistically to the driving oscillation in $\delta\beta$ (particularly in whooping cough after 1785).

Table 11.3. *Interepidemic interval (T) and seasonal drivers of lethal infectious diseases in London, 1750–1812*

	1750–1785		1785–1812	
	T (yr)	Seasonal drivers	T (yr)	Seasonal drivers
Smallpox	2	Low autumn rain Low spring rain	2	Low autumn rain Low spring rain
Whooping cough	3	High autumn temperature Low winter temperature Wheat prices	5	Wheat prices
Measles	3	Low autumn temperature	2	Low autumn temperature

In conclusion, this comparative study of mortality in London suggests that all three diseases were systems that were driven and that it is not necessary to suggest that the epidemics were maintained by stochastic, spatial or age-structure effects.

11.13.2 Interactions between the three lethal diseases

The interepidemic intervals of smallpox, measles and whooping cough in London during the period 1750–1812 are shown in Table 11.3 and cross-correlation analysis between the three series (Table 11.4) shows that, in general, the measles epidemics did not occur in years when smallpox or whooping cough were epidemic and the lags suggest that the smallpox and measles epidemics came in alternate years. This observation is in agreement with the different seasonal drivers for the two diseases: smallpox epidemics correlated with dry conditions in autumn and spring, whereas measles was driven by low temperatures in autumn (Table 11.3). The epidemics of whooping cough tended to synchronise with those of smallpox; the diseases had different drivers, although whooping cough was also strongly linked to wheat prices. All the correlations became weaker after 1785.

11.13.3 Effects of the deaths from infectious diseases on the population dynamics in London

The mean annual deaths from each of the three infectious diseases are presented in Table 11.5, which shows that deaths from smallpox in the

Table 11.4. *Correlation between the epidemics of smallpox, whooping cough and measles in London, 1750–1812*

Cohort		Smallpox v. measles	Smallpox v. whooping cough	Whooping cough v. measles
1750–1784	Phase shift	180°	0°	180°
	ccf	−0.15	+0.25	−0.4
	Notes	Positive correlation at −1 year	Negative correlation at −1 year	Positive correlation at −1 year
1785–1812	Phase shift	270°	0°	180°
	ccf	Weak correlation	Weak correlation	−0.2

Table 11.5. *Mean annual deaths from smallpox, measles and whooping cough in London in the 18th century*

Years	Smallpox	Measles	Whooping cough	Total
1701–1749	1888	154	55	2097
1750–1799	2018	230	296	2544
1800–1812	1229	526	632	2387
1701–1812	1869	231	230	2330

Note:
Data taken from the London Bills of Mortality (Creighton, 1894).

18th century were some four-fold greater than the combined deaths from measles and whooping cough. In this section we consider the contribution made by these deaths to the overall mortality cycles in London in the period 1750–1812. The mortality from the three diseases in each year (which would have been mostly the result of childhood deaths) are subtracted from the annual total mortality in London and the residuals are plotted in Fig. 11.5, which shows short and medium wavelength oscillations, but the 2–3-year oscillation has now been lost, suggesting that it was predominantly associated with smallpox deaths. The residual mortality, compounded mainly of infant and adult deaths, now shows a progressive fall.

Spectral analysis of the series of residuals (1750–1812) that is illustrated in Fig. 11.5 shows two dominant short wavelength oscillations at 8 and 6 years. During this period the wheat price series also displayed a strong short wavelength oscillation which spectral analysis shows to be in the 5- and 8-year wavebands during 1750–1785, but predominantly at 5 years after 1785. Did wheat prices contribute to driving the cycles in infant and adult mortality? As we have seen in previous chapters, wheat prices rose sharply after 1785 causing, it is suggested, a rise in susceptibility and a change in the dynamics of smallpox, measles and whooping cough epidemics in London. In contrast, the residual mortality shown in Fig. 11.5 clearly falls steadily during this period, confirming that the major effect of the *trend* in wheat prices was the exacerbation of child mortality from the lethal diseases. Adult and infant deaths were falling at this time in spite of an increasing population in London.

However, the wheat series and the residual mortality of Fig. 11.5 cross-correlate significantly in the short waveband and these studies may be summarised as follows:

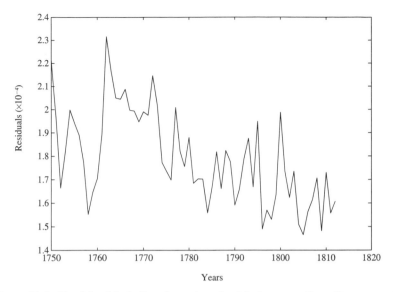

Figure 11.5. Total burials in London minus burials because of smallpox, measles and whooping cough ('residuals series'), 1750–1812 (ordinate). Steadily falling trend.

1750–1784: positive cross-correlation with 1- to 2-years lag; ccf = +0.65; coherence, $P < 0.01$ in the 5- to 8-year waveband.

1785–1812: positive cross-correlation at 0- to 1-year lag; ccf = +0.55; coherence, $P < 0.001$ in the 6- to 10-year waveband.

This suggests that the short wavelength oscillation in the mortality of the residuals is associated with raised wheat prices. Malnutrition could affect the mortality of both infants (acting via pregnancy for neonates and via suckling and weaning for post-neonates, as described in section 7.6) and adults (via deaths in the weak and elderly). Rising wheat prices probably also promoted the influx of people from the country on a cyclical basis (see section 9.10 and Landers, 1986) which may have contributed to the deaths which were not associated with the three infectious diseases.

To conclude: the studies presented in this section have shown how the dynamics of smallpox, measles and whooping cough interacted with, and contributed to, the overall demography of London in the 18th century. It also reveals evidence for the hitherto undetected effects of nutrition on the mortality of adults and infants, in addition to its effects on susceptibility to infectious diseases.

12

Integration of the dynamics of infectious diseases with the demography of London

The results of a time-series analysis of smallpox mortality in London are given in Chapter 9 and are shown in Chapter 10 to be consistent with linearised and non-linear models in which the epidemics are driven by an oscillation in susceptibility ($\delta\beta$) produced by seasonal climatic conditions when the frequency of this is at, or close to, ω_r. These mathematical models are, necessarily, simplified and are not integrated into the population dynamics. An extended model of a driven system is introduced in this chapter; it includes the mortality from smallpox, the rate of vaccination and changes in population size. These are potentially important factors where the disease is lethal and a substantial proportion of those infected die or where the population is increasing steadily (as in London in the 18th century). The objectives of this modelling of the smallpox epidemics in London are:

(1) To test the robustness of the model when these additional parameters are included and to confirm, in particular, that the system can be driven by an oscillation in $\delta\beta$.

(2) To simulate the pattern and detailed characteristics of the smallpox epidemics in London and so verify the model.

(3) To study the effect of varying the parameters, for example $\delta\beta$ or the proportion of the infectives dying, on the behaviour of the model. From such studies it is possible to predict some details of the epidemiology and biology of the disease in London in the 18th century, before the major impact of inoculation and vaccination.

(4) To integrate the smallpox epidemics with the overall population dynamics of London. Some of these interactions of epidemiology and demography has been described previously; for example, it is suggested that the long wavelength cycle in smallpox mortality in London, that is evident during the later part of the 17th century and continues in the

18th century, is the consequence of a corresponding population cycle that follows the Great Plague (section 9.11). In addition, the secondary, 5-year oscillation in smallpox is suggested to be the consequence of the cyclical immigration of susceptibles following the 5-year oscillation in wheat prices (section 9.10; Landers, 1993).

12.1 Incorporation of the death rate from the disease into the mathematical model

The further development of the full, non-linear model presented in section 10.5 is described in this section, but readers who do not welcome the mathematics can proceed directly to section 12.2. In this modelling, the population is not assumed to remain constant.

A simple model of the disease uses the coupled differential Equations 9.1 to 9.4 to describe the rate of transmission between the different classes of the population. These equations can be replaced by:

$$dX/dt = \gamma N(t) - \mu X(t) - \eta X(t) - \beta(t)X(t)Y(t) \tag{12.1}$$
$$dY/dt = \beta(t)X(t)Y(t) - \mu Y(t) - \nu Y(t) - \alpha Y(t) \tag{12.2}$$
$$dZ/dt = \eta X(t) + \nu Y(t) - \mu Z(t) \tag{12.3}$$

where

$X(t)$ is the number of susceptibles;
$Y(t)$ is the number of infectives;
$Z(t)$ is the number of immunes;
γ is the birth rate;
μ is the death rate *excluding* deaths owing to smallpox;
η is the rate of vaccination, see section 12.7;
ν is the rate of recovery;
α is the death rate because of the disease;
$\beta(t)$ is the 'force' of the infection.

Since the total size of the population, $N(t)$, satisfies $N(t) = X(t) + Y(t) + Z(t)$, the third differential equation can be replaced by:

$$dN/dt = (\mu + \nu)X(t) + (\mu + \nu)Y(t) - \mu N(t) \tag{12.4}$$

The rate of death excluding those resulting from smallpox is determined from the average age at death, which varied significantly over the period of study from around 20 years in the period 1700 to 1749 to nearly 35 years after 1800 (Landers, 1993). Consequently, μ changed from 1/20 to 1/35 over the period of study. N did not remain constant but changed with time.

If the force of infection remains constant, so that $\beta(t) = \beta_0$, the behaviour of the population depends upon the difference between the birth rate, γ, and the rate at which people are dying, both because of the disease and from other causes. We are concerned in this modelling with the effects of periodic changes in the force of the infection about a mean level, β_0, so that $\beta(t)$ is assumed to have the form

$$\beta(t) = \beta_0 + \beta_1 \sin \omega t \tag{12.5}$$

where ω is the frequency of the periodic variation and β_1 its magnitude. If $X_0(t)$, $Y_0(t)$ and $N_0(t)$ denote the solution of the differential equations when $\beta(t) = \beta_0$, then it is convenient to define

$$X(t) = X_0(t) + X_1(t) \tag{12.6}$$
$$Y(t) = Y_0(t) + Y_1(t) \tag{12.7}$$
$$N(t) = N_0(t) + N_1(t) \tag{12.8}$$

where $X_1(t)$, $Y_1(t)$ and $N_1(t)$ denote the *variations* from the solution obtained when β_0 is constant. Substituting these expressions into the differential Equations 12.1, 12.2 and 12.4 leads to

$$\begin{bmatrix} \dot{X}_1(t) \\ \dot{Y}_1(t) \\ \dot{N}_1(t) \end{bmatrix} = A(t) \begin{bmatrix} X_1(t) \\ Y_1(t) \\ N_1(t) \end{bmatrix} + b(t) \sin \omega t + \begin{bmatrix} -1 \\ 1 \\ 0 \end{bmatrix} f(X_1(t), Y_1(t), \beta_1) \tag{12.9}$$

where

$$A(t) = \begin{bmatrix} -\mu - \eta - \beta_0 Y_0(t) & -\beta_0 X_0(t) & \gamma \\ \beta_0 Y_0(t) & \beta_0 X_0(t) - \mu - \nu - \alpha & 0 \\ \mu + \eta & \mu + \nu & -\mu \end{bmatrix} \tag{12.10}$$

$$b(t) = \begin{bmatrix} -\beta_1 X_0(t) Y_0(t) \\ \beta_1 X_0(t) Y_0(t) \\ 0 \end{bmatrix} \tag{12.11}$$

and:

$$f(X_1(t), Y_1(t), \beta_1) = \beta_0 X_1(t) Y_1(t) + X_0(t) Y_1(t)\beta_1 \sin \omega t$$
$$+ X_1(t) Y_0(t)\beta_1 \sin \omega t + X_1(t) Y_1(t)\beta_1 \sin \omega t \tag{12.12}$$

The term $f(X_1(t), Y_1(t), \beta_1)$ describes the non-linearities inherent within the system, but in cases where the variations in the force of the infections are small, the system can be approximated by the (time-varying) *linear* system:

$$\begin{bmatrix} \dot{X}_1(t) \\ \dot{Y}_1(t) \\ \dot{N}_1(t) \end{bmatrix} = A(t) \begin{bmatrix} X_1(t) \\ Y_1(t) \\ N_1(t) \end{bmatrix} + b(t)\sin\omega t \qquad (12.13)$$

As will be seen below, this approximation is reasonable when one is modelling variations in the number of infectives around an endemic level. The time-varying nature of the linear system is a result of the changes in $X_0(t)$ and $Y_0(t)$ because of the increasing population size. For the birth rates and death rates appropriate for London during the period under study, these values are changing slowly relative to the oscillations in the force of the infection. As a result, the behaviour of the system can be determined by the roots of the characteristic equation. For the values of the parameters used in the model, the characteristic equation takes the form

$$(s - q)(s^2 + 2\zeta\omega_n + \omega_n^2) \qquad (12.14)$$

where there are a complex conjugate pair of roots in the left-half plane and a real root at $s = q$, which lies in the right-half plane. This unstable real root is a consequence of the increase in the population because the birth rate exceeds the death rate. Because the rate of population growth is relatively slow, q is small and this root is close to the origin of the s-plane.

The presence of the complex conjugate pair of roots indicates that the system has a resonance at frequency

$$\omega_r = \omega_n\sqrt{1-2\zeta^2} \qquad (12.15)$$

If q is taken to be small, then the natural frequency of the system, ω_n, can be approximated by

$$\begin{aligned} \omega_n^2 \approx &-\mu\beta_0 X_0(t) + \mu(\mu + \nu + \alpha) + \mu(\mu + \eta + \beta_0 Y_0(t)) \\ &-\beta_0 X_0(t)(\mu + \eta + \beta_0 Y_0(t)) + (\mu + \nu + \alpha)(\mu + \eta + \beta_0 Y_0(t)) \\ &+\beta_0^2 X_0(t) Y_0(t) - \gamma(\mu+\eta) \end{aligned} \qquad (12.16)$$

Similarly, ζ, the damping factor for the resonance is approximately given by

$$\zeta \approx \frac{3\mu + \eta + \nu + \alpha + \beta_0(Y_0(t) - X_0(t))}{2\omega_n} \qquad (12.17)$$

For typical values of the parameters used in this model, ζ is small, indicating that the system is lightly damped and, as a result, will amplify any periodic variations in the force of infection, $\beta(t)$ that have a frequency close to ω_r.

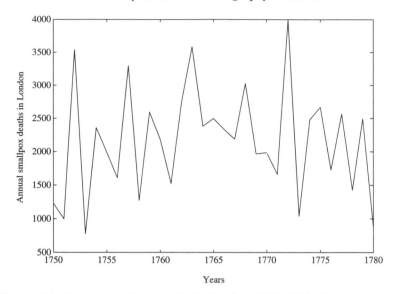

Figure 12.1. Annual smallpox deaths in London, 1750–1780, the period selected for modelling in section 12.3.

12.2 Criteria to be satisfied by the model

The modelling is based on the London smallpox mortality in cohort III that is shown in Fig. 9.1 and the starting point for running the model is 1750; the smallpox deaths for the next 30 years are shown in detail in Fig. 12.1. The population of London at that time is estimated to be 6.8×10^5, which rose over 30 years to 8.2×10^5, and the mid-range life expectancy was 29.7 years for males and 27.9 years for females (Landers, 1993). The period of the epidemics was 2 years in cohort III, and in 1750 the endemic level of annual deaths from smallpox was some 800 superimposed on which were some additional 2200 deaths in the epidemics (see Figs. 9.1 and 12.1), and in the modelling that follows the epidemic ratio is defined as:

$$\frac{\text{(total number dying in an epidemic year)} - \text{(endemic level)}}{\text{endemic level}}$$

12.3 Modelling the London smallpox mortality in 1750–1780

The basic variables used in the model were based on the conclusions in the previous section and the theoretical considerations developed in Chapters 9 and 10:

Age at death, $\mathring{e}_0$ = 30 years.

Average infectious period = 25 days. This has been extended from the value quoted by Anderson & May (1991) to allow for infectivity via the crusts.

Initial size of population of London in 1750 = 6.8×10^5.

Interepidemic interval, T = 2 years.

$N\beta$ = 250.

The other, 'optional', variables in the model were then set to simulate the population dynamics and the characteristics of smallpox mortality shown in Fig. 12.1 as follows:

Fraction of infectives dying from smallpox = 0.45.

Magnitude of the oscillation in $\delta\beta$ = 0.12.

Ratio of the number of births to deaths, *excluding* deaths from smallpox = 2.15.

Period of variation in $\delta\beta$ = 2 years (i.e. at ω_r).

The effect of vaccination (η) is not considered in this initial modelling.

The number of infectives in the population in each of the following 30 years is shown in Fig. 12.2A; the mean number and the endemic level of infectives rises steadily, whereas the number of infectives in the epidemic years remains steady at 6000. The fraction of the population infected in the epidemics is shown in Fig. 12.2B and the corresponding annual number of deaths is shown in Fig. 12.2C. Even with some 3000 deaths in the epidemics, the model shows that the population would grow over 30 years from 6.8 $\times 10^5$ to 8.4×10^5 (Fig. 12.2D), corresponding to the population growth in London (section 12.2) and it is concluded that Fig. 12.2C closely mirrors the dynamics of smallpox mortality in London for the 30 years after 1750, as shown in Fig. 12.1. The early epidemic mortality of some 2200 deaths superimposed on an endemic level of some 800, a rising basal endemic level with time, a T of 2 years, $\mathring{e}_0$ and the rising level of the population in London (Fig. 12.2D) predicted by the model all agree with the criteria laid down in section 12.2. The modelling therefore tells us a great deal about the epidemiology and demography that underlies the annual smallpox mortality shown in Fig. 12.1: (a) changes with time of the annual number of infectives (Fig. 12.2A), (b) the fraction of the population infected (Fig. 12.2B), and (c) the progressive, albeit fluctuating, rise in the population of London (Fig. 12.2D).

Changing the values chosen for the variables shows that the model system operates under tight constraints: the characteristics of the

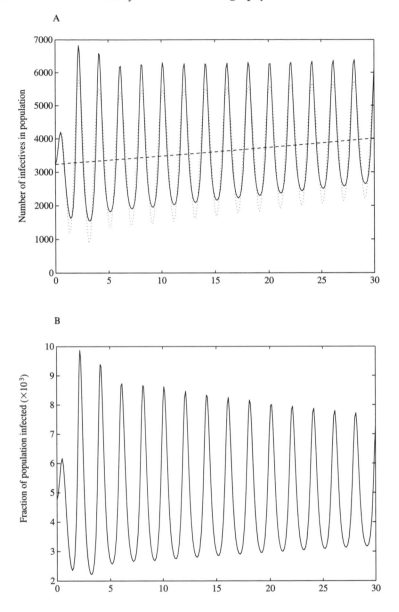

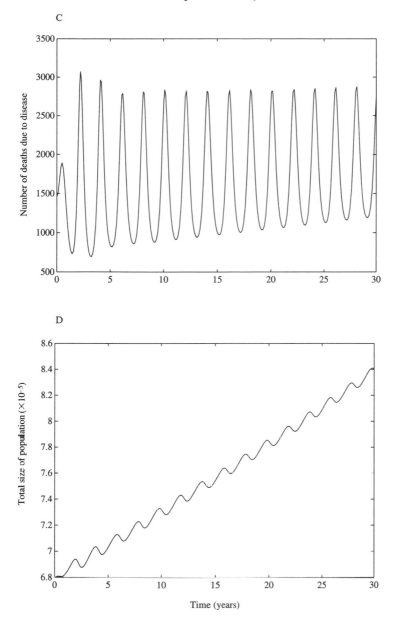

Figure 12.2. Results of running the smallpox model for 30 years to show the changes in the dynamics of the epidemics and population size. Abscissa: time (years). (A) Predicted number of infectives in London (ordinate). (B) Predicted fraction of population infected (ordinate). (C) Predicted number of deaths because of smallpox (ordinate), compare with Fig. 12.1. (D) Predicted changes in the total population size of London (ordinate).

epidemics, particularly the heavy smallpox mortality experienced in London, cannot be replicated if any of the optional variables are markedly changed. The striking features of the modelling are, firstly, the high value (0.12) that is predicted for the magnitude of the oscillation in susceptibility ($\delta\beta$) needed to drive the system. This is in contrast with the much lower amplitude of $\delta\beta$ predicted for measles (section 12.6) or scarlet fever (section 14.9). Secondly, the model also predicts that mortality from smallpox was very high, with 45% of those infected dying from the disease, a value that is very much higher than is suggested in rural towns at this time (see Chapter 13 and Razzell, 1977).

These surprisingly high values were tested by fine-tuning the model, with small changes in either $\delta\beta$ or in the fraction of infectives dying. The magnitude of $\delta\beta$ was changed over the range 0.08 to 0.14; raising the value to 0.14 exaggerated the epidemic/endemic ratio above that seen in Fig. 12.2B, whereas changing $\delta\beta$ from 0.12 to only 0.11 reduced both the total number of deaths and the epidemic/endemic ratio. When $\delta\beta$ is reduced to 0.08, the model predicts that total deaths in the epidemic years were only some 2400 and the epidemic/endemic ratio would fall to 1.6.

The fraction of infectives dying in the model was changed over the range 0.35 to 0.5. Raising the fraction from the standard value of 0.45 used in the modelling to 0.5 resulted in much too small a population growth together with a very high epidemic/endemic ratio. In contrast, the population rose enormously to over one million if the fraction was reduced to 0.35.

12.4 Modelling smallpox mortality in London during cohort II
(1710–1740)

For comparison, the mortality in cohort II, when the interepidemic interval was 3 years, is modelled in this section, starting at 1710. Maximum deaths in the epidemic years were some 3000, which compounded 1800 epidemic and 1200 endemic deaths (see Fig. 12.3, which shows the annual smallpox deaths in London from 1710 to 1740). The following parameters were therefore chosen:

Initial population of London in 1710: 6×10^5 (Landers, 1993).
Population of London in 1740: 6.7×10^5.
Average infectious period: 25 days (as above).
$N\beta = 139$.
$T = 3$ years.
Period of variation in $\delta\beta = 3$ years.
Average age at death, $\overset{\circ}{e}_0$: 20 years (Landers, 1993).

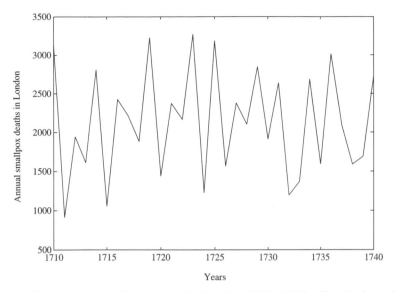

Figure 12.3. Annual smallpox deaths in London, 1710–1740 (ordinate), the period selected for modelling in section 12.4.

The 'optional' variables that gave the response of the model which corresponded with the criteria above and the annual deaths shown in Fig. 12.3 were

Ratio of births to deaths *excluding* deaths because of smallpox: 1.86.
Fraction of infectives dying from smallpox: 0.45.
Magnitude of $\delta\beta$: 0.12.

The number of smallpox deaths predicted by the model is illustrated in Fig. 12.4, with over 3000 in the first epidemic and an epidemic/endemic ratio of 1800/1200, corresponding to Fig. 12.3. The population numbers predicted by the model rose in an oscillatory fashion to 6.7×10^5 after 30 years and, again, the model provides a good approximation to the events in cohort II.

In conclusion, the extended model developed in this chapter not only confirms the findings of the earlier modelling of driven systems but greatly increases our understanding of the underlying dynamics, as will be shown in the next section. Biological systems are invariably noisy and obviously the modelling will not replicate exactly the fluctuations in the mortality in London which is not a 'fully stirred' system. Changes in $\overset{o}{e}_0$ over time, fluctuating immigration of susceptibles, changes in N producing a change in $N\beta$ and changes in nutritive levels in the short and medium term, modifying β, will all have modulating effects.

Figures 12.1 and 12.3 show that the total number of smallpox deaths and

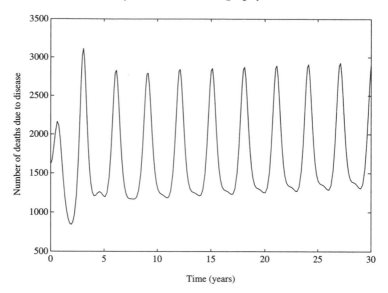

Figure 12.4. Prediction from the modelling of the number of smallpox deaths in London, 1710–1740 (ordinate). Compare with Fig. 12.3.

the epidemic/endemic ratios were broadly comparable in 1710 and 1750 and yet the underlying demographic features were very different. The population size was smaller in 1710; the average age at death ($\overset{\circ}{e}_0$) changed markedly between 1710 and 1750 (Landers, 1993), which would have had a marked effect on the dynamics of the epidemics; the interepidemic period was 3 years in 1710 and 2 years in 1750. However, in spite of these differences, the values of the fundamental variables in the model necessary to replicate the smallpox mortality series remained the same, with the fraction of the infectives dying = 0.45 and the magnitude of the oscillation in $\delta\beta = 0.12$, suggesting that the basic biology of the disease was unchanged and the major difference in the dynamics lay in the change of $N\beta$.

12.5 The effect of changing the variables on the response of the model

The following variables that we have applied to the model have been changed progressively: (a) $\delta\beta$, (b) ratio of births/deaths, (c) fraction of infectives dying, (d) length of infectious period, (e) initial population size, (f) $\overset{\circ}{e}_0$, and (g) $N\beta$. The responses of the model have been monitored by determining the variation in the predicted values of (a) ratio of epidemic/endemic deaths, (b) average number of infectives, and (c) number of deaths at the peak of the epidemics, and the findings are summarised in Table 12.1.

Table 12.1. *Summary of the effects of a progressive increase in each variable on the output of the smallpox model*

Variable	Effects			
	Epidemic/endemic ratio	Mean number of infectives	Total deaths in epidemic years	Changes in population size
Variation in $\delta\beta$	Rises as $\delta\beta$ rises	Constant	Rises as $\delta\beta$ rises	Constant
Births/deaths ratio	Falls exponentially	Rises linearly	U-shaped response	Rises rapidly at > 1.45 Falls slowly at < 1.4
Fraction of infectives dying	Rises progressively but irregularly	Constant	Rises linearly	Falls at > 0.35 Rises at < 0.35
Infectious period (D)	Falls exponentially	Rises linearly	Rises quasi-exponentially	Falls slightly, linearly
Population size (N)	Rises slightly but irregularly	Rises linearly	Rises linearly	Percentage rise constant
Life expectancy ($\mathring{e}_0$)	Rises exponentially (but very flat over ages 15–23 years)	Falls exponentially	Complex. Min at $\mathring{e}_0 = 23$yr. Max at $\mathring{e}_0 = 33$yr.	Falls
$N\beta$	Complex. Max at $N\beta = 130$	Constant	Complex. Max at $N\beta = 130$	Falls exponentially

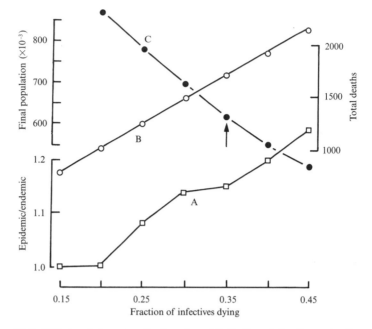

Figure 12.5. Effects of changing the fraction of infectives dying from the disease in the model (abscissa). Line A: epidemic/endemic ratio (open squares). Line B: deaths from smallpox at the peak of the epidemics (open circles). Line C: final population size of London after 30 years (solid circles); arrow indicates the initial size of population at a fraction of 0.35; i.e. smaller fractions generate a rising population, greater fractions generate a falling population.

The basic model is established with the following values which approximates to the smallpox mortality conditions: (a) $\overset{o}{e}_0 = 19$ years, (b) birth/deaths $= 1.5$, (c) infectious period $= 25$ days, (d) fraction of infectives dying $= 30\%$, (e) size of population $= 6.25 \times 10^5$, (f) $N\beta = 270$, (g) $\delta\beta = 0.1$, and (h) period of $\delta\beta = 2$ years.

12.5.1 Variation in the fraction of infectives dying of smallpox

As would be expected, the model predicts that, as the fraction of infectives dying is raised, the number of infectives is unaffected, whereas the total number of deaths at the peak of the epidemics rises linearly (Fig. 12.5). More surprising is the effect on the epidemic/endemic ratio (defined as (total number of deaths during an epidemic)−(endemic mortality)/(endemic mortality)); with the $\delta\beta$ selected, this ratio rises linearly from 1.0 (when 20% of the infectives die) to 1.26 (with a 45% mortality of the infec-

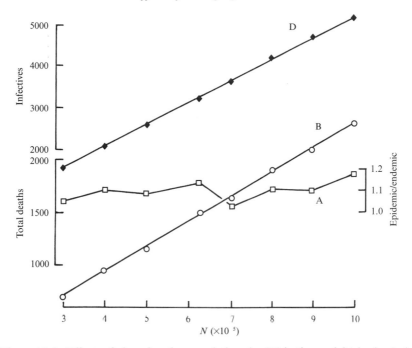

Figure 12.6. Effects of changing the population size (N) in the model (abscissa). A: epidemic/endemic ratio (open squares). B: deaths from smallpox at the peak of the epidemics (open circles). D: number of infectives (solid diamonds).

tives), and thus we see that a change in the fraction of infectives dying from the disease profoundly alters the characteristics of the epidemics. Such a situation might occur where malnutrition rose sharply, weakening resistance, increasing susceptibility to the disease and increasing the chance of dying.

12.5.2 Variation in total population size (N)

The value of N was changed over the range from 3×10^5 to 10^6, with the expected result: the mean number infected and the number of deaths at the peaks of the epidemics rose linearly (Fig. 12.6). The epidemic/endemic ratio (at the value of $\delta\beta$ selected) rose erratically from 1.06 to 1.18. Figure 12.2D of the modelling of smallpox mortality starting from 1750 predicts a rising population over 30 years and hence a predicted progressive change in the epidemic/endemic ratio, as shown in Fig. 12.6 which may be compared to actual events in Fig. 12.1. A situation with an effective *falling* N would occur following the introduction of inoculation or vaccination into the

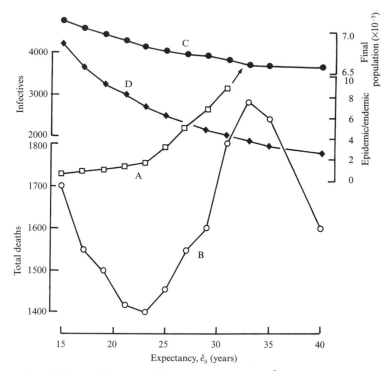

Figure 12.7. Effects of changing life expectancy at birth, $\mathring{e}_0$, in the model (abscissa). Line A: epidemic/endemic ratio (open squares). Line B: deaths from smallpox at the peak of the epidemics (open circles). Line C: final population size of London after 30 years (solid circles). Line D: number of infectives (solid diamonds).

population, which would rapidly reduce the pool of susceptible children and so effectively reduce N. A rising N would also produce a small rise in $N\beta$ and so modify the characteristics of the epidemics (see section 12.5.7).

12.5.3 Average age at death ($\mathring{e}_0$)

The predicted smallpox dynamics proved to be profoundly and unexpectedly affected by $\mathring{e}_0$ which, in the modelling, was changed over the range from 15 years to 40 years. The mean number of infectives falls exponentially (Fig. 12.7), whereas the total number of deaths at the peak of the early epidemics has a complex response, falling from 1700 deaths when $\mathring{e}_0$ = 15 years, to a minimum at 23 years (1400 deaths), then rising to a maximum when $\mathring{e}_0$ = 33 years and falling again thereafter (see Fig. 12.7).

The response of the predicted epidemic/endemic ratio is even more remarkable. The ratio is around 1.0 and rises only slightly over the lower range of $\overset{o}{e}_0$ of 15 to 24 years, but at values of $\overset{o}{e}_0$ of over 25 years the ratio rises sharply and dramatically, reaching 9.0 at 31 years and 18.0 at 33 years, i.e. with large amplitude epidemics and a very low endemic level. By present-day standards, an average life expectancy at birth of 33 years is still very low. Improved living and nutritional standards produced a steady fall in infant mortality through the 17th and 18th centuries and a corresponding change in life tables and in $\overset{o}{e}_0$ and, as Fig. 12.7 shows, this must have had subtle, but important effects on the dynamics of the epidemics.

Landers (1993) estimate the mid-range life expectation for male Quakers in London as:

1650–1699:   27.3 years.
1700–1749:   20.6 years.
1750–1799:   29.7 years.
1800–1849:   34.2 years.

The appropriate values have been incorporated into the modelling of London smallpox mortality in sections 12.3 and 12.4 and it is evident that these changes in $\overset{o}{e}_0$ would have had profound effects on the dynamics of the smallpox epidemics during the 18th century.

12.5.4 Variation of the births/deaths ratio

This parameter was used during the modelling to adjust the population growth during the 30-year period of study to correspond to the estimated values given by Landers (1993) for London. The population is predicted to rise rapidly when the ratio of the number of births to deaths (excluding deaths from smallpox) is set at 1.5, but falls slowly when the ratio is set at 1.4 and it is evident that the dynamics are very sensitive to the ratio of births/deaths in the population. Raising the births/deaths ratio from 0.9 to 1.7 caused the mean number of infectives in the population to rise linearly, whereas the epidemic/endemic ratio fell exponentially (Fig. 12.8). The latter had dramatic effects under conditions when the population was falling sharply, as shown in Fig. 12.9 (when the births/deaths ratio = 0.9) where the response of the model is almost completely epidemic. However, the effects of changing the births/deaths ratio at higher values are more modest (Fig. 12.8).

Raising the births/deaths ratio from 0.9 to 1.3 (conditions when the population levels were falling; see Fig. 12.8) produced a progressive fall in the total number of deaths during an epidemic, whereas these numbers rose progressively when the ratio was increased above 1.4. Changing the births/deaths ratio (perhaps by a rising birth rate or improved infant

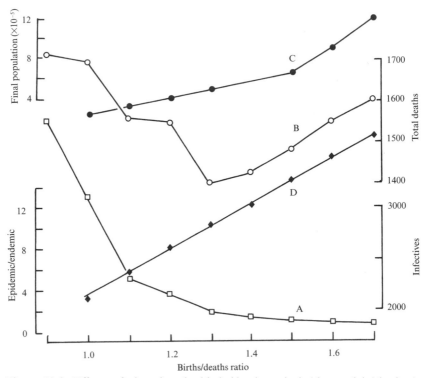

Figure 12.8. Effects of changing the births/deaths ratio in the model (abscissa). Line A: epidemic/endemic ratio (open squares). Line B: deaths from smallpox at the peak of the epidemics (open circles). Line C: final population size of London after 30 years (solid circles). Line D: number of infectives (solid diamonds).

mortality) not only changes population growth and the number of infectives (Fig. 12.8), but the model also predicts how the characteristics of the epidemics are fundamentally affected.

12.5.5 Variation in the magnitude of $\delta\beta$

Figure 12.10 shows how a variation in $\delta\beta$ profoundly affects the detailed characteristics of the epidemics whilst the basic demography remains unaltered: $\delta\beta$ does not modify the growth of the population, nor the mean number of infectives. The system is not driven when $\delta\beta = 0$ and so, obviously, no epidemics occur and the epidemic/endemic ratio = 0, but when $\delta\beta$ is raised over the range 0 to 0.14 the system is driven and both the epidemic/endemic ratio and the total number of deaths in the epidemics rise exponentially (see Fig. 12.10).

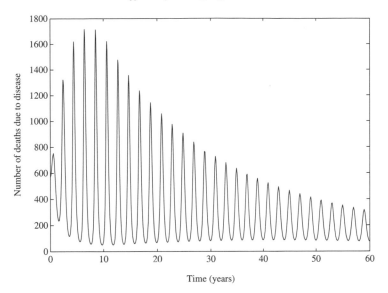

Figure 12.9. Prediction from the modelling of the number of smallpox deaths (ordinate) when the births/deaths ratio = 0.9 and the population was falling sharply. Smallpox is almost completely epidemic.

12.5.6 Variation in the infectious period

The predictions from the model for changing the infectious period of the disease over the range 9–30 days are shown in Fig. 12.11: the mean number of infectives rises linearly and the growth of the population decreases slightly. However, whilst the total deaths in the epidemics rise exponentially, broadly in parallel with the number of infectives, the epidemic/endemic ratio fell exponentially and it can be seen from Fig. 12.11 that any extension of the infectious period, as by spreading the dried crusts in smallpox, would have major effects on the dynamics of the disease. Furthermore, the detailed epidemiology and dynamics of two infectious diseases would differ if they had different infectious periods. Figure 12.11 allows us to predict what these differences in the dynamics might be.

12.5.7 Changing the value of $N\beta$ used in the model

The value of $N\beta$ was raised over the range 90 to 500; the number of infectives remained unaltered whereas the growth of the population was reduced exponentially (Fig. 12.12). However, the characteristics

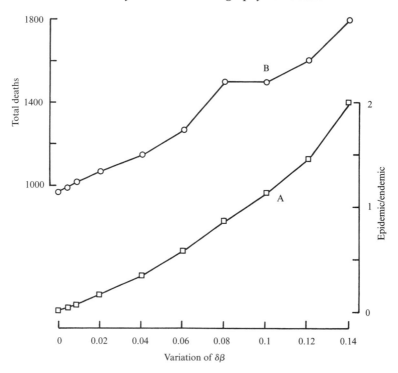

Figure 12.10. Effects of changing the value of $\delta\beta$ in the model (abscissa). Line A: epidemic/endemic ratio (open squares). Line B: deaths from smallpox at the peak of the epidemics (open circles).

of the epidemics, the epidemic/endemic ratio and the total deaths in the epidemics, showed the same complex response, rising sharply to a maximum at $N\beta = 130$ and then falling exponentially at higher values of $N\beta$. The model is less sensitive to changes in $N\beta$ around 250–270, the value used to predict the dynamics of smallpox in large cities.

Apart from a change in the interepidemic interval from 3 to 2 years, the pattern and characteristics of the smallpox epidemics in 1710 and 1750 were very similar and the predicted values for $\delta\beta$ and the fraction of infectives dying were identical. However, N and $\overset{\circ}{e}_0$ had changed markedly over this 40-year period and Fig. 12.12 shows that changing $N\beta$ from 133 to 250 has a marked effect on the response of the model and not only allows the system to oscillate at a period of 2 years (the observed value of T), but, more importantly, also modifies the response to the new, observed demographic parameters.

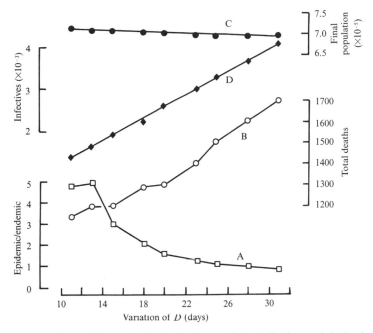

Figure 12.11. Effects of changing the infectious period, D, in the model (abscissa). Line A: epidemic/endemic ratio (open squares). Line B: deaths from smallpox at the peak of the epidemics (open circles). Line C: final population size of London after 30 years (solid circles). Line D: number of infectives (solid diamonds).

12.6 Modelling the measles epidemics in London

The annual measles deaths (shown in Fig. 12.13) in London during 1750–80 (the same period for smallpox as that described in section 12.3) are modelled in this section for comparison with the foregoing. Can the model developed in section 12.1 for smallpox also simulate the measles epidemics in London? The number dying in the epidemics in 1750 was about 250 but this rose progressively to a maximum of some 750 before the amplitude of the epidemics fell steadily. The endemic level was very low in 1750 but this rose steadily over the following 30 years (Fig. 12.13). The same basic demographic parameters for London for this period are used in the model as before, namely $\mathring{e}_0 = 30$ years, initial population size (N) in 1750 $= 6.8 \times 10^5$, final N in 1780 $= 8.2 \times 10^5$ (Landers, 1993).

The other variables were set as follows so as to simulate the pattern of epidemics shown in Fig. 12.13:

Ratio of births/deaths excluding deaths from measles $= 1.5$.
Average infectious period $= 12$ days (Anderson & May, 1991).

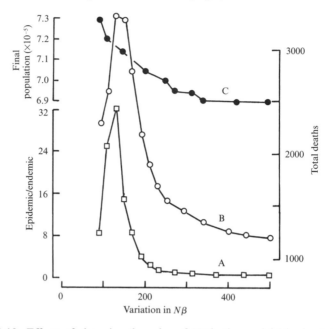

Figure 12.12. Effects of changing the value of $N\beta$ in the model (abscissa). Line A: epidemic/endemic ratio (open squares). Line B: deaths from smallpox at the peak of the epidemics (open circles). Line C: final population size of London after 30 years (solid circles).

Fraction of infectives dying = 0.23.
$N\beta = 133$.
$T = 3$ years.
Magnitude of oscillation in $\delta\beta = 0.021$ (note the very low value necessary compared with smallpox).
Period of oscillation in $\delta\beta = 3$ years.

The mortality from measles predicted by the model is shown in Fig. 12.14 and this can be compared to the actual deaths recorded in the Bills of Mortality and shown in Fig. 12.13. The total population size is predicted by the modelling to rise to 8.2×10^5 in 1780, corresponding to the actual estimate for London, and it is concluded that the model represents a satis-factory simulation of the measles epidemics.

12.7 Theoretical considerations of the effect of vaccination

The generalised, non-linear model of the epidemics of infectious diseases presented in section 12.1 is developed in this section to include the effects

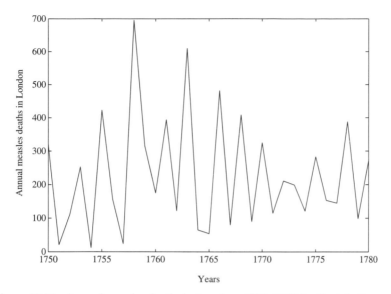

Figure 12.13. Annual measles deaths in London, 1750–1780 (ordinate), the period selected for modelling in section 12.6. Data source: Bills of Mortality (Creighton, 1894).

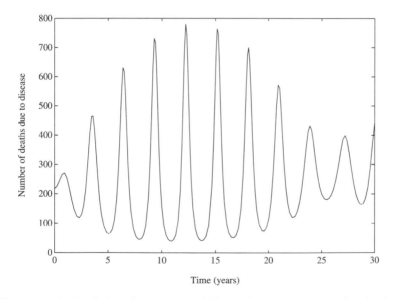

Figure 12.14. Prediction from the modelling of the annual measles deaths in London, 1750–1780 (ordinate). Compare with Fig. 12.13.

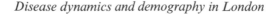

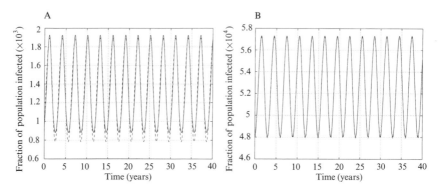

Figure 12.15. Modelling the effects of vaccination on the dynamics of the epidemics of an infectious disease. Solid line: results from full, non-linear model. Dashed line: results from linearised model. Vaccination rate, η, is 0.1. (A) No vaccination. (B) With vaccination. Note different scales on the ordinate.

of vaccination, which moves a proportion of the susceptibles, X, directly to the immune category, Z. From Equation 12.17 and for the range of values appropriate for the model, it can be shown that as η increases, ζ increases. Consequently, as the vaccination rate is increased, the system becomes more damped.

In the preliminary modelling for illustrative purposes that follows, the rate of vaccination, η, is taken as 0.1 year^{-1}, i.e. the overall average age of vaccination $= 1/\eta = 10$ years. $N\beta = 123$; $\delta\beta = 0.05$; $\mu = 0.04$; $\nu = 24$; period of driver $= 3$ years. The results of running the non-linear model are shown in Fig. 12.15 (solid line) and can be compared with the linearised response (dashed line). Figure 12.15A shows the standard response with no vaccination and can be compared with Fig. 12.15B, where the vaccination rate, η, is 0.1.

Vaccination clearly reduces the fraction of the population infected during the interepidemic years (note the different scales on the ordinate in the two figures), falling by about 50% from 0.9×10^{-3} to 4.8×10^{-4}. However, the amplitude of the epidemics fell much more dramatically by 90%, even with this relatively low rate of vaccination. This is because (a) vaccination damps the system so that there is much less amplification, and (b) frequency response plots show that vaccination shifts the resonant frequency of the system, so that the driver (the frequency of which is unchanged at 3 years) is no longer operating at the resonant period.

12.8 Conclusions: interacting effects of nutrition on the detailed epidemiology of infectious diseases

The non-linear model developed in Chapter 10 has been extended to take account of known population changes (i.e. not operating at constant N) and to include the deaths from the infectious disease; the latter has proved to be a significant component of the modelling of smallpox in London, where it produced heavy mortality (see section 11.13). The model appears to give good simulations of both the smallpox and measles deaths in London, the only caveats being the amplitude of $\delta\beta$ and the fraction of the infectives that die from smallpox. Both values have to be set high to reproduce the large number of deaths reported in the London Bills of Mortality in the simulation with varying N. The value of $\delta\beta$ for the smallpox modelling, 0.12, may be compared with the very much lower value for measles which was set at 0.021 in the modelling and, although surprisingly high, may reflect a real difference in the biology of the two diseases. The 45% death rate from smallpox predicted by the model certainly seems too high for an absolute value, but probably reflects accurately the severity of the mortality relative to measles where the model predicts a death rate from the disease of only 23%; as we have shown in section 11.13 (Table 11.5), the mortality rate from smallpox in London during the last half of the 18th century was some eight times that of measles.

If the modelling is accepted as providing a good approximation of the biology of these two lethal infectious diseases, this study integrates the epidemiology into the demography of London in the 18th century. The deaths from the diseases contribute to the oscillations in population numbers and modulate population growth. Equally, oscillations and long-term changes in population size and density will modify the characteristics of the epidemics (the interepidemic interval and the epidemic/endemic ratio). Changes in nutritional levels, as discussed below, can have far-reaching effects, including modifying the infant mortality and $\overset{o}{e}_0$, and so modulating the characteristics of the epidemics.

This modelling also illustrates how the basic characteristics of a disease may be predicted from the annual mortality, given only the demographic parameters of population size and $\overset{o}{e}_0$. T can be determined by time-series analysis of the mortality data series. The changing pattern of the epidemics (the epidemic and endemic levels), the fluctuating numbers of infectives, the percentage of the population infected, the relative lethality of the disease and the relative sensitivity to the driver may all be predicted. The epidemiology and demography of two lethal diseases (e.g. measles and

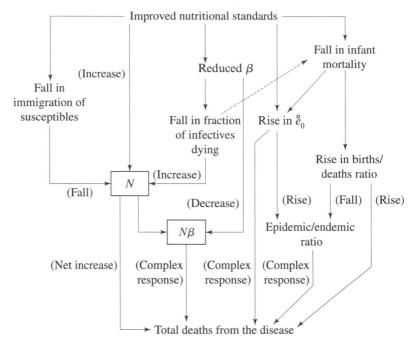

Figure 12.16. Diagram of the suggested interacting effects of improved nutritional standards on the demography and dynamics of smallpox epidemics, based on the results summarised in Table 12.1. The dotted line represents only a small change in infant mortality for a change in the fraction of infectives dying.

smallpox) may be compared in a conurbation over the same time period. Alternatively, the basic characteristics of a disease may be compared during two time periods (e.g. smallpox during 1710–1740 and 1750–1780) when the basic dynamics (e.g. T and the endemic level) are different.

The effects of systematically altering the variables on the response of the modelling are summarised in Table 12.1, above. Some of the results are obvious: the mean number of infectives rises linearly with N but is unaffected by the fraction of infectives dying. The other findings reveal the complex web of interacting factors that determine the changing pattern of the disease, and small changes in some of the variables markedly modify the predicted epidemiology and demography. This imposes severe constraints on the chosen values of the variables when one is producing a simulation of the annual deaths from a disease recorded in the London Bills of Mortality.

In Chapter 14 we describe the mortality from infectious diseases for the whole of England and Wales in the 19th century and show that the model is applicable on a much wider scale to what is a metapopulation (a population of populations).

Changes in nutritional levels have many short-, medium- and long-term, direct and indirect effects on population dynamics, as has been suggested in many of the preceding chapters. They will also have subliminal, and sometimes opposing, effects on the epidemiology of infectious diseases and some suggestions of how the dynamics of the system can be modulated, based on the findings in Table 12.1, are summarised in Fig. 12.16. All these factors can introduce 'apparent noise' into the system. The secondary effect of the short wavelength oscillation in wheat prices which probably promoted the influx of susceptibles from the countryside into London is described in section 9.10.

Thus, Fig. 12.16 shows that improved nutritional standards in a population can potentially directly affect immigration, population size, susceptibility to lethal infectious diseases, life expectancy and infant mortality. These parameters can then, in turn, interact and secondarily modify the fraction of infectives dying from the disease, the epidemic/ endemic ratio and the births/deaths ratio. Finally, this web of synergistic interactions culminates in modulating the total deaths from the disease.

13

Smallpox in rural towns in England in the 17th and 18th centuries

Smallpox was a lethal infectious disease and was persistent in England throughout the period 1600–1800; perhaps 20% of smallpox victims died (although a very much higher mortality in London in the 18th century is suggested by the modelling in Chapter 12) and the survivors retained an immunity for many years. Evidence suggests that a particularly virulent strain began to afflict people of all ages and social backgrounds in the middle and later decades of the 17th century.

When smallpox was fully established in large conurbations (with high $N\beta$) it was endemic and was characterised by 2-yearly epidemics, the evolution of which, from 4-yearly through 3-yearly epidemics, can be traced clearly in London (section 9.5) and Chester (section 10.2). It has been suggested that smallpox was also endemic in such cities as Nottingham, Chester, Northampton, Norwich, and Manchester after 1725 and before it was brought under control by inoculation and then by vaccination (Mercer, 1985). There are no long runs of data for deaths or cases of smallpox in rural England outside the major cities during the 17th and 18th centuries, although there are sporadic references to smallpox deaths in many parish registers and many accounts of outbreaks of smallpox in rural England in the 18th century (Creighton, 1894; Razzell, 1977), but this does not necessarily mean that the disease was endemic; indeed, accounts of spectacular outbreaks with widespread mortality indicate a population that had not recently experienced the disease and in which most individuals were susceptible. An example is the outbreak in the Island of Foula (Shetland Islands) in 1720, where only about six persons survived out of a population estimated at 200 (Razzell, 1977).

Smallpox was widely recognized as a serious, often fatal disease. For example, 'It was a major source of loss of life through the [18th] century and a disease relatively easily identified. In rural parishes and small towns it appeared every four years or so, usually in summer and sent up child mortality sharply' (Flinn, 1977).

To understand fully the demography of rural England we need to know the details of the biology of this disease which formed an important component of childhood mortality. What were the interepidemic periods? Did the epidemics follow SEIR dynamics, decaying progressively (section 9.2) or was the system driven by an oscillation in susceptibility? Was the disease endemic in some rural communities?

13.1 Smallpox epidemics in a rural town

Penrith is a rural market town that has been chosen as an area for the intensive study of its population dynamics (Chapter 7) and it is used here as an example of a much smaller town in which smallpox epidemics were specifically recorded in the parish registers in 1656 and 1661 (the cause of death was not usually reported in the registers until the late 18th century). Many historical reports (Creighton, 1894; Razzell, 1977; Hopkins, 1983; Mercer, 1985) show that the disease was confined largely to children who formed the bulk of susceptibles in endemic or epidemic situations, and the series of child burials, determined from the parish registers, has been analysed to determine indirectly the evidence for the incidence of smallpox, using the techniques of time-series analysis as described in section 10.2 for the determination of the smallpox epidemics at Chester. Spectral analysis of child burials at Penrith for the period 1600–1812 has a major peak at a frequency of 0.2 showing that this 5-yearly oscillation is the dominant cyclical feature of child mortality; it is shown after filtering in Fig. 7.1 (autocorrelation function, acf, at 5 years = 0.63) and the years of recorded smallpox epidemics at Penrith synchronize with the major peaks in the filtered series. It is tentatively suggested that this oscillation in child mortality may represent periodic epidemics of this lethal disease.

Since smallpox epidemics exploded suddenly but burnt out quickly, evidence for outbreaks of the disease at Penrith have been studied by time-scries analysis, following the procedure used for analysing the burial series at Chester (section 10.2). Child burials at Penrith have been divided into four periods and plotted on a monthly basis. Linear filtering revealed clear oscillations with a wavelength of approximately 5 years, i.e.

1600–1650: 71 months, acf = 0.18.
1650–1700: 63 months, acf = 0.29.
1700–1760: 59 months, acf = 0.3.
1750–1812: 66 months, acf = 0.19.

These oscillations are illustrated in Fig. 13.1 in which the known smallpox years (1656, 1661) are indicated.

Inspection of the child burial series at Penrith shows periodic aggregations of deaths with high mortality for 10–12 weeks and the series has therefore been further analysed by determining the largest total of burials for three consecutive months in each year. Spectral analysis shows the major peak at wavelength 5 years, with a smaller peak at 2–3 years; the filtered series (1600–1800) is shown in Fig. 13.2. The oscillation has a wavelength of 5 years for 1600–1812 (acf = 0.63), but if the analysis is confined to the middle period 1660–1775 (thereby eliminating the effects of widespread famine during the early part of the 17th century, as described in Chapter 8, and the rise in the population at the end of the 18th century) a higher acf of 0.71 is revealed. These oscillations seen in Fig. 13.2 become more pronounced and of greater amplitude after 1700.

We conclude that this analysis of the child burial series at Penrith reveals a 5-year oscillation of an infectious, lethal disease which is confined largely to children and has a strong seasonality in which the epidemic rapidly burnt out; we suggest that it provides indirect evidence of periodic epidemics of smallpox. A comparable study of the adult burials showed no oscillation with these characteristics. The known smallpox epidemics at Penrith in 1656 and 1661 coincide with the peaks of these 5-year oscillations. Finally, there is no evidence to suggest that there were outbreaks of the disease in the interepidemic years, suggesting that, in this rural market town, with an estimated population of 1500–2000, smallpox was not endemic and its dynamics were completely different from those described in Chapters 9 to 11 in large cities.

13.2 What drives the smallpox epidemics at Penrith?

There is good evidence that infection in many diseases is linked to poor nutrition (Scrimshaw *et al.*, 1968) and it has been suggested that smallpox epidemics have been related specifically to poverty and famine (Flinn, 1977), although other studies have suggested that it is not closely related to nutritional status (Rotberg & Rabb, 1985; Livi-Bacci, 1991). It was shown in Chapter 7 that the 5-year oscillation in child burials at Penrith synchronizes with the corresponding oscillation in the wheat price series (i.e. the maximum cross-correlation value is at zero lag). The thesis that child deaths correlate with wheat prices was tested by analysing the coherence of the two series without filtering, and wheat prices and child burials were found to be significantly coherent in the frequency bands of 5 to 6 years

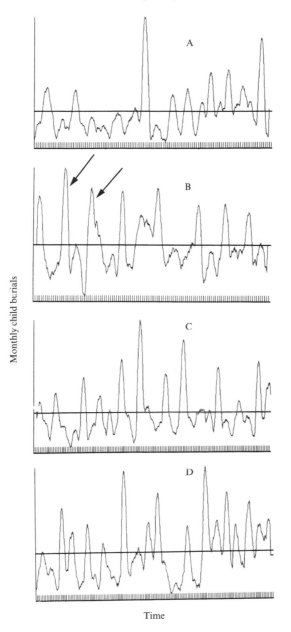

Figure 13.1. Child burials at Penrith plotted on a monthly basis. (A) 1600–1650; (B) 1650–1700; (C) 1700–1760; (D) 1750–1812. Arrows indicate known smallpox years at Penrith in 1656 and 1661. Each interval on the abscissa = 5 months. Note 5-year (60 months) cycles.

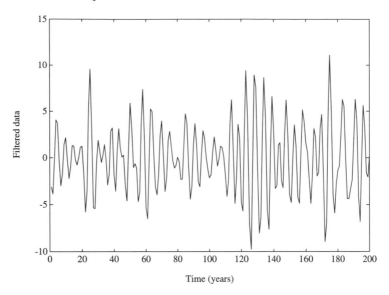

Figure 13.2. Child burials at Penrith, 1600–1800, plotted as the highest total for three consecutive months in each year. Filtered to show the short wavelength oscillation. Filter window = 4 to 10 years.

($P < 0.025$). We have suggested (Chapter 7) that there is evidence that regular cycles in wheat prices drove oscillations in child deaths at Penrith, and that these deaths were associated both directly and indirectly with malnutrition. The 5-year oscillation in wheat prices became clearly established only after 1550 (see Fig. 6.1) and the 5-year cycle in child burials at Penrith developed during this time and high mortality was cross-correlated with high wheat prices.

We conclude that the 5-year oscillation in wheat prices generated the 5-year oscillation in child deaths during the period after 1560, and 100 years later the smallpox epidemics were superimposed on this pre-existing mortality cycle. Epidemics were probably initiated by travellers because Penrith lay on the main road to Scotland and the spread of the disease during epidemic years would be facilitated if outbreaks of smallpox in any nearby towns with similar dynamics were locked to the same cycles of hardship and famine. We suggest that regular oscillations of famine and malnutrition produced periodic fluctuations in susceptibility (= the transmission coefficient, β, see section 9.3) and so drove the epidemics. In summary, regular fluctuations in the degree of hardship and malnutrition generated corresponding driving oscillations in susceptibility to the disease ($\delta\beta$) and thereby greatly enhanced the likelihood of an epidemic explosion when an infective entered the population. Once an epidemic was initiated, all susceptible members of the community would be exposed and equally likely to become infected. Market towns would be particularly vulnerable to smallpox epidemics, being of sufficient size and density and with the regular movement and crowding resulting from incomers from the surrounding farms and villages.

13.3 Dominant effect of the size of the pool of susceptibles

In the basic SEIR models of infectious diseases (section 9.2) the population is divided into susceptibles (X), latents (infected, not yet infectives, H), infectious (Y) and recovered and hence immune (Z). Thus, $N = X + H + Y + Z$.

It is assumed that the net rate at which infections occur is proportional to the number of encounters between susceptibles and infectives, βXY (where β is a transmission coefficient or susceptibility). Individuals move from latent to infectious at a *per capita* rate, σ, and recover, so becoming immune, at rate γ. The dynamics of the infection are then described by the four basic equations, 9.1 to 9.4.

The disease will maintain itself within the population provided that R (the 'reproductive rate' of the infection) is greater than, or equal to, unity; R is the expected number of secondary cases produced by an infectious individual in a population of X susceptibles where R is defined by Equation 9.5. The criterion $R > 1$ for the establishment of the disease can be expressed as the requirement that the susceptibles (X) exceed a threshold density, $X > N_T$, where

$$N_T = (\gamma + \mu)(\sigma + \mu)\beta\sigma$$

It is this criterion that the susceptibles exceed a threshold density that is of critical importance in determining the interepidemic interval in rural towns. Once an epidemic had exploded within the community, most of the survivors would be immune, having been infected in this or in previous outbreaks, and hence the disease could not explode again until a sufficient pool of susceptibles had been built up by new births. This process clearly took 5 years, during which, with a mean number of 60 births per year at Penrith, a maximum pool of 300 susceptibles would be built up, perhaps potentially 18% of the population. Razzell (1977) recorded that in 1791 Haygarth published a letter than he had received from the Council of Geneva: 'An epidemic of smallpox is of almost regular occurrence every five years and between the epidemics it frequently happens that we have no natural smallpox whatever, little in the City or its vicinity.' This was a large conurbation, where N would be high, but where inoculation had been practised for 40 years with progressively more children treated, so that build-up of the pool of true susceptibles was delayed, effectively changing the dynamics of the disease from that of a major conurbation to that of a medium-sized, rural market town.

Thus, the epidemics at Penrith were critically dependent on the time taken to build up an adequate pool of susceptibles, which took about 5 years. The epidemics were then simply locked into the pre-existing 5-year cycle in child mortality, with periodically rising wheat prices driving the system and maintaining the epidemics. This is another example where malnutrition has subliminal effects that are not easily detectable in studies of the population dynamics. All sections of the community, rich and poor alike, caught smallpox, so that it is not suggested that the well-nourished individuals escaped from being infected (although they may have been more likely to have survived an epidemic); rather, time-series analysis and modelling of the dynamics suggest that an oscillation in malnutrition and hardship generated an oscillation in susceptibility ($\delta\beta$), particularly among the poorer members of the community, that need have been of only very small amplitude but was sufficient to drive the system. Once an epidemic was started, all susceptibles who came in contact with the virus were infected.

13.4 Did infants have a natural immunity to smallpox?

Razzell (1977) recorded that there were very few infants under the age of 6 months dying of smallpox in the 1770s and suggested that one possible explanation is the non-registration of smallpox deaths because of the fulminating form of the disease among this group. He suggested that another explanation, for which there is good evidence, is that infants are born with a form of natural immunity (the exact nature of which is unknown; Dixon, 1962) which protects them from attack by smallpox for four or five months after birth until this immunity declines with age.

However the 5-yearly epidemics detected in Penrith and other rural towns, with few or no infectives in the interepidemic years, would mean that only one in five infants would be born in years when there was a smallpox epidemic, so that 80% would inevitably escape infection during infancy.

13.5 Non-linear modelling of the smallpox epidemics in rural towns

The linearised model shows (see Fig. 10.16A) that, if it is established with an appropriate $N\beta$ for the size and density of population of a medium-sized community, the resonant frequency (ω_r) of the system is 5 years, and if it is driven by an oscillation in susceptibility ($\delta\beta$) with a frequency of 5

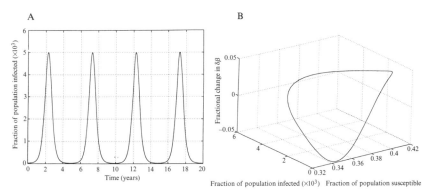

Figure 13.3. Modelling the smallpox epidemics at Penrith. $N\beta = 65$; $\delta\beta = 0.05$; period of sinusoidal input = 5 years. (A) Fraction of population infected; 5-year, non-sinusoidal oscillatory output, smallpox is not endemic; abscissa = time (years). (B) Phase diagram of fraction infected versus fraction susceptible versus fractional change in $\delta\beta$.

years, clear 5-yearly epidemics are generated. The striking result from this modelling (see section 10.14) is the very small amplitude in $\delta\beta$ (0.003) that is sufficient to drive the system and maintain the epidemics.

However, Fig. 10.16A does not completely represent the dynamics of smallpox at Penrith; the oscillation in infectives does not return to the baseline during the interepidemic interval so that the modelling suggests that the disease would be endemic whereas, in reality, Penrith was probably characterised by having no or few infectives in the interepidemic years. The linearised model is, therefore, not valid for the non-endemic situation and in this section we consider the dynamics of smallpox in medium-sized towns in more detail, using the full, non-linear model and giving examples of different types of driving inputs. As before (see section 10.8), the following assumptions are made: the system is assumed to start out in steady-state, the original oscillations being damped out. The dynamics of the population are simulated assuming, $\mu = 0.04$, $\alpha = 4.0$, $\gamma = 20.0$ (i.e. the average age at death = 25 years, the latent plus infectious period = 15 days and 1/6 of those infected die of the disease). $N\beta$ is slightly raised from 65 to 85. The model is run for 250 years and the figures show the results for the last 20 years (fraction of population infected or susceptible) or the last 50 years (phase diagrams).

Example 1

The period of the sinusoidal input of a variation in susceptibility is 5 years; amplitude of $\delta\beta = 0.05$ (5%). The resonant frequency of the system, ω_r, is close to 5 years and, with only this small $\delta\beta$, Fig. 13.3A shows that very large epidemics are generated at a periodicity of 5 years and that there are virtually no infectives in the interepidemic period, so that the disease was not endemic in this modelling. The response of the model system shown in Fig. 13.3A is non-sinusoidal, so that a sinusoidal driving input of a variation in susceptibility ($\delta\beta$) has been converted into an epidemic output. The corresponding simulation for the number of susceptibles shows the progressive build-up by new births during the interepidemic period which follows the dramatic fall at each epidemic. The phase diagram of susceptibles versus infectives versus $\delta\beta$ is shown in Fig. 13.3B; it touches the *x*-axis, confirming that the disease was not endemic.

In summary, the full non-linear model provides a good description of the smallpox epidemics in market towns of which Penrith represents an example. The dynamics of the disease are simply explained: the population takes 5 years to build up the pool of susceptibles to threshold size/density ($X > N_T$); the natural frequency of the system is determined by $N\beta = 85$; the epidemics are driven by a very small change in β so that smallpox epidemics become phase-locked to the 5-yearly oscillations in wheat prices.

Example 2

The possibility that a 1-yearly (annual) cycle of susceptibility might drive the smallpox epidemics in large cities, where the disease was endemic, has been explored in section 10.8. Could a simple annual cycle in susceptibility associated with the usual seasonal changes of temperature and weather modify the dynamics of the disease in a smaller town? The amplitude of the variation in susceptibility ($\delta\beta$) is chosen at 0.08 but the sinusoidal input is compounded of 75% (dominant) 1-year cycle and 25% 5-year cycle. The resulting oscillation in the numbers infected each year is irregular, but retains its 5-year periodicity (Fig. 13.4A). However, neither the number of infectives nor the number of susceptibles (Fig. 13.4B) falls to zero in the interepidemic period (i.e. the system is endemic) and it is concluded that this is not a completely satisfactory model of the conditions at Penrith. The Penrith model, with $N\beta = 65$, is robust so that, even when only 25% of the input is a 5-year oscillation, the epidemics are still established at 5-year intervals. Indeed, with $N\beta = 65$, the model was found to lock onto the 5-year component, even if the ratio of the 1-year cycle to the 5-year cycle was 9:1.

Example 3

$\delta\beta$ is raised to 0.13 and the sinusoidal input again comprises 75% 1-year cycle, 25% 5-year cycle. The 5-year oscillation in infectives shows

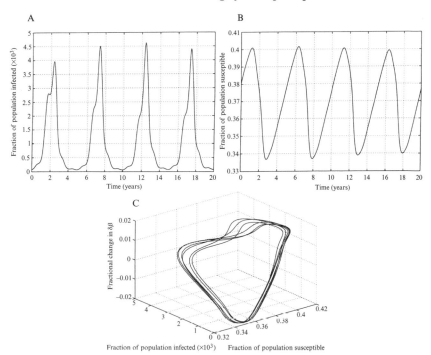

Figure 13.4. Modelling the smallpox epidemics at Penrith with a compound input composed of 75% 1-year cycle plus 25% 5-year cycle; $\delta\beta = 0.08$; $N\beta = 65$. (A) Fraction of the population infected (ordinate): 5-year, non-sinusoidal oscillatory output; number of infectives does not fall to zero in the interepidemic years. (B) Fraction of population susceptible (ordinate). Abscissa: time (years). (C) Phase diagram, fraction infected versus fraction susceptible versus fractional change in $\delta\beta$ associated with 5-year cycle.

clearly with this higher $\delta\beta$ of 13% (Fig. 13.5A), even though the 5-year driving input has again been reduced to 25% of $\delta\beta$. The build-up of the number of susceptibles during the interepidemic periods is shown in Fig. 13.5B.

We conclude from examples 2 and 3 that a 1-year seasonal cycle has little effect on the dynamics of smallpox at Penrith, which is a robust system and responds primarily with 5-yearly epidemics.

Modelling of the Penrith epidemics also shows that the changes induced by variations in the susceptibility are the most important factor in determining the dynamics of the epidemics. The system is markedly less sensitive to other possible drivers, such as fluctuations in the disease-induced death rate or in the general mortality rate that is not induced by smallpox.

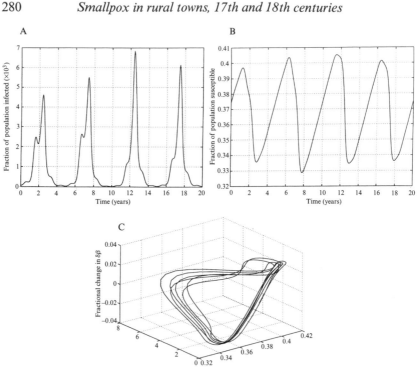

Figure 13.5. Modelling the smallpox epidemics at Penrith with a compound input composed of 75% 1-year cycle plus 25% 5-year cycle; $\delta\beta = 0.13$; $N\beta = 65$. (A) Fraction of the population infected (ordinate). (B) Fraction of population susceptible (ordinate). Abscissa: time (years). (C) Phase diagram, fraction infected versus fraction susceptible versus fractional change in $\delta\beta$ associated with 5-year cycle.

13.6 Could a noisy input drive the epidemics in rural towns?

The Penrith model (with $N\beta$ raised to 85) has been tested with random noise inputs of $\delta\beta = 0.05$ (corresponding to the London model; see section 10.7), 0.055, 0.06 and 0.075 and the results for $\delta\beta = 0.05$ are shown in Fig. 13.6A and for $\delta\beta = 0.075$ in Fig. 13.6B. Five-year oscillations in the infectives are generated when $\delta\beta$ is at the high value of 0.075 (i.e. peak-to-peak = 45%) but we conclude that this does not adequately simulate the conditions at Penrith. Firstly, the amplitude of the input required is too large and, secondly, the number of infectives does not drop to zero in the interepidemic years, in contrast with the true situation at Penrith, where smallpox epidemics were explosive and confined to a 3–month period with no further infectives until the next epidemic.

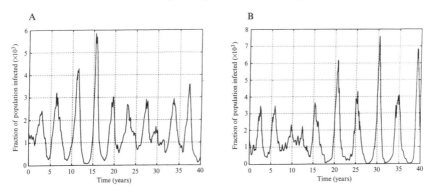

Figure 13.6. Introduction of white noise in the variation of β in the Penrith model. $N\beta = 85$. (A) $\delta\beta = 0.05$; (B) $\delta\beta = 0.075$.

13.7 Case fatality rate from smallpox

Razzell (1977) suggested that smallpox could potentially have attacked everyone except for a small minority of about 5% with natural immunity. Where communities were geographically isolated and had not been exposed to the disease, the mortality was devastating when smallpox arrived. It was first brought to Greenland in 1734, when nearly two-thirds of the population of the country (some 6000 to 7000) died. Of 200 families living within a radius of 3 miles from the Danish settlement into which smallpox was brought, only 30 remained alive. Only six people were left alive out of a population of about 200 after smallpox came to the Island of Foula in the Shetland Islands in 1720. Comparable highly fatal epidemics have not been recorded in mainland Britain, although more than one-fifth of the population of Hanbury, Worcester, died in an epidemic in 1725 and 190 persons are recorded as dying of smallpox out of a population of 1200 in the market town of Burford, Oxfordshire, in 1758. Razzell (1977) concluded that the population of Britain had been periodically affected for a long period of time and that all the evidence points to a gradual but highly significant increase in the virulence and case fatality rate of smallpox which persisted from the late 16th to the end of the 19th century.

Razzell (1977) has provided a detailed discussion of the statistics of smallpox mortality originally compiled during the 1720s (i.e. when the lethal epidemics were firmly established) when censuses were conducted in 31 market towns spread fairly evenly throughout England. Of the total of the 13 192 people who caught the disease, 2167 died and the mean case-fatality rate of the individual towns was 18.5%, with a standard deviation of 6.1% (range = 9.1% to 36.4%).

The pattern of a smallpox epidemic at Penrith during 1650–1750 can be described as follows, and can be compared with the results of this census. Baptisms at Penrith remained remarkably constant during 1650–1750, with an average of 65 per year. Since the interepidemic interval was 5 years, approximately 325 children would be born during the interval between epidemics to establish a potential pool of susceptibles. The total population between 1650 and 1750 was perhaps 2000–2200 (Scott *et al.*, 1996) so that, after 5 years, potentially 15% of the population would have become susceptible.

Of the epidemics at Penrith recorded in the parish registers, 28 children and 2 adults died in 1656 and 31 children died in 1661. We estimate that between 1635 and 1670 the mean number of children dying within a 3–month period during the epidemics was 26; this figure fell to 17 from 1670 to 1710 but rose to 28 thereafter. Probably the mean total deaths from smallpox in each epidemic was about 26. The mortality curves for the population at Penrith have been determined by family reconstitution (Duncan *et al.*, 1994b); 38% of children born during 1650–1700 died before reaching the age of 6 years. Thus, of the potential pool of 325 susceptible children born during the 5-year interepidemic period, 124 (38%) died, of which, on average, 26 died of smallpox during the epidemic. So that, of the original pool of 325 susceptibles, 201 (325 minus 124) survived both smallpox infection and the other hazards of childhood. A proportion of the population, particularly those in outlying and isolated farms, may have avoided exposure to the virus throughout their lifetime. If (say) 10% of the 201 1- to 6-year olds were never infected with smallpox during their lifetime, 180 recovered from the disease and became immune. Hence, 206 (180 + 26) were infected, of which 26 died and 180 recovered, and the mortality of those children who caught smallpox in this rural community was approximately 13% – a serious threat in childhood, but it should be remembered that 22% of the children in Penrith died of other causes in the first year of life at that time.

This estimate of 13% child mortality is a little below the mean percentage mortality determined from the censuses of 31 market towns (Razzell, 1977), but is well within the range of values and it must be remembered that the latter results will include adult deaths from the disease. However, the estimates for smallpox mortality at Penrith agree well with data for larger conurbations in the northwest. The Bills of Mortality for Carlisle compiled by Heysham for the years 1779 to 1787 shows that, unlike Penrith, the disease was certainly endemic at that time (it was a larger conurbation): the number of deaths per year are given as 90, 3, 19, 30, 19, 10, 39, 1, 30

(Lonsdale, 1870). During these 9 years, smallpox deaths accounted for 13.1% of total deaths, a figure comparable with the 13.8% found in Manchester during 1754–1774 (Mercer, 1985).

13.8 Smallpox at Thornton-in-Lonsdale

Thornton-in-Lonsdale is a small, upland parish on the western edge of the Pennines on the Lancashire–West Yorkshire borders, about 10 miles northwest of Settle; its population dynamics in the early 17th century have been briefly discussed in sections 2.2.2, 8.7 and 8.8 and it illustrates well how a small farming community, prior to expansion, had too small a population at low density for epidemics to explode. After 1750, the population was of sufficient size to sustain epidemics on a regular basis. The parish can be compared to Penrith: both are situated in upland north-west England, in marginal agricultural country, both populations expanded dramatically after 1750, and deaths from smallpox are recorded in the parish registers. However, the population at Thornton-in-Lonsdale differs in several important respects. Firstly, it is much smaller and, although the population in the 1801 census was 1060, it was probably below 500 prior to 1750. Secondly, the parish was apparently more scattered and lacked the central concentration of a market town like Penrith. Thirdly, it did not suffer major mortality crises from plague, typhus or famine, and the burials series shows no marked peaks in 1587, 1597 and 1623, although 31 people died in 1598 and 43 in 1664. Appleby (1978) described Thornton-in-Lonsdale as an untouched island in a sea of mortality during the crisis of 1623.

The annual baptisms at Thornton-in-Lonsdale from 1576 to 1812 are shown in Fig. 13.7; there is a small falling trend up to 1725, whereupon there was a marked change and the annual number of baptisms rose sharply. Evidently, the population burgeoned at this time. Spectral analysis of the annual child burial series over the same time period reveals a peak at a wavelength of 6 years ($P < 0.05$) and this oscillation is shown in the filtered series in Fig. 13.8, where the change after 1750 is evident. Again, therefore, there is a persistent short wavelength oscillation in child burials that is strongly developed after 1750 ($P < 0.01$) but it has a 6-year wavelength (acf $= 0.8$) which is in clear distinction from the situation at Penrith, where the short wavelength oscillation was 5-yearly.

Before 1750, the amplitude of the oscillations at Thornton-in-Lonsdale is smaller (Fig. 13.8) and analysis shows that the wavelength varies between 5 and 8 years. It was shown in section 8.8 that child mortality at

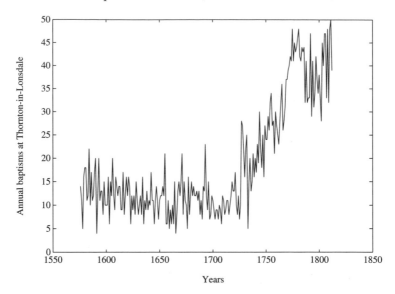

Figure 13.7. Thornton-in-Lonsdale baptisms series, 1576–1812. Note the marked rising trend after 1725. Data source: Chippindall (1931).

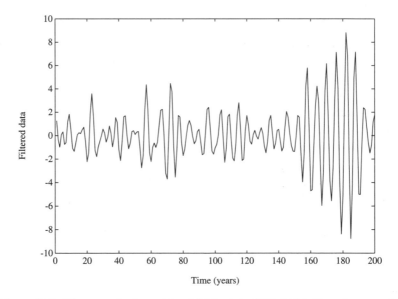

Figure 13.8. Thornton-in-Lonsdale, child burials, 1600–1800, filtered to reveal the short wavelength oscillation that emerges strongly after 1750 (year 150). Filter window = 4 to 10 years.

Thornton-in-Lonsdale (unlike adult mortality) was not related to the wheat price series in the 17th century (see Table 8.4) and the cross-correlation function at this time shows a strong *negative* correlation at a lag of zero or +1 years.

One adult is recorded of dying of smallpox in the parish registers in 1687 in Thornton-in-Lonsdale but the disease apparently did not spread and analysis of monthly child burials and of the maximum number of children dying in a 3–month period in the years prior to 1750 shows no evidence of any explosive epidemics of infectious diseases among children. Apparently the population of susceptibles was too small and of insufficient density for an epidemic to be established. In 1750/51 (October to April) 5 children and 1 adult died of smallpox and in 1756 (February to November) 19 children and 4 adults died of the disease. These outbreaks spanned a longer period than at Penrith (perhaps because of the lower population density at Thornton-in-Lonsdale) and if mortality were 13%, some 175 people may have been infected in 1756, possibly 30% of the population. Eighty per cent of those dying in 1756 were children, suggesting that many of the adults may have been immune from previous exposure to the disease. Inspection of the monthly data for child burials from 1756 to 1790, when the population was increasing rapidly, shows mortality peaks, confined to some 6 to 8 months in each year, in 1756, 1762, 1768, 1774, 1780/1, and 1785–6; these can be seen in Fig. 13.8 and probably reflect smallpox epidemics. Figure 13.8 also shows that the size of the epidemics was clearly reduced after 1790, possibly because the community was beginning to inoculate the children.

Thornton-in-Lonsdale is suggested as an example of a population that, prior to 1750, exhibited low amplitude oscillations of variable periodicity in child deaths, but the density of susceptibles at that time was too low to establish a smallpox epidemic following the introduction of an infective, as in 1687. Thornton-in-Lonsdale was on a packhorse route and the virus may have been introduced by this means, either directly or by crusts carried in the loads. However, the increase in the population and in $N\beta$ after 1725, allowed the build-up of an adequate pool of susceptibles and smallpox outbreaks began in 1750, with an interepidemic period (T) of 6 years, the time taken to rebuild the pool of susceptibles; this value for T is higher than that for Penrith, reflecting a lower $N\beta$ for the population, probably associated with a lower density. Thus, smallpox epidemics came to Thornton-in-Lonsdale some 100 years later than at Penrith when the population density had risen sufficiently, following the rapid rise in the annual number of births post-1725.

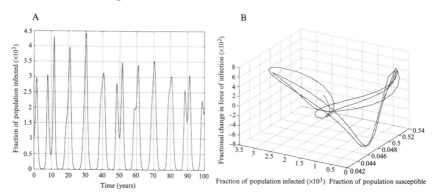

Figure 13.9. Modelling the 6-year smallpox epidemics at Thornton-in-Lonsdale with a 5-yearly driving input. $N\beta = 50$ (ω_r=6 years); $\delta\beta = 0.063$. (A) Fraction of population infected (ordinate). (B) Phase diagram of fraction of population infected versus fraction of population susceptible versus fractional change in $\delta\beta$.

13.9 Driving the epidemics at Thornton-in-Lonsdale

The striking feature of the biology of smallpox at Thornton-in-Lonsdale is the 6-year periodicity of the epidemics which do not correlate with annual wheat prices (which is clearly different from the situation at Penrith) and, apparently, they are not driven by an oscillation in suscepti-bility ($\delta\beta$) associated with malnutrition. How is the system driven at its res-onant frequency (ω_r) of 6 years? The dynamics of smallpox at Thornton-in-Lonsdale has been simulated using the full non-linear model and driving it with a sinusoidal input of $\delta\beta$ with a 5-year periodicity, so as to determine whether a system will oscillate at its resonant frequency with 6-yearly epidemics in response to a 5-year driver (thereby mimicking the wheat price series).

Example 1

$N\beta$ is defined as 50, giving a natural, resonant frequency of the system of 6 years. The input is an oscillation of susceptibility ($\delta\beta$) of a relatively high amplitude of 0.063 and with a periodicity of 5 years. The results of the modelling show that there are no infectives in the interepidemic periods (Fig. 13.9A), so that smallpox was not endemic and, to this extent, the model accurately reflects the situation at Thornton-in-Lonsdale. However, the epidemics generated are irregular and obviously not at a 6-year period-icity, so that the system is not oscillating at its resonant frequency. The progressive build-up of the susceptibles between epidemics takes approx-imately 10 years instead of the 6 years observed. The irregular nature of the

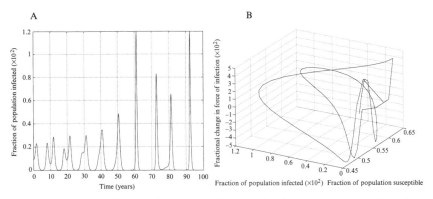

Figure 13.10. Modelling the 6-yearly smallpox epidemics at Thornton-in-Lonsdale with a 5-yearly driving input. $N\beta = 45$ ($\omega_r = 6.87$ years); $\delta\beta = 0.047$. (A) Fraction of population infected (ordinate). (B) Phase diagram, fraction of population infected versus fraction of population susceptible versus fractional change in $\delta\beta$.

epidemics is shown in the phase diagram of Fig. 13.9B and we conclude that this is not a satisfactory model.

Example 2

$N\beta$ is defined as 45 ($\omega_r = 6.87$ years); the driver is an oscillation in $\delta\beta$ of amplitude 0.047 and wavelength 5 years. Again, the system is not endemic, with no infectives in the interepidemic years (Fig. 13.10A) but the epidemics have a periodicity of approximately 10 years, only a small proportion of the susceptibles are infected, the output is irregular (Fig. 13.10B) and this model is also unsatisfactory.

Example 3

$N\beta$ is 45 and the driving input, $\delta\beta$, is of high amplitude (0.15) and comprises a 20% 5-year oscillation (simulating the oscillation in wheat prices) and an 80% 1-year oscillation (simulating an additional and major contribution from a simple annual cycle). The complex output of infectives is shown in Fig. 13.11A; the response is not truly epidemic and the power spectrum shows that the epidemics, although fairly regular, are 5-yearly and not 6-yearly (i.e. not at the predetermined ω_r, corresponding to the real data series at Thornton-in-Lonsdale). Only a small proportion of the susceptibles are infected in each epidemic and the irregularity of the response is illustrated in Fig. 13.11B.

Example 4

As in the previous example, $N\beta = 45$ and the input is compound, with 20% 5-year and 80% 1-year wavelengths, but the amplitude of $\delta\beta$ has been raised

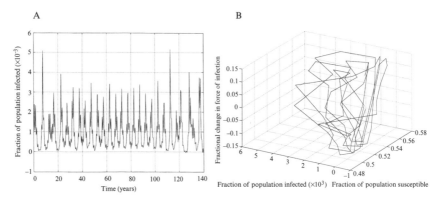

Figure 13.11. Modelling the 6-yearly smallpox epidemics at Thornton-in-Lonsdale with a compound driving input. $N\beta=45$ ($\omega_r=6.87$ years); $\delta\beta=0.15$, compounded of 20% 5-year oscillation plus 80% 1-year oscillation. (A) Fraction of population infected (ordinate). (B) Phase diagram, fraction of population infected versus fraction of population susceptible versus fractional change in $\delta\beta$.

from 0.15 to 0.16. The output is superficially very similar to that of example 3, but the power spectrum of the resulting infectives shows that the major periodicity of the epidemics is now 8 years. Only a very small change in the amplitude of $\delta\beta$ produces a dramatic change in the wavelength of the epidemics.

In summary, when the model is established at a resonant frequency of the epidemics of 6 years, even large amplitude driving inputs of wavelength 5 years (simulating a wheat price cycle of malnutrition) cannot generate the true 6-year epidemic situation at Thornton-in-Lonsdale.

In searching for a suitable driver for the smallpox epidemics (post-1750) and childhood mortality cycles (pre-1750) at Thornton-in-Lonsdale (Fig. 13.8), the data for the 18th century has been divided into two sections, 1700–1749 and 1750–1812, and correlations have been sought between annual child deaths and mean seasonal rainfall and temperatures, as described in section 9.6. Three techniques have been used (multiple regression, coherence and cross-correlation function) and the results are summarised in Table 13.1. Child burials at Thornton-in-Lonsdale were *inversely* correlated with wheat prices during the low amplitude oscillations of 1700–1750 and were not associated with this series during the period of the suggested smallpox epidemics. There was a strong correlation (but, obviously, not necessarily a causal connection) of child deaths with low autumnal rainfall in 1700–1750 and with high autumnal rainfall during the epidemics, 1750–1800. Probably, more importantly, the suggested epidemics were correlated with low wool prices.

Table 13.1. *Analysis of the factors affecting child mortality at Thornton-in-Lonsdale, 1700–1812*

Factors	1700–1750	1750–1812
Seasonal temperatures	NS	NS
Low autumn rainfall	$P < 0.001$	NS
High autumn rainfall	NS	$P = 0.001$
Low wheat prices	$P < 0.001$	NS
Low wool prices	NS	$P = 0.01$

Note:
NS, not significant.

Can these findings be related to the dynamics of smallpox epidemics at Thornton-in-Lonsdale? What constituted the driver for the disease in this apparently healthy community that was largely untouched by the major mortality crises suffered by other parishes in northwest England? The following suggestions can be made:

(1) The rising trend in national wheat prices post-1750 probably contributed to a general rise in susceptibility and hence to an increase in $N\beta$ at Thornton-in-Lonsdale, so allowing the establishment of the epidemics at 6-yearly intervals.

(2) The epidemics were initiated once the rising birth rate had established an adequate level for $N\beta$; the 6-year interepidemic interval (compare with $T = 5$ years in the larger town of Penrith) and the longer duration of the individual epidemics probably reflects the low population density at Thornton-in-Lonsdale. SEIR dynamics, where the epidemics decay because they are not driven (see section 9.2), are probably truly applicable only to the endemic situation in large cities. In rural towns, particularly at low $N\beta$, given a regular supply of infectives coming into the community, epidemics may well occur at the resonant frequency of the system, once the pool of susceptibles has built up. An undriven system is probably the explanation of the epidemiology of many smaller communities and, indeed, analysis of the smallpox epidemics at Penrith suggests that they may have come out of synchrony with wheat prices for a short period in the first half of the 18th century.

(3) The epidemics were driven by a low amplitude oscillation in $\delta\beta$ caused by seasonal conditions, namely high autumn rainfall, although this would be surprising since smallpox epidemics in London (Chapter 9) and scarlet fever epidemics in England and Wales (Chapter 14) were

Table 13.2. *Years of smallpox epidemics in rural England in the 17th and 18th centuries*

Place	Sherbourne	Taunton	Godalming	Skipton	Maidstone
Year	1634	1658	1672	1716	1734
T	8	12	14	6	7
Year	1642/3	1670	1686	1723	1741
T	6	7	15	3	4
Year	1649/50	1677	1701	1726/7	1745
T	7	7	9	5	8
Year	1657/8	1684	1710/1	1732	1753
T	9		12	4	7
Year	1667		1723/4	1736	1760
Mean T	7.5	8.7	12.5	4.5	6.5

Notes:
Epidemics at Sherbourne (Dorset); Taunton (Somerset); Godalming (Surrey); Skipton-in-Craven (Yorks.); Maidstone (Kent); data from Razzell (1977).
The dates of the successive epidemics in each of the towns is given in the columns, together with the corresponding intervals between them. *T* is interepidemic interval (years).

correlated with dry conditions. Probably there was no direct causal connection between wet autumns and smallpox epidemics at Thornton-in-Lonsdale.

(4) The 6-yearly epidemics at Thornton-in-Lonsdale were dependent primarily on the time taken to build up a sufficient density of susceptibles, as summarised in paragraph (2), but the system may have been weakly driven by the price of wool.

13.10 Smallpox in other rural communities

The foregoing are presented as examples of case studies of single rural communities where time-series analysis of the parish register series can be used to elucidate the biology of a serious infectious disease, to integrate the findings with the mathematical modelling of the dynamics and to incorporate the results into the overall mortality cycles of the population, as shown in Chapter 7. The results presented show clearly that if the records of two or more populations with differing dynamics are pooled, an understanding of the underlying epidemiology of the disease would be lost.

The story of the origins and biology of smallpox epidemics at Penrith, which were developed on a pre-existing oscillation in child mortality, where the resonant frequency of the system, defined by population size and density ($N\beta$), coincided with the wavelength of the dominant, exogenous factor, is deceptively straightforward and the case study at Thornton-in-Lonsdale reveals that the overall dynamics in some populations, when studied individually, are much more complex. This conclusion is borne out by some short runs of data of smallpox epidemics in rural England that have been compiled from the records of the deaths in parish registers by Razzell (1977) and are shown in Table 13.2. The mean interepidemic interval varied from 4.5 to 12.5 years and there was little regularity in the outbreaks of the disease, although only five epidemics are recorded. The epidemics at Skipton correspond with the 5-year periodicity at Penrith (although they are apparently not synchronous with high wheat prices over this short time period) and mean T at Maidstone corresponds approximately with the periodicity at Thornton-in-Lonsdale, but the interepidemic intervals in the three other communities are much greater.

It would be of interest to have further studies using time-series analysis of other rural communities, exploring the occurrence of smallpox epidemics from 1630 to 1800, particularly within a common geographical area. Initially, indirect evidence would be sought for epidemics, their timing, regularity and interval. Can T and the emergence of the epidemics be related to population size and density? Did the epidemics originate at about 1750 with the population boom (N) that was experienced by many communities at that time and with the steep rise in national wheat prices (causing a rise in susceptibility, β) in the second half of the 18th century? Is there evidence for decaying epidemics after about 1780 as the community began practising inoculation? Were the epidemics in synchrony over a wide area, promoted by the movement of infectives in epidemic years? Is there evidence of a specific, exogenous driver?

A start has been made to answer some of these questions and it seems clear that in rural England (outside the endemic situation of the large conurbations), regular epidemics did not occur in small or scattered communities (i.e. with a low $N\beta$), as at Thornton-in-Lonsdale prior to 1750 when the disease did not explode following the introduction of an infective. This confirms an earlier observation by Razzell (1977), who wrote:

A small relatively isolated village is likely to have had epidemics only infrequently, and when such epidemics did occur they would affect the majority of the population, adults as well as children, as many children would grow to adulthood without being attacked by the disease. An example of this is to be found at Aynho,

Northants, which was a village with a population of about 350 in 1723–24 when the epidemic occurred. Over forty per cent of all smallpox attacks in this epidemic occurred amongst adults of 20 years and above: this age distribution can only occur when epidemics return relatively infrequently . . . Not all the population at Aynho were attacked during the 1723–24 epidemic but this was probably because many of them had caught the disease in previous epidemics.

A preliminary study of the oscillations in child mortality has been made in several parishes as follows:

Area A: Highland zone. Crosby Ravensworth, Crosthwaite, Kirkoswald and Newton Reigny (Cumbria). All low density communities.

Area B: Barnstaple (Devon) was chosen because it suffered from reported smallpox epidemics, was approximately the same size as Penrith, and because its situation on the edge of the highland zone of North Devon has been compared to Cumbria (Slack, 1979).

Area C: Nantwich and Wybunbury (Cheshire), relatively affluent lowland parishes of large size but low density (Wyatt, 1987).

Area D: St Bees (Cumbria), coastal.

Area E: Thornton-in-Lonsdale (Yorkshire/Lancashire borders, described above) and Great Harwood (Lancashire); upland communities in the northwest, low density.

Area F: Lancaster. A large market town with a population some 50% greater than that of Penrith, with which it can be compared. It was a moderately busy seaport so there would have been considerable movement through the town. Its population dynamics have been described in section 8.9.

The results are summarised in Table 13.3. The parish registers of these communities, particularly the child burial series, have been studied by spectral analysis to determine whether an underlying 5–6-year oscillation in mortality that is coherent with wheat prices exists. If so, is there evidence that it drove smallpox epidemics, particularly in the 18th century when the population was rising, thereby establishing a suitable level of $N\beta$? Outbreaks of severe childhood mortality largely confined to 3–4 months in the year during which adult mortality remained at normal levels is regarded as possible evidence of sporadic epidemics of smallpox.

Area A

Newton Reigny is a small parish, with only 220 inhabitants in 1801, situated in the Eden Valley three miles to the northwest of Penrith. The population was buoyant until the early 17th century but declined progressively thereafter. It suffered mortality crises in 1587/8 (mostly adults), 1596 (mostly adults) and 1623 (children and adults) suggestive of an economy based on both wool and wheat. Although spectral analysis shows a 5-year oscillation in adult and child burials before 1650 there is no firm evidence of a 5-year mortality cycle thereafter. Nine smallpox deaths in children are reported in the registers in 1727 but the disease did not spread further and inspection of the child burial series suggests that there were no major outbreaks of the disease. In spite of their close proximity, Newton Reigny did not suffer from the smallpox epidemics experienced at Penrith.

Kirkoswald is situated on the eastern slope of the Eden Valley, 8 miles north of Penrith. The population is estimated to have fluctuated between 450 and 561 during the period 1642–1688 (Clark *et al.*, 1989). It suffered the mortality crises in 1587, 1597 and 1623 (when the deaths were confined to adults), typical of the Eden Valley. There is evidence of a 5-year oscillation in adult burials coherent with wheat prices during the period 1580–1685, and in child burials during 1685–1812, although the correlation with wheat prices is not at a significant level. There is possible evidence of outbreaks of smallpox in 1657 and 1711 but we conclude that the community was too small to experience regular epidemics.

Crosby Ravensworth is another small and scattered parish situated on the river Lyvennet, a tributary of the Eden, some 4 miles east of Shap. It suffered the usual mortality crises in 1587, 1597 and 1623 and regression analysis (child and adult mortality versus wheat and wool prices) for the period confirms that the economy was dominated by wool prices. There is no evidence of 5-yearly mortality crises (perhaps because wheat was of secondary importance) nor of any major outbreaks of smallpox.

The parish of Crosthwaite, which included the market town of Keswick, lies towards the northern boundaries of the Lake District. It had a large population with mean annual baptisms from 1613 to 1622 of 92, about 50% higher than Penrith, but was probably of low density. It suffered the mortality crises in 1587 (mainly adults) and 1623 (adults and children), and regression analysis for the period 1587–1641 confirms that the economy was dominated by wool. A 5-year oscillation in child mortality coherent with wheat prices is found only during 1587–1642. There is no evidence of major smallpox epidemics; $N\beta$ may have been of sufficient magnitude but the parish was probably off the main trading routes and so there may not have been a regular supply of infectives.

Table 13.3. *Correlation of 5-year cycles in child burials with wheat prices and smallpox epidemics in different geographical areas*

	Area	Dates of registers studied	5-year child burial cycles	Coherent with wheat	Smallpox epidemics	
					Sporadic	Regular
Newton Reigny	A	1572–1812	Pre-1649	No	Small outbreak in 1727	No
Kirkoswald	A	1580–1812	1685–1812	NS	1657, 1711	No
Crosby Ravensworth	A	1600–1811	No	—	No	No
Crosthwaite	A	1562–1812	1587–1642	Yes	No	No
Barnstaple	B	1540–1812	1590–1730	Yes	1652–1715 (mean T = 21 years)	1715–1796 (varying, mean T=5-yearly)
Nantwich	C	1680–1812	1680–1812	NS	1688–1746 (mean T = 14.5 years)	1746–1793 (varying, mean T=5 or 6 years)
Wybunbury	C	1680–1812	1680–1812	Weak coherence 1710–1780	Possible small outbreaks in 1779 and 1789	No
St Bees	D	1538–1837 (incomplete)	—	—	1636–1710	No

Great Harwood	E	1560–1805	No	—	1725–1790 during boom (mean T = 11 years)	No
Thornton-in-Lonsdale	E	1576–1812	6-yearly, 1576–1812	No	No	1750–1790 (T = 6 years)
Lancaster	F	1600–1785	1600–1785	Yes	1655–1735 (mean T= 20 years)	1735–1785 (mean T= 5 years)

Data sources: Newton Reigny (Haswell, 1934); Kirkoswald (Thornley, 1901); Crosby Ravensworth (Haswell, 1937); Crosthwaite (Brierley, 1931); Barnstaple (Wainwright, 1903); Nantwich and Wybunbury (Wyatt, 1987); St Bees (Stout, 1963); Great Harwood (Sparke, 1937); Thornton-in-Lonsdale (Chippindall, 1931); Lancaster (Brierley, 1908)

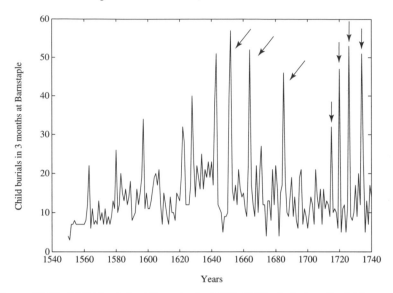

Figure 13.12. Child burials at Barnstaple, 1550–1740, plotted as the highest total for 3 consecutive months in each year (ordinate). Arrows indicate suggested small-pox epidemics. Data source: Wainwright (1903).

Area B

The registers of the market town of Barnstaple in Devon are incomplete during 1740–1759, but it is evident that the population was buoyant during the period 1540 to 1630 and then fell steadily until 1760, rising again there-after. Annual baptisms and burials numbered about 100 during peak times, some 66% above the average at Penrith. It suffered from a major mortality crisis, predominantly among children, in 1546 and further mortality crises in 1597 and 1623, indicative of an economy sensitive to wool prices. A 5-year oscillation in child mortality associated with wheat prices ($P = 0.05$) emerges after 1590 and persists until 1730. The child burial series has also been analysed on the basis of the greatest total in three consecutive months (Fig. 13.12) and this shows that there is good evidence for the first small-pox epidemic occurring in 1651/2 with further outbreaks in 1664 and 1685. Thereafter, the epidemics became more regular, occurring in 1715, 1720, 1726 and 1734 before the gap in the registers (see arrows in Fig. 13.12); after 1760, epidemics were detected in 1775, 1781, 1790, 1796 and possibly occurred again in 1812. In conclusion, it is suggested that in spite of a large population pre-1620, sharply falling numbers reduced $N\beta$ to a lower level than at Penrith and so early smallpox epidemics (pre-1715) were sporadic with a mean interepidemic interval (T) of 21 years and were governed by

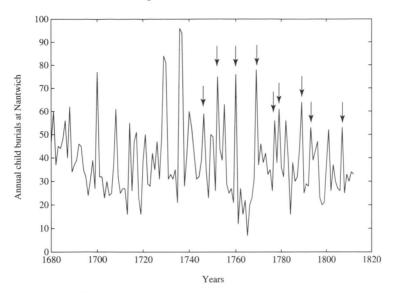

Figure 13.13. Child burials at Nantwich, 1680–1812. Suggested smallpox epidemics are indicated by arrows. Data source: Wyatt (1987).

the build-up of an adequate pool of susceptibles. After 1715, the epidemics were established on a more regular basis (approximately 5–6 yearly) and continued until 1796.

Area C

Nantwich is a large Cheshire parish which had a mean of 100 annual baptisms during 1680–1812 and with a rising trend after 1750. Spectral analysis shows a variable short wavelength oscillation in child burials that was not coherent with wheat prices. Peaks of child mortality are clearly seen in the burial series and those that are believed to be smallpox epidemics by detailed examination of the monthly burials are indicated on Fig. 13.13. The epidemics begin in 1688 but are irregular and there is a gap of 32 years between 1714 and 1746. Excluding this period, the mean T was 7 years (1688–1807). There was high child mortality in 1755 and 1782 which may have been because of smallpox and, if these are included, mean T was 6 years. In conclusion, it is suggested that $N\beta$ had risen sufficiently by 1688 to allow explosive sporadic smallpox epidemics to develop with a mean interepidemic interval of 14.5 years; see Fig. 13.13. After 1746, a rising population associated with a boom in baptisms, produced a rise in $N\beta$ with epidemics at mean intervals of 5 or 6 years (1746–1793), although these lacked the regularity of the epidemics at Penrith.

Wybunbury is a small and scattered parish (mean annual baptisms over the period 1680–1812 were only 21) adjacent to Nantwich with which it may be directly compared. Both parishes suffered the mortality crisis in adults and children in 1729 which, although widespread in England (see Wrigley & Schofield, 1981), was not experienced in Cumbria. Spectral analysis shows a short wavelength oscillation in child burials which was coherent with wheat for a limited period (1710–1780; $P = 0.025$). There is no convincing evidence of smallpox epidemics, although there were 4 years with mortality peaks when child burials exceeded adult burials; two of these years (1779 and 1789) coincided with suggested smallpox epidemics at Nantwich. Otherwise, Wybunbury did not suffer from major outbreaks of the disease, unlike its neighbour.

Area D

The registers of St Bees (Cumbria) are confused, but this was probably quite a large parish; the community suffered the mortality crises in 1597 and 1623 that are typical of Cumbria. Analysis of the largest number of child burials in three consecutive months suggests that there may have been smallpox epidemics in 1636, 1650, 1656 and 1668 followed by quite large epidemics during the period 1680–1710. After 1740, some very small epidemics with a mean T of 14 years are suggested by analysis, although they do not coincide with the years in which smallpox deaths are listed in the registers (1780, 1781, 1784). In conclusion, St Bees experienced sporadic epidemics in the 17th century but the disease became almost endemic after 1740 with no explosive, spreading epidemics.

Area E

Great Harwood lies on the western edge of the Pennines, close to the Ribble Valley, 80 miles south of Penrith. It experienced small crises in mortality in 1587 and 1597 (crisis mortality ratios = 1.6 and 2.0, respectively) but was unaffected by the crisis of 1623. There was a population boom after 1740. Only a non-significant 4- to 5-year oscillation in child burials is shown by spectral analysis. There is evidence of perhaps six smallpox epidemics after 1725 during the population boom, but they were at very variable intervals, with a mean T of 11 years.

Area F

The printed published registers for Lancaster are available for the period 1600–1785 and it is evident from the baptism series that the population boom began in about 1705, much earlier than at Penrith. Spectral analysis

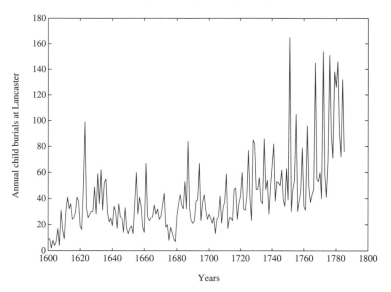

Figure 13.14. Child burials at Lancaster, 1600–1780 (ordinate). Data source: Brierley (1908).

shows a short wavelength oscillation in the child burials series that was coherent with wheat prices throughout the period of study. There are records of smallpox deaths in the registers in 1772 and good evidence of sporadic epidemics from 1655 to 1735, with a mean T of 20 years (see Fig. 13.14). Regular epidemics were established after 1735 associated with the population boom and are clearly seen after 1750 in Fig. 13.14; mean T during this period was 5 years and the epidemics were probably triggered by the peaks in wheat prices with which they correlated.

13.11 Classification of smallpox epidemics and integration with population dynamics

It is evident from the foregoing and from the results given in Chapter 9 that the biology of smallpox infections was markedly different in the separate communities in England in the 17th and 18th centuries. The pattern and evolution of the epidemics reflect the underlying dynamics of the population and a classification of the different smallpox epidemics is attempted in this section. The most obvious difference between populations is the endemic nature of the disease, with clear epidemics superimposed in cities and major conurbations, in contrast to the epidemics experienced in rural England where there were no significant outbreaks in the interepidemic years. The factor that determines the inherent properties of any single population is $N\beta$ (see sections 9.3 and 9.4), namely the interaction of population size/density and susceptibility to smallpox. With respect to N in rural communities, density will be a factor that is just as important as the total number of people; the parish may cover a very wide area (Greystoke in Cumbria is a good example of such a parish; it lies close to Penrith and covers some 65 square miles, making it one of the largest in England at that time; Armstrong, 1994) and if the farmsteads and hamlets are widely scattered an epidemic will not explode. Overall susceptibility (β) may change progressively, for example with the rising trend in wheat prices during the second half of the 18th century. This rise in β may be an important contribution to a rise in $N\beta$ in many communities which were experiencing a population boom at that time (e.g. Lancaster, Penrith).

Parishes with a focus, with a substantial town centre, would be more likely to experience smallpox epidemics. Market towns, with regular movements of incomers and the consequent mixing of infectives and susceptibles would be particularly vulnerable. If a town were situated on a drovers' road (Penrith) or a packhorse route (Thornton-in-Lonsdale) or on a major road or was a busy port (Lancaster) there would be a steady supply of infectives, possibly bringing crusts, which would ensure that an epidemic would explode as soon as the pool of susceptibles had built up to a sufficient level.

The arrival of inoculation and vaccination, as we have seen in London (section 9.7), had profound effects on the dynamics of smallpox by reducing the supply and build-up of the pool of susceptibles and so, effectively, reducing $N\beta$.

The following categories are arranged in order of increasing $N\beta$ but probably form a continuum. Obviously, a community can alter its underlying population characteristics and its pattern of infection and so change categories. In some cases, a parish may simply move to the next higher category, but others may leap-frog to a very different pattern of epidemics (e.g. York in 1635, section 10.4; Thornton-in-Lonsdale in 1750). The history of smallpox in many cities shows a progressive evolution through several categories. For the purpose of this classification of lethal smallpox epidemics in England the story is assumed to begin in about 1630 when a more lethal form of smallpox is believed to have emerged (Razzell, 1977).

Category 1. Low $N\beta$. Small, scattered population. No epidemics; if an outbreak of smallpox occurs the disease does not spread and explode into a full epidemic because of the low density. Many of the inhabitants remain as susceptible and would be at risk if they migrated to cities where smallpox was endemic. Examples: Newton Reigny, Kirkoswald, Wybunbury, Thornton-in-Lonsdale (before 1750).

Category 2. Larger parishes, probably with a slowly rising $N\beta$. Large, but very sporadic epidemics. T varied widely from 3 to 30 years. Probably many susceptibles escaped infection. $N\beta$ may have been marginal for epidemics to occur or the infection may have come at only irregular intervals. An undriven system.

Some parishes may have remained in category 2 until inoculation began. Examples: Great Harwood, Anyo, Godalming and Taunton (see Table 13.2) and probably many of the 31 market towns listed by Razzell (1977, p. 131). Other communities may evolve into a higher category when a population boom began. Examples: Lancaster (1655–1735), Nantwich (1688–1746), Barnstaple (1652–1715).

Category 3. Generally larger towns, perhaps only during the boom post-1750, with a steady supply of infectives. Regular, clear epidemics with a frequency of 7 or 6 years. T governed by the time taken to build up a pool of susceptibles (X) of sufficient density for a population to explode i.e. X must exceed a critical threshold density, $X > N_T$, where $N_T = (\gamma + \mu)(\sigma + \mu)\beta\sigma$ (see section 9.2). The system may not have been driven. Examples: Thornton-in-Lonsdale after 1750, Maidstone and Sherbourne (see Table 13.2), but many rural towns seem to have evolved from category 2 to category 4 via this category.

Category 4. Typically rural market towns with a higher $N\beta$, population movement and a regular supply of infectives coming into or through the parish. Epidemics on a regular, 5-yearly basis with no infections in the interepidemic years. This category represents the climax epidemic situation for rural England from *c.* 1630 to the early 19th century. T is governed by $N\beta$ and the length of time taken to build up the necessary pool of susceptibles, whereupon an epidemic will explode. Most of the other inhabitants will be immune. The epidemics may be triggered by high wheat prices or other external factors causing a periodic change in β. Examples: Penrith, Nantwich (after 1746), Lancaster (after 1735), Barnstaple (after 1715), Skipton (see Table 13.2).

Category 5. High $N\beta$, as in cities and major conurbations, but smallpox probably still not fully endemic. Epidemics at 4- or 3-yearly intervals. Examples: Chester before 1729 (see section 10.2).

Category 6. Endemic smallpox in cities. High $N\beta$; 4- and 3-yearly epidemics, driven by climatic factors. Examples: the evolving epidemics at York, Chester and London.

Category 7. Endemic smallpox with 2-yearly epidemics driven by climatic factors in large cities. High $N\beta$. Climax smallpox epidemics. Examples: London 1750–1800, Edinburgh, Glasgow and Chester after 1790.

Category 8. Endemic smallpox in London after inoculation and vaccination had been introduced (1800–1840). Epidemics of very low amplitude (see section 9.7). See also St Bees after 1740.

Category 9. Decaying oscillations on a low endemic level. Weakly driven; the system obeys SEIR dynamics. Example: London 1840–1900 (section 9.8); compare with diphtheria in England and Wales in the 19th century (section 14.11).

14

Infectious diseases in England and Wales in the 19th century

The birth and death rates in England and Wales are known with greater certainty after 1837, and the continued growth of the population was in part because of the excess of births over deaths and in part because of a continuing decline in mortality (McKeown & Record, 1962). By the mid-19th century, over half of the population of Britain could be classified as urban and there is clear evidence of a rising standard of living during the second half of the century, with rising real wages, a falling cost of living (Woods & Woodward, 1984) and a fall in food prices (Woodward, 1984). Imports of meat trebled between 1870 and 1890 and the imports of butter and margarine more than doubled between 1880 and 1890 (Cronje, 1984). However, there is no positive evidence to show that there was any increase in the heights or weights of school children; working-class diets were still composed principally of carbohydrates and any movement towards proteins was limited to small increases in the consumption of dairy products rather than meat (Oddy, 1982).

McKeown & Record (1962) concluded that the amelioration of the effects of infectious diseases made the predominant contribution to this decline in mortality in Britain in the 19th century and the following diseases had the most important effects:

Tuberculosis: the progressive improvement in the standard of living had the dominant influence, although some workers (Burnet, 1953) have suggested that the elimination of susceptible individuals must have had a profound influence on the history of the disease.
Typhus: the virtual elimination of typhus from England and Wales is attributed to an improvement in the standard of living.
Typhoid: the decline of typhoid is attributed to improvements in the water supply and other sanitary measures, such as efficient sewage disposal and the protection of food.

303

Scarlet fever: McKeown & Record (1962) accepted the view that the most important influence was a change in the nature of scarlet fever and this is discussed in greater detail below.

Cholera: the elimination of cholera is attributed to improvements in the water supply and other sanitary measures.

Smallpox: vaccination is regarded as having the major effect in the elimination of smallpox although some have concluded that another influence, probably a change in the character of the disease itself, must also have contributed substantially.

A comparative study of four lethal infectious diseases in England and Wales in the 19th century is presented in this chapter. The dynamics of measles epidemics in London and of smallpox epidemics in rural towns as well as in London have been presented in earlier chapters, but hitherto these analyses and models have been concerned with single, identified populations and have usually concentrated on earlier centuries. Are these models applicable to the spread of infectious diseases across the whole country? Do epidemics occur with regularity and, if so, is the system driven? Do the dynamics of the diseases interact with one another?

The diseases considered are measles, scarlet fever, smallpox and diphtheria and the data have been taken from the Registration of Deaths, as recorded by Creighton (1894), and it must be emphasized again that these analyses are based on deaths and not on case reports.

14.1 Measles in England and Wales, 1847–1893

Annual measles deaths are shown in Fig. 14.1; the annual fatality rate rose steadily from about 6000 in 1850 to about 14 000 by the end of the 19th century. Regular epidemics are detectable by eye and spectral analysis confirms that the national epidemics in the first half of this period (1847–1869) were 3-yearly whereas they changed to 2-yearly after 1870. This change in the interepidemic interval for the whole country may be compared to the development of the pattern of epidemics of measles in London in the preceding century (Table 11.1) where, 100 years earlier, T was 3 years during 1750 to 1785 but was reduced to 2 years from 1785 to 1837. Measles epidemics in the mid-19th century, therefore, were probably 2-yearly in London and basically 3-yearly in the country. This difference reflects the difference in $N\beta$ for the population in London and the metapopulation (a population of populations) of England and Wales. The corresponding absolute sizes of the populations (N) would be of the order of 10^6 (London)

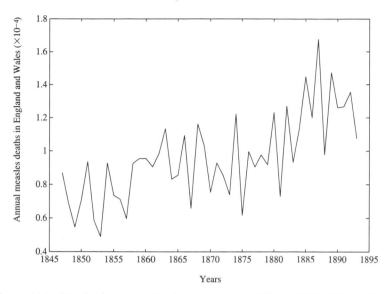

Figure 14.1. Deaths from measles in England and Wales, 1847–1893 (ordinate).
Data source: Creighton (1894).

and 22×10^6 (England and Wales); it is evident that the much greater concentration of the population in London accounts for the high value of N there and emphasizes the importance of the density component within $N\beta$. Rising $N\beta$ during the 19th century would stem from a progressively increasing population size, but also improved communication and transport would promote an effective increase in density.

Regression analysis, cross-correlation function and coherence all show that the measles epidemics in England and Wales correlated with low autumn temperature and low summer rain. There was no correlation with the other seasonal climatic variables. The overall regression equation is:

Annual number of measles deaths =
$$24486 - 1295 \ (\text{autumn temperature}) - 25.7 \ (\text{summer rain}) \qquad (14.1)$$

(constant, $P < 0.001$; autumn temperature, $P = 0.035$; summer rain, $P = 0.029$; regression, $P = 0.017$.) Such findings suggest that the driver for measles in England and Wales at that time could have been a combination of a dry summer followed by a cold autumn.

These conclusions may be compared to the dynamics of measles infections in London during the period from 1785 to 1837 where $T = 2$ years and where the epidemics correlated with low autumn temperature which is suggested to act as a driver for the system. Thus, the transition from 3-

yearly to 2-yearly measles epidemics occurred in London about 100 years before that in the whole of England and Wales, apparently using the same seasonal driver.

Equation 14.1 can be used to compute a series of *predicted* annual measles deaths driven by autumn temperature and summer rain and this has oscillations that are coherent with the actual measles epidemics ($P =$ 0.001 in the 2- to 3-year waveband), supporting the suggestion that the epidemics correlate with these seasonal conditions. The predicted-minus-actual measles deaths series is strongly coherent with actual measles epidemics, so that this series of residuals still displays the main epidemics, suggesting that their amplitude is not linearly related to the magnitude of the climatic change which simply acts as a driver or trigger. The absolute amplitude of the epidemic will depend on such factors as the effective size of the national pool of susceptibles and which areas of the country are affected.

In conclusion, the characteristics of measles mortality in London in the 18th century and in England and Wales in the 19th century, with a smooth evolution from 3- to 2-yearly epidemics in both systems, are consistent with a system driven by an oscillation in $\delta\beta$ caused by fluctuating seasonal weather conditions.

14.2 Modelling the measles epidemics in England and Wales

The population model developed in Chapter 12 is used here to describe the development of the measles epidemics and the demography of England and Wales during the 19th century. The absolute numbers in the population are very much higher than in the London models but, of course, the overall effective density is much less, the metapopulation comprising widely dispersed subpopulations. The pattern of epidemics after 1875 to be satisfied by the model is shown in Fig. 14.1, where T has been shown to be 2 years and the trend in measles deaths is rising. Although the amplitude of the epidemics is fluctuating, the starting 'endemic level' in 1875 is some 7000 deaths per annum, superimposed on top of which are maximum epidemic deaths of some 5000.

Landers (1993) gives the mean age at death for London Quakers (males and females combined) as 35 years for the cohort 1800–1849 (the last period for which he gives data) and $\overset{\circ}{e}_0$ for the mid point of this modelling, starting in 1875, has been assumed to be 40. The population of England in 1871 was given by Wrigley & Schofield (1981) as 21.3×10^6, and N to include Wales is taken as 22×10^6 for the purposes of the present model.

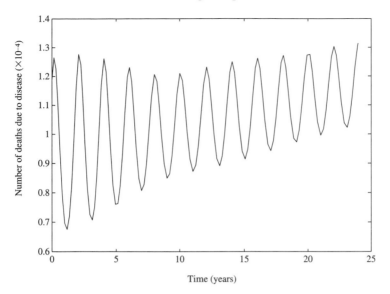

Figure 14.2. Modelling the deaths from measles in England and Wales, 1875–1900 (ordinate). Compare with Fig. 14.1.

Creighton (1894) quoted the annual death rate from measles in England and Wales during 1871–1880 as 377 per million living. A mean annual death rate from measles of some 9000 p.a. in 1875 suggests that the population would be 23 million, agreeing with the estimate above.

The other parameters chosen for the modelling are as follows:

Ratio of births to deaths (excluding deaths from measles) = 1.85.
Average length of infectious period – 12 days (Anderson & May, 1991).
$T = 2$ years.
Fraction of those infected dying = 0.28.
$N\beta = 270$.
Magnitude of $\delta\beta = 0.0075$ (i.e. a very low amplitude).
Period of oscillation in $\delta\beta = 2$ years.

The result of running the model is shown in Fig. 14.2, in which the first 5 years, whilst the model settles, is omitted. The simulated epidemics are more regular than those recorded in real life (Fig. 14.1) but otherwise the essential features are duplicated and it appears that using the same $N\beta$ as for London (i.e. 270 for $T = 2$ years, as predicted by Equations 9.18 and 9.19) is satisfactory, in spite of the population being so large and scattered. The value of $\delta\beta$ (0.0075) is both critical and noteworthy; the system was extremely sensitive to only very small changes in $\delta\beta$ which produced an

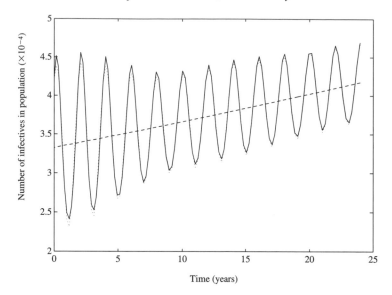

Figure 14.3. Modelling the number of measles infectives in England and Wales, 1875–1900 (ordinate).

alteration in the epidemic:endemic ratio. A $\delta\beta$ of 0.0075 suggests that in reality only a very low amplitude oscillation in susceptibility was necessary to drive the epidemics.

Using the ratio of births:deaths of 1.85, the model predicts that the total population would rise from the starting point of 22×10^6 in 1875 to over 27×10^6 by the end of the 19th century. The number of infectives (those catching measles) each year predicted by the model is shown in Fig. 14.3. To simulate the characteristics of the mortality of the epidemics it was necessary to raise the fraction of the infectives that died from measles to 0.28 (or 28%) and the model therefore provides an estimate of the mortality from the disease during the 19th century.

These results suggest that the population modelling developed for London epidemics is also applicable to a metapopulation represented by the whole of England and Wales and that some insight into the dynamics of measles can be gained from these models. Finally, the studies of measles in London (Chapter 11) and in England and Wales in the 19th century, both of which show a smooth evolution from 3-yearly to 2-yearly epidemics, are consistent with the hypothesis that the systems are driven by a low amplitude oscillation in $\delta\beta$ and are not dependent on an annual or stochastic forcing.

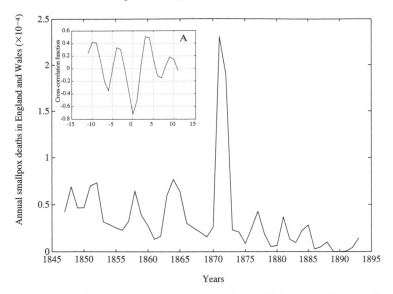

Figure 14.4. Deaths from smallpox in England and Wales, 1847–1893 (ordinate). Inset A: cross-correlation function (ordinate), wheat prices versus smallpox deaths in England and Wales, unfiltered data, 1847–1869. Minimum ccf (−0.7) at zero lag. Abscissa: lag (years).

14.3 Smallpox deaths in England and Wales, 1847–1893

The annual smallpox deaths in England and Wales for the second half of the 19th century are shown in Fig. 14.4 and the pattern is comparable to London at this time: the picture is dominated by the enormous epidemic of 1871 which was associated with the Franco-Prussian War, wherein 23 000 died in England and Wales. This was superimposed on an endemic level which fell steadily from some 5000 deaths per annum in 1845 to disappear by the end of the century as vaccination became progressively widespread. The amplitude of the epidemics also fell.

Spectral analysis of this series shows a strong peak at 6.7 years, which corresponds with a 6.7-year oscillation in national wheat prices at this period. The cross-correlation function, wheat prices versus smallpox deaths (Fig. 14.4A) shows that the two series are completely out of phase and that wheat prices do not directly drive the epidemics. The epidemics did not correlate with any of the seasonal weather conditions. High wheat prices may produce susceptible children (who die in the next smallpox epidemic) via the effects of malnutrition during pregnancy or during the first year of life and so contribute to maintaining the epidemics, but it is probable that, as in London at this period (see section 9.8), the decaying oscillations reflect an undriven system that is obeying simple SEIR dynamics. These decaying epidemics show much more clearly in the London data series (i.e. in a single population) in Fig. 9.1, cohort V.

14.4 Scarlet fever in England and Wales

Scarlet fever is a bacterial disease caused by a haemolytic streptococcus (*Streptococcus pyogenes*) which also causes streptococcal tonsillitis and erysipelas in humans. It has been regarded as becoming relatively benign over the last 150 years (Quinn, 1989) but the disease is not mild everywhere and no one can forecast what its epidemic future may be (Christie, 1980). A recent, unexplained increase in severe streptococcal diseases in the USA and UK has been compared to the 1825–1885 pandemic of fatal scarlet fever (Katz & Morens, 1992).

There was an enormous number of deaths from scarlet fever in England and Wales during 40 years in the middle of the 19th century whereas this period was preceded and followed by decades with very much lower levels of annual mortality from the disease. This major outbreak of scarlet fever with a high mortality during 1825–1885 is regarded as remarkable by historical epidemiologists (Creighton, 1894) and the biology of the disease and the characteristics of the epidemics during this critical period are determined by time-series analysis in the next section.

14.5 Annual scarlet fever deaths in England and Wales, 1847–1893

Annual scarlet fever deaths in England and Wales taken from registration details for the period 1847–1893 are shown in Fig. 14.5A; there are clear epidemics from 1847 to 1880 but thereafter the endemic level of deaths falls rapidly and the fatal epidemics virtually disappear. Spectral analysis of the series for the period 1847–1880 shows a peak at wavelength 5.3–5.6 years, showing that the interepidemic interval (T) was 5 to 6 years. $N\beta$ for this value of T is 60.5 (calculated from Equation 9.18), so that the damping factor, ζ, of the system is 0.046 (where ζ lies between 0 and 1; Equation 9.15). Because the system is so lightly damped, it will oscillate, and large amplitude epidemics will be maintained, in response to an oscillation in susceptibility ($\delta\beta$) of very small amplitude (0.003) (see section 10.14), provided that its frequency is at the resonant frequency (ω_r) of the system.

14.6 Seasonal drivers for the scarlet fever epidemics

Is there evidence of an oscillation in seasonal weather conditions that could cause a regular fluctuation in susceptibility and so drive the epidemics of scarlet fever? No significant correlation was found between seasonal temperatures and the epidemics, unlike the dynamics of whooping cough where the epidemics were significantly correlated with low temperatures in autumn and winter (see section 11.10 and Duncan *et al.*, 1996b). However, during the major epidemics of 1847–1880, the scarlet fever deaths were significantly correlated with low mean spring and low mean summer rainfall (i.e. dry conditions). Analysis was carried out with the following tests. (a) Squared coherence relations; scarlet fever deaths correlated significantly with low summer rainfall ($P < 0.001$) in the 5- to 6-year waveband and with low spring rainfall ($P < 0.01$) in the 5-year waveband, both series at zero lag. (b) Cross-correlation function shows that scarlet fever deaths in the epidemics correlated with low summer rainfall (ccf $= -0.8$) and with low spring rainfall (ccf $= -0.5$), both seasons at zero lag.

The possible interacting effects on scarlet fever mortality of the three variables, spring rainfall, summer rainfall and wheat prices were further studied by multivariate analysis which confirmed these findings. The overall regression was highly significant ($P = 0.002$), with the correlations for low spring rainfall and low summer rainfall at $P < 0.04$ and $P = 0.004$, respectively.

These correlations suggest that periodic dry conditions in spring and summer were sufficient to produce a low amplitude oscillation in susceptibility which drove the system and maintained the epidemics. Creighton (1894) also noted that high mortality from scarlet fever was apparently associated with a rainfall below average and Waddy (1952) has shown that the infectivity of certain respiratory infections is increased in air of low absolute humidity in both Ghana and England and Wales and suggests that such air dries the nasopharyngeal mucosa more rapidly and may thereby lower its resistance. This sensitivity to seasonal dry conditions parallels the findings with smallpox epidemics (Table 9.1).

14.7 Effects of malnutrition on the biology of scarlet fever

The annual wheat price series for 1847–1893 is shown in Fig. 14.5B; it closely mirrors the scarlet fever deaths series with clear oscillations up to 1880 and a sharp fall in the index thereafter; spectral analysis of the wheat price series for this period shows a dominant peak at 6.7 years. The cross-correlation between scarlet fever deaths and wheat price series during the

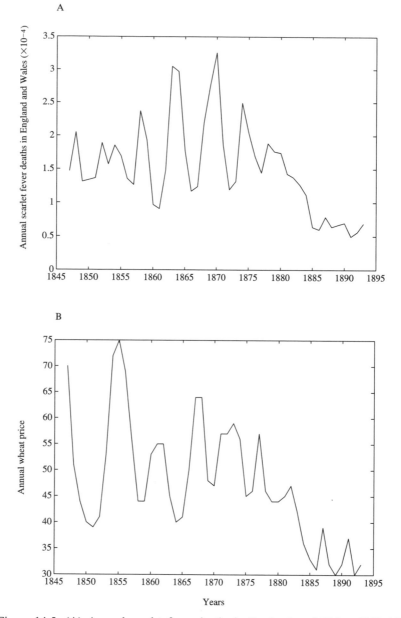

Figure 14.5. (A) Annual scarlet fever deaths in England and Wales, 1849–1893 (ordinate). (B) National wheat prices (shillings; ordinate). Marked falling trend in both series after 1875. Data sources: Creighton (1894) and Stratton (1970).

period of the epidemics, 1847–1880, was studied by the following techniques: (a) Cross-correlation function: there is a strong correlation between the two series (ccf $= +0.87$), but with a clear lag of 2 to 3 years. (b) The coherence programme shows that wheat prices and scarlet fever deaths are significantly correlated in the 5- to 6-year waveband ($P < 0.001$), again with a lag of 3 years.

It is clear that after 1880 both the scarlet fever mortality (Fig. 14.5A) and the wheat price series (Fig. 14.5B) fall sharply and progressively. The *trends* in the two data series correlate closely ($P < 0.001$) during this period when scarlet fever eventually ceased to be a lethal disease. Dietary standards in the UK improved in the second half of the 19th century, with real wages rising particularly after 1870. Imported food supplemented and improved the diets of many sections of the population (Cronje, 1984). The findings in the present study suggest that the greatly improved general nutrition associated with low wheat prices in the last quarter of the 19th century contributed to the steady fall in the lethality of the disease. Records for scarlet fever deaths are incomplete before 1847 but the scattered records show that mortality doubled in 1839 from the preceding year and was particularly severe in 1840 when there were 20 000 deaths from the disease. The endemic level of annual deaths then continued at a high rate until 1880. Inspection of the annual wheat price series shows that the index rose in 1838 and the mean level remained high until 1880 (see Fig. 14.5B), suggesting that the remarkable 40 years of high scarlet fever mortality (Creighton, 1894) was initiated and was dependent on the poor nutritive levels at that time.

In addition to the effect on the overall endemic level and the final falling trend, the scarlet fever epidemics during 1847–1880 were also significantly correlated with the oscillation in wheat prices although with a lag of 2 to 3 years between the two series. This lagged effect suggests that high wheat prices and inadequate nutrition of the mother during pregnancy caused greater susceptibility to the disease in the subsequent children who then contracted it and died in the next epidemic. Neonatal mortality has been shown to be associated with malnutrition in pregnancy, whereas postneonatal mortality was primarily directly dependent on exogenous causes in the first year of life, both in England in the 17th century (Scott *et al.*, 1995) and in the Dutch hunger winter between September 1944 and May 1945 (Stein *et al.*, 1975; Hart, 1993; see section 7.7). Malnutrition during pregnancy has also been suggested to increase the susceptibility of the progeny to measles (see Chapter 11) and the critical importance of a good diet during pregnancy has been elucidated by Barker in his studies of historical epidemiology (Barker, 1992a). Although correlation does not prove causality, it is suggested that an oscillation of malnutrition, in this way, indirectly produced an oscillation of susceptibility to scarlet fever in young children which interacted synergistically with periods of low rainfall in spring and/or summer to produce an oscillation in $\delta\beta$ which drove the system and maintained the epidemics at its resonant frequency.

14.8 Age of children dying of scarlet fever

During the period of the 5-yearly epidemics in scarlet fever, it would be expected from Equation 9.19 that the mean age of contracting scarlet fever was approximately 13 years, much higher than for the 2-yearly epidemics of smallpox and measles. However, Creighton (1894) reported that, in the last half of the 19th century in England and Wales, two-thirds of the deaths from scarlet fever occurred in children under the age of 5 years; the attacks were much more fatal in the first years of life and the fatality decreased rapidly after five. The results presented here (see Fig. 14.5A) are for scarlet fever deaths which therefore will be predominantly of young children. Possibly, in each epidemic those dying in the age groups 0 to 2 years within one interepidemic interval of 5 years were born mainly to undernourished mothers whilst those in age groups 2 to 5 years may have suffered from increased susceptibility associated with periodic seasonal dry conditions.

14.9 Modelling the dynamics of scarlet fever in England and Wales, 1847–1877

The scarlet fever mortality for the country shown in Fig. 14.5A can be modelled in the same way as measles. The epidemics were clearly 5-yearly. Before 1870, with a mortality of over 25 000 in the peaks of the epidemics, the following parameters were chosen to produce a satisfactory simulation.

Age at death = 40 years.

Ratio of births to deaths (excluding deaths from scarlet fever) = 1.5.

Average length of infectious period = 25 days (this is longer than the infectious period of 15–20 days quoted by Anderson and May (1991) to allow for spread by infected fomites; the epidemics can be modelled with the shorter infectious period by adjusting the magnitude of $\delta\beta$ but the level of mortality is then below that shown in Fig. 14.5A and is only 50% of actual values).

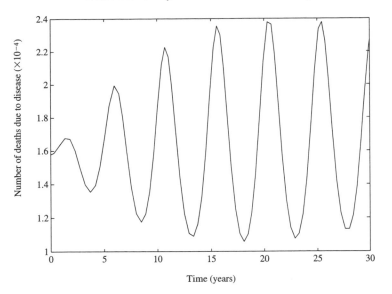

Figure 14.6. Modelling the scarlet fever deaths in England and Wales over the period 1847–1877. Compare with Fig. 14.5.

$T = 5$ years.
Fraction of infectives dying from scarlet fever $= 0.35$.
Initial size of population $= 21 \times 10^6$.
$N\beta = 60$.
Magnitude of $\delta\beta = 0.007$ (i.e. very low amplitude).
Period of the oscillation in $\delta\beta = 5$ years.

The annual deaths from scarlet fever predicted by the model are shown in Fig. 14.6, with some 24 000 dying at the peak of the epidemics and an interepidemic (i.e. 'endemic') death rate of some 11 000 per annum, corresponding to Fig. 14.5A. Again, this epidemic:endemic ratio is produced only by setting the magnitude of $\delta\beta$ at 0.007; only a very low amplitude oscillation in susceptibility is necessary to drive the system. The fraction of infectives that died of the disease in the model was set at 0.35, this value being necessary to produce the drastic mortality in the scarlet fever epidemics seen in Fig. 14.5A and suggesting that the disease took a heavy toll during this 40-year period in the 19th century.

14.10 Reasons for the decline in scarlet fever mortality

No specific measures of prevention or treatment of scarlet fever were available in the 19th century and McKeown & Record (1962) concluded that the only possibilities for the marked reduction in the lethality of the disease towards the end of the century were environmental improvement or a change in the nature of the disease. Scarlet fever was described as a mild disease in 1676 and has since exhibited at least four cycles of severity followed by remission. It was very serious in the late 18th century (probably coincident with the rising wheat prices at that time) and again in the mid-19th century, as we have described in this chapter. It was still a relatively important cause of death at the start of the present century, but has declined progressively and is today a mild disease.

McKeown & Record (1962) believe these modifications in the behaviour of scarlet fever to have been largely independent of environmental changes and conclude that there is no reason to differ from the general opinion that they have resulted from a change in the nature of the disease, probably because of a variation in the virulence of the haemolytic streptococcus rather than to an alteration of the human response to it.

However, whilst agreeing that changes in the bacterium have contributed to the diminished lethality of scarlet fever, particularly in the 20th century world-wide, we have presented evidence in this chapter that the remarkable rise in scarlet fever mortality in England and Wales in the mid-19th century, which persisted for some 40 years, was probably dependent on poor nutritive levels during that time; furthermore, mortality was sharply reduced after 1880, in parallel with falling wheat prices and rising standards of living. It is suggested that epidemics in this lightly damped system were maintained during this period by a low amplitude oscillation in susceptibility produced by the synergistic interaction of cyclical dry conditions in spring/summer and the short wavelength oscillation in wheat prices which caused malnutrition in pregnancy and increased the susceptibility in the subsequent children at a lag of 3 years.

14.11 Diphtheria in England and Wales, 1855–1893

Diphtheria is a bacterial infection of the throat, nose or larynx and, although the causative organism, *Corynebacterium diphtheriae*, remains localised, it produces a powerful exotoxin which becomes widely distributed and may cause serious or fatal effects on other parts of the body. The amount of exotoxin produced by different strains of the organism varies and that is one reason why some infectives are much more severely ill than others. Another reason for the variation in clinical severity is the state of the patient's immunity at the time of infection. The bacterium withstands

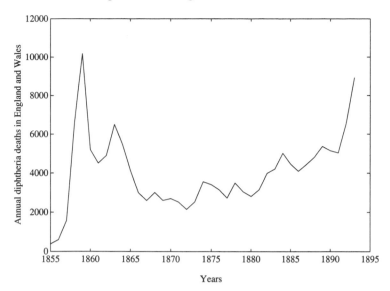

Figure 14.7. Annual deaths from diphtheria in England and Wales, 1855–1893. Data source: Creighton (1894).

drying, may be isolated from the dust round the beds in diphtheria wards and remains virulent for 5 weeks. It may also be isolated from the floordust of classrooms, even after all known carriers have been removed, although spread is normally directly by droplets from an infective. The number of cases of diphtheria per year in England and Wales between 1915 and 1942 was about 50 000 and the number of deaths was around 4000 per year at the beginning and 2500 per year at the end of this time. During this period in the 20th century, the disease ranked first as a cause of death in children aged 4 to 10 years and second in the 3- to 4-year age-group. Mass immunization then began to show its effect and by 1950 the number of cases had fallen to 962 with 49 deaths.

The biology of diphtheria epidemics in the 19th century is considered in this section. The annual deaths from the disease in England and Wales during the period 1855–1893 taken from the registration details are shown in Fig. 14.7. There was an impressive rise in mortality during the pandemic of 1858/9 when it first appeared world-wide; it was only in some parts of France, Norway and Denmark that diphtheria had been epidemic in the generation before. Creighton (1894) stated that diphtheria came as a novelty to the medical profession in England and referred to the first public notice of a fatal throat epidemic in the Registrar-General's third quarterly report of 1857 and to the many accounts of the epidemic in the medical journals in 1858. The two years of the epidemic coincided with the River Thames running so low in summer as to give out a stench, which was the consequence of a succession of years when rainfall was below average.

This epidemic was followed by a second, smaller outbreak in 1863, but thereafter the endemic level fell to some 2500 deaths per year, with very low amplitude epidemics superimposed, and spectral analysis reveals that their period was 5 years. The trend in the endemic level of deaths then rose progressively after 1880 (Fig. 14.7), leading to its ranking first as the cause of death in the 4–10 year olds in the early 20th century.

A possible driver for these low-level, 5-yearly epidemics of diphtheria has been sought in the standard, seasonal weather conditions using multivariate analysis, cross-correlation function and coherence. In summary, the analysis suggests that the epidemics were associated with dry seasons (i.e. low rainfall), although the correlation is not good. It is noteworthy that the first epidemic of 1858 coincided with severe drought conditions. The effect of warm winters is more significant (multivariate analysis shows $P = 0.03$) and spectral analysis of the winter temperature series reveals a strong 5-year oscillation which cross-correlates with the diphtheria epidemics. The two series are significantly coherent in the 5-year waveband ($P < 0.01$). Creighton (1894) recorded that winter appeared to be the most fatal season for diphtheria.

The 5-yearly diphtheria epidemics also cross-correlate strongly at zero lag with *low* wheat prices in both the filtered and unfiltered series, i.e. there is a 3-year lag in the positive correlation with high wheat prices. This finding corresponds with the effects of wheat prices on the epidemiology of scarlet fever and it is concluded that malnutrition is having a similar effect in the two diseases by acting in pregnancy to produce susceptible children who die in the next epidemic.

However, the initial outbreak of diphtheria in 1858/9 was followed by a sharply decaying oscillation, suggestive of a system obeying SEIR dynamics and we conclude that it is only weakly driven by an oscillation in susceptibility. The rising trend in the endemic level seen at the end of the 19th century is probably linked to the sharply rising population numbers but may also have been associated with the virtual disappearance of smallpox (because of vaccination) and scarlet fever (probably because of improved nutrition) as lethal diseases. The pool of potential susceptibles to diphtheria and measles rose as the population increased and as many more children escaped from these other previously serious diseases.

14.12 Overview of the interactions of lethal infectious diseases in England and Wales in the 19th century: effects of malnutrition

It is evident from the foregoing that these infectious diseases were a major factor in determining the demography of England in earlier centuries. In 1851, the greatest mortality was from scarlet fever, followed by, in descending order, whooping cough, measles, smallpox and diphtheria, whereas in 1891 this sequence had become measles, whooping cough, diphtheria, scarlet fever and smallpox.

The acceptance of vaccination (it was made compulsory in 1854, but the law was not enforced until 1871) ensured that smallpox ceased to be the most feared killer of the 17th and 18th centuries and progressively became a spent force. McKeown & Record (1962) have estimated that its contribution (about 6%) to the reduction of mortality during the second half of the 19th century was small. The exception is the great and inexplicable mortality in the smallpox epidemic of 1870.

With the progressive reduction in smallpox mortality a greater proportion of an ever-growing population of young children joined the pool of those susceptible to measles. The epidemics became firmly established at 2-year intervals with seasonal climatic drivers and mortality rose steadily.

The two bacterial diseases, scarlet fever and diphtheria, have features in common and there was confusion in their diagnosis until 1855 (McKeown & Record, 1962). Coherence and cross-correlation studies suggest that both were associated with dry conditions and the two diseases show positive cross-correlation at zero lag. Both diseases emerged or re-emerged with high mortality in the 19th century, the gradual disappearance of smallpox providing a greater pool of susceptibles, but their underlying dynamics were very different. Scarlet fever epidemics lasted for some 40 years, with an interepidemic interval of 5–6 years and is suggested as an example of a system driven by an oscillation in susceptibility. The epidemics of diphtheria decayed and are believed to follow SEIR dynamics and the system was only weakly driven. Unlike scarlet fever, the endemic level of diphtheria did not decrease but, instead, started to rise during the last part of the 19th century.

Evidence is presented in this and earlier chapters that nutritive levels could have affected the dynamics and lethality of infectious diseases in profound, but hitherto undetected and unquantified ways. Firstly, malnutrition and accompanying hardship may directly increase overall susceptibility and lethality and raise the value of $N\beta$; examples include smallpox in London in the late 18th century and scarlet fever in the mid-19th century. Deaths from diphtheria, in contrast, rose at the end of the

19th century when conditions were improving. Secondly, a short wavelength oscillation in wheat prices may generate an oscillation in $\delta\beta$ and so drive the epidemics directly; examples are whooping cough in London during 1785–1812 and the smallpox epidemics at Penrith. Thirdly, malnutrition during pregnancy, lactation or weaning may produce more susceptible children and so contribute to the cyclical mortality of the epidemics (see section 7.6). These situations can be identified when the epidemics of a disease cross-correlate with the short wavelength oscillation in wheat prices but at a lag of 2 to 3 years. Examples are measles in London in the 18th century and scarlet fever and diphtheria in the 19th century. Some of these interacting effects of changed nutritive levels are summarised in Fig. 12.16.

15

Prospectives – towards a metapopulation study

Time-series analysis is a valuable technique for historical demographers in their studies of population cycles and the epidemiology of diseases. This statistical technique can be applied to runs of data, including parish register series, commodity prices, Bills of Mortality and meterological records and the significance of their cross-correlation can be determined. We have shown how both endogenous and exogenous oscillations can be uncovered by this means in single populations (section 3.5). Matrix modelling of a community maintained in steady-state suggests that synchronous, long wavelength cycles in births and deaths (section 4.1) are endogenous and dependent on the inherent properties of the system and are triggered by a mortality crisis. Such endogenous cycles, which have been detected in different populations probably living under density-dependent constraints, appear to have a wavelength of about 43 or 44 years which reflects the interaction of the demographic parameters and the dynamics of the population (i.e. the fertility function and the gain of the feedback; see section 5.5).

In contrast, short wavelength, exogenous, mortality cycles can be detected quite commonly in the dynamics of many populations; infant, child and adult burial series probably oscillate independently but all three are driven, either directly or indirectly (via effects in pregnancy, section 7.7), by commodity prices, usually the price of grain (Chapter 7). Severe mortality crises were produced in communities in the northwest when the adverse effects of two commodities synchronised and interacted synergistically (Chapter 8). The exogenous short wavelength oscillation in births is driven by the mortality oscillation but is exactly out of phase, in accordance with the predictions from matrix modelling (section 7.8). The child mortality cycles were sharpened up in some rural towns by the superimposition of smallpox epidemics that may have been initially triggered in years in which wheat prices were high and exacerbated malnutrition.

321

The epidemiology of lethal infectious diseases can be understood only by modelling the epidemics, which illustrates the subject of this book, namely the complex interaction between human demography and disease. We present an overview and classification of the characteristics of small-pox epidemics in different communities in England in section 13.11, based on time-series analysis and mathematical modelling and show how these can be correlated with the population dynamics. These different categories probably form a continuum, but two main conditions can be recognised, the epidemic and endemic situations. Smallpox was epidemic in medium-sized market towns, with no outbreaks in the interepidemic years, where the interepidemic interval was determined primarily by the time taken after an epidemic to build up a sufficient density of susceptibles by new births, although the initial outbreaks were probably triggered by a year of malnutrition. In contrast, smallpox was gradually established in cities and large conurbations as an endemic disease with superimposed epidemics as the population progressively increased in size and density; the evolution of the dynamics of these epidemics, with a climax situation of regular, 2-yearly epidemics, is described in Chapters 9 and 10. The conclusion from time-series analysis and from linearised and non-linear modelling of a number of lethal infections in large conurbations is that the results are con-sistent with a system driven by a low amplitude cycle of susceptibility which could be caused by a variety of external factors provided that they oscil-lated at the resonant frequency of the system.

One theme of this study is the underlying importance of sharply chang-ing levels of malnutrition which are the result of the short wavelength oscillation in grain prices (Chapter 6). This appears, at first sight, to go against current accepted opinion which is summarised by Livi-Bacci (1991) as follows: 'The picture that emerges casts doubt upon the existence of any long-term interrelationship between subsistence or nutritional levels and mortality, showing that the level of the latter was determined more by the epidemiological cycles than by the nutritional level of the population'. However, although there are significant correlations between the trend in grain prices and the endemic levels of smallpox (Chapter 9) and scarlet fever (section 14.7), the major and significant effects of malnutrition were in the short term. These effects were important, but were subliminal and not readily detectable other than by time-series analysis, which also pro-vides estimates of the confidence limits for the observed correlations, although correlation does not prove causality. Thus, wheat prices did not appear to affect the 'baseline' mortality rates (except, perhaps, scarlet fever), but the oscillations of malnutrition which they introduced caused a

Table 15.1. *Weekly budget of a poor rural family of seven in 1841*

Bread	9s
Rent	1s 2d
Sugar	3½d
Washing blue	½d
Candles	3d
Coal and wood	9d
Cheese	3d
Potatoes	1s
Tea	2d
Soap	3d
Thread	2d
Salt	½d
Butter	4½d
Total weekly earnings	13s 9d

Source: The Health of Adult Britain 1841–1994; the Stationary Office, 1997.

corresponding, superimposed mortality cycle in which the weak and disadvantaged probably died. The effects of malnutrition during pregnancy on the health and susceptibility to disease of the subsequent children is described in detail in sections 7.7 and 11.6. For these reasons the infant, child and adult mortalities would respond to a sharp rise in wheat prices with different lags. Changes in infant mortality have the most important effects on $\overset{o}{e}_0$ and so, in turn, modify the dynamics of lethal infectious diseases (section 12.5.3).

Figures 4.6 and 4.7 reveal the marked teenage subfertility that existed at Penrith over a period of 250 years, a feature that is found in Third World countries today. Current studies show that girls born to malnourished mothers carry a handicap forward and grow up to become unhealthy mothers themselves, even when given an adequate diet as children. In this way, the adverse effects of female malnutrition were perpetuated in successive generations and we suggest that this effect may account for the characteristic teenage subfertility found in communities living under marginal conditions.

Table 15.1 gives the average weekly budget of a poor rural family of seven in 1841 and it is striking that, even into the 19th century, 65% of income was spent on bread. Not only was this protein-deficient but rises in the price of grains would have had severe consequences for the nutritive levels of this family. It is not surprising that the poorer classes in earlier centuries in England were so sensitive to the short wavelength oscillation in grain prices and we suggest comparisons between the demography and the effects of malnutrition in 17th and 18th century England and under-developed countries today.

15.1 Mortality cycles in 404 aggregated parishes

In this book we have mainly been concerned with exploring the dynamics of single populations and our conclusions therefrom are summarised above. How do the results from single communities compare with the findings from multi-parish studies which may display different dynamics and have experienced diverse economic circumstances? Wrigley & Schofield (1981) gave the annual, aggregate totals of baptisms and burials from their study of 404 parishes from 1539 to 1871, and short wavelength oscillations in the plotted data are evident by eye. These short-term variations have been studied by Lee (1981), who concluded that mortality was increased by cold temperatures in winter and by hot temperatures in summer and that variation in the price of grain accounted for only a small proportion of the variance in mortality. We have studied the aggregated data series of total burials provided by Wrigley & Schofield for the harvest years 1539–1870 by time-series analysis: when it is detrended the short wavelength oscillation shows clearly on spectral analysis. It was non-stationary, with a wavelength varying between 5 and 7 years ($P < 0.01$), and correlated with the wheat price index as follows:

(1) 1539–1600: ccf = +0.58, lag = −2 years.
(2) 1600–1650: ccf = +0.6, zero lag.
(3) 1650–1700: ccf = +0.24, zero lag.
(4) 1700–1750: ccf = +0.4, lag = 0 to −1 years.
(5) 1750–1800: ccf = +0.4, but lag now = +1 to +2 years.
(6) 1800–1873: ccf = only +0.17, lag = −1 year.

Thus, the short wavelength mortality cycle in the aggregated data cross-correlates well with the wheat price index during the years 1539 to 1750, although the association was much weaker from 1650 to 1700. The amplitude of the mortality oscillations during the boom, after 1750, was much smaller and was not significantly correlated with wheat prices.

These findings reflect, and are comparable with, the persistent exogenous mortality cycles at Penrith which correlated with grain prices and which are described in Chapter 7. Child mortality, driven by smallpox deaths, was particularly correlated with grain prices at Penrith during the period 1650 to 1700, whereas adult mortality was less significantly associated at this time. The data from 404 parishes is not divided into child and adult deaths and, furthermore, many of these communities were probably too small to have regular epidemics (section 13.11) and this probably accounts for the weaker association with wheat prices during 1650 to 1700 in the national burial series.

The oscillation in baptisms in the series from 404 parishes is of smaller amplitude than that for burials; its wavelength was 5 to 6 years and its significance on spectral analysis was weaker. Nevertheless, the cycle in baptisms was strongly and negatively correlated with burials (i.e. 180° out of phase):

(1) 1539–1650: ccf = −0.4; zero lag.
(2) 1650–1750: ccf = −0.7; zero lag.
(3) 1750–1871: ccf = −0.25; zero lag (i.e. the correlation was weaker in this cohort).

Again, this finding corresponds with the demographic analysis at Penrith and with the predictions of the matrix modelling (section 7.8), where the oscillations in births and deaths are 180° out of phase.

We conclude that the *exogenous* oscillations, characterised and described in single communities in this book reflect the picture nationally in earlier centuries, particularly pre-1750, suggesting that malnutrition could have had subtle and not readily detectable effects on mortality cycles at that time. This effect of grain prices pre-1750, therefore, was not confined to marginal farming communities but must have existed to some extent throughout the country; indeed, the Northern Province is underrepresented in the 404 parishes studied by Wrigley and Schofield.

However, we suggest that much valuable information (e.g. endogenous oscillations) is lost by simply combining data from disparate communities and that one way forward is to begin by exploring the interactions between the communities in a geographical region, namely a metapopulation study.

15.2 Metapopulation dynamics

The term metapopulation is used by ecologists to describe a population of populations. The study of metapopulation dynamics in biology is normally concerned with the behaviour of a single species over time; there are no static populations and likewise there is no such thing as a static metapopulation. The metapopulation concept in ecology is closely linked with the processes of population turnover, extinction and the establishment of new populations, and the study of metapopulation dynamics is essentially the study of the turbulent conditions under which these processes are in balance (Hanski & Gilpin, 1991).

Ecological metapopulation theory, with one exception, has not been applied to human populations; indeed, as originally defined, it is not strictly applicable because it deals with extinctions and recolonisations and makes the simplifying assumption that each habitat patch or ecological site is regarded as being in one of two alternative states, either empty (extinct) or filled to their local carrying capacity (Ebenhard, 1991), characteristics that were rarely found in pre-industrial England during the period of study. The exception concerns studies of spatial heterogeneity and the epidemic spread of infectious diseases through a human metapopulation, the extension of the modelling developed in Chapters 9 to 14 and an example of the interaction between human demography and disease. Rhodes & Anderson (1996) described a model of the spread of measles or another communicable disease in a spatially extended host population which used lattice-based simulation as a way of incorporating spatial effects. Each non-empty site on the lattice is either susceptible, infective or recovered (see section 9.2). The modelling shows that a population threshold exists which is affected by the rate of population mixing and below which the disease dies out and above which it settles to an endemically stable state. Similar models have been used to study epidemic spread through stationary populations on lattices (Cardy, 1983; Grassberger, 1983; Cardy & Grassberger, 1985).

Spatial heterogeneity is believed to play an important role in the persistence and dynamics of epidemics because asynchrony between populations within different regions allows global persistence, even if the disease dies out locally. An ecological multi-patch (metapopulation) model for epidemics shows that the patches in non-seasonal deterministic models often oscillate in phase; synchronization is also seen for stochastic models, although slightly stronger coupling is needed to overcome the random effects (Lloyd & May, 1996).

Although the basic equations of ecological metapopulation dynamics are not applicable to the human populations that we have studied, we suggest that it should be possible to provide a demographic description of the dynamics of an identifiable region over time by assembling and studying the interactions between them. Present-day geographers are well versed in considering regions as combinatorial structures in the planning process of aggregating subareas into regions (Cliff *et al.*, 1975). We have laid the foundations in this book for such a metapopulation study of an area of northwest England circumscribed by the Pennines to the east, the hills of the Lake District to the west and the Westmorland fells to the south over a period of 250 years, and the responses of different communities in the region to prices of grains and wool are illustrated in Chapter 8. The classification of the different types of dynamics that may be found in separate communities in the metapopulation are summarised in Chapter 5 and Fig. 5.1.

Caswell (1989) has introduced the concept of stage-classified life cycles into matrix modelling and has drawn a distinction between the state of an individual (an *i*-state) and the state of a population (a *p*-state). In addition to age, environmental variables, spatial subdivision, climate, marital status, and reproductive socio-behaviour are examples of *i*-state variables, and density functions are an example of *p*-state variables. Multiregional studies are an extension of these stage-classified matrix models (Caswell, 1989) and, initially, the plan would be to study the basic dynamics of adjacent populations. (a) Was the population booming, declining or in steady-state? (b) Does the population size/density determine the impact of lethal epidemics such as the plague or smallpox (section 13.11)? (c) Are steady-state conditions with feedback a requirement for the generation of long wavelength (endogenous) oscillations (Chapter 4)? (d) What effect do different *i*-state variables have on the dynamics of different but adjacent populations? (e) Can cycles in emigration from one centre be correlated with immigration elsewhere? Can these migratory movements be explained in terms of *i*-state variables? (f) There is currently considerable debate concerning the relative importance of nutritional status versus socio-economic and behavioural factors in regulating the incidence and impact of infectious diseases (Scrimshaw *et al.*, 1968; Landers, 1986; Livi-Bacci, 1991) and we expect that, in addition to population density, these factors were complex and interrelated in the Eden Valley. (g) Do all, or most, populations in the region display a short wavelength, exogenous mortality cycle? If so, were they synchronized? The time-series analysis described in section 15.1 for the 404 parishes suggests that they probably were, although the statistical significance of the correlation may be poor, particularly after 1700.

The arrival of the plague in the northwest, with its catastrophic mortality (section 3.6), did not bring about conditions that approached extinction, as required in classical metapopulation theory, but it greatly exacerbated migratory movements within the region. The spread of the plague in 1597/8 in northwest England is described in the next section; it triggered major demographic changes in the metapopulation.

15.3 The spread of the plague in northwest England, a study in metapopulation dynamics

A pandemic persisted throughout the north of England at the end of the 16th century. The plague had raged severely in northeast England in 1589 following years of food scarcity, and in 1597 the combination of famine and plague afflicted the area again: the plague was in Newcastle in January 1597 and spread through the northern counties (Creighton, 1894). By September, the disease was increasing in virulence in Newcastle and was also at Darlington and Durham.

Concomitant with this persistent and severe plague in Northumberland and Durham, there was an equally devastating epidemic in the North Riding of Yorkshire, particularly in the parish of Richmond. The characteristics of this outbreak closely resembled those observed at Penrith (section 3.6): both were market towns and, although the plague reached Richmond a month earlier (August), deaths also finally ceased by December 1598. The population appeared to suffer as grievously as at Penrith, with many victims having to be buried on the fells. From Richmond, the disease spread across the Pennines to the counties of Westmorland and Cumberland. The plague moved along trade routes from east to west via the Stainmore/Bowes Moor gap, thence northwards from market town to market town and eventually crossed the border to southern Scotland. It also moved southwards from Kendal, as shown in Fig. 15.1, so that its effects were felt throughout the northwest. Identification of parishes that were affected by plague is hampered by the fact that most parishes in Cumberland and Westmorland recorded serious food shortages and above-average mortality in 1597, and a number of authors have attributed this increase in burials to the plague simply because the disease was known to be present in the northwest by autumn 1597 (Howson, 1961). Inspection of the registers of a number of smaller parishes shows that there was neither a mention of plague as the cause of death, nor an increase in the number of burials during the period that the disease was prevalent in the area and the parishes shown in Fig. 15.1 are those where the occurrence of the plague has been identified with certainty.

The pandemic affected a number of the settlements in the area, being far more prevalent in the market towns in the Eden Valley than in the surrounding countryside. The only exception was the market centre of Brough-under-Stainmore where the disease did not gain a strong foothold; only eight deaths occurred in November 1597, albeit over 20 days, and there were no further deaths from the plague until July 1598, when seven more fell victim.

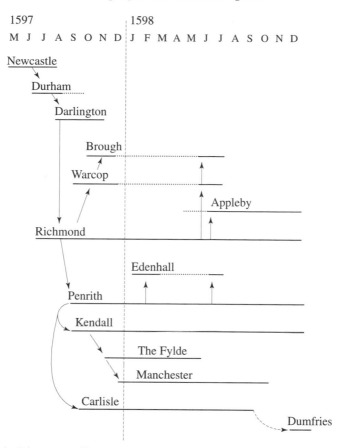

Figure 15.1. Diagram to illustrate the timing and duration of plague epidemics in the northwest, 1597/8. Arrows indicate probable spread of the disease, although Kendal may have received the infection directly from Richmond rather than via Penrith. Lines indicate the duration of the epidemic: dotted lines indicate probable persistence of the disease but with no recorded cases; broken line indicates suggested movement of the plague from Carlisle to Dumfries. Months are shown at the top of the figure.

Between 1 August 1598 and the following 25 March 1599, 128 persons died at Appleby and its environs, and it is inferred that death was because of the plague. Burials of the first plague victims in both Kendal and Carlisle occurred on 3 October 1597, 12 days after the first burial at Penrith, indicating a rapid spread of the infection. At Carlisle, the number of households visited by the plague was 242 from a total of 316 (Hughes, 1971) and the scale of infection was similar to that seen at Penrith where it was estimated that 242 families out of 323 had been affected (Scott *et al.*, 1996).

The infection spread outwards from Kendal, causing major mortality crises in larger communities in the Fylde and arrived in Manchester in December 1597 (France, 1939). The infection also appeared in some of the smaller parishes adjacent to the afflicted market centres but only on a very small scale. Edenhall, a small parish to the east of Penrith, had 4 deaths in one family in March 1598 with a further 31 deaths in the following summer. At Warcop, the disease appeared to be confined to one part of the parish and to only two families.

The following conclusions concerning the relationship between the epidemiology of the disease and the demography of the metapopulation can be drawn:

(1) There is little difference in the timing and severity of the epidemics in Kendal, Carlisle, Penrith and Richmond (Fig. 15.1) and the plague evidently spread rapidly.
(2) The dynamics of the disease, again, were probably dependent on the density and size of the constituent populations (see section 9.4); the epidemics did not explode in the smaller communities and the minimum population size was probably about 1300 (Scott *et al.*, 1996).
(3) Northwest England suffered a major mortality crisis in the year preceding the plague, stemming from famine and hardship, as described in Chapter 8, and this may have contributed to the explosion of the plague, via malnutrition, and also to the movements of vagrants and beggars disseminating the infection.
(4) The nature of the causative agent that was responsible for the mortality in the northwest is briefly discussed in section 3.6.

The most important demographic consequence of the mortality of the plague, once the fear of infection was past, was extensive migratory movement. The populations of these towns were not extinguished after this catastrophe, as in classical metapopulation theory, but a large proportion died, leaving many ecological niches to be filled by incomers from the surrounding, untouched communities. This immigration was a major factor in the initiation of the endogenous oscillations at Penrith described in Chapters 3 and 4.

15.4 Migration and dispersal in the metapopulation

Paradoxically, dispersal is the glue that keeps local populations together in a biological metapopulation (Hansson, 1991). It is of primary importance to biologists (and to historical demographers studying marginal communities which lived under the constraints of food supply and available ecological niches) to know what factors trigger dispersal and whether these are density-dependent or not. It is interesting to compare the demographer's view of dispersal with that of a biologist which can be stated as follows: density-dependent dispersal will increase the role of large or growing populations in metapopulation dynamics. If, on the other hand, the tendency to disperse is inherent, and a constant fraction of individuals emigrate, then large 'mainland' populations would play a relatively less important role in metapopulation dynamics. Differences in proneness to dispersal between population categories (age, sex, etc.) will determine which kind of individuals will arrive at the receiving populations. The genetic constitution of dispersing and non-dispersing individuals may differ and affect the genetic structure of the metapopulation. Habitat requirements (sheltered environments, corridors, etc.) during dispersal may crucially influence the distances moved and may thus determine the spatial extension of a metapopulation. The time of dispersal may affect the potential contribution to the reproductive output in the receiving population. The health or fitness of the immigrating individuals is also of prime importance for their influence (Hansson, 1991).

Biologists regard the factors that promote dispersal in animal metapopulations as falling into three categories; again, there is correspondence with the views of human demographers:

(1) Economic thresholds. An individual disperses, as a proximate response, when its food supply (or some other resource) diminishes below a critical level. An increase in the perceived number of individuals in the neighbourhood may release emigration as a possible indicator of impending food shortage.

(2) Conflicts over resources. The resource may be food or shelter (i.e. the patch or ecological niche) but is often mates. A possible conflict between parents and offspring over breeding opportunities (the Oedipus hypothesis) is another example. Inferior individuals are forced to disperse, usually before the conflicts escalate to actual fights. Such conflicts may ultimately select for an innate dispersal biased towards inferior social categories.

(3) Inbreeding avoidance has been considered both as an ultimate adaptation and a proximate cause of dispersal. Individuals of one sex should disperse from each litter to mate with unrelated conspecifics. Dispersal is typically male-biased in mammals whereas it is female-biased in birds.

Migration can be defined in the light of the demographic balancing equation

$$Pt = Po + B - D + IM - OM \qquad (15.1)$$

where:

Pt   = population at the close of interval.
Po   = population at the beginning of the interval.
B   = number of births in the interval.
D   = number of deaths in the interval.
IM   = number of in-migrants in the interval.
OM = number of out-migrants in the interval.

The rate of migration is defined as

$$m = \frac{M}{P} \times K \qquad (15.2)$$

where:

m = migration rate.
M = number of migrants.
P = population at risk.
K = a constant, usually 100 or 1000.

Human migration is a fundamental spatial process and is a major cause of social change and can be viewed as an independent, as well as a dependent, variable in the examination of change. An area may grow in population size by an influx of people or it may decline by an outflow of its members, and it is now recognized that migration is usually the most important factor in differential population trends. Differences in natural increase (in birth rates and death rates) between areas are often smaller than differences in migration rates. If such movements are selective of individuals in terms of age, sex or economic or social attributes, they will determine the differences in the demographic and socio-economic composition of the metapopulation. Moreover, the migrant can initiate further change in his new place of residence by the introduction of new ideas, values, skills and even reproductive behaviour. In other words, migration is a two-way process: it is a response to economic and social change and, equally, it is a catalyst for change for those areas gaining or losing migrants. Migration has widespread consequences for the individual migrant, for the community of origin and of destination, and for the society within which the movement takes place (Lewis, 1982).

Migration and dispersal in Penrith and the Eden Valley in the 17th century appears to have been largely density dependent. Inheritance customs in Cumberland, whereby each son had a piece of their father's holding led to the progressive subdivision of holdings and the establishment of a large number of cottagers with tiny amounts of lands which exacerbated the effects of scarcity. This practice of partible inheritance and the extreme parcelization of land over generations which it produced, eventually provided too small a living and thereby increased the pressure to migrate.

The plague in Penrith (which the surrounding communities escaped) left a surplus of niches and resources available, and substantial immigration took place (category (1)). Widowers sought second wives in the adjoining parishes (Scott, 1995). As a consequence, the population started to recover, initiating the endogenous, density-dependent oscillations (Chapters 3 and 4). Mathematical modelling of the vector that describes the contribution of migratory movements at Penrith to the feedback is described in section 4.7 and the detection of migration cycles is described in section 4.6. The cycles of migratory incomers were also associated with concomitant rises of illegitimacy. The association between an influx of migrants and illegitimacy was particularly noticeable at Penrith after the mortality crises of the late 16th and early 17th centuries and it has been shown from the family reconstitution study that the children of immigrant families also tended to produce illegitimate offspring (Scott & Duncan, 1997a), an interesting socio-economic consequence of mortality crises and population movements.

In 1750, the optimum level of population at Penrith that could be supported by the resources available clearly rose. This change in the dynamics reflected the general population increase in England at this time, as recorded in the aggregate data from 404 parishes (Wrigley & Schofield, 1981). Fertility at Penrith did not increase, but total childhood mortality fell progressively. Adult mortality also fell, with an improved life expectancy, but this had little effect on the birth rate because the number of offspring per marriage did not rise. A sustained period of low mortality would cause an increase in the total population, but the boom was certainly accompanied by substantial movements, both immigration and emigration (Scott, 1995).

This population boom probably resulted from improvements in agriculture and transport in Cumberland (McKeown, 1983). The turnip was introduced as a field crop in 1755, with improved crop rotation and the provision of winter feed as important consequences, so that the autumn slaughter of beasts was unnecessary and milk, butter and fresh meat became available all the year round. By 1800, turnips were apparently 'cultivated to perfection' in the Eden Valley, where the soil was particularly suitable, and Scottish Highland sheep were imported and fattened on them. Maize was also introduced, together with manuring and improved drainage (Bouch & Jones, 1961). Fleming wrote in 1810: 'Agriculture . . . has become so improved within the last 25 years . . . that the Produce is five Times as much . . . the People live better by one-half, and most of the industrious are becoming professed of independence. Land is become three Times the Value, not only from the increased produce of Grain but also of those productions most suitable and useful for Animals on the Farm . . .'. Together these measures probably led to a progressively greater exploitation of the resources of the community and consequently there was a change in the level of population that could be sustained with a net influx of migrants (Scott, 1995) and a corresponding fall in the population of the surrounding, smaller communities in the metapopulation.

References

Anderson, O. (1984). The decline in Danish mortality before 1850 and its economic and social background. In *Pre-Industrial Population Change*, ed. T. G. Bengtsson, G. Fridlizius & R. Ohlsson, pp. 115–126. Stockholm: Almquist & Wiksell.

Anderson, R. M. (1994). The Croonian Lecture, 1994. Populations, infectious disease and immunity: a very nonlinear world. *Philosophical Transactions of the Royal Society* B, **346**, 457–505.

Anderson, R. M.,Grenfell, B. T. & May, R. M. (1984). Oscillatory fluctuations in the incidence of infectious disease and the impact of vaccination: time series analysis. *Journal of Hygiene*, **93**, 587–608.

Anderson, R. M. & May, R. M. (1982). Directly transmitted infectious diseases: control of vaccination. *Science*, **215**, 1053–1060.

Anderson, R. M. & May, R. M. (1985). Vaccination and herd immunity to infectious diseases. *Nature*, **318**, 323–329.

Anderson, R. M. & May, R. M. (1991). *Infectious Diseases of Humans*. Oxford: Oxford University Press.

Anderson, R. M.,May, R. M.,Boily, M. C.,Garnett, G. P. & Rowley, J. T. (1991). The spread of HIV-1 in Africa: sexual contact patterns and the predicted demographic impact of AIDS. *Nature*, **352**, 581–589.

Appleby, A. B. (1973). Disease or famine? Mortality in Cumberland and Westmorland 1580–1640. *Economic History Review*, **26**, 403–432.

Appleby, A. B. (1975). Nutrition and disease: the case of London, 1550–1750. *Journal of Interdisciplinary History*, **6**, 1–22.

Appleby, A. B. (1978). *Famine in Tudor and Stuart England*. Liverpool: Liverpool University Press.

Appleby, A. B. (1979). Grain prices and subsistence crises in England and France, 1590–1740. *Journal of Economic History*, **39**, 865–887.

Appleby, A. B. (1981). Epidemics and famine in the little ice age. In *Climate and History*, ed. R. I. Rotberg & T. K. Rabb, pp. 65–83. Princeton: Princeton University Press.

Armstrong, D. (1994). Birth, marriage and death in Elizabethan Cumbria. *Local Population Studies*, **53**, 29–41.

Aron, J. L. (1990). Multiple attractors in the response to a vaccination programme. *Theoretical Population Biology*, **38**, 58–67.

Aron, J. L. & Schwartz, I. B. (1984). Seasonality and period-doubling bifurcations in an epidemic model. *Journal of Theoretical Biology*, **110**, 665–679.

335

336 *References*

Ashworth, A. & Feacham, R. G. (1985). Interventions for the control of diarrhoeal diseases among children, prevention of low birthweight. *Bulletin of the W.H.O.* **64**, 165.

Bailey, J. & Culley, G. (1794). *General View of the Agriculture of the County of Cumberland. Drawn up for the Boards of Agriculture.* London.

Bamgboye, E. A. & Familusi, J. B. (1990). Mortality pattern at a children's emergency ward, University College Hospital, Ibadan, Nigeria. *African Journal of Medical Science,* **19**, 127–132.

Banks, J. A. (1968). Historical society and the study of population. *Daedalus,* **97**, 397–414.

Barclay, A. J. G.,Foster, A. & Sommer, A. (1987). Vitamin A supplements and mortality related to measles: a randomised clinical trial. *British Medical Journal,* **294**, 294–296.

Barker, D. J. P. (1992a). *The Fetal and Infant Origins of Adult Disease.* London: British Medical Journal.

Barker, D. J. P. (1992b). Fetal growth and adult disease. *British Journal of Obstetrics and Gynaecology,* **99**, 275–282.

Barker, D. J. P.,Godfrey, K. M.,Fall, C.,Osmond, C.,Winter, P. D. & Shaheen, S. O. (1991). Relation of birth weight and childhood respiratory infection to adult lung function and death from chronic obstructive airways disease. *British Medical Journal,* **303**, 671–675.

Barker, D. J. P. & Martyn, C. N. (1992). The maternal and fetal origins of cardiovascular disease. *Journal of Epidemiology and Community Health,* **46**, 8–11.

Barker, D. J. P. & Osmond, C. (1986a). Infant mortality, childhood nutrition and ischaemic heart disease in England and Wales. *Lancet,* **i**, 1077–1081.

Barker, D. J. P. & Osmond C. (1986b). Childhood respiratory infection and adult chronic bronchitis in England and Wales. *British Medical Journal,* **293**, 1271–1275.

Barker, D. J. P.,Winter, P. D.,Osmond, C.,Margetts, B. & Simmonds, S. J. (1989). Weight in infancy and death from ischaemic heart disease. *Lancet,* **ii**, 577–580.

Barnes, H. (1889). Visitations of the plague in Cumberland and Westmorland. *Transactions of the Cumberland and Westmorland Antiquarian and Archaeological Society,* **XI**, 158–186.

Bartlett, M. S. (1957). Measles periodicity and community size. *Journal of the Royal Statistical Society,* **120**, 48–70.

Bartlett, M. S. (1960). The critical community size for measles in the U. S. *Journal of the Royal Statistical Society,* **123**, 38–44.

Beckett, J. V. (1982). The decline of the small landowners in eighteenth and nineteenth–century England. *Agricultural History Review,* **30**, 97–111.

Benenson, A. S. (1989). Smallpox. In *Viral Infections of Humans: Epidemiology and Control,* ed. A. S. Evans, pp. 633–658. New York: Plenum Press.

Bengtsson, T. & Ohlsson, R. (1984). Age-specific mortality and short-term changes in the standard of living: Sweden 1751–1860. Paper presented at the Social Science History Association Annual Meeting in Toronto.

Bergthorsson, P. (1985). Sensitivity of Icelandic agriculture to climatic variations. *Climatic Change,* **7**, 111–127.

Berman, S. (1991). Epidemiology of acute respiratory infections in children in developing countries. *Review of Infectious Diseases,* **13**, S454–S462.

Bernardelli, H. (1941). Population waves. *Journal of the Burma Research Society,* **31**, 1–18.

Black, F. L. (1966). Measles endemicity in insular populations: critical community size and its evolutionary implication. *Journal of Theoretical Biology*, **11**, 207–211.

Bolker, B. & Grenfell, B. (1992). Are measles epidemics chaotic? *Biologist*, **39**, 107–110.

Bolker, B. M. & Grenfell, B. T. (1993). Chaos and biological complexity in measles dynamics. *Philosophical Transactions of the Royal Society* B, **251**, 75–81.

Bolker, B. M. & Grenfell, B. T. (1995). Space, persistence and dynamics of measles epidemics. *Philosophical Transactions of the Royal Society* B, **348**, 309–320.

Bos, R.,van Dijk, G.,Kruyt, C. & Roessingh, H. K. (1986). Long waves in economic development. *AAG Bijdragen, Netherlands*, **28**, 57–92.

Bouch, C. M. L. & Jones, G. P. (1961). *A Short Economic and Social History of The Lake Counties 1500–1830*. Manchester: Manchester University Press.

Bowden, P. J. (1967). Agricultural prices, farm profits, and rents. In *The Agrarian History of England and Wales*, ed. J. Thirsk, vol. IV, *1500–1640*, pp. 593–695. Cambridge: Cambridge University Press.

Bowden, P. J. (1971). *The Wool Trade in Tudor and Stuart England*. London: Frank Cass.

Bowden, P. J. (1985). Agricultural prices, wages, farm profits and rents. In *The Agrarian History of England and Wales*, ed. J. Thirsk, vol. V, *1640–1750*, pp. 1–117. Cambridge: Cambridge University Press.

Brierley, H. (1908). The registers of the Parish Church of Lancaster. *Lancashire Parish Register Society*.

Brierley, H. (1923). Brough under Stainmore, Westmorland, 1556–1706. *Cumberland and Westmorland Antiquarian and Archaeological Society, Parish Register Series*, IX.

Brierley, H. (1931). Crosthwaite, Cumberland, 1562–1812. *Cumberland and Westmorland Antiquarian and Archaeological Society, Parish Register Series*, XVI-XIX.

Brierley, R. N. (1952). Kendal, Westmorland, 1596–1631. *Cumberland and Westmorland Antiquarian and Archaeological Society, Parish Register Series*, XXXVI.

Brierley, R. N. & Dickinson, R. (1907). *The Registers of the Parish Church of Cartmel*. Lancashire Parish Register Society.

Brown, J. & Beecham, H. A. (1989). Crop pests and diseases. In *Agrarian History of England and Wales*, ed. G. E. Mingay, vol. VI, 1750–1850, pp. 311–313. Cambridge: Cambridge University Press.

Bryson, R. A. & Padoch, C. (1981). Climates of history. In *Climate and History*, ed. R. I. Rotberg & T. K. Rabb. Princeton: Princeton University Press.

Burnet, H. (1953). *Natural History of Infectious Diseases*. Cambridge: Cambridge University Press.

Caldwell, P. (1996). Child survival: physical vulnerability and resilience in adversity in the European past and the contemporary Third World. *Social Science and Medicine*, **43**, 609–619.

Cardy, J. (1983). Field theoretic formulation of an epidemic process with immunisation. *Journal of Physics, A: Mathematical and General*, **16**, L709–L712.

Cardy, J. & Grassberger, P. (1985). Epidemic models and percolation. *Journal of Physics, A: Mathematical and General*, **16**, L267–L271.

Caswell, H. (1989). *Matrix Population Models*. Sunderland, MA: Sinauer Associates, Inc.

Champion, J. (1993). Epidemics and the built environment in 1665. In *Epidemic Disease in London*, pp. 35–52. University of London: Centre for Metropolitan History Working Papers Series No. 1.

Chen, L. C. & Chowhury, A. K. M. (1977). The dynamics of contemporary famine. *Mexico International Population Conference*, vol. 1, pp. 409–425. Liège: International Union for the Scientific Study of Population.

Chippindall, W. H. (1931). Thornton-in-Lonsdale, Lancashire, 1576–1812. *Leeds Lancashire Parish Register Society*, **67**.

Christie, A. B. (1980). *Infectious Diseases*. Edinburgh: Churchill Livingstone.

Clark, P.,Gaskin, K. & Wilson, A. (1989). *Population estimates of English small towns 1550–1851*. Centre for Urban History, University of Leicester, Working Paper No. 3.

Cliff, A. D. & Haggett, P. (1988). Atlas of disease distributions: analytic approaches to epidemiological datA. Oxford: Blackwell Reference.

Cliff, A. D.,Haggett, P.,Ord, J. K.,Bassett, K. A. & Davies, R. B. (1975). *Elements of Spatial Structure. A Quantitative Approach*. Cambridge: Cambridge University Press.

Cliff, A. D.,Haggett, P.,Ord, J. K. & Versey, G. R. (1981). *Spatial Diffusion. An Historical Geography of Epidemics in an Island Community*. Cambridge: Cambridge University Press.

Clutton-Brock, T. H. (1991). *The Evolution of Parental Care*. Princeton: Princeton University Press.

Coale, A. J. & Demeny, P. (1966). *Regional Model Life Tables and Stable Populations*. Princeton: Princeton University Press.

Corfield, P. J. (1987). Introduction. In *The Speckled Monster, Smallpox in England, 1670–1970*, ed. J. R. Smith, pp. 1–2. Hunstanton, Norfolk: Witley Press.

Crampton, J. M. (1994). Approaches to vector control – new and trusted. 3. Prospects for genetic manipulation of insect vectors. *Transactions of the Royal Society of Tropical Medicine*, **88**, 141–143.

Crampton, J. M.,Warren, A.,Lycett, G. J.,Hughes, M. A.,Comley, I. P. & Eccleston, P. (1994). Genetic manipulation of insect vectors as a strategy for the control of vector-borne disease. *Annals of Tropical Medicine and Parasitology*, **88**, 3–12.

Creighton, C. (1894). *History of Epidemics in Britain*. Cambridge: Cambridge University Press.

Cronje, G. (1984). Tuberculosis and mortality decline in England and Wales, 1851–1910. In *Urban Disease and Mortality in Nineteenth-Century England*, ed. R. Woods & J. Woodward, pp. 79–101. London: Batsford Academic.

DeVries, J. (1981). Measuring the impact of climate on history: the search for appropriate methodologies. In *Climate and History*, ed. R. I. Rotberg & T. K. Rabb, pp. 19–50. Princeton: Princeton University Press.

Dietz, K. (1976). The incidence of infectious diseases under the influence of seasonal fluctuations. In *Lecture Notes in Biomathematics*, ed. J. Berger, W. Buhler, R. Repges & P. Tantu, pp. 1–15. Heidelberg, Berlin: Springer Verlag.

Dixon, C. W. (1962). *Smallpox*. London: Churchill Livingstone.

Downie, A. W. (1970). Smallpox. In *Infectious Agents and Host Reactions*, ed. S. Mudd, 487–518. Philadelphia: Saunders.

Drake, M. (1962). An elementary exercise in parish register demography. *Economic History Review*, XVI, 427–445.

Dunbar, R. I. M. (1982). Life history tactics and alternative strategies of reproduction. In *Mate Choice*, ed. P. Bateson, pp. 423–434. Cambridge: Cambridge University Press.

Duncan, C. J.,Duncan, S. R. & Scott, S. (1996a). Whooping cough epidemics in London, 1701–1812: infection dynamics, seasonal forcing and the effects of malnutrition. *Proceedings of the Royal Society* B, **263**, 445–450.

Duncan, C. J.,Duncan, S. R. & Scott, S. (1996b). The dynamics of scarlet fever epidemics in England and Wales in the 19th century. *Epidemiology and Infection*, **117**, 493–499.

Duncan, C. J.,Duncan, S. R. & Scott, S. (1997). The dynamics of measles epidemics. *Theoretical Population Biology*, **52**, 155–163.

Duncan, S. R.,Scott, S. & Duncan, C. J. (1992). Time series analysis of oscillations in a model population: the effects of plague, pestilence and famine. *Journal of Theoretical Biology*, **158**, 293–311.

Duncan, S. R.,Scott, S. & Duncan, C. J. (1993). An hypothesis for the periodicity of smallpox epidemics as revealed by time series analysis. *Journal of Theoretical Biology*, **160**, 231–248.

Duncan, S. R.,Scott, S. & Duncan, C. J. (1994a). Modelling the different smallpox epidemics in England. *Philosophical Transactions of the Royal Society* B, **346**, 407–419.

Duncan, S. R.,Scott, S. & Duncan, C. J. (1994b). Predictions from time series analysis of the oscillations in parish register series. *Journal of Theoretical Biology*, **168**, 95–103.

Easterlin, R. A. (1968). *Population, Labor Force and Long Swings in Economic Growth: The American experience*. New York: National Bureau for Economic Research.

Easterlin, R. (1980). *Birth and Fortune*. New York: Basic Books.

Ebenhard, T. (1991). Colonization in metapopulations: a review of theory and observations. *Biological Journal of the Linnean Society*, **42**, 105–121.

Eckstein, Z.,Schultz, T. P. & Wolpin, K. I. (1985). Short-run fluctuations in fertility and mortality in pre-industrial Sweden. *European Economic Review*, **26**, 295–317.

Eden, F. M. (1797). *The State of the Poor*, vol. I. London: J. Davis.

Editorial. (1968). Measles in Africa. *Lancet*, **1**, 239.

Ellner, S. (1993). Detecting low-dimensional chaos in population dynamics data: a critical review. In *Chaos and Insect Ecology*, ed. J. A. Logan & F. P. Hain, pp. 63–90. Upland, PA: Diane.

Espenshade, T. J.,Bouvier, L. F. & Arthur, W. B. (1982). Immigration and the stable population model. *Demography*, **19**, 125–133.

Everitt, A. (1967). The marketing of agricultural produce. In *The Agrarian History of England and Wales*, ed. J. Thirsk, vol. IV, *1500–1640*, pp. 466–592. Cambridge: Cambridge University Press.

Farrall, L. M. (1914). Chester, Holy Trinity, 1598–1812. Chester: G. R. Griffith.

Ferriere, R. & Gatto, M. (1993). Chaotic population dynamics can result from natural selection. *Proceedings of the Royal Society* B, **251**, 33–38.

Fine, P. E. M. (1993). Herd immunity: history, theory, practice. *Epidemiologic Review*, **15**, 265–304.

Fine, P. E. M. & Clarkson, J. A. (1982). Measles in England and Wales. I: An analysis of factors underlying seasonal patterns. *International Journal of Epidemiology*, **11**, 5–14.

Flinn, M. (ed.) (1977). *Scottish Population History from the 17th century to the 1930s*. Cambridge: Cambridge University Press.

Floud, R. C.,Wachter, K. W. & Gregory, A. (1990). *Height, Health, and History: Nutritional Status in the United Kingdom, 1750–1980.* Cambridge: Cambridge University Press.

Fogel, R. W. (1994). Economic growth, population theory, and physiology: the bearing of long-term processes on the making of economic policy. *American Economic Review*, **84**, 369–395.

Foster, S. O. (1984). Intervening variables and parasitic diseases. In *Child Survival: Strategies for Research,* ed. W. H. Mosley & L. C. Chen. Supplement to *Populations and Development Review*, **10**, 130.

France, R. S. (1939). A history of plague in Lancashire. *Transactions of the Historic Society*, **90**, 1–175.

Franklin, G. F.,Powell, J. D. & Emani-Naeini, A. (1994). *Feedback Control of Dynamic Systems*, 3rd edn. Reading, MA: Addison-Wesley.

Fraser, K. B. & Martin, S. J. (1978). *Measles Virus and its Biology*. London: Academic Press.

Frauenthal, J. & Swick, K. (1983). Limit cycle oscillations of the human population. *Demography*, **20**, 285–298.

Galley, C. (1994). A never-ending succession of epidemics? Mortality in Early-Modern York. *Social History of Medicine*, **7**, 29–57.

Galley, C. (1995). A model of early-modern urban demography. *Economic History Review*, **48**, 448–469.

Galloway, P. R. (1985). Annual variations in deaths by age, deaths by cause, prices, and weather in London 1670–1830. *Population Studies*, **39**, 487–505.

Galloway, P. R. (1988). Basic patterns in annual variations in fertility, nuptiality, mortality, and prices in preindustrial Europe. *Population Studies*, **42**, 275–302.

Garnett, G. P. & Anderson, R. M. (1993a). Factors controlling the spread of HIV in heterosexual communities in developing countries: patterns of mixing between different age and sexual activity classes. *Philosophical Transactions of the Royal Society* B, **342**, 137–159.

Garnett, G. P. & Anderson, R. M. (1993b). Contact tracing and the estimation of sexual mixing patterns: the epidemiology of gonococcal infections. *Sexually Transmitted Diseases*, **20**, 181–191.

Gaulin, S. J. & Robbins, C. J. (1991). Trivers–Willard effect in contemporary North American society. *American Journal of Physical Anthropology*, **85**, 61–69.

Gentleman's Magazine (1766). XXXVI, 582.

Gilpin, M. E. (1979). Spiral chaos in a predator–prey model. *American Naturalist*, **107**, 306–308.

Glasziou, P. P. & Mackerras, D. E. (1993). Vitamin A supplementation in infectious disease: a meta-analysis. *British Medical Journal*, **306**, 366–370.

Godfrey, K. M.,Forrester, T.,Barker, D. J. P.,Jackson, A. A.,Landman, J. P.,Hall, J. S.,Cox, V. & Osmond, C. (1994). Maternal nutritional-status in pregnancy and blood pressure in childhood. *British Journal of Obstetrics and Gynaecology*, **101**, 398–403.

Goodwin, G. C.,Evans, R. J.,Leal Lozano, R. & Feik, R. A. (1986). Sinusoidal disturbance rejection with application to helicopter flight data estimation. *IEEE Transactions on Acoustics, Speech and Signal Processing*, **ASSP-24**, 479–484.

Gottman, J. M. (1981). *Time-Series Analysis*. Cambridge: Cambridge University Press.

Grassberger, P. (1983). On the critical behaviour of the general epidemic process and dynamic percolation. *Mathematical Biosciences*, **63**, 157–172.

Gregson, N. (1989). Tawney revisited: custom and the emergence of capitalist class relations in north-east Cumbria, 1600–1830. *Economic History Review*, XLII, 18–42.

Grenfell, B. T. (1992). Chance and chaos in measles epidemics. *Journal of the Royal Statistical Society* B, **54**, 383–398.

Hansson, L. (1991). Dispersal and connectivity in metapopulations. *Biological Journal of the Linnean Society*, **42**, 89–103.

Hanski, I. & Gilpin, M. (1991). Metapopulation dynamics: brief history and conceptual domain. *Biological Journal of the Linnean Society*, **42**, 3–16.

Harper, G. J. (1961). Airborne micro-organisms: survival tests with four viruses. *Journal of Hygiene*, **59**, 479–482.

Harrison, C. J. (1971). Grain price analysis and harvest qualities, 1465–1634. *Economic History Review*, **19**, 135–155.

Hart, N. (1993). Famine, maternal nutrition and infant mortality: a re-examination of the Dutch hunger winter. *Population Studies*, **47**, 27–46.

Hastings, A. & Powell, T. (1991). Chaos in a three-species food chain. *Ecology*, **72**, 896–903.

Haswell, C. S. (1938). Penrith, Cumberland, 1557–1812. *Cumberland and Westmorland Antiquarian and Archaeological Society, Parish Register Series*, XXVI–XXX.

Haswell, J. F. (1927). Bridekirk, Cumberland, 1584–1812. *Cumberland and Westmorland Antiquarian and Archaeological Society, Parish Register Series*, XIV.

Haswell, J. F. (1932). Cliburn, Westmorland, 1565–1812. *Cumberland and Westmorland Antiquarian and Archaeological Society, Parish Register Series*, XX.

Haswell, J. F. (1934). Newton Reigny, 1571–1812. *Cumberland and Westmorland Antiquarian and Archaeological Society, Parish Register Series*, XXII.

Haswell, J. F. (1937). Crosby Ravensworth, Westmorland, 1570–1812. *Cumberland and Westmorland Antiquarian and Archaeological Society, Parish Register Series*, XXV.

Henderson, D. A. (1974). Importation of smallpox into Europe. *WHO Chronicle*, **28**, 428–430.

Herlihy, D. (1977). Deaths, marriages, births and the Tuscan economy (c. 1300–1550). In *Population Patterns in the Past*, ed. R. D. Lee, pp. 135–164. New York: Academic Press.

Hill, K. & Kaplan, H. (1988). Tradeoffs in male and female reproductive strategies among the Ache: part 2. In *Human Reproductive Behaviour*, ed. L. L. Betzig, M. Burgerhoff Mulder & P. W. Turke, pp. 291–304. Cambridge: Cambridge University Press.

Hinchliffe, S. A.,Howard, C. V.,Lynch, M. R. J.,Sargent, P. H.,Judd, B. A. & Vanvelzen, D. (1993). Renal developmental arrest in sudden-infant-death-syndrome. *Pediatric Pathology*, **13**, 333–343.

Holderness, B. A. (1989). Prices, productivity, and output. In *Agrarian History of England and Wales*, ed. G. E. Mingay, vol. VI, 1750–1850, pp. 84–189. Cambridge: Cambridge University Press.

Hollingsworth, T. H. (1968). The importance of the quality of the data in historical demography. *Daedalus*, **97**, 415–433.

Hopkins, D. R. (1983). *Princes and Peasants: Smallpox in History*. Chicago: University of Chicago Press.

Hoskins, W. G. (1964). Harvest fluctuations and English economic history, 1480–1619. *Agricultural History Review*, **12**, 28–45.

Hoskins, W. G. (1968). Harvest fluctuations and English economic history, 1620–1759. *Agricultural History Review*, **16**, 15–31.

Howell, F. & Jennings, S. (1992). The epidemiology of pertussis in the Republic of Ireland. *Communicable Disease Report Review*, **2**, R31–R33.

Howson, W. G. (1961). Plague, poverty and population in parts of North-West England 1580–1720. *Transactions of the Historic Society of Lancashire and Cheshire*, **112**, 29–55.

Hughes, A. L. (1986). Reproductive success and occupational class in eighteenth century Lancashire England. *Social Biology*, **33**, 109–115.

Hughes, J. (1971). The plague at Carlisle 1597/8. *Transactions of the Cumberland and Westmorland Antiquarian and Archaeological Society*, **71**, 52–63.

Hugo, G. J. (1984). The demographic impact of famine: a review. In *Famine as a Geographical Phenomenon*, ed. B. Currey & G. Hugo, pp. 7–31. Dordrecht: D. Reidel Publishing Company.

Hutchinson, W. (1794). *The History of the County of Cumberland*, 2 vols. Carlisle: F. Jollie.

James, J. W. (1972). Longitudinal study of the morbidity of diarrhoeal and respiratory infections in malnourished children. *American Journal of Clinical Nutrition*, **25**, 690–694.

Kahn, C. (1963). History of smallpox and its prevention. *American Journal of Diseases of Children*, **106**, 597–609.

Kailath, T. (1980). *Linear Systems*. Eaglewood Cliffs, NJ: Prentice Hall.

Katz, A. R. & Morens, D. M. (1992). Severe streptococcal infections in historical perspective. *Clinical Infectious Diseases*, **14**, 298–307.

Kerridge, E. (1969). *Agrarian Problems in the Sixteenth Century and After*. London: Allen & Unwin.

Keusch, G. T. (1991). Nutritional effects on response of children in developing countries to respiratory tract pathogens: implications for vaccine development. *Review of Infectious Diseases*, **13**, S486–S491.

Lamb, H. H. (1978). *Climate: Present Past and Future*. vol. II, *Climate History and the Future*. London: Methuen.

Landers, J. (1986). Mortality, weather and prices in London 1675–1825: study of short-term fluctuations. *Journal of Historical Geography*, **12**, 347–364.

Landers, J. (1987). Mortality and metropolis: the case of London 1675–1825. *Population Studies*, **41**, 59–76.

Landers, J. (1993). *Death and the Metropolis*. Cambridge: Cambridge University Press.

Landsberg, H. E. (1981). Past climates from unexploited written sources. In *Climate and History*, ed. R. I. Rotberg & T. K. Rabb, pp. 51–62. Princeton, NJ: Princeton University Press.

Large, E. C. (1958). *The Advance of the Fungi*. London: Jonathan Cape Publishers.

Lawes, J. B. & Gilbert, J. H. (1880). Our climate and our wheat crops. *Journal of the Royal Agricultural Society of England*, XVI, 175–195.

Laycock, T. (1844). *Report on the State of York, in reply to the Questions Circulated by the Commissioners for Inquiry into the state of Large Towns and Populous Districts*. London.

Lee, R. D. (1974). Estimating series of vital rates and age structure from baptisms and burials: a new technique, with applications to pre-industrial England. *Population Studies*, **28**, 495–512.

Lee, R. D. (1981). Short-term variation: vital rates, prices and weather. In *Population History of England and Wales, 1541–1871. A reconstruction*, ed. E. A. Wrigley & R. S. Schofield, pp. 356–401. Cambridge: Cambridge University Press.

Lee, R. D. (1985). Population homeostasis and English demographic history. *Journal of Interdisciplinary History*, **15**, 635–660.

Lee, R. D. (1987). Population dynamics of humans and other animals. *Demography*, **24**, 443–465.

Leslie, P. H. (1945). On the use of matrices in certain population mathematics. *Biometrika*, **33**, 183–212.

Leslie, P. H. (1948). Some further notes on the use of matrices in population mathematics. *Biometrika*, **35**, 213–245.

Levins, R. (1969). Some demographic and genetic consequences of environmental heterogeneity for biological control. *Bulletin of the Entomological Society of America*, **15**, 237–240.

Levins, R. (1970). Extinction. In *Some Mathematical Problems in Biology*, ed. M. Gerstenhaber, pp. 77–107. Providence, RI: American Mathematical Society.

Lewis, E. G. (1942). On the generation and growth of a population. *Sankhya: The Indian Journal of Statistics*, **6**, 93–96.

Lewis, G. J. (1982). *Human Migration. A Geographical Perspective*. London: Croom Helm.

Livi-Bacci, M. (1986). Fertility, nutrition and pellagra: Italy during the vital revolution. *Journal of Interdisciplinary History*, XVI, 431–454.

Livi-Bacci, M. (1991). *Population and Nutrition*. Cambridge: Cambridge University Press.

Lloyd, A. L. & May, R. M. (1996). Spatial heterogeneity in epidemic models. *Journal of Theoretical Biology*, **179**, 1–11.

Long, M. & Pickles, M. (1986). An enquiry into mortality in some mid-Wharfedale parishes in 1623. *Local Population Studies*, **37**, 19–35.

Lonsdale, H. (1870). *The Life of John Heysham, M. D.* London: Longman's Green.

McKeown, T. (1976). *The Modern Rise of Population*. London: Arnold.

McKeown, T. (1983). Food, infection and population. *Journal of Interdisciplinary History*, **14**, 227–247.

McKeown, T. & Record, R. G. (1962). Reasons for the decline of mortality in England and Wales during the nineteenth century. *Population Studies*, **16**, 94–122.

MacLean, A. M. (1911). *The Registers of the Parish of Greystoke, 1559–1757*. Kendal.

McLean, A. R. (1986). *Lecture Notes in Biomathematics* **65**, 171–197.

MacLulich, D. A. (1937). Fluctuations in the numbers of the varying hare (*Lepus americanus*). *University of Toronto Studies. Biological Series*, **43**, 3–126.

Malthus, T. R. (1798). *An Essay on the Principle of Population*. Reprinted for the Royal Economic Society London, 1926.

Manley, G. (1974). Central England Temperatures: monthly means 1659–1973. *Quarterly Journal of the Royal Meteorological Society*, **100**, 389–405.

Marshall, J. D. (1980). Agrarian wealth and social structure in pre-industrial Cumbria. *Economic History Review*, **33**, 503–521.

Mercer, A. J. (1985). Smallpox and epidemiological demographic change in Europe: the role of vaccination. *Population Studies*, **39**, 287–307.

Millward, P. (1983). The demographic crisis of 1623 in Stockport, Cheshire. *Historical Social Sciences Newsletter*, **1**, 3–6.

Nelson, M. C. (1994). Diphtheria in late nineteenth-century Sweden: policy and practice. *Continuity and Change*, **9**, 213–242.

Oddy, D. J. (1982). The health of the people. In *Population and Society in Britain, 1850–1980*, ed. T. C. Barker & M. Drake, pp. 121–139. London: Batsford.

Odum, E. P. (1959). *Fundamentals of Ecology*. Philadelphia: W. B. Saunders Co.

Olsen, L. F. & Schaffer, W. M. (1990). Chaos versus noisy periodicity: alternative hypothesis for childhood epidemics. *Science*, **249**, 499–504.

Olsen, L. F.,Truty, G. L. & Schaffer, W. M. (1988). Oscillations and chaos in epidemics: a nonlinear dynamic study of six childhood diseases in Copenhagen, Denmark. *Theoretical Population Biology*, **33**, 344–370.

Pascual, M. (1993). Diffusion-induced chaos in a spatial predator-prey system. *Proceedings of the Royal Society* B, **251**, 1–7.

Perrenoud, A. (1991). The attenuation of mortality crises and the decline of mortality. In *The Decline of Mortality in Europe*, ed. R. Schofield, D. Reher & A. Bideau, pp. 18–37. Oxford: Clarendon Press.

Pfister, C. (1988). Fluctuations climatiques et prix céréaliers en Europe du XVIe au XXe siécle. *Annales: Économies, Sociétés, Civilisations*, **43**, 25–53.

Pielou, E. C. (1969). *An Introduction to Mathematical Ecology*. New York: Wiley–Interscience.

Pool, R. (1989). Is it chaos or is it just noise? *Science*, **243**, 25–28.

Post, J. D. (1985). *Food Shortage, Climatic Variability, and Epidemic Disease in Preindustrial Europe: The Mortality Peak of the Early 1740s*. Ithaca, NY.: Cornell University Press.

Priestley, R. H. (1978). Detection of increased virulence in populations of wheat yellow rust. In *Plant Disease Epidemiology*, ed. P. R. Scott & A. Bainbridge. Oxford: Blackwell Scientific Publications.

Quinn, R. W. (1989). Comprehensive review of morbidity and mortality trends in rheumatic fever, streptococcal disease, and scarlet fever: the decline of rheumatic fever. *Review of Infectious Diseases*, **11**, 928–953.

Rand, D. A. & Wilson, H. B. (1991). Chaotic stochasticity: a ubiquitous source of unpredictability in epidemics. *Proceedings of the Royal Society* B, **246**, 179–184.

Razzell, P. (1977). *The Conquest of Smallpox: The Impact of Inoculation on Smallpox Mortality in Eighteenth-Century Britain*. Sussex: Caliban.

Razzell, P. (1994). *Essays in English Population History*. Sussex: Caliban.

Razzell, P. (1995). The growth of population in eighteenth century England. A critical reappraisal. *Genealogists' Magazine*, **25**, 137–142.

Rhodes, C. J. & Anderson, R. M. (1996). Persistence and dynamics in lattice models of epidemic spread. *Journal of Theoretical Biology*, **180**, 125–133.

Richards, T. (1983). Weather, nutrition, and the economy: short-run fluctuations in births, deaths, and marriages, France 1740–1909. *Demography*, **20**, 197–212.

Robinson, R. J. (1992). Introduction. In *Fetal and Infant Origins of Adult Disease*, ed. D. J. P. Barker, pp. 1–20. London: British Medical Journal.

Roehner, B. (1991). Liaison entre les conjonctures de prix des produits de base: le cas de l'Allemagne au XIXe siécle. *Histoire et Mésure*, **6**, 31–49.

Rogers, C. D. (1975). *The Lancashire Population Crisis of 1623*. Manchester: Manchester University Press.

Rotberg, R. I. (1983). Nutrition and history. *Journal of Interdisciplinary History*, **14**, 199–204.

Rotberg, R. I. & Rabb, T. K. (1985). *Hunger and History.* Cambridge: Cambridge University Press.

Royama, T. (1992). *Analytical Population Dynamics*. London: Chapman & Hall.

Sarkar, J. K.,Ray, S. & Manji, P. (1970). Epidemiological and virological studies in the off-season smallpox cases in Calcutta. *Indian Journal of Medical Research*, **58**, 829–839.

Schofield, R. S. (1977). An anatomy of an epidemic: Colyton November 1645–November 1646. In *The Plague Reconsidered*, pp. 95–126. Stafford: Hourdsprint.

Schofield, R. S. & Wrigley, E. A. (1979). Infant and child mortality in England in the last Tudor and early Stuart period. In *Health, Medicine and Mortality in the Sixteenth Century*, ed. C. Webster, pp. 61–95. Cambridge: Cambridge University Press.

Scott, S. (1995). Demographic study of Penrith, Cumberland, 1557–1812, with particular reference to famine, plague and smallpox. Ph.D. thesis, Liverpool.

Scott, S. & Duncan, C. J. (1993). Smallpox epidemics at Penrith in the 17th and 18th centuries. *Transactions of the Cumberland and Westmorland Antiquarian and Archaeological Society*, **93**, 155–160.

Scott, S. & Duncan, C. J. (1996). Marital fertility at Penrith, 1557–1812 – evidence for a malnourished community? *Transactions of the Cumberland and Westmorland Antiquarian and Archaeological Society*, **96**, 105–114.

Scott, S. & Duncan, C. J. (1997a). Interacting factors affecting illegitimacy in preindustrial northern England. *Journal of Biosocial Science*, **29**, 151–169.

Scott, S. & Duncan, C. J. (1997b). The mortality crisis of 1623 in North-West England. *Local Population Studies*, **58**, 14–25.

Scott, S.,Duncan, C. J. & Duncan, S. R. (1996). The plague at Penrith, Cumbria, 1597/8: its causes, biology and consequences. *Annals of Human Biology*, **23**, 1–21.

Scott, S.,Duncan, S. R. & Duncan, C. J. (1995). Infant mortality and famine: a study in historical epidemiology in Northern England. *Journal of Epidemiology and Community Health*, **49**, 245–252.

Scott, S.,Duncan, S. R. & Duncan, C. J. (1997). The interacting effects of prices and weather on population cycles in a preindustrial community. *Journal of Biosocial Science*, **30**, 15–32.

Scrimshaw, N. S.,Taylor, C. E. & Gordon, J. E. (1968). *Interaction of Nutrition and Infection*. Geneva: World Health Organization.

Searle, C. E. (1983). The odd corner of England: a study of a rural social formation in transition Cumbria c.1700–1914. Ph.D. thesis, University of Essex.

Searle, C. E. (1986). Custom, class conflict and the agrarian capitalism: the Cumbrian economy in the eighteenth century. *Past & Present*, **110**, 106–133.

Shumway, R. H. (1988). *Applied Statistical Time Series Analysis*. Wisconsin: Prentice Hall International Editions.

Slack, P. (1979). Mortality crises and epidemic disease in England 1485–1610. In *Health, Medicine and Mortality in the Sixteenth Century*, ed. C. Webster, pp. 9–59. Cambridge: Cambridge University Press.

Smith, A. & Dickinson, R. (1951). *The registers of the Parish Church of Walton-on-the-Hill*. Lancashire Parish Register Society.

Smith, J. R. (1987). *The Speckled Monster, Smallpox in England 1670–1970*. Hunstanton, Norfolk: Witley Press.

Sparke, A. (1937). The parish register of Great Harwood, 1546–1812. *Lancashire Parish Register Society*, **45**.

Stein, Z.,Susser, M.,Saenger, G. & Marolla, F. (1975). *Famine and Human Development: The Dutch Hunger Winter of 1944–45.* Oxford: Oxford University Press.

Stout, H. B. (1963). St. Bees, Cumberland, 1538–1837. *Cumberland and Westmorland Antiquarian and Archaeological Society, Parish Register Series,* XLI.

Stratton, J. M. (1970). *Agricultural Records A. D. 220–1968.* London: John Baker.

Strebel, P.,Hussey, G.,Metcalf, C.,Smith, D.,Hanslo, D. & Simpson, J. (1991). An outbreak of whooping cough in a highly vaccinated urban community. *Journal of Tropical Pediatrics,* **37**, 71–76.

Sugihara, G.,Grenfell, B. & May, R. M. (1990). Distinguishing error from chaos in ecological time series. *Philosophical Transactions of the Royal Society,* **330**, 235–251.

Sugihara, G. & May, R. M. (1990). Nonlinear forecasting as a way of distinguishing chaos from measurement error in time series. *Nature,* **344**, 734–741.

Syedabubakar, S. N.,Matthews, R. C.,Preston, N. W.,Owen, D. & Hillier, V. (1995). Application of pulsed field gel electrophoresis to the 1993 epidemic of whooping cough in the U.K. *Epidemiology and Infection,* **115**, 101–113.

Thirsk, J. (ed.) (1967). *The Agrarian History of England and Wales,* vol. IV. Cambridge: Cambridge University Press.

Thirsk, J. (ed.) (1984). Regional farming systems, 1640–1750. In *Agrarian History of England and Wales,* vol. 5, part I, pp. 3–58. Cambridge: Cambridge University Press.

Thornley, J. J. (1901). *The Ancient Church Registers of the Parish of Kirkoswald, Cumberland. Births, marriages, burials, 1577–1812.* Workington: G. H. Smith & Co.

Tidd, C. W.,Olsen, L. K. & Schaffer, W. M. (1993). The case of chaos in childhood epidemics. II. Predicting historical epidemics from mathematical models. *Proceedings of the Royal Society* B, **254**, 257–273.

Tromp, S. W. (1980). *Biometeorology: The Impact of the Weather and Climate on Humans and their Environment.* London: Heyden.

Twigg, G. (1984). *The Black Death: A Biological Appraisal.* London: Batsford Academic.

Voland, E. (1988). Differential infant and child mortality in evolutionary perspective: data from late 17th to 19th century Ostfriesland (Germany). In *Human Reproductive Behaviour,* ed. L. L. Betzig, M. Burgerhoff Mulder & P. W. Turke, pp. 253–261. Cambridge: Cambridge University Press.

Wachter, K. W. (1991). Elusive cycles: are there dynamically possible Lee–Easterlin models for US births? *Population Studies,* **45**, 109–135.

Wachter, K. W. & Lee, R. D. (1989). US births and limit cycle models. *Demography,* **26**, 99–115.

Waddy, B. B. (1952). Climate and respiratory infections. *Lancet,* **2**, 674–677.

Wainwright, T. (1903). *The parish register of Barnstaple, 1540–1812, Devon.* Exeter: J. G. Commin.

Wales-Smith, E. G. (1971). Monthly and annual totals of rainfall representative of Kew, Surrey, from 1697–1970. *Meteorological Magazine C,* 345–362.

Walker, J. (1860). *The History of Penrith from the Earlier Period to the Present Time.* Penrith: Hodgson Printers.

Walter, J. & Schofield, R. S. (1989). *Famine, Disease and the Social Order in Early Modern Society.* Cambridge: Cambridge University Press.

Weir, D. R. (1984). Life under pressure: France and England, 1680–1870. *Journal of Economic History*, **44**, 27–47.

Wigley, T. M. L. & Atkinson, T. C. (1977). Dry years in south-east England since 1698. *Nature*, **265**, 431–434.

Wilmshurst, P. (1994). Temperature and cardiovascular mortality. *British Medical Journal*, **309**, 1029–1030.

Wilson, C. (1984). Natural fertility in England 1600–1799. *Population Studies*, **38**, 225–240.

Woods, R. & Woodward, J. (1984). Mortality, poverty and the environment. In *Urban Disease and Mortality in Nineteenth-Century England*, ed. R. Woods & J. Woodward, pp. 19–36. London: Batsford.

Woodward, J. (1984). Medicine and the city: the nineteenth-century experience. In *Urban Disease and Mortality in Nineteenth-Century England*, ed. R. Woods & J. Woodward, pp. 65–78. London: Batsford.

Wright, P. F. (1991). Pertussis in developing countries: definition of the problem and prospects for control. *Review of Infectious Diseases*, **13**, S528–S534.

Wrigley, E. A. (ed.) (1966). *Introduction to English Historical Demography*. London: Weidenfeld and Nicholson.

Wrigley, E. A. (1977). Births and Baptisms: the use of Anglican Baptism registers as a source of information about the numbers of births in England before the beginning of Civil Registration. *Population Studies*, **31**, 281–312.

Wrigley, E. A. (1989). Some reflections on corn yields and prices in pre-industrial economies. In *Famine, Disease and the Social Order in Early Modern Society*, ed. J. Walter & R. Schofield, pp. 235–278. Cambridge: Cambridge University Press.

Wrigley, E. A., Davies, R. S., Oeppen, J. E. & Schofield, R. S. (1997). *English Population History from Family Reconstitution 1589–1837*. Cambridge: Cambridge University Press.

Wrigley, E. A. & Schofield, R. S. (1981). *The Population History of England and Wales, 1541–1871. A reconstruction*. London: Arnold.

Wrigley, E. A. & Schofield, R. S. (1983). English population history from family reconstitution: summary results. *Population Studies*, **37**, 157–184.

Wyatt, G. (1987). A demographic study of Cheshire parishes: Nantwich and Wybunbury, 1680–1819. M.Phil. thesis, University of Liverpool.

Young, J. Z. (1950). *The Life of Vertebrates*. Oxford: Oxford University Press.

Index

Numbers in *italics* refer to pages with figures and tables.

Ackerman's pole placement, 72, *73*
aggregative analysis, 16, 161
Appleby, plague, 329, *329*
autoregressive effects
  burials, 142–3
  wheat series, 105–6, 109
Aynho, 291, 292, 301

baptisms
  England and Wales, 325
Barker, D. J .P., 6, 7, 12, 113, 125, 129, 135, 313–14
barley, 37, *93, 96*
  cycles, 92–6, *93, 95*, 105
  prices, 90, 96, 114, 146
Barnstaple, 292, *294*, 296–7, 301
  baptisms, 296
  burials, 296, *296*
  economy, 296
  mortality crisis, 296
  smallpox epidemics, 296, *296*
beef prices, 156
bigg, 37
Bills of Mortality, 171, *172*, 187, *187*, 188, *196*, 197, 223, 231, *232*, 239, *242*, 264, 267, 282, 321
births loop, 49–51, 77, 81, 140
  delay, 82
  gain, 49–51, *50*
birthweight, 6, 125, 231
Bode diagrams, 204, *205*, 218, 237,
boom, 45, 46, 47, 114, 140, *141*, 299, 300, 301, 324, 327, 333
boom and bust
  fertility in the USA, 4–5
  rust cycles, 108, *108*
Bridekirk, 157, *158*
Brough, 157, *158*, 328, *329*
Burford, 281
burial rates, *120*, 136

Carlisle, 37, 282
  plague, 328, 329, *329*, 330,
Cartmel, 157, *158*, 161, *162*
Caton, *158*
cattle prices, 146, 153, 156, 161
chaos, 178, 202, 208, *211*, 214
  and epidemics, 214–18, 223
Chester, smallpox, 189, 190–7, 270, 271, 301, 302
  child burials, 191–5, *192, 193, 194*, 196–7
  correspondence with London, 196–7, *196*
  drivers, 195–7
chickenpox, 216, 217
cholera, 304
Cliburn, 157, *158*
Cockerton, *158*
control cycles, 4, 64
crisis mortality, 70, *76, 154*
  Cheshire, 157
  Cumbria, 145, 154, 157–63, *158*
  Lancashire, 157, 158, 159, 160, 161, *162*, 163
  Lancaster, 164
  northwest England, 146, 147, *147*, 150, *154*, 155, 157–63, *158*
  Penrith, *48*, 70, 125, 127–9, 150, 157
  Scotland, 157
  York, 165, 168
  Yorkshire, 157, *158*, 160
crisis mortality ratio (CMR), 157, *158*, 160
Crosby Ravensworth, *158*, 161, *162*, 292, *294*
  adult burials, *162*, 293
  child burials, *162*, 293
  economy, 293
  mortality crises, 293
Crosthwaite, *158*, 160, 161, *162*, 292, *294*
  baptisms, 293
  economy, 293
  mortality crises, 161

348

Cumberland, *see* Cumbria
Cumbria, 6, 34, 327, 333
  crisis mortality, 145, 154, 157–63, *158*
  crops, 37
  economy, 138, 139, 140, 155–7
  farming conditions, 34–8, 334
  inheritance customs, 333
  mortality crises, 145–63
  parishes, 145–63
  plague, 327, 328–30, *329*
  sheep, 37
  size of holdings, 35–7, 333
  tenant right, 35–7
  wool produced, 37, 146
cycles
  births in France, 83
  deaths in Florence, 83
  fertility, 83
  population size, 83
  real wages, 83
  30-year, 77, 80

damping, *76*
damping, factor, 176, 228, 237, 247, 316
  definition, 180
Darlington, 328, *329*
demographic balancing equation, 332
density-dependent, 55–74, 136, 140, 333
  grain prices, effect of, 142
diet, 223, 225, 303, 313, 323, *323*
diphtheria, 302
  drivers, 318
  England and Wales, 316–18, *317*
  interactions, 319–20
  SEIR dynamics, 318
  wheat prices, 318
dispersal, 330–3
driver, for epidemics, 176, 240, 320
  diphtheria, 318
  measles, 217, *226*, 228–9, *240*
  scarlet fever, 289–90, 311
  smallpox, *179*, 185–6, 181–3, 195–7, *196*,
    203, 206, 211, 216, 217, 219, 220,
    221, 230, *240*, 266, 272–5, 277, 279,
    286–90, 301
  whooping cough, 234–6, *235*, 237, 238,
    240
Dumfries, 157, *329*
Dunfermline, 157
Durham, plague, 328, *329*

ecological niches, 331, 333
economic thresholds, 331
Edenhall, plague, *329*, 330
Eden Valley, 6, 34, 37, 52, 71, 114, 146, 292,
  293, 327, 328, 333, 334
Edinburgh, smallpox, 190, *190*, 302

eigenvalues, 3, 57–8, 59, 78
endogenous cycles, 51–3
  definition, 2
  Kirkoswald, 52–3
  London, 53
  matrix modelling, 55–63, 83-6
  Penrith, 44–7, 51, 75–86
  York, 51–2, 53, 54
epidemic/endemic ratio, 252, 253, 254, *255*,
    256, 257, *257*, 258, *258*, *260*, 262,
    262, *263*, *264*, *265*, *268*, 315
  definition, 256
exogenous cycles
  definition, 2
  Penrith, 44–7, 113–44, *133*, *141*

family reconstitution, 17
  methods, 17
  Penrith, 17, 38, 64, 69, 114, 120, 123, 125,
    126, 131, 137, 138, 140, 282
  validation of matrix model, 64–9
famine, 5–8, 272
  Dutch winter, 130, 313
  Northern Province, 34–5, 145, 146
  Penrith, 70, 127–9, *128*, 137, 150
feedback, 58, 60–3, *60*, 78, 83–6, *133*
  Ackerman's pole placement, 72, *73*
  density-dependent, 55–74, *60*, *72*, *73*, 136,
    139, 140, 142
  gain, 60–1, 75, 84, 86
  migration (*b*) vector, 71–4, *72*
  population dynamics, 136, 139
  positive, 135, 142
fertility function, 32, 55–6, 58–9, 77–80, *78*,
    79, *80*
  estimation, 77–80
  mean, 84
  standard deviation, 78–80, 84, 85
Florence, cycles in deaths, 83
frequency, definition, 19, *19*

Geneva, smallpox, 275
Germany, Waldeck parishes, *67*
Glasgow, smallpox, 189–90, *191*, 302
Godalming, *290*, 301
grain prices, 87–112
  correspondence between, 94–6
  cycles, 87–9, 90–4
  predicted price series, 103–4, 111–12
  rust epidemics, 106–9
  weather, effect of, 87–9, 97–104
Great Harwood, 292, *294*, 301
  child burials, 298
  mortality crises, 298
  smallpox epidemics, 298
Greenland, 281
Greystoke, 34, 157, *158*, 300

Hanbury, 281
hardship index, 151–3, *151*, *152*, *153*, 155–6, *156*
hare, *22*, *23*, *24*, *25*
    population cycles, 21–5
hide prices, 161
homeostasis, *see* steady-state population
Hutterites, 65–6, *67*

i-state, 327
illegitimacy, 333
inbreeding, 331
infectious diseases, 8–10, 113
    interactions, 224–8, 267–9, 319–20
    theory of, 173, 175–80, 244–8
infectious period
    measles, 307
    scarlet fever, 314
    smallpox, 175, 177, 249, 252, *255*, 256, 261, *263*
influenza, 145, 197
Ingleton, 157, *158*, 160
inoculation (variolation), smallpox, 172, 183, 270, 275, 285, 291, 300, 301, 302
    definition, 183
interepidemic interval (*T*)
    interactions, 239, 240
    measles, 223, 225, 227, 228, *240*, 264, 304, 305, 306, 307
    scarlet fever, 310, 315
    smallpox, 172–3, 177, 178, 180, 181, 184–5, 188, 195, 196, 204, 208, 218, *240*, 249, 252, 271, 275, 277, 278, 282, 285, 289, 291, 296, 297, 298, 299, 301
    whooping cough, 231, 233, 236, 237, *240*

Kalman filtering, 83
Kendal, 45, 157, *158*, 328, 329, *329*, 330
Keswick, *see* Crosthwaite
Kirkoswald, 52–3, 292, *294*, 301
    adult burials, 293
    child burials, 293
    mortality crises, 293
    smallpox, 293
Kondratieff cycle, 4
Kuznets cycle, 4

Lancashire
    economy, 163
    parishes, 157, 158, 159, 160, 161, *162*, 163
Lancaster, 157, *158*, 163–5, *164*, 292, *294*, 298–9, 300
    adult burials, 164–5, *164*
    baptisms, 163, 298
    boom, 298, 299

child burials, 163, 164, *164*, 165, 299, *299*
    economic factors, 164–5
    mortality crises, 164
    population dynamics, 163–5
    smallpox epidemics, 299, 301
    wool and wheat, effect of, 164–5
latitude, effect on infant mortality, 160
Leslie Matrix, *see* matrix modelling
life expectancy, 4, 175, 201, 245, 247, 248, 249, 252, 253, 254, *255*, 256, 258–9, *258*, 263, *268*, 314
limit cycles, see control cycles, 4
linearised model, 174, 175, 177, 188, 218, 219–20, *220*, 276, 277
London
    deaths, *187*, *243*
    endogenous cycles, 53
    interaction of diseases, 238–43, *241*, 319–20
    long wavelength cycles, 76, *187*
    measles, 222–31, *224*, *226*, *227*, *240*, 263–4, *265*
    migration, 185, 186, 187, 269
    modelling smallpox, *207*, *209*, *210*, *212*, *213*, 248–54, *250*, *251*, *254*
    plague, 53, 172, *172*, *173*, 186, 187
    population dynamics, 244–69
    Quakers, 306
    smallpox, 113, 171–3, *172*, *173*, 177, *179*, 180–1, 184–7, *186*, 239, 240, *240*, *241*, 242, *242*, 243, *248*, *253*, 289, 300, 301, 302
        correspondence with Chester, 196–7, *196*
    typhus, 113
    whooping cough, 231–7, *232*, *233*, *235*, *240*, *242*
Lowther, *158*
lynx, *22*, *23*, *25*
    population cycles, 21–5

Maidstone, *290*, 291, 301
malnutrition, 5–8, 322–4
    birthweight, effect on, 6
    child mortality, 125–31, 145, 243
    infant mortality, 125–31, 145, 243
    population dynamics, effect on, *268*
    population growth, effect on, 7
    in pregnancy, 6, 8, 113, 125–31, 142, 229–30, 243, 313, 316, 318, 320
    and susceptibility to disease, 181, 185, 186, 188, 229–31, 237, 238, 267–9, *268*, 272–5, 276, 286, 309, 311–14, 316, 319–20
Manchester, 270, 283, 330, *329*
marital fertility, 64–6, *65*, *67*
market towns, 271, 275, 300

marriage
  mean age, 80–1
  oscillations, 80–1
maternity, mean age at, 77
matrix modelling, 31–3, *59*, *60*, *62*, *63*, 71–4, *72*, 77–80, *82*
  Ackerman's pole placement, 72, *73*
  baptisms, 58–9
  eigenvalues, 32–3, 57–8, 59, 78
  of endogenous oscillations, 55–63, 83–6
  feedback, 58, 60–3, *60*, *72*, *78*
  fertility function, 32, 55–6, 58–9, 77–80, *78*, *79*, *80*
  identity (*I*) matrix, 72
  loop gain, 50, *50*
  migration (*b*) vector, 71–4, *72*, *73*
  mortality function, 61–3
  survival function, 32
  validation, 64–9
  vectors, 55, 56, *72*, *73*
measles, 178, 197, 206, 215, 217, 318
  and chaos, 215, 216, 217, 252
  death rate, 307
  driver, 217, *226*, 228–9, *240*
  in England and Wales, 304–6, *305*, 306–8, *307*
  infectious period, 307
  interactions, 238–43, *241*, 319–20
  in London, 222–31, *226*, *227*, *242*, 265
  malnutrition in pregnancy, 229–30
  mean age of infection, 228
  modelling, 263–4, *265*, 306–8, *307*, *308*
  predicted deaths, 306
metapopulation, 11, 83, 217, 306, 308, 325–34
  definition, 2, 325
  epidemic spread, 326
  lattice-based simulation, 326
  migration, 327
  feedback (*b*) vector, 71–4, *72*
  in homeostasis, 69–71
  immigration index, 71
  in London, 185, 186, 187, 269
  in metapopulation, 330–4
  oscillations at Penrith, *70*, 131–2, 141, 142
  smallpox, effect on, 185, 186, 187, 188, 269, 300
  wheat prices, effect of, 131–2, 136, 269
Morland, *158*
mortality
  child, rate of, 81, 85
  function, 81–3
  theory, 3
mumps, 217

Nantwich, 292, *294*, 298, 301
  baptisms, 297

child burials, 297, *297*
  smallpox epidemics, 297, *297*, 298
natural frequency, *see* resonant frequency
natural immunity, 276, 281
neonatal mortality, 123–31, *124*, *128*, 138, 230, 243
Newbiggin, 157, *158*
Newcastle, 328, *329*
Newton Reigny, 292, 293, *294*, 301
  adult burials, 293
  child burials, 293
  economy, 293
noise
  white, 19, 110, 142, 143, 206, 207, *207*, 208, 220, 280, *281*
  non-white, 110, 143
non-linear model, 175, 188, 189–221, *220*, 278, 286
North Meols, 157, *158*
Northampton, 270
Northern Province, 37, 325
Northumberland, plague, 328
Norwich, 270
Nottingham, 270

oats, 37
  cycles, 92–4, *93*, *94*, *95*, 96, 105
  prices, 90, *93*, 96, 114, 146
oscillations
  overdamped, 75, *76*
  stable, 75, *76*
  underdamped, 75, *76*
  unstable, 75, *76*
  see also wavelength, cycles

p-state, 327
parish registers
  aggregative analysis, 16
  as a database, 16
  family reconstitution, 17
  underregistration, 31, 121
Penrith
  age at marriage, 80–1, 131
  age at maternity, 77
  age-specific mortality, 49, *126*
  baptisms, 39–47, *41*, *42*, *43*, *44*, *45*, 131, 135–6, 138, 140, 282
  birth loop, 49–51, *50*
  boom, 45, 46, 47, 140
  burial rates, *120*
  burials, 38–9, *38*, *39*, *40*, *44*, *45*, 83
  description, 37–8
  endogenous cycles, 44–7, 51, 75–86
  exogenous cycles, 44–7, 113–142, *133*, *141*
  family reconstitution, 17, 38, 64, 69, 114, 120, 123, 125, *126*, 131, 137, 138, 140, 282

Penrith (*cont.*)
  famine, 70, 127–9, *128*, 137, 150
  feedback, 135–6, 142
  hardship index, *151*, 153
  marital fertility, 64–6, *65*, *67*, 131, 139,
    140
  as a market town, 271, 283
  marriages, 80
  matrix modelling, 55–74
  migration, 69–71, *70*, 131–2, 136, 139,
    141, 142
  modelling smallpox, *277*, *279*, *280*, *281*
  mortality, adult, 116, 118–20, *119*, 132,
    133–4, 138, 139, 140, 142, 147, *150*,
    156, 157, *158*, *162*
  mortality, child, 115–18, *115*, *117*, 127,
    138, 139, 142, 147, *150*, 156, 157,
    158, *162*, 271–6, *273*, *274*
  mortality crises, *48*, 70, 125, 127–9, 150,
    157
  mortality, infant, 114, 120–31, *121*, *122*,
    123, *128*, 135, 138, 139, 141, 147,
    150, *151*, 156, *158*, *162*
  plague, 38, 45, 47–9, *48*, *49*, 70, 75, 77,
    137, 187, 328–30, *329*
  population size, 47–8, 272, 282
  smallpox, 116, 134, 138, 139, 271–5, *273*,
    276–80, *277*, *279*, *280*, *281*, 282, 289,
    291, 301
  stationarity of data series, 142–3
  steady-state, 46–7, 50, 55, 114, 136, 140,
    141
  survival curve, 67–9, *68*, 83
  30-year cycle, 82–3
  underregistration, 44, 121
  wheat prices, *150*, *151*
  wool prices, 147–51, *150*, *151*, 155–7
phase diagrams, 206, *207*, 208, *209*, 210,
    210, *212*, *213*, 215, 216, *277*, 278,
    279, *280*, *286*, 287, *287*, *288*
phase-shift, 203, 204, *205*, *241*
placenta, 135
plague, 4, 145, 327, 328–30
  Cumbria, 327–30
  Kendal, 45, 328–30, *329*
  Kirkoswald, 52–3
  London, 53, 172, *172*, *173*, 186, 187
  Penrith, 38, 45, 47–9, *48*, *49*, 70, 75, 77,
    137, 187, 328–30, *329*
  spread, 328–30, *329*
  as a trigger, 75, 77, 186–7, 188
  York, 51–2, 198
population growth
  boom, 45, 46, 47, 114, 140, *141*, 299, 300,
    301, 324, 327, 333
  fertility, effect of, 3
  food supply, 6

Malthusian checks, 3, 34
  mortality, effect of, 3, 7
  nuptiality, effect of, 3
  optimal level, 60
  positive check, 3
  preventive check 3
population size/density, (*N*)
  changes, 304–5, 306–8
  in classification of epidemics, 300–2
  definition, 174, 175, 178
  determination of interepidemic interval,
    177, 183, 196, 201, 285, 289, 291
  determination of resonant frequency,
    178, 209, 286, 291
  effect on dynamics of epidemics, 225–8,
    230, 233–4, 236–8, 253, 254, 296
  in modelling, 177, 203, 218–19, *255*,
    257–8, *257*, 261–2, *264*
  predicted, *179*, 180
  relative measure of, 180
post-neonatal mortality, 123–31, *124*, *128*,
    138, 139, 243
Poulton-le-Fylde, 157, *158*
pregnancy, nutrition in, 6, 8, 113, 125–31,
    142, 229–30, 243, 313, 316, 318, 320
Prestwich, *158*

rainfall
  driver, *179*, 181–2, 183, 196, 240, 288,
    289, *289*, 305–6, 311, 318
  predicted price series, 103–4, 111–12
  principal component analysis, 110–11
  seasonal mean, 89
  soil moisture deficit, 102
  wheat prices, effect on, 101–2
reproductive rate, (*R*), 174, 275
resonant frequency, 18, 176, 177, 178, 180,
    182, 183, 204, 206, 208, 211, 217,
    219, 220, 221, 228, 229, 230, 234,
    236, 237, 238, 239, 247, 276, 277,
    286, 288, 291
resources, 331
Richmond, plague, 328–30, *329*
rubella, 217
rural towns, smallpox in, 270–302
  modelling, 276–80
rust, 106–9
  Berberis vulgaris, as secondary host, 106
  eradication, 109
  epidemics, 106–9
  life cycle, *107*, *108*
  Puccinia spp. 106–7
rye, 37, 96

St Bees, 292, *294*, 298
  mortality crises, 298
  smallpox epidemics, 298, 302

scarlet fever, 289, 304
  drivers, 289–90, 311
  England and Wales, 289, 310–16, *312, 315*
  epidemics, 219, 252
  infectious period, 314
  interactions, 319–20
  interepidemic period, 310, 315
  malnutrition, 311–14, 316, 318
  mean age of infection, 314
  modelling, 314–15, *315*
  mortality, 315–16
seasonal forcing, 178, 223
Sefton, *158*
SEIR/SIR dynamics, *173*, 174, 177, 184,
    188, 206, 215, 271, 275, 289, 302,
    310, 318, 319
sheep, 37
  wool prices, 146, 154, 156
Sherbourne, *290*, 301
Shetland Islands, 270, 281
sine wave, 18, *19*
Skipton, *290*, 291, 301
smallpox, 4
  at Chester, 189, 190–7, 270, 271, 301, 302
  classification of epidemics, 299–302
  drivers, *179*, 181–3, 185–6, 195–7, *196*,
    203, 206, 211, 216, 217, 219, 220,
    221, 230, *240*, 266, 272–5, 277, 279,
    286–90, 301
  England and Wales, 309–10, *309*
  epidemics, *268, 290, 294, 296, 297*
  fatality rate, 169, 281–3
  history, 169–71
  inoculation, 172, 183
  interactions, 238–43, *241*, 319–20
  lethality, 169, 270
  London, 113, 171–3, *172, 173*, 177, *179*,
    180–1, 184–7, *186*, 239, 240, *240*,
    241, 242, *242*, 243, *248, 253*, 289,
    300, 301, 302
    interepidemic interval, 172–3, 180
    mean age of infection, 177, *179*, 184–5,
      191, 206
  long wavelength oscillations, 186–7
  modelling, *207, 209, 210, 212, 213*,
    244–69, *250, 251, 254, 255, 277, 279*,
    280, 281, 283–90, *286, 287, 288*
  natural immunity, 276
  Penrith, 116, 134, 138, 139, 271–5,
    276–80, *273, 277, 279, 280, 281*, 282,
    289, 291, 301
  in rural towns, 270–302, *294*
  seasonal weather conditions, 181–3
  Thornton-in-Lonsdale, 29, 283–90, *286*,
    287, 288
  vaccination, 172, *173*, 183, 184, 188, 264–6,
    266, 270, 300, 302, 304, 318, 319

virus, 170
York, 197, 198, 200
spatial dynamics of infectious diseases, 178,
    223, 240, 326
  in metapopulations, 332
stationarity, analysis, 110, 142–4
steady-state population, 46–7, 55–74, 277,
    327
  Penrith, 46–7, 50, 55, 114, 136, 140, 141
stochastic effects, driving epidemics, 178,
    206, 207, 216, 221, 223, 240, 308, 326
Stockport, 157
survival curve, 67, *68*, 72, 83, 84
susceptibility, *see* transmission coefficient

Taunton, 301, *290*
temperature, seasonal
  adult burials, effect on, 132, 133–4, 142
  average, *98*
  driver, *179*, 181, 182, 183, 196, *226*, 229,
    230, 231, *235*, 236, 237, 240, 278,
    288, *289*, 305–6, 318
  predicted price series, 103–4, 111–12
  principal component analysis, 101, 110–11
  seasonal mean, 89
  wheat prices, effect on, 97–101, *100*
Third World countries, 9, 10, 66, *67*, 131,
    222, 230, 238, 311
Thornton-in-Lonsdale, 157, *158*, 160, 161,
    162, 291, 292, *294*, 300, 301
  baptisms, 283, *284*
  burials, 25–31, *26, 27, 28, 29, 30, 31*
  child burials, *26, 27, 28, 29, 30, 31*, 283,
    284, 288
  drivers, 286–90, *289*
  population dynamics, 289
  smallpox epidemics, 29, 283–90, *286, 287*,
    288
  wool prices, 288, 290
threshold density, 136, 137, 174, 180, 275,
    278, 301
time-series analysis, 18–31
  autocorrelation function (acf), 21, 143
  coherence (input–output), 20
  cross-correlation function (ccf), 21
  delay (lag), 21
  fast Fourier transform, 18
  filtering, 20
  Kalman filtering, 83
  spectral analysis, 20
  worked examples, 21–31
transmission coefficient (β)
  measles, 225, 229, 230, 307, 308
  smallpox, 174, 175, 176, 178, 195, 202,
    203, 208, 209, 218, 252, 253, 274,
    275, 276, 277, 278, 279, 280, 286,
    287, 288, 289, 291, 300, 301

transmission coefficient (β) (*cont.*)
  whooping cough, 234, 236, 237
trend, definition, 19
tuberculosis, 303
typhoid, 303
typhus, 4, *48*, 113, 137, 145, 303

Urswick, *158*

vaccination, smallpox, 172, *173*, 183, 184,
  188, 264–6, *266*, 270, 300, 302, 304,
  318, 319
  definition, 183
  theoretical effects, 264–6, *266*
vitamin A, 223, 231

Walton-on-the-Hill, *158*, 161, *162*
Warcop, *158*
  plague, *329*, 330
wavelength (λ),
  definition, 18, 19, *19*
  damping, 75
  long, 19, 39, 41, 44, 45, *52*, *187*
  medium, 19, 43, 47
  short, 19, 39, 41, 43, 46
Westmorland, *see* Cumbria
Whalley, 157, *158*
wheat, 37
  autoregressive effects, 105–6, 109
  causes of short wavelength oscillation,
    105–12
  cycles, 90–112, *92*, *95*, *149*, 209
  medium wavelength oscillation, 90–1,
    98–101
  predicted price series, 103–4, 111–12
  rust epidemics, 106–9
  seasonal rainfall, effect of, 101–2
  seasonal temperatures, effect of, 97–101,
    100
  short wavelength oscillation, 90–1,
    97–112
wheat prices, 90, *90*, *91*, *92*, 94, *96*, 97, *100*,
    114, 145, *162*, *164*
  adult mortality, effect on, 118, *150*
  and baptisms, 131
  child mortality, effect on, *117*, 118, 126,
    127, 145–55, *150*, *201*
  as a driver, *186*, 206, 209, *226*, 227, 228,
    229, *235*, 237, 238, 240, 242, 243,

272–5, 276, 278, 285, 288, 289, *289*,
    294, 299, 309, 311, *312*, 318, 320,
    324–5
  hardship index, 151–3, *151*, *152*, *153*,
    155–6, *156*
  infant mortality, effect on, 122–31, *123*,
    124, 145, *150*, *151*
  and migration, 131–2
  non-stationarity, 110
  and susceptibility, 181, 185–6, 188, 231,
    233, 237, 239, 242
  and wool prices, 146–57, *147*, *149*, *154*,
    161–3
whooping cough, 231–7, 319–20
  in Cape Town, 238
  drivers, 234–6, *235*, 237, 238, *240*
  interactions, 238–43, *241*, 306–8
  interepidemic interval, 231, 233, 236, 237,
    240
  in London, 231–7, *232*, *233*, *235*, *240*, *242*
  mean age of infection, 234
wool prices, 146–57, *148*, *155*, *162*, *164*, *289*
  hardship index, 151–3, *151*, *152*, *153*,
    155–6, *156*
  mortality, effect on, 147–57, *150*, 161–8
  and smallpox epidemics, 288, 289, 290
  and wheat prices, 146–57, *147*, *149*, *154*,
    161–3
  York, 165, 167, *167*, 168, 200
Wrigley & Schofield, 1, 4, 16, 66, *67*, 69, 77,
    81, 83, 157, 160, *172*, *224*, *235*, 298,
    306, 324, 325, 333
Wybunbury, 292, *294*, 301
  child burials, 298
  mortality crises, 298
York
  baptisms, *52*
  child mortality, 167, 168, *198*, *199*, 200,
    200, *201*
  crisis mortality, 165, 168
  endogenous oscillations, 51–2, 53, 54
  infant mortality, 165, *166*, 167, *167*, 168
  market centre, 168
  mortality, effect of wheat prices, 167, 168
  mortality, effect of wool prices, 165, 167,
    168
  plague, 51–2, 198, *198*
  smallpox, 167, 197–201, 300
  wool prices, 165, 167, *167*, 168, 200